Exploring
CONSTRUCTION
Systems

Designing ◆ Engineering ◆ Building

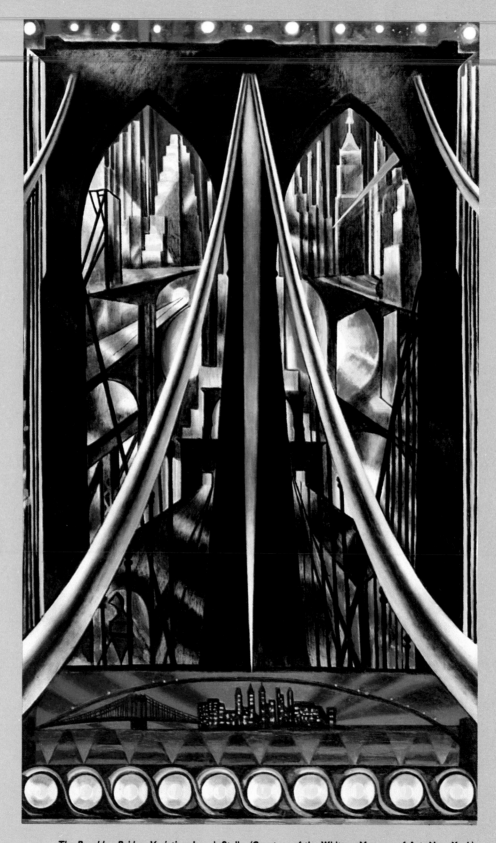

The Brooklyn Bridge, Variation. Joseph Stella. (Courtesy of the Whitney Museum of Art, New York).

Exploring
CONSTRUCTION
Systems

Designing • Engineering • Building

Andrew Horton, St. Cloud State University,
St. Cloud, Minnesota

Stanley A. Komacek, California University of
Pennsylvania, California, Pennsylvania

Brian W. Thompson, Concord Developmental Center,
Concord, West Virginia

Peter H. Wright, Indiana State University,
Terre Haute, Indiana

Paul W. DeVore
Consulting Editor
West Virginia University,
Morgantown, West Virginia

Davis Publications, Inc.
Worcester, Massachusetts

The authors dedicate this text to all those, past and present, who have designed, engineered and constructed safe, efficient and humane structures.

Copyright 1991
Davis Publications, Inc.
Worcester, Massachusetts, U.S.A.

Cover:
Old and new: Trinity Church, Boston, 1877, designed by Henry Hobson Richardson; and the John Hancock Building, Boston, 1973, designed by I.M. Pei. (Courtesy of Arthur D. Little, Inc.)

Library of Congress Catalog Card Number:

ISBN 0-87192-224-X

Graphic Design: Janis Capone Owens
Editing and Page Layout: Julia Runk Jones
Photo Acquisition: Victoria Hughes
Typesetting and Production: Devlin Graphics, Inc.

Printed in the United States of America
10 9 8 7 6 5 4 3 2 1

Acknowledgements

The creation of this book took many hands and minds at every stage. In particular, we received important critiques early on from the following technology educators: Lloyd Gober, Austin, Texas, Independent School District; W.A. Mayfield, University of Texas at Tyler; Margaret Rutherford, Goliad, Texas, Middle School; and, Larry Stiggins, Lubbock, Texas, Independent School District. Their comments steered us toward a text suited for today's technology education needs. James Dean and Richard Bresnahan of St. Cloud, Minnesota, helped us in our research of design and indigenous materials.

Paul DeVore, of West Virginia University, has spent many years critiquing us during our graduate programs in his department. He has continued this review process with his invaluable comments during the writing of this book.

We also thank the many companies and design firms that provided photographs. In particular, George Barford, author of *Understanding Modern Architecture* (Davis Publications, Inc.), generously provided us with his photographs of structures from around the world.

We have also come to realize that no authors can write without the support of their families. We thank our spouses and children for their help and understanding.

A.H.   February, 1990
S.A.K.
B.W.T.
P.H.W.

Understanding one's culture is a measure of cultural literacy. Today, we live in a highly technological society. Thus, understanding technology is essential to cultural literacy.

A significant and critical part of our technological society is our constructed world—our buildings, highways, dams, airports and marine terminals. Understanding our constructed world is an essential part of the cultural literacy of an educated person.

We at Davis Publications are pleased to provide students preparing for the future with a leading edge textbook—part of our Technology Education Series. It is a textbook designed to provide the learner with knowledge, insight and understanding of the technological concepts essential to comprehending our constructed world.

Paul W. DeVore,
February 1990
Morgantown, WV

Contents

Construction of a geodesic dome. (Photo by Stan Komacek)

■ Part II Process   190

Pouring concrete. (Courtesy of GSA)

Saddledome, with Space Needle in the background, Calgary, Alberta. (Courtesy of Gerald Brommer)

. . . .

Construction: Stage Center

◼ Hey! We're Having an Earth . . . !

At 5:04 P.M., October 17, 1989, just as Game 3 of the World Series was beginning in San Francisco's Candlestick Park, a tremor shook the stadium. The ground rippled under the players' feet, sending them running for cover. The top of the bleachers rolled and buckled. "Hey!" cried the TV announcer, "we're having an earth . . . !" and then television screens all over the United States went blank as CBS went off the air.

San Francisco was indeed having an earthquake. It registered 6.9 on the Richter scale, making it one of the strongest in modern history—as strong as the quake that killed 25,000 people in Armenia just a year before.

Within hours, crews from all the networks were in San Francisco, recording the damage to one of our largest cities. On our TV sets, we saw three-story buildings that sank 2 stories into the ground, beautiful old apartment houses leaning precariously to one side while people crawled out through buckled windows, a busy double-decker highway horribly crumbled onto itself, and over and over we watched the replay of the collapse of a section of the San Francisco Bay Bridge, a little red car disappearing into the hole and bouncing up again to smash against the concrete.

This three-story building sank two stories deep into the ground during the earthquake. It was constructed on landfill, which tends to "liquefy" during earthquakes. (Courtesy of the San Francisco Chronicle)

The failure of two small bolts (connectors) caused the collapse of this span on the San Francisco Bay Bridge. (Courtesy of the San Francisco Chronicle)

Overnight, technical terms like *shear, stress,* and *resonance* became household words. We heard talk about reinforced concrete and retrofitting. Base isolation for skyscrapers became something people discussed over breakfast.

But what is it really about? Why, in a city of almost 1 million people, did only 50 people die, when many thousands died in smaller, less populated areas of Armenia? Why did only one small section of the city sink into the ground? Why did a delicate masonry chimney next to the Nimitz Freeway remain intact while the roadway collapsed? And why did only a one-mile section of that freeway collapse while the rest was undamaged? Three answers are clear:

- Earthquakes do not usually kill people; human-made structures, such as bridges, roads, dams and buildings, kill people in earthquakes.

- Structures react to stress in predictable ways, following basic principles of design and construction.

- Buildings do not have to fall down for you to learn something about them.

The Nimitz Freeway collapsed due to the stresses on improperly reinforced concrete. This one-mile stretch lay directly along the center line of the earthquake. (Courtesy of the San Francisco Chronicle)

■ Understanding Construction Systems

Construction must be understood as a whole. Building a structure without understanding the principles behind it is like working in the dark. This book is not just about the nuts and bolts of construction (the *how*), but also about the *what* and, especially, the *why*.

In order to make these principles clearer, this book is divided into four parts: Inputs, Processes, Outputs and Feedback.

Inputs cover materials and why they behave as they do. Concrete reacts to stress one way, steel another. We will look at how these materials are put together into the basic elements of structures—the beam, the arch, the truss, etc.—and how loads or stresses affect these structures.

Process examines the actual design and building of structures. After an in-depth look at all the basic tools and processes, we will "walk through" the construction of a house.

Outputs are the results of all this knowledge and work—in short, the many structures humans have created to shelter and serve them, such as buildings, roads, dams, even space shuttles. By looking closely at the structures and their use, we can better understand why they are built the way they are.

Feedback is a critical but often overlooked part of construction. What are the short-term and long-term effects of building systems? What will happen in the future?

Activities at the end of each part encourage a "hands-on" approach through design briefs and problem-solving.

Once you know more about construction, events like the San Francisco earthquake will not be so confusing. As you explore this book, use it to open up your eyes to the world of construction around you.

. . . .

Chapter 1

Construction, Technology, and Society

Chapter Concepts

■ The basic technologies can be categorized as either production technology (manufacturing and construction) or service technology (communication and transportation).

■ Construction, communication, manufacturing, and transportation are interrelated and interdependent technologies. Each system uses parts of the other systems and depends on their safe and efficient operation.

■ Mathematics and science are a necessary part of the processes and operations of construction.

■ The systems approach can be used to simplify complex systems of technology, including construction.

■ There are two systems approach methods: identifying subsystems and the universal systems model.

■ The universal systems model includes the inputs, processes, outputs, and feedback used to make the system work.

■ All of the institutions of society (family, community, state, religion, trade, recreation, and education) require structures that, when in place, influence the behavior of the people who use the structures.

Key Terms

Beanstalk Principle
culture
feedback
four basic technologies
inputs
interdependent
interrelated
outputs
processes

production technology
service technology
society
subsystem
systems approach
technical means
tradeoff
universal systems model

A group of people gather at the cliff dwellings of Mesa Verde. This thousand-year-old structure was created by an intensely communal society. (Courtesy of the U.S. Department of the Interior)

. . . .

```
┌──────────────────────┐
│      TECHNOLOGY       │
└──────────────────────┘
         │
    ┌────┴────┐
    │         │
┌──────────────────┐  ┌──────────────────┐
│   PRODUCTION     │  │     SERVICE      │
│   TECHNOLOGY     │  │   TECHNOLOGY     │
│                  │  │                  │
│ - Construction   │  │ - Communication  │
│                  │  │                  │
│ - Manufacturing  │  │ - Transportation │
└──────────────────┘  └──────────────────┘
```

Biotechnology is a relatively new field that simultaneously holds great promise and poses difficult problems for our society. It involves the manipulation of living organisms to invent new or different organisms. Some of the promises of biotechnology are artificial foods, drugs that might stop or reverse the aging process, and processes that will permit us to make human clones. These science fiction-type promises pose ethical issues related to how biotechnology may be abused for the control or manipulation of human beings.

Our society is made up of a highly complex web of systems of technology. Both our large cities and small towns are artificial environments that have been created by these systems of technology. Today, our society is totally dependent on technology for its most basic needs. Most of us could not provide our own food, water, shelter, and energy. Without technology, we could not survive.

Each technology is dependent on all the others. There are often discussions about which is the most important technology; but in truth, they are **interrelated** and **interdependent.** No one technology could exist without the aid of other technologies.

There are four **basic technologies:**

- communication
- construction
- manufacturing
- transportation

These basic technologies provide the industrial, technical and economic base upon which our society is built. In addition, there are other technologies, such as agricultural and medical technologies and biotechnology. These technologies are important to our society, as well.

All technologies can be categorized as **production technologies** or **service technologies.** Production technologies produce goods or products to meet the needs of society. Construction, manufacturing and biotechnology are examples of production technology. Each of these systems produce a good or product. Construction produces structures, such as buildings, bridges, dams, roads and tunnels. Manufacturing produces products for consumers. Biotechnology is already being used to produce new drugs.

Examples of service technology include the systems of communication, transportation and medical technology. Communication provides the services related to transmitting information. Transportation services include moving people and goods from one place to another. Medical technology provides for the health-related services that people need.

Communication systems depend upon construction systems. The base of this satellite dish had to be strong enough both to support and to rotate the huge dish.

Importance of Construction to Other Technologies

Each of the basic technologies is dependent on construction. Consider these examples:

Manufacturing and Construction ■ Manufacturing factories and plants are often huge, very specialized buildings that house large machines and equipment. Construction technologies are used to build these structures.

Transportation and Construction ■ Some of the most obvious examples of interrelated technologies can be found in the relationship between construction and transportation. Roads, highways, bridges, tunnels and railroad tracks are just a few examples of constructed projects essential to safe, efficient land transportation.

An often overlooked but very important form of transportation is the pipeline. Every city and community is dependent on pipelines for the transportation of water, natural gas and sewage. Pipelines, like roads and bridge, are constructed projects.

Communication and Construction ■ Construction provides the system of communication with a wide range of structures, from the lowly telephone pole to the great towers that support and rotate satellite dishes. The trans-oceanic cable was not only a communication success; it was also a construction task of enormous proportions.

Below left: Factories such as this must be specially built to house the large machines and equipment necessary to manufacture steel. (Courtesy of Bethlehem Steel)

Below right: Construction of the Trans-Alaska pipeline was important for the transportation of oil from the North Slope to the port of Valdez. (Courtesy of Alyeska Co.)

Right: I-beams are a critical part of structural support. If this steel I-beam is not manufactured to exact specifications, the structure using it may be unsafe. (Courtesy of Bethlehem Steel)

Below: Drafters and other artists must draw plans correctly before the structure is built. Projects are sold and approved on the basis of drawings such as these. (*Bottom* courtesy of Robert Ward, architect)

Importance of Other Technologies to Construction

Construction is not only necessary to the other technologies; it is dependent upon them as well. Workers in communication fields draw the plans and blueprints needed for construction projects. Manufacturing technologies produce the tools, machines and equipment used in construction. All standard building materials, such as structural metals and woods, glass, fasteners and paints and finishes, are manufactured products. Construction depends on systems of transportation, among other things, to deliver building materials to the construction site on time and to move large quantities of earth for excavation.

The quality of work performed in one system of technology affects the quality of work in other systems. For example, if a structure is to be built properly and safely, the materials used, such as steel I-beams, lumber and plywood, must be manufactured to the correct specifications. Drafters must draw the plans correctly and materials and supplies must be delivered on time. In order for one field of technology to improve productivity and efficiency, all systems of technology must work together.

Transportation systems are essential for the delivery of materials to construction sites.

Construction, Math and Science

Construction is also interrelated and interdependent with the fields of mathematics and science. Workers in construction must be able to understand and use both of these fields. Throughout the construction field there are numerous examples of the importance of applying mathematics and understanding scientific principles.

Being able to measure accurately is one obvious example. Construction workers must be able to read customary measuring devices in inches and fractions of an inch. This requires the ability to add, subtract, multiply and divide whole numbers and fractions. Geometry is used in measuring the length of angled structural components like roof rafters or laying out a square angle between two components. This means being able to multiply and calculate square roots.

Fractions of an inch can make a big difference in a constructed project. This pipe must be exactly the right length and diameter specified in the plans. (Courtesy of Riley-Stoker)

Construction managers must estimate the cost of a project, determine the cubic yards of concrete needed or compute the total number of board feet of lumber for a job. Surveyors measure lengths in feet and decimal parts of an inch and angles in degrees, minutes and seconds of an arc. Each of these processes requires the ability to use mathematics.

Many scientific principles must be considered in construction. Aerodynamics is one example. When you think of aerodynamics, you usually think of automobile and airplane design, but it is also extremely important to construction technology. For example, all tall buildings sway back and forth like a pendulum when heavy winds blow. For some skyscrapers, this sway from one side to the other can be measured in seconds. Designers and engineers must take this aerodynamic effect into consideration when designing tall buildings.

The scientific principle that explains expansion and contraction of materials is another example. All construction materials expand in heat and contract when cold. A bridge 300 feet long in 32° Fahrenheit weather can expand almost 1-1/4 inches in 90° F weather. This may not seem like very much expansion, but all bridges subjected to such conditions must be designed with expansion joints to prevent buckling.

These are just a few examples of the importance of math and science in construction. Throughout this text, math will be applied to the design, engineering, building and analysis of structures.

The Sydney Opera House, Sydney, Australia, was built on a promotory jutting out into the harbor. Its roof was designed to look like a series of gigantic sails. Such innovative design would be impossible without modern construction techniques.

THE SYSTEMS APPROACH

Over the past two hundred years, there have been dramatic changes in the structures people build. In the past, structures were fairly simple. People used basic structural elements, such as the post-and-beam or the arch. They also used natural building materials like stone and wood. Today, these basic elements and materials are still used. However, there are also many new elements, materials and techniques used by builders.

Some of these techniques can be very complex. Look at the Epcot Center in Disney World or the Sydney Opera House in Australia. These could not have been built by construction workers of the past. Both structures use new materials, new building techniques, and structural designs that are made possible only by advancements in the field of construction technology.

This book will give you a better understanding of how structures like these are constructed and used. But how can you possible understand something so complex? One technique used to make complex technology less complex is called the systems approach. The **systems approach** breaks a whole into its basic parts. When you understand the basic parts, you can better understand the entire system.

Introduction

There are two different methods of using the systems approach. One method is to examine the subsystems that make up a complex system. The other method is to use the universal systems model to analyze a complex system. Let's look at each of these methods.

. . . .

Subsystems: Systems within Systems

All complex systems have **subsystems,** which are systems within a system. Your school building is a system with several technical subsystems. Each subsystem is necessary. Most of these subsystems can be found in any type of structure, but the way the subsystems are put together makes them a school building.

These are also human subsystems in your school. All technological systems need people to make them work. Each of these technical and human subsystems is important to the school. If any of the subsystems are missing, the school cannot function properly to educate students.

Identifying the subsystems simplifies a complex technological system and gives you a clear picture of how the entire system works.

Applying the Subsystems Approach

The subsystems approach can be applied to any type of system. The chart below identifies the subsystems for a human body (a system of biology) and compares them to the subsystems found in a house (a system of construction technology)

SUBSYSTEM	HUMAN BODY	HOUSE
structure	bones, muscle	wood, concrete, plywood
ventilation	respiration	windows, doors
waste removal	digestion	sewage lines
protection	skin	siding, roof shingles
support	feet	foundation
fasteners	tendons, cartilage	nails, screws, glue
circulation	blood	plumbing
energy	food	heating, electrical system

. . . .

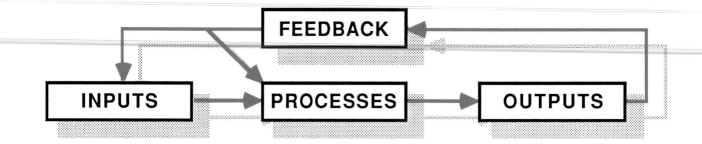

Universal Systems Model

The second systems approach method is the **universal systems model,** which breaks complex systems into four basic parts: inputs, processes, outputs and feedback.

Inputs are everything that must be put into a system to make it work. **Processes** are the actions performed by people using the inputs. **Outputs** are the results of the process. **Feedback** are the means of monitoring (checking) and adjusting the inputs, processes, and outputs to make sure the goal of the system is achieved.

This universal systems model can be applied to any kind of system. Let's look at a biological system: growing tomatoes. The inputs needed to grow tomatoes include soil, tools, seeds, fertilizer, water and a farmer who knows how to use these inputs. The processes the farmer performs include digging the soil, planting the seeds, and watering and fertilizing the plants. If everything goes well, tomatoes will grow on the plants. The tomatoes are the outputs of the system. During the entire process, the farmer monitors the system and makes necessary adjustments, such as providing extra water during dry spells or controlling bugs that might eat the plants. This monitoring and adjusting is the feedback.

The universal systems model can also be applied to technological systems. Let's look at the inputs, processes, outputs, and feedback found in construction.

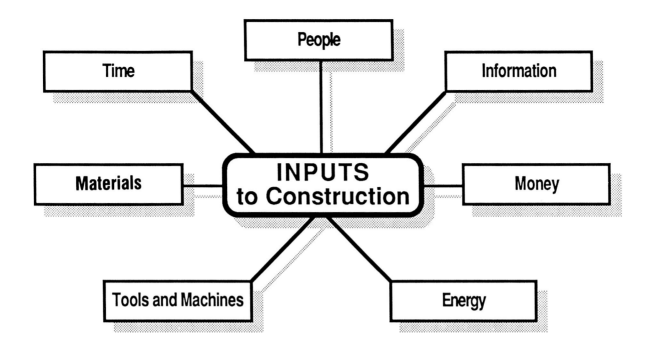

```
                    ┌──────────┐
                    │  People  │
                    └──────────┘
  ┌──────────┐           │          ┌──────────────┐
  │   Time   │           │          │ Information  │
  └──────────┘           │          └──────────────┘
        \                │                /
         \      ╔════════════════╗       /
  ┌──────────┐  ║     INPUTS     ║  ┌──────────┐
  │Materials │──║ to Construction║──│  Money   │
  └──────────┘  ╚════════════════╝  └──────────┘
         /             │             \
        /              │              \
┌──────────────────┐   │   ┌──────────┐
│ Tools and Machines│  │   │  Energy  │
└──────────────────┘   │   └──────────┘
```

Inputs to Construction

There are eight major inputs for all systems of technology:

- people,
- information,
- money,
- energy,

- tools,
- machines,
- materials, and
- time.

Let's look at each of these inputs and see how they relate to construction.

■ People

People are the most important input. They perform the four processes of construction: designing, managing, producing (building) and using structures. Architects and engineers are the designers. Supervisors and owners manage construction. Skilled workers, such as ironworkers, carpenters, masons, electricians and plumbers, build the structure. All this is done to meet the needs of the users.

People are the most important input. The materials and machinery in this picture are vital to the construction project, but without the skilled craftsman they mean very little. (Courtesy of U.S. Forest Service)

In addition to drawings and blue prints, models are used to communicate design information. This highly detailed model was used to sell an urban renewal project.

Information

Each person in the construction system needs special information or knowledge. Owners want a certain type of structure. To design the structure, designers must interpret the wishes of the owners within the limitations of building regulations. Drawings, blueprints and other specifications are used to communicate the design information to managers and construction workers.

Every person involved in construction also must have the knowledge and skill needed to use the special tools, materials and processes of their job safely and efficiently.

Money

Construction projects can cost hundreds of thousands or even millions of dollars. Money is needed to pay for all the other inputs in the construction system. The land where the structure will be built, all the necessary tools, machines and materials must be purchased and workers must be paid. Having enough money is critical to a successful construction project.

■ Energy

A lot of energy is needed in construction. Materials used in construction must be extracted, processed and transported. This takes fuel for chain-saws, sawmills and trucks. Large earth-moving equipment, such as bulldozers, graders and backhoes use large amounts of diesel fuel. Most structures must have energy systems built in for later use. Lighting, heating, electrical service and air conditioning are all energy systems.

■ Tools and Machines

Workers in construction use very specialized tools. Designers use drawing tools, such as T-squares, triangles and pencils. Carpenters use saws, hammers and measuring devices; masons use trials, floats and levels. Many large machines, such as piledrivers, tower cranes, and specialized road paving and tunneling equipment are used only in construction.

■ Materials

Construction materials are used for structural, protective or decorative purposes. Steel, stone, wood and concrete are examples of structural materials that support the structure. Protective materials protect the structure from the environment. Paint, aluminum siding, roof shingles and insulation, for example, protect structural materials from decay and deterioration. Decorative materials are used to make the structure look more appealing. Colors, special designs and certain details are often added to structural and protective materials to improve the appearance of a structure. Paint, colored sidings, wood molding and ornamental metals are examples of decorative materials. Materials may serve more than one purpose; notice in the examples above that paint is both protective and decorative.

■ Time

Construction projects can take years to complete. Owners usually have a time schedule in mind for the completion of the structure. Managers are responsible for following the time schedule. They plan the delivery of materials and hire workers with the schedule in mind. Running past the scheduled completion date can mean increased costs for the owner or builder. It can be very difficult to keep to a schedule, because of factors beyond the control of managers, such as unexpected weather conditions or accidents. The schedule is so important that often owners will provide on-time incentives for the managers and workers. By offering bonus pay if the job is completed on time, an owner can reduce cost overruns that result when projects run past the original completion date.

Highly specialized equipment is used in the building of roads.

PROCESSES of Construction

- Designing Structures
- Managing Construction
- Building Structures
- Using Structures

Processes of Construction

Processes are what people do in construction. In general, construction processes can be divided into designing, managing, producing and using.

Designing processes include determining the needs of the owner, analyzing the environmental and social impact of the structure, designing the structure to withstand loads and forces, and presenting the design in the form of drawings and specifications. Managing processes include arranging financing, hiring workers and coordinating the building of the structure. Supervisors on the job site are responsible for coordinating the arrival of materials with progress of the work and inspecting the quality of construction. Construction workers are responsible for building the structure.

The three categories of material processes workers perform with their tools and machines are separating, combining and forming.

- *Separating processes* reduce the shape and size of materials by removing some of the material. Examples of separating processes include sawing, drilling, shearing and other cutting processes.

- *Combining processes* are used to add one material to another. Gluing, welding, riveting, nailing and screwing are examples of combining processes.

- *Forming processes* change the external shape of materials. Bending metals and casting concrete are two common forming processes.

All of the people who work in construction must cooperate in the design and building of a structure. The processes each group performs are important to the entire construction system.

OUTPUTS of Construction

- Structures
- New Knowledge
- Impacts
  - positive
  - negative

Outputs of Construction

There are three outputs of construction: structures, new knowledge and techniques, and impacts (effects).

The main outputs of construction are, of course, structures. The type of structure depends on the needs of the owner. Structures can be built for a variety of purposes, including sheltering, supporting, containing, directing and transporting. The design and final form of the structure should follow the intended use.

A second output is new knowledge and new techniques that may be developed during the construction process. As structures are built, people learn new and improved ways of doing construction. This new information is added to the knowledge base available to other construction workers. Improving and expanding the information and efficiency available in a field has always been an important part of technology.

A third output of construction is its impact. Impacts are the effects construction has on people, society and the environment. All systems of technology have both positive and negative impacts. Construction projects, for example, are intended to meet human needs and wants. Owners and workers begin the process with the hopes of having a positive impact on some aspect of life. However, negative impacts occur. Every time a structure is built, the natural resources available for building materials is reduced, limited energy resources are consumed and the land where the structure is built can not be used for other purposes, often for many years.

Extreme examples of negative impacts occur when structures fail, such as when a bridge collapses, a dam gives way, or storage tanks burst. In such cases, the most tragic negative impact is, of course, the loss of human life.

Every time technology is used, both positive and negative impacts occur. As a society, we are willing to accept this tradeoff. A **tradeoff** is when people accept negative impacts in order to receive the positive benefits of a technology. Tradeoffs are associated with the impacts of all technology. One of the most common tradeoffs in construction is the money we pay (negative impact) in order to receive the positive benefits of a newly built home. Other tradeoffs are not so easy to understand and predict. Usually, we can not predict or anticipate all the possible negative impacts of technology.

· ·

Feedback

Feedback mechanisms are used to make sure the goal of the system is met and to control or prevent negative impacts. Feedback monitors the system and makes adjustments when necessary. Construction supervisors inspect

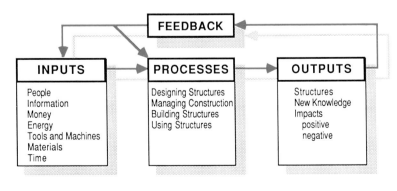

· ·

the work of a carpenter, engineers analyze the load-bearing capabilities of a beam before building and managers make sure the project doesn't go over budget or past the scheduled deadlines. These are examples of monitoring the system. When problems are recognized, adjustments can be made. Some examples of adjustments include replacing inferior materials, firing incompetent workers, using reinforcing techniques for a weak beam and hiring more workers to finish a project on time.

This monitoring and adjusting of feedback goes on constantly during the input, process, and output stages of construction. The best time to monitor and make adjustments is during the input and process stages, before the structure is finished. Fixing problems when the structure is in use, in the output stage, can be very expensive or impossible.

CONSTRUCTION & INSTITUTIONS OF SOCIETY

We shape our buildings and thereafter,
our buildings shape us.
—Winston Churchill

Winston Churchill, the famous British Prime Minister, was referring to the oblong shape of the Commons Room, a room where British legislators meet. Because the room is long and narrow, members of the two political parties tend to group together at opposite ends. Churchill believed that the room's shape encouraged opposition rather than cooperation among the legislators.

If it is possible for buildings to influence how a group of politicians behave, it is also possible for structures to affect how society itself behaves. **Culture,** or the unique characteristics of a group of people, is highly influenced by the **technical means** employed by that group of people.

Numerous studies reinforce this idea. In one case, it was found that people living near the ends of a U-shaped apartment complex had half as many friends as those living in the middle of the U. Another study, showed that the arrangement of furniture could increase or decrease conversation. It was found, for example, that fixed row seating in railway waiting rooms discouraged conversation.

These findings suggest that the design of living habitats as well as our placement within these habitats influence our social behavior. Friendship and social interaction can be increased or discouraged by the design of social or public places in structures. In some cases, crime, vandalism and other hostilities have been directly tied to poorly designed housing projects.

People living near the middle of a U-shaped apartment complex have twice as many friends as those living near the ends.

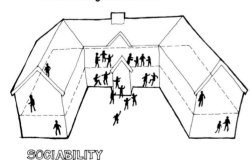

SOCIABILITY

Introduction

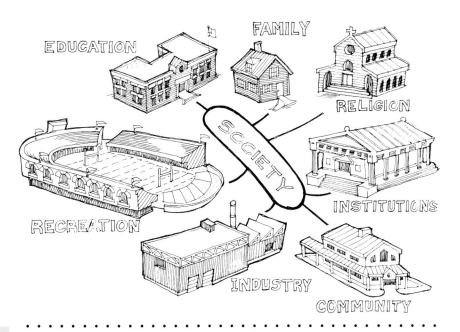

EDUCATION
FAMILY
RELIGION
SOCIETY
INSTITUTIONS
RECREATION
INDUSTRY
COMMUNITY

Societal Institutions

All societies, regardless of how advanced or primitive have social institutions. Some societies have more formal institutions than others. Sociologists, people who study social behavior, categorize a society by the following institutions.

1. Family
2. Community
3. State
4. Religion

5. Trade
6. Recreation
7. Education

These societal institutions create the need for structures and dictate their design. But construction systems and structures also influence societal institutions. To understand the complex relationship between societal and construction systems let us look at the seven institutions of society.

■ Family

The family unit differs from culture to culture, but usually consists of children, parents, grandparents, great grandparents and the extended family (including aunts, uncles, cousins, nieces, and nephews). Construction systems in the form of shelters generally are used by a single family, which sometimes includes the extended family as well.

Social collapse has also been attributed to poorly designed structures. For example, the Pruit-Igoe housing project in St. Louis was designed without any public places. Residents could not formally or informally meet their next door neighbors. The usual social networks did not form and paranoia, mistrust, fear, and other negative emotions became dominant.

Respect Your Elders

In Houkanese homes of China's Guang Dong province, the grandparents are the chief decision makers. This family power is reflected by the design of the shelters the family lives in. The very center of the house usually contains a small Buddhist shrine where family members worship. The grandparents' rooms are located near this center, indicating their importance.

The wings of the structure are used for storage until a son marries. He then moves into one of the wings of the house with his new wife. As the newlyweds grow older, their room position

shifts toward the center, closer to the Buddhist shrine. This dynamic design keeps the generations of family members together, while giving them their

A Houkanese family compound.

proper significance. Family members move throughout the house from birth to death.

Triple decker houses were originally intended to keep several generations of one family under the same roof. (Courtesy of Mary Pat True)

Shelters are often referred to as houses. But "a house is not a home." The physical structure (the shelter) must combine with the social structure (family harmony and interaction) to create that positive climate we call "home." A well designed shelter can add to the social harmony of the family. Important family behaviors such as cooperation, compromising and sharing may be enhanced by certain shelters and stifled by others. Family harmony is often attributed to well designed, well built shelters.

In some families, a sense of history is enhanced by those shelters that include space for extended family members. Grandparents who live with their children and grandchildren in a shelter designed to include them often have dignity and play an influential role in the family decision-making process. Some shelters are designed not to include grandparents and this affects how a family social structure develops.

During the early 1900's, generational housing known as "three-deckers" were designed and constructed in New England (northeastern United States). Worcester, Massachusetts, was one New England mill town that became well known for its three-deckers. Three apartment "flats" were placed on top of one another. Each flat usually had a front porch and a back porch, with clothesline.

The three decks were designed so that the grandparents could live on the first floor. This saved them a long and difficult climb upstairs. The parents lived on the second floor. Young energetic newly married children lived on the third floor. When the grandparents died, the parents would move down to the first floor. In some areas, these three-deckers are still used as generational houses, and help keep the extended family together.

In colonial America, the fireplace hearth was the unifying area of the home. The hearth served more than one practical purpose. Not only were meals cooked on the hearth, family members also gathered there for wintertime warmth. But, even more importantly, because the family tended to group together for long hours at the hearth, it became the area where they discussed and solved common problems that faced the family as a whole.

The increasing popularity of the wood stove and fireplace is once again creating a hearth as a central family gathering place. The radiant heat provided by the fire is very comforting on cold winter nights. Family members are drawn together naturally around the wood stove and fireplace. Problems can be discussed and solved just as they were in early colonial American families.

Although family shelters vary with culture, the most important concern should be how to design and construct shelters to increase family harmony. This problem is complex. There are many other variables affecting family behavior today. However, shelters and the technology within shelters play an important role in shaping the social behavior of the family.

hearth is the psychological center of the
e. On cold nights, family members are
rally drawn together around the fire. There,
lems can be discussed; decisions made. The
ern wood stove can be considered a type of
th. (*Right:* copyright Southern Living, 1988.
inted with permission. *Above:* photo by
Stang)

Cliff Palace.

Mesa Verde, a flat-topped mountain in Colorado, was the site for hundreds of prehistoric cliff dwellings. The Anasazi, ancestors of the Pueblo Indians, began building these structures on the cliffs 1,500 years ago. Incredible construction skill was needed to build the sandstone and clay based structures. Some of these structures have stood over 800 years. Within the Anasazi communities, individual family dwellings were secondary to the larger community structures. Cliff Palace was one such community. It included a community building over three hundred feet long and one hundred feet wide. Similar to modern apartment buildings, Cliff Palace stood four stories tall. Archaeologists believe that these cliff dwellings of the Anasazi people were community-built.

■ Community

Most anthropologists believe that the social institution of the community actually preceded the institution of family. This is because the tribe, clan or troop was necessary for survival. Banding together in a cooperative group helped humans survive in a hostile environment. The community, usually thought of as groups of 500 people or less, is still considered extremely important to the well being of individuals.

A stone wall can be built by hand with stones cleared from the fields.

Urban environments are often stressful places to live.

Sociologist Kirkpatrick Sale, using the analogy of the folktale Jack and the Beanstalk developed the **Beanstalk Principle,** which deals with the optimal size or scale of systems. The principle reads:

For every system, there is an optimal limit beyond which it ought not to grow, or elements of the system will be affected adversely.

The Beanstalk principle can be applied to the social institution of community and to the structures of the community.

What does the size or scale of community have to do with construction systems? When the size of a group of people was kept to a small number (around 500), the scale of the constructed systems was kept to the community scale. Members of a community could walk easily to the house of any other member of the community. Buildings were small. (Kirkpatrick Sale believes that structures taller than five stories are beyond scale.) Materials for structures could be produced locally. Many small towns would have a sawmill and/or brickyard (depending on the region) to support construction projects. In agricultural areas, the stones cleared from fields were used as fence and/or foundation material.

Community-scaled structures did not require the technical expertise of engineers and architects. Therefore, community members could participate in the construction of many structures that were needed in the community. This unified the community. The spirit of construction systems came from the spirit of the persons who needed them, designed them, built them, and more importantly used them.

Construction systems, such as shelters were the responsibility of the group or community. Community fiber and spirit were enhanced through the need to cooperate during the construction process.

It is harder to foster community spirit in urban environments. High-rise apartment buildings are often stressful living environments. In many cases, persons living directly next door do not even know one another. The entrances of apartments are often characterized by a series of bolts and locks on the door.

This is not an attack on urban communities, which often offer great cultural diversity. It is an illustration of the beanstalk principle in action. When human populations grow beyond an appropriate size or scale, the structures that support these populations may have characteristics detrimental to the total well-being (physical and emotional) of the people.

■ State

In this context, "state" refers to the governing institutions at all levels: community, regional, state and federal. There are two areas of interaction between state and construction: structures used or inspired by government, and state-sponsored, large-scale construction projects.

• •

Monuments help unify groups. *Top:* the Sphinx and pyramids are enduring memorials to the pharoahs of Egypt. (Courtesy of the Egyptian Tourist Board) *Below:* A small town war memorial. This simple monument serves the town by honoring its history. (Photo by Sonia Stang)

Government Structures ■ The state plays an important role in the building of society's historical monuments. A quick drive around Washington, D.C. reveals the importance of monuments. Many of these structures have the sole purpose of communicating stability, security and power. Others are memorials to important events in the society's history; they unify group emotions.

Monuments and memorials are also found on a less grandiose scale in small communities. Many town halls, fire departments, and town parks display monuments and memorials. These monuments help unify a community by honoring its history.

The White House, perhaps the most famous building in the United States, unifies Americans in a symbolic sense. Although most of the citizens in the United States have never seen the White House, all people know what it looks like. It represents wealth, power, stability and goodness.

On local government levels, such as in the small town, government buildings often parallel the structures throughout the town. This is because community participation and direct involvement are characteristics of small-town government. The building tools, materials and processes are often similar to the tools, materials, and processes used in the houses of the local residents. There is a community sense of ownership of such structures.

State-Sponsored Construction Projects ■ The state, with its greater power and wealth, can sponsor projects beyond the scope of the community. Our complex road systems and large dams are examples. Without state involvement, such large-scale projects could not be built.

However, the power of the state versus the power of individuals and communities will always invite debate in the planning of construction projects.

These projects become controversial when they impact other institutions such as the family and community. For example, controversy often sur-

The building of the Hoover Dam. One of the world's largest dams, it stands 727 ft. high and 1180 ft. long. A project of this size could not be successful without the involvement of the government. (Courtesy of U.S. Department of Interior)

Religious structures are often built to inspire. *Top:* The Parthenon, Athens, Greece. *Below:* The chapel at the Air Force Academy, Colorado Springs, Colo. (Courtesy of George Barford)

rounds the planning of a major highway. Such a highway will usually displace people. Houses, farms, families, even whole communities may be destroyed. Large scale hydroelectric dams often draw criticism from environmental groups. Difficult questions arise such as, does meeting energy demand have a higher priority than protecting the natural environment?

The social, technical and environmental impact of large construction projects are complicated and difficult to measure. How does society weigh the positive and negative impacts of such projects?

■ Religion

Virtually all societies design and construct religious structures. Some of these structures are grand while others are simple. Because religious beliefs vary greatly, the structures of religion also vary greatly. Some structures may be formed of a simple ring of stone, while others are magnificent in scale.

Nowhere is the "two-way street" of construction and society more clearly seen than in social institution of religion. Religious belief inspires people to build structures. These buildings are often so grand and beautiful that they themselves inspire belief. Grand structures related to religion have been prominent throughout history: Notre Dame cathedral in France, the Parthenon in Greece, and the Hagia Sophia Mosque in Istanbul are just a few examples.

■ Trade

Trade (or commerce) is the manufacture and distribution of goods produced by the society. It requires a construction infrastructure. Historically, societies with advanced construction techniques (such as ship building or road building) have had the most advanced and powerful trade systems.

Societies with the most advanced construction systems usually have the most powerful trade systems. Large airports, such as Logan Airport in Boston, Mass., help ensure the nation's economic power. (Courtesy of Massport)

The Metrodome in Minneapolis, Minn. Large sports arenas contribute to the psychological and physical well-being of cities. (Photo by Brent Miller)

Good school design balances economics, tradition and function. This small schoolhouse *(top)* is an example of traditional school design serving the needs of a small community. (Photo by Rhonda Fournier) The courtyard at Loyola Law School, Los Angeles, Calif. *below* uses innovative design, reflecting modern university philosophy.

In technological societies such as ours, the construction infrastructure is complex, including manufacturing buildings, transportation systems (i.e. roads, bridges), retail outlets, and so on. Housing for the labor force of trade and industry is also part of the construction infrastructure. Industrialization (characteristic of a very complex trade system) requires a nearby labor force; this leads to urbanization. The urban landscape of our country is a result of our elaborate trade system.

■ Recreation

Recreation is an important part of a healthy society. In addition to promoting mental and physical health, recreational activities unite the community. Specific structures are usually needed to support the many different types of recreation. A baseball stadium is one example of a recreation requiring a specialized structure.

Recreational structures provide a rallying point for the community. These structures are so important to communities that cities wanting a professional athletic team will sometimes build a stadium first in order to attract a team to their area. Community spirit is enhanced by local athletic teams. Many high schools include basketball, football, swimming, track, gymnastics, volleyball, baseball, music, and theater programs that require special structures or facilities.

■ Education

Most societies design and build educational structures. These structures may take the form of a simple school house or a complex of buildings that serve multiple functions.

There is a direct relationship between education and classroom design. In the early 1900s the classroom with its rectangular shape, straight rows of chairs and wide windows was designed to provide adequate ventilation and lighting, quick departure, behavior surveillance and a host of other functions. Before the advent of electric light, windows were located so that light came over students' left shoulders. Desks were arranged so that students would not block the natural light of other students. Even though there are new developments in lighting, acoustics and structures, the design of most school classrooms continue to follow this traditional layout.

Some educators believe that there are other ways to organize a classroom that are more conducive to learning. Some schools have broken the traditional pattern. Innovations in classroom design include removing walls between classrooms in order to promote team teaching and student interaction. This is referred to as open planned architecture. There has also been a recent trend toward flexible rooms, which have large movable tables instead of fixed desks. Good school design must balance these changes with economics and tradition, in order for a school to function well in a community.

SUMMARY

The technological society of today is a complex web of interrelated and interdependent systems. The basic technologies of construction, communication, manufacturing and transportation work cooperatively to keep our society alive and growing. No one system of technology could exist without the products and services provided by the other systems. The fields of mathematics and science are also important to construction. Workers must be able to understand and apply math operations and scientific principles for construction systems to operate safely and efficiently.

Construction systems can be very complex in today's technological world. In order to use construction safely and efficiently people must understand how the system works. The systems approach can be used to break construction systems into its basic parts. Analyzing the basic parts can make a complex technology like construction easier to understand.

Two systems approach methods that can be used to help people understand construction technology are examining subsystems and using the universal systems model. Apply these techniques to structures in your community to learn more about local construction systems.

All cultures design and build structures that serve the societal institutions of family, community, state, religion, trade, recreation and education. Although culture influences the design of constructed systems, some sociologists believe that once structures are in place, they influence society as well.

. . . .

Study Questions

1. What are the four basic technologies?

2. There are two categories of basic technologies. Name and define these two categories and give one example of each.

3. Technology systems are interrelated and interdependent. Give one example of the importance of construction to the fields of communication, manufacturing and transportation. Then give one example of how construction depends on the other three basic technologies.

4. Why are math and science important to construction?

. . . .

5. Subsystems are systems within systems. Can you give examples of subsystems in your home?

6. What are the four parts of the universal systems model?

7. Can you name the seven inputs found in all systems of technology? Which is most important? Which inputs do you think could be eliminated?

8. List structures that you use every day and place them into the various societal institution categories.

9. Explain the meaning of Winston Churchill's statement, "We shape our buildings and, thereafter, our buildings shape us."

10. List and describe interesting structures from another culture. Why do you find these structures interesting? Which social institutions do you think they relate to?

Suggested Activities

1. Make a chart that illustrates the interdependence of the basic technologies in your local community.

2. Interview a worker or manager in the construction field and ask him or her to describe the math and science used as a part of the job.

3. As a group project, analyze a structure in your community using the subsystems method or the universal systems model. Make a chart identifying the basic components of the structure.

4. Rank the seven inputs to construction systems from most important to least important. Give your reasons for ranking the inputs in a certain way. Can any of the inputs be eliminated from the construction system?

Glossary

Beanstalk Principle   The principle that states that for every system, there is an optimal limit beyond which it ought not to grow, or elements of the system will be affected adversely.

Culture   The unique characteristics of a group of people.

Feedback   The fourth step in the universal systems model. Feedback are the means of monitoring (checking) and adjusting the inputs, processes, and outputs to make sure the goal of the system is achieved.

Four basic technologies   Communication, construction, manufacturing and transportation are basic technologies found in all technological societies.

Inputs   The first step in the universal systems model. Inputs are everything that must be put into a system to make the system work.

Interdependent   Each system of technology depends on the others for safe, efficient operations.

Interrelated   All systems of technology are related; one can not exist without the others.

Outputs   The third step in the universal systems model. Processes are the actions performed by people using the inputs to a system.

Production technology   A technology that produces or makes goods and products to meet the needs of society, including construction and manufacturing technologies.

Service technology   A technology that produces services to meet the needs of society, including communication and transportation technology.

Society   An organized group of people sharing similar institutions such as family, community, state, religion, trade, recreation and education.

Subsystem   A system within a larger system; all complex systems have subsystems.

Systems approach   A technique used to make a complex system of technology less complex by breaking the whole system into its basic parts.

Technical means   The tools, materials and technical knowledge used by people.

Tradeoff   Accepting the negative impacts of technology in order to receive the positive benefits.

Universal systems model   A systems approach method that breaks complex systems into inputs, processes, outputs and feedback.

Part I

Inputs

Chapter 2

Construction Materials

Chapter Concepts

■ Proper selection of construction materials depends on cost, geographic location, and availability.

■ Materials can be grouped into three overlapping categories: structural, protective and decorative.

■ Common structural materials are wood, concrete, brick, stone, and steel.

■ Protective materials are used in many sheltering systems including windows, siding, insulation and roofs.

Key Terms

admixture
aggregate
alloy steel
brick
decorative material
dimension lumber
indigenous resource
insulation
particleboard
pressure treating
protective material

R value
reflective glass
retarders
rock wool
shake
skeleton construction
structural material
tempered glass
terne
thatch
waferboard

(Previous page) Materials, such as this dimension lumber, are one of the key inputs to construction systems.

(Left) Modern uses of materials allow for well-lighted and spacious interiors. How many different materials can you find in this photograph? Why do you think they were used in the construction of this shopping and library complex? (Courtesy of County of Orondaga, New York)

Glass, stone and wood are the main materials of this solar house. (Courtesy of Deck House, Inc.)

ook around any building material or hardware store and you will see an amazing variety of types, styles and forms of construction materials. The number of different materials is increasing steadily as new products enter the marketplace. Entire books have been written on the subject without covering all of the materials commonly available. This chapter is intended to provide only a broad overview of some of the most commonly used construction materials.

It is said that there is no substitute for experience; this is certainly true with construction materials. This information is only useful if supplemented with hands (and eyes) on experience. Knowing that Number Three (economy) grade lumber is the lowest quality commercially available is good to know, but looking through a stack of this grade lumber, noting its various strengths and weakness and thereby becoming familiar with the material, is even more beneficial.

Selection of Materials

The proper selection of the most appropriate building material must be based on several criteria. One of the most obvious of these is cost. Often many different materials can be used to perform the same function, but with large differences in final cost. It is important to note that there is a difference between the real cost and the price of a material. If a material that is low in purchase price requires significant labor, or quickly deteriorates with age, its real cost may be quite a bit higher than that of a more durable, easier to install and maintain material with a higher purchase price.

Geographic location also plays an important role in the selection of building materials. The location itself is perhaps not as significant as are local consumer demands, dominant weather patterns and available resources.

Differing areas often have a dominant, and unique, style of architecture. A particular material may be very fashionable and therefore in great demand by consumers in one area, and yet be unpopular in others.

Different weather patterns require different types of structures. A home that is excellent for a Florida location would most likely be unacceptable in Alaska, and vice versa. However, differing needs of structures are not always based on such an extreme geographic separation. A structure built on the shore where it is constantly exposed to highly corrosive salt spray and mist might require different materials than would a similar structure built only a few miles inland.

Geographic location directly influences the cost of materials. If the material to be used is an **indigenous resource,** something found naturally in the area, it will usually be substantially less expensive than another material

The House That Trash Built

This house is made of bottles and cans.
(Courtesy of Walter M. Kroner, Professor and
Director, Center for Architectural Research,
RPI)

Every so often newspapers and magazines have featured articles describing a home or other structure that is made partly, or entirely, from materials gathered from the local scrap pile. The designer/builder of these structures is often quoted as saying that this is the wave of the future, that soon all houses will use unprocessed scrap materials as their main building material.

Obviously these predictions never came true, at least not to the extent that was predicted. There is increased interest in using recycled materials in modern construction applications, but these materials are almost always processed into new, more commonly acceptable, forms.

Nevertheless, in a time when new buildings are often criticized for being unimaginative and indistinct clones, these structures serve as glowing examples of imagination and creativity. They demonstrate how countless numbers of materials can be utilized in the construction process to create new patterns and effects. The designers of these structures were able to free themselves of preconceived ideas as to what a building material is, and look around to find inventive new uses for existing products.

Earlier attempts at this method were inspired by much simpler considerations. In 1912, wood was relatively rare and expensive in parts of Nevada. Solution? Build a bottle house from discarded bottles. This bottle house was built primarily because discarded bottles were plentiful and free.

More recent attempts have often used bottles, not only because of their low cost but also because they are strong, durable and can be used to create a beautiful visual effect as sunlight filters through the different colored glass.

Aluminum, steel and tin cans have all been used as a construction material. Cans used in this fashion are strong enough to meet building code for structures up to two stories tall.

Fieldstone, an indigenous resource in some areas, provides a durable and attractive construction material. (Photo by Stan Komacek)

This composite concrete panel fulfills all three functional categories of construction materials—it is structural, protective and decorative.

that must be transported from far away. Wood and marble provide an excellent example of this. Throughout most of the world, marble is an expensive and high-status material, while wood is considered more common and less prestigious. But in many parts of Italy marble is an abundant indigenous resource, while high-quality wood is relatively rare. For this reason many builders in Italy will use marble as a protective and decorative material instead of wood, because it is significantly less expensive.

Classifying Materials

There is no easy way to classify the materials used in the construction process. Every method yet devised to organize construction materials has some major limitations or shortcomings. One method, the one used in this chapter, is to group materials by their intended function. Any material may be classified by function as being **structural, protective** or **decorative.**

Structural materials are those elements of a structure that support weight and/or assist in maintaining the shape and form of the structure. Protective materials shelter the structure and its contents from adverse environmental conditions such as precipitation, wind, high or low temperatures, noise, insects and intrusion. Decorative materials make the structure more appealing to the senses, particularly visual.

A major drawback of this system is that one material may serve more than one function. Glass block may be used to form an exterior entrance to a commercial or residential building. The block is structural, because it supports the roof or door frame. It also protects against moisture, noise and intrusion. Yet, its selection as a material may have been based on the desire to form an inviting and visually appealing entrance. Therefore, in this application, the glass block serves all three functions.

Because of the way the functions of materials can overlap, this chapter does not contain a section devoted strictly to decorative materials. Many of the materials that can be classified as being decorative are also protective (ie. siding and shingles) or structural (ie. stone and brick) and are covered in other sections. In addition, there is an overwhelming variety of materials that may be considered strictly decorative, most of which have limited use. These materials have been omitted to allow a more detailed discussion of the more significant and widely used structural and protective materials.

. . . .

Structural Materials

Structural materials are those elements used to form the framework of a structure. Concrete, steel, wood and stone are all commonly used structural materials. These materials are used for structural frameworks because they are able to maintain their shape while supporting a static (stationary) or dynamic (moving) load.

A structural material may be selected based on its aesthetics (how it looks), but more often the decision is a function of the size and shape of the building. For example, while a typical suburban, single-family home can use wood as its primary structural element, it would not be appropriate for a skyscraper. The tremendous weight of a multi-story building would cause it to collapse if steel and/or concrete were not extensively used.

A structural material may be exposed, as in a steel suspension bridge or stone house, or covered by a protective or decorative material. If left exposed, the material must be resistant to the various climatic conditions.

The structural materials of this bridge, concrete and steel, must support both static and dynamic loads. (Courtesy of PCI Journal)

Structural lumber is the backbone of the construction trade. The frame of this house is made up of a variety of dimensional lumber. Carpenters are sheathing the house with wafer board. (Courtesy of Mitek Industries)

■ Wood

Wood was one of the first materials ever used by humans to construct a shelter and it is still widely used today. There are a number of reasons for this popularity, among them strength, availability, versatility and low cost.

Categories of Wood ■ Wood is broadly classified into two categories. **Softwood** comes from conifers, needle-leaved evergreen trees. **Hardwood** is cut from trees that are deciduous; they have broad leaves that are shed at the end of the growing season. These terms can be misleading. Hardwoods are not always hard and softwoods can be stronger than some hardwoods. For example, balsa, a wood commonly known by model builders for its extreme light weight and ease of cutting, is from a deciduous tree and is therefore classified as a hardwood.

Softwoods generally grow faster, straighter, taller and closer together than hardwoods. These factors make softwoods much cheaper than hardwoods. This low price is the main reason why softwoods are used much more often than hardwoods as a structural material.

Inputs

Wood is also classified by size:

- **Dimension lumber** is most commonly used for structural purposes. The familiar 2 × 4 and 4 × 4 are examples of dimension lumber.

- **Boards** have at least one side thinner than 2 inches. Boards are not extensively used for structural applications. Sometimes they are used as a flooring, but they are more commonly used for shelving, siding, furniture and cabinet making.

The dimensions of wood are based on the size of green, rough-cut pieces. The milling process (to produce a smooth surface) and the drying process both cause the final dimensions to be notably smaller than the given size. A standard 2 × 4 is very close to 2 inches by 4 inches when rough cut and wet, but actually only 1½ by 3½ inches by the time it is ready for use.

American Standard Softwood Lumber Sizes

| | Thickness | | | | Face width | |
| | Actual size Minimum dressed | | | | Actual size Minimum dressed | |
Item	**Named Size**	**Dry**	**Green**	**Named Size**	**Dry**	**Green**
	(in.)	(in.)	(in.)	(in.)	(in.)	(in.)
Board	1	¾	²⁵/₃₂	2	1½	1⁹/₁₆
	1¼	1	1¹/₃₂	3	2½	2⁹/₁₆
	1½	1¼	1⁹/₃₂	4	3½	3⁹/₁₆
				5	4½	4⅝
				6	5½	5⅝
				7	6½	6⅝
				8	7¼	7½
				9	8¼	8½
				10	9¼	9½
				11	10¼	10½
				12	11¼	11½
				14	13¼	13½
				16	15¼	15½
Dimension	2	1½	1⁹/₁₆	2	1½	1⁹/₁₆
	2½	2	2¹/₁₆	3	2½	2⁹/₁₆
	3	2½	2⁹/₁₆	4	3½	3⁹/₁₆
	3½	3	3¹/₁₆	5	4½	4⅝
	4	3½	3⁹/₁₆	6	5½	5⅝
	4½	4	4¹/₁₆	8	7¼	7½
				10	9¼	9½
				12	11¼	11½
				14	13¼	13½
				16	15¼	15½
Timbers	5 and greater		½ less than named size	5 and greater		½ less than named size

Lumber in this shop is remanufactured into kitchen cabinetry panels. This machine sands panels on both top and bottom before assembly. (Courtesy of Conestoga Wood Specialities, Inc.)

Softwood is grouped into three categories by its intended use.

Yard Lumber is intended for general building or construction use. Lumber in this category may be dimension or further processed into forms suitable for siding and flooring (tongue-and-grooved, beveled, shiplaped). Yard lumber has two grades; select and common. Select is used when a good appearance is wanted. Common grade is significantly less expensive, but its appearance makes it suitable for those applications where it is hidden from view or when appearance is not considered to be important.

Shop or Factory lumber is intended for remanufacturing purposes such as door frames, window sashes and decorative trim. Grading for shop and factory lumber is based on the amount and size of high-quality pieces that can be obtained from a board.

Structural lumber is used when, for architectural reasons, the piece must be able to resist a specified amount of bending, compression and tension. Structural lumber is grouped based on its size.

- **Structural light framing** is the grade given the smallest structural lumber. Lumber in this group has thickness of 2 inches to 4 inches and widths of 3 inches to 4 inches.

- **Structural joists and planks** is lumber that is 2 to 4 inches thick and wider than 5 inches.

- **Beams and stringers** are at least 5 inches thick with widths more than 2 inches greater than the thickness.

- **Post and timbers** are similar in size to beams and stringers, but are closer to a square shape. The minimum thickness for posts and timbers is 5 inches; widths must not be more than 2 inches greater than the thickness.

All of the above sizes are further graded by quality. Select is the premium grade, followed by structural number one, two and three. Structural light framing wood has a fourth grade, "stud,"—the lowest grade of the size.

Pressure-Treated Wood ■ Pressure-treated wood is primarily used for outdoor applications or when the wood is expected to be in contact with moisture or insects. The pressure-treating process applies chemicals to the wood that are toxic to insects and fungus. The most commonly used chemicals are coal-tar compounds and water-borne inorganic compounds.

Coal-tar compounds include creosote, a dark brown substance distilled from coal tar. Creosote may be used alone or mixed with coal tar or petroleum. A creosote mixture is generally less expensive, but not as efficient as straight creosote for resisting insects and fungus. This resistance is due to the complex chemical structure of creosote. It contains over 160 different compounds known to be toxic to wood-eating insects, fungi and marine borers.

If you have ever sat on a newly constructed pier or leaned against a newly installed utility pole, you are probably familiar with one of the main disadvantage of creosite-treated wood. It is extremely dirty. Another significant

Safety Tip

Pressure-treated wood contains a wide variety of toxic compounds. Burning this wood releases these compounds into the atmosphere, creating a potential health hazard. For this reason, all pressure-treated wood should be properly disposed of, not burned or buried at the job site.

disadvantage is its toxicity. Some of the compounds in creosote that are toxic to insects are also harmful to humans.

Water-borne inorganic compounds are commonly used in residential construction. The pale green lumber often found in decks and patios is pressure treated with chromated copper arsenate (CCA). As with creosote-treated wood, lumber treated with CCA or other water-borne inorganic compounds is toxic to insects and fungi that cause wood to decay. Wood treated with these compounds is clean, odorless and can be painted, stained or left to weather to a natural gray color. Wood treated with CCA is available in most lumber yards or hardware stores.

Regardless of the agent used, the preservative rarely is absorbed completely through the entire thickness of the wood. For this reason, pressure-treated wood that is cut after the treatment process should have the cut ends retreated to avoid the possibility of infestation entering from the exposed cut.

Plywood ▪ Plywood is one of the most commonly used construction materials. It is an inexpensive means of forming a large, flat, durable surface and is relatively lightweight and easy to work with. Plywood has a wide variety of applications including subflooring, sheathing, roof decking and forms for concrete.

Plywood is manufactured by peeling thin layers of wood from logs. These layers are then cut to size, glued, stacked with the grain running in alternate directions and then subjected to high temperatures and pressure. The finished product should have an odd number of layers (3, 5, or 7). If an even number of layers is used, the finished sheet will have the grain on both outside layers running in opposite directions, thereby allowing a greater amount of warping.

Plywood thicknesses typically range from 1/4 to 3/4 inches. The standard size is 4 by 8 feet (48 by 96 inches), accounting for over 75 percent of all the plywood sold. Plywood marked "sized for spacing" is cut one-half inch shorter (95-1/2 inches). This allows workers to leave a small gap between plywood sheets, to allow for expansion, while still having each joint fall evenly on a joist, rafter or stud. Plywood has been made in lengths of up to fifty feet, but 5 × 10 feet is the more common maximum size for special orders.

Grading of plywood is based on the quality of the veneer (the outermost layers of wood) and on its ability to withstand moisture. Veneer quality is graded N, A, B, C, C plugged and D. "N" is the premium grade; it is suitable for highly visible applications where appearance is important. "D" is the poorest quality grade; it is used primarily for subflooring or roof decking, where it is completely covered and concealed from view. Plywood often has two letters used to describe the quality of its veneer. These letters refer to the quality of the individual sides of the sheet. A sheet that is marked A–C has one high quality (A) side and one poorer quality (C) side. Since the cost of plywood increases with the quality of its veneer and plywood is often used in applications that expose only one face, significant savings can be achieved by opting for a poorer quality backing.

Veneer machines peel a thin layer of wood from a log—the first step in making plywood.

The layers of plywood are arranged with the grain running in alternate directions to increase strength.

The moisture resistance of plywood is classified into four groups:

- **Exterior** panels are made with completely waterproof glue that prevents delamination (the separation of the individual layers) when exposed to high-moisture areas or precipitation. The wood used in this grade is the most durable of all the grades.

- **Exposure 1** (commonly called CDX plywood) is bonded with the same glue used in exterior grade, but the wood is not as durable. CDX plywood, if properly sealed, can be used in a limited number of outdoor applications.

- **Exposure 2** also uses a waterproof glue, but the wood is poorer quality than that used in exposure 1 grades. Plywood graded exposure 2 should not be used for outdoor applications unless it is protected from direct, long-term contact with water.

- **Interior** panels are made with glue that is not water resistant; as a result contact with water will result in delamination. For this reason, interior grade should only be used in indoor applications where there is no contact with water or extremely high humidity.

Wafer board can be made with different finished surfaces for a variety of indoor and outdoor uses. (Courtesy of Boise Cascade)

Manufactured Wood Panels ■ Manufactured wood panels are increasingly being used in the construction process to replace plywood. There are several varieties available. Their names and applications are based primarily on the size of the wood fragments being used.

Particleboard is manufactured from small wood particles that are mixed with a bonding resin, heated and pressed to form solid panels. These panels are most commonly made in 4 foot widths. Thicknesses range from 3/8 to 3/4 inch; lengths include the standard 8 foot, as well as 10 and 12 foot. The small wood fragments used to produce particleboard do not provide a great deal of strength; therefore its use as a structural material is limited.

Waferboard is manufactured by a process similar to particleboard but uses thin wood chips that are up to 1-1/4 inches square. The greater strength of the larger wood fragments allow waferboard to be made thinner (1/4 inch minimum) and longer (up to 16 feet) than particleboard. The strength of waferboard makes it a suitable substitute for plywood in many construction applications. These applications include roof decking, sheathing, subflooring and exterior coverings. Waferboard can be purchased unsanded, sanded on one or both sides and in plain or patterned forms. Patterned panels are usually grooved to appear as tongue-and-groove planking when painted and used as an exterior covering.

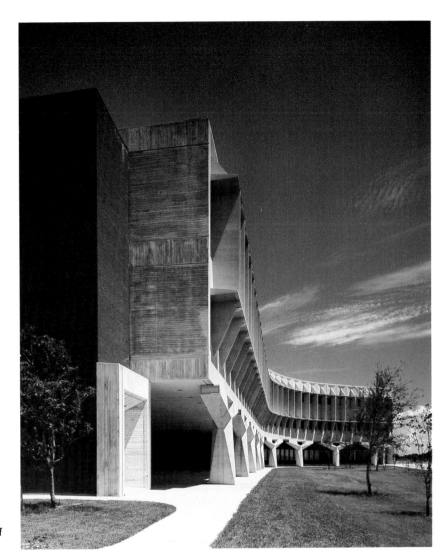

White portland cement gives this building a pleasing color. The precast cement window units function as walls, windows and sunshades. (IBM Building, Boca Raton, Florida. Courtesy of Marcel Breuer and Assoc.)

■ Concrete

Concrete is one of the most abundantly used structural materials in use in the construction industry. Many people will be surprised to know that it is by no means a modern invention. It is believed to have been first used before the second century B.C., when the Romans used it to construct buildings and monuments.

Concrete is a mixture of cement, aggregate, water and, on occasion, an admixture. Each of these components have several different types and varieties that directly affect the nature and strength of the finished concrete.

Cement ■ Cement is the most critical element in the production of concrete. In 1825, Joseph Aspdin invented a mixture that he called "Portland cement." Although this mixture has been improved upon and slightly modified with time, it is still the most common form of cement used in the produc-

· ·

TYPICAL SOURCES OF RAW MATERIAL USED IN THE MANUFACTURE OF PORTLAND CEMENT

COMPONENTS

Lime	Silica	Alumina	Iron
Cement rock	Sand	Clay	Iron ore
Limestone	Traprock	Shale	Iron calcine
Marl	Calcium silicate	Slag	Iron dust
Alkali waste	Quartzite	Fly ash	Iron pyrite
Oyster shell	Fuller's earth	Copper slag	Iron sinters
Coquina shell		Aluminum ore refuse	Iron oxide
Chalk		Staurolite	Blast furnace flue
Marble		Diaspore clay	dust
		Granodiorite	
		Kaolin	

tion of concrete. The components of modern portland cement are shown above. Portland cement is manufactured in three main types and for five different applications.

Standard portland cement is most commonly used for construction applications. If someone mentions "cement", without further specifying the type, it can be safely assumed that this person is referring to standard portland cement.

White portland cement has all of the structural and physical properties as standard portland. Careful selection of raw materials produce a very light colored cement. The advantages of white portland cement are strictly visual. The lighter tint is more visually appealing than is the drab gray of standard portland cement. Coloring agents may be added to white portland cement to produce a finished surface tinted with any desired color. Higher costs limit the use of this product to applications where appearances are important.

Air Entraining portland cement produces billions of microscopic air bubbles within the concrete. These air bubbles provide greater resistance to potentially destructive freezing and thawing cycles. Less water is needed to produce a workable consistency in air entraining concrete.

Cement Applications ■ These cements are commonly available for five different applications. The type needed is dependent on the job site, manner of construction, desired strength and size of the structure.

Type I normal is the most commonly used for all applications, including construction. If cement is ordered without further specification, type I normal is assumed. Type I cement will disintegrate if exposed to sulfates or alkaloids, produces significant amounts of heat that can damage extremely large blocks, sets relatively slowly and takes months or years to develop full strength.

Type II moderate-sulphate resistant is used for foundations, drainage and floor slabs in areas that contain moderate amounts of sulfates in the

Do concrete carpenters use stone hammers?

Some carpenters work for weeks on a project, leave it standing for a few days, and then tear it down. Their projects are sometimes the size of a house, other times smaller than a compact car. It is not dissatisfaction with the results of their work that causes them to tear it down; it was planned that way from the start. In fact, they even use special nails with two heads that are designed to be easily removed.

These people are concrete carpenters, their job is to make forms that will shape and hold concrete until it sets. Evidence of their craft can often be seen underneath highway bridges or other large-scale concrete works. When concrete has a texture that resembles wood, complete with knotholes and grains, it is a sure sign that the forms used to pour the concrete were wood, and they were made by concrete carpenters.

soils. Type II cement sets slower than does type I and produces less heat during the curing process.

Type III high early strength is primarily used when time is critical. After three days, Type III cement is almost twice as strong as the same age Type I. This is important consideration in some applications, particularly in high-rise building construction, when forms must be set, concrete poured and forms removed as quickly as possible. Type III cement generates considerable amounts of heat as it sets. This combination of high heat and fast setting also makes Type III useful in applications where freezing temperatures may be present during pouring and setting.

Type IV low heat of hydration is not universally available. It is specifically designed for massive applications, such as large concrete dams. The heat generated by most cements would cause significant problems if used in the enormous amounts required for these structures. Type IV cement sets slower than any other type.

Type V sulfate resistant is used in structures that are exposed to higher than normal amounts of sulfates or highly alkaline water. Type V cement takes longer to reach full strength and produces less heat than do Types I, II and III.

APPROXIMATE RELATIVE STRENGTH OF CONCRETE AS AFFECTED BY TYPE OF CEMENT

Types of Portland Cement	Compressive Strength—Percent of Strength of Normal (Type I) Portland-Cement Concrete			
	1 Day	7 Days	28 Days	3 Months
10 Normal	100	100	100	100
20 Moderate	75	85	90	100
30 High-early-strength	190	120	110	100
40 Low-heat	55	55	75	100
50 Sulfate-resistant	65	75	85	100

These carpenters are building a very large concrete form. Note their safety harnesses. (Courtesy of the United Brotherhood of Carpenters)

• •

And you thought it was all marble

Scientists and professionals in the construction industry around the time of the American revolution knew less about the nature and uses of concrete than did the ancient Romans. In the first century A.D. the Roman author Vitruvius wrote; "There is also a powder which from natural causes produces astonishing results. . . . This substance, when mixed with lime and rubble, not only lends strength to buildings of other kinds, but even when piers are constructed in the sea, they set hard underwater."

Vitruvius and his peers had no understanding of the chemical reactions taking place in curing concrete, but they had developed its use to impressive degrees. The Pantheon, built around 123 A.D., still stands as an example of Roman understanding and use of concrete. Its ceiling span of 143 feet was not exceeded for almost 1500 years. It is interesting to note that its seven-foot-thick walls used a mixture of aggregates. Stone, brick and pottery shards were used in the lower levels. Lightweight aggregates such as pumice, imported from Mount Vesuvius, and hollow clay tubes and even empty wine and oil bottles were used for the higher levels.

During the dark ages, much of

Built in the second century A.D., the Pantheon is perhaps the best example of the ancient Romans understanding of the use of concrete. When empty wine and oil bottles were first discovered inside the walls it was believed to be the result of sloppy workers. Further investigation revealed that these bottles were used as a form of lightweight aggregate.

the knowledge concerning concrete was lost. It was the late eighteenth century before any further major research was done on the development of concrete cement. The primary reference material for this research was the writing of Vitruvius, written over 1600 years earlier. It was not until 1811 that a cement (portland cement) superior in quality to the Romans' was developed.

Aggregates ■ Aggregates make up two thirds to three quarters of the volume of concrete. An aggregate is a material that does not react with water or cement and is used to add both strength and inexpensive volume to a concrete. Sand and gravel are the most commonly used aggregates, but the choice of materials is by no means limited to those two. All aggregates can be classified by their weight and their size. The proper selection of the aggregate has a direct effect on the weight, durability, strength and other qualities of the finished concrete.

Lightweight aggregates include perlite, vermiculite, pumice, expanded slag and expanded clay. All of these aggregates produce a concrete that is significantly less dense than standard weights. Perlite and vermiculite have the advantage of improving insulation characteristics of the concrete. Unfortunately, this added insulation is gained only at the expense of lost strength. Therefore concretes that use perlite or vermiculites as an aggregate have limited structural applications.

Slag is a waste material created during the production of metals. If slag is sprayed with water while it is still extremely hot it expands or foams. This process traps tiny air bubbles inside the material, greatly reducing its density.

Lightweight aggregates are being used in greater amounts in recent years. Part of the reason for this is reduced cost. Lighter concrete means reduced costs caused by decreased amounts of space, materials and labor needed to support the weight of the material.

Standard-weight aggregates are usually sand, stone, gravel and unexpanded slag. All of these materials provide good bonding with the cement and are inexpensive.

Heavyweight aggregates are rarely used. Although uncommon, there are structures that require a specific high weight as well as structural strength. In such cases, or when the finished concrete is used for a radiation shield, masgnetite, barite or steel and iron punchings (scrap from a manufacturing process) are used as an aggregate.

Water ■ When it comes to adding water to make concrete, many people go by the adage "If it's wet, it will work." Unfortunately, this is not always true. Even some texts and "how-to" books will specify "water fit for human consumption;" this is not always correct either. Drinking water in some areas has relatively high levels of sulfates or other impurities that can cause a reduction in the quality and strength of the finished mixture.

Cement and concrete do not dry in the conventional sense. Rather than evaporating, the water combines with the cement into a new chemical compound. Water content of concrete must be carefully controlled: too much water will weaken the final product and too little water will cause incomplete setting, which also decreases the strength.

Admixtures ■ Admixtures are specially designed chemicals or materials that are added to the concrete mixture before pouring. These agents allow the concrete to be tailored to meet specific requirements of the site or application.

Accelerators reduce the time taken for concrete to form its initial set. Calcium chloride is the most common accelerator used. The amount of accelerator should not exceed two percent of the total weight of the concrete mixture.

Retarders increase the amount of time taken for concrete to form its initial set. These slower rates are desirable in hot, dry or windy weather conditions that would cause normal concrete to set without adequate time for working and finishing. The steel framework of some structures, most notably highway bridges, are designed to bend slightly as the weight placed upon them is increased. If some of the concrete placed around this steel work hardened before all the weight was applied, stress and cracks might result as the framework continued to bend. By adding a retarding agent, this problem can be eliminated or reduced.

Hardeners are used to extend the life expectancy of concrete that will be exposed to heavy wear. hardeners are usually applied to the top of the freshly poured slab and worked into the concrete using a float or trowel.

Super plasticizers are used when a strong, high-quality concrete is needed. When mixed with water, cement has a tendency to clump together, much like lumps in gravy. A super plasticizer coats each cement particle and gives it a negative electrical charge. This causes the lumps to break up and dissolve evenly in the concrete mixture. The resulting mixture is more workable and requires less water, thereby increasing the strength of the concrete.

Buying Concrete and Cement ■ The method of buying and mixing concrete depends on the size of the job. For small jobs, bags of dry, ready-mixed concrete can be purchased in 60-pound bags to be mixed with water. Mixing can be done by hand or motorized mixer. For slightly larger jobs, portland cement is purchased in 94-pound bags, mixed with water, damp sand and other aggregates. Larger pours usually have premixed concrete delivered by truck ready for immediate use. Concrete delivered by truck is sold by the cubic yard.

To support the weight of large buildings, concrete is poured in columns.

Trucks deliver premixed concrete for large jobs such as this slab foundation.

Inputs

Brick is an extremely versatile material. This special order brick was assembled into a sculptural panel depicting the Civil War General Stonewall Jackson. (Photo by John Carnes, Courtesy of General Shale)

■ Brick

Brick may be defined as earthen material that is formed and dried into a rectangular block. Various kinds of brick have been used in construction applications for thousands of years. If properly made and installed, brick can be one of the most durable and long-lived building products in common use.

There is a staggering variety of types and styles of brick available. The following section will discuss a few of the most common of these.

Kiln-Burned Brick ■ Kiln-burned brick is the most commonly used brick. Anyone living in a industrialized country has undoubtedly seen the traditional red kiln-burned brick. These bricks are made from sand, clay or shale. Slight differences in the material used in the production of brick or slight changes in the firing process can have a profound effect on the final product.

• •

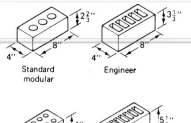

Standard modular

Engineer

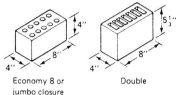

Economy 8 or jumbo closure

Double

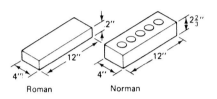

Roman

Norman

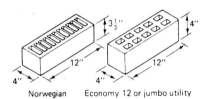

Norwegian

Economy 12 or jumbo utility

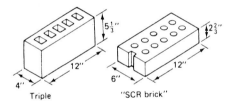

Triple

"SCR brick"

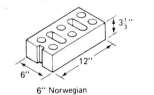

6" Norwegian

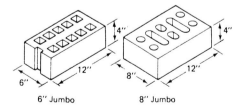

6" Jumbo

8" Jumbo

Bricks are commonly made in a variety of styles and sizes.

The weather resistance of brick is graded into three groups:

- **Grade SW** is intended for severe weather (SW) conditions. The high strength of this brick makes it less likely to suffer damage from freeze-thaw cycles and water contact. SW grade brick is ideal for below ground or other locations where it may be subjected to both water and freezing conditions.

- **Grade MW** is intended for moderate weather (MW) exposures. This brick can withstand freezing temperatures, but should be used where there is limited exposure to water. Walls built above ground are usually constructed using this grade.

- **Grade NW** (no weathering) is used for indoor applications or where there is little likelihood of freezing or water contact. NW grade brick has the lowest compressive strength of all three grades.

Standard brick can be used to create great depth and texture. (Photo by John Carnes, Courtesy of General Shale)

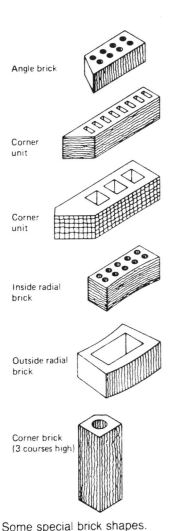

Angle brick

Corner unit

Corner unit

Inside radial brick

Outside radial brick

Corner brick (3 courses high)

Some special brick shapes.

Special brick shapes provide flexibility of design.

Brick is further classified by size, function and style:

Common Brick is the cheapest and most frequently used brick in construction. Common brick is used when there is no need for special colors, textures or shapes. The color varies from a deep red to a dark orange, depending on the clay material found in the area of production.

Face Brick is made under more controlled conditions than is common brick. Face brick is graded into three types depending on intended use.

- **FBX** is for general use in exposed walls and partitions when variations in size and color must be within certain strict limits.

- **FBS** is also used for walls and partitions, but when color and size requirements are less stringent than FBX.

- **FBA** is used when subtle variations in color, texture and size are desired in order to produce a specified visual effect.

  Glazed face brick is given a glazed facing during the manufacturing process. This glazing may be glossy, mottled, satin or dull. The addition of metallic salts to the glaze creates a range of colors, textures and finishes.

  Fire Brick is used in applications where it will be subjected to extreme heat, such as in fireplaces, chimneys and furnaces. Fire brick is softer than common brick and is usually a light brown color.

  Sand Lime Brick uses lime and washed sand to produce a pearl gray colored brick. The uses and grading of sand lime brick are similar to kiln-burned brick.

  Special Brick refers to brick with a form and/or appearance made to order. Brick made in a special form is often used as a sill, corner or door frame. Bricks that are special ordered for appearance may be specified by an architect or designer, who is attempting to create a certain visual effect. They may also be used to create a sense of uniformity and distinction for a chain of retail stores, housing developments or similar projects. Special brick made to meet construction demands include radial brick used to form a curved wall, corner brick and angled brick.

Adobe Brick ■ Adobe brick is traditionally made by mixing clay and straw, forming it into rough rectangular blocks and placing it in direct sunlight to dry. These bricks were then stacked to form the walls of a structure. Another traditional method used the same material stacked while it was still somewhat wet.

Modern adobe brick uses emulsified asphalt as a stabilizing agent. Walls are reinforced with steel, particularly in areas susceptible to earthquakes. Bricks are assembled on a concrete foundation that extends at least six inches above ground. Overhanging roofs are used in conjunction with a water-resistant outer coating for protection for precipitation and moisture.

In terms of cost and thermal efficiency, adobe can be a fantastic building material. Adobe walls are usually at least 16 inches thick and relatively heavy. The large amounts of mass used in the walls absorbs heat during the day, maintaining a cool and comfortable indoor temperature. At night this heat is slowly released keeping the home warm despite chilly evening temperatures.

Adobe is an excellent example of a geographically appropriate building material. While adobe is a relatively common sight in arid and semiarid areas, it is not used in areas with moderate or greater amounts of precipitation. The reason for this is simple: adobe will disintegrate in rain.

Structural Clay Tile ■ Structural clay tile may be used as a structural element for an unfinished wall, a faced wall or as a plastered load-bearing wall. Clay tile that is designed to be used in an unplastered wall is referred to as structural clay facing tile. Structural facing tile is graded into two groups.

- **Grade FTX** has a smooth finish. It is used when the tile needs to be easily cleaned, resistant to stains and uniform in color and dimensions.

- **Grade FTS** may have either a smooth or textured surface. FTS tiles have a greater color range, slightly less precise dimensions and may have a limited number of flaws in the finish and/or small chips on the surface.

  Clay tile that is made to provide structural support while covered by a facing or stucco is called structural clay load-bearing tile. It is also graded in two groups:

- **Grade LBX** is suitable for applications where the tile will be exposed to freezing temperatures.

- **Grade LBS** must be protected from freezing temperatures. This grade, therefore, can be used primarily in tropical climates and protected indoor areas. If it is used in cold areas, it must be covered by at least three inches of facing.

Structural clay tile varies according to its application.

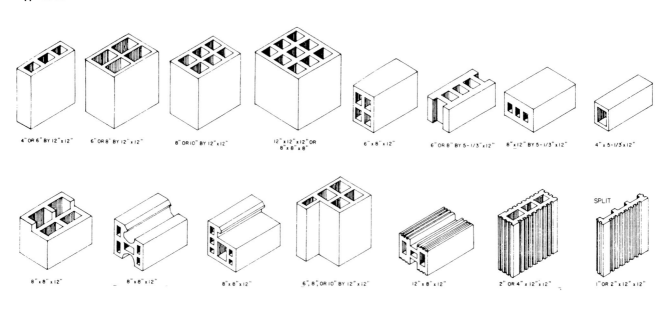

Concrete block foundations are favored in some cases over poured concrete. Foundations such as this one can be built without building wooden forms. (Courtesy of Gary Bolyard)

■ Concrete Blocks

Concrete blocks are often referred to as cinder blocks. This name is not always correct. Cinder block is a type of concrete block that uses cinders as an aggregate. There are a variety of other aggregates used in concrete blocks. These aggregates directly influence the strength and weight of the block. Concrete blocks are commonly used much like large bricks to form walls. These walls are constructed using a mortar between the individual blocks, or are stacked into shape and covered with a fiberglass-reinforced mortar mix, a process called surface bonding.

Block Types ■ Block types are grouped by form and function. Concrete block forms include pierced, glazed, textured and detailed.

Pierced Blocks are manufactured with openings on the face side. These openings allow light and air through while still providing security and limited amounts of privacy. A wide variety of sizes and styles are available. Pierced blocks are most commonly used in outdoor areas, particularly in gardens and for privacy fences.

Glazed Face have at least one side covered with a glazed finish. A glazed finish has a smooth, colored finish as well as increased durability, impact and abrasion resistance. The smooth finish does not allow germs and bacteria to flourish as they might in a rougher surface. For this reason, glazed block is used when sanitation is important, such as in public bathrooms, dairies and restaurant kitchens.

Detailed block is formed with a textured or patterned face, such as grooves, indented triangles or squares. Detailed block can be used to create an interesting and visually appealing appearance, particularly if exposed to direct sunlight, which creates shadows on the face surface.

Functional classifications of block include hollow load-bearing, solid load-bearing, hollow non-load-bearing, concrete brick and specialty block.

• •

Hollow load-bearing block is defined as a block with walls at least 3/4 to 1-1/2 inches thick, depending on the size of the block. The designation "hollow" indicates that the area of the core is greater than one quarter (25%) of the total surface area of the block. For example, if the area of the hollow core is 30 square inches, and the area of the entire block is 100 square inches, the block would be considered hollow.

Solid load-bearing block is not necessarily completely solid. Like hollow load-bearing block, its walls must be at least a certain thickness. Solid block must have at not more than 25% of its load-bearing face comprised of hollow core.

Hollow non-load-bearing block is similar to load-bearing block but with thinner face wall thicknesses.

Concrete brick does not have a hollow core; it is completely solid.

Specialty concrete block is used for a variety of specific applications. Drainage tile, chimney block and lawn-edging block are all examples of specialty block.

■ Stone

Stone is a prime example of a construction material that can be used for either structural, protective or decorative applications. As a structural material, stone can be used to build home or retaining walls, or as a base for concrete floor slabs or foundations. The protective sheathing of an entire high-rise building may be cut and polished granite. Stone is also widely used as a decorative material. Interior walls, floors and fireplaces are the most common of these applications.

The major considerations in the selection of a stone building material are strength, hardness, workability, durability, appearance (color and grain) and accessibility.

The ancient builders of England's Stonehenge (ca. 1500 B.C.) transported these 7-ton stone blocks over 140 miles from the quarry site. This structure may have been an astronomical observatory and religious site. (Courtesy of Gerald Brommer)

The high compressive strength of stone makes it suitable for the pier foundations of this 18th century Japanese footbridge. The wooden walkway is constructed without any metal fasteners. (Courtesy of George Barford)

Strength is most important when the stone is to be used in structural applications. Compressive strength of more than 5000 pounds per square inch (psi) is considered to be satisfactory for most uses.

The **hardness** of stone varies greatly. Some stone, sandstone for example, is much too soft for many applications, such as floors or steps. Other stone is actually harder than steel.

Workability is often directly related to hardness. Harder stone is usually more difficult to cut and shape. Stone that is not easy to work with requires greater amounts of time and labor to form to size, thereby increasing its cost.

Durability refers to the stone's ability to withstand environmental conditions such as moisture, freezing, heat, air pollution, wind and spray. Durability is directly related to the life expectancy of a material. Depending on the stone used, this life expectancy can range from less than a decade to hundreds of years.

The **appearance** of stone building materials can vary greatly. Colors range from pure white to jet black and almost every conceivable color in between. Pure, unbroken colors are often available as are wild mixtures of colors that rival even the most abstract modern art. The grain, or surface appearance, of stone also varies considerably.

The **accessibility** of stone has the greatest impact on its cost. Questions concerning the accessibility of the stone include: How much of it is available?

Stone is quarried using drilling, cutting and blasting techniques.

How easy is it to quarry? Where is it found? Stone that is rare or difficult to quarry will be more expensive. Stone found at the job site, nearby stream beds or local farm fields usually costs nothing but time and labor. It is not uncommon for stone to be shipped hundreds and sometimes thousands of miles from the quarry to the job site. The transportation costs in such cases can greatly increase the total price of the material.

Commercially available stone is classified by its form:

■ **Rubble** is also referred to as "fieldstone," or even more commonly as "rocks." Rubble may be completely unprocessed stone or stone that is roughly broken to a desired size.

■ **Dimensional** stone, the most commonly used stone, is cut and/or finished to given specifications.

■ **Flagstones** are flat slabs of stone that may have their face dimensions cut to a specified size.

■ **Crushed** stone ranges in size from 3/8 to 6 inches. Although stone of this size does have some applications as a decorative material, its primary use is as a base or aggregate for concrete.

There are five types of stone commonly used in construction processes: These stones are granite, slate, limestone, marble and sandstone.

The United States Navy Memorial in Washington, D.C., includes a 100-foot diameter granite map of the world. Special high power water cutters were developed to slice the granite into the intricate outlines of the continents and oceans. (Courtesy of the U.S. Navy)

Granite ■ Granite is available in textures ranging from natural to mirror smooth and polished. There are also a great variety of colors and grain types available. Granite has a very high compressive strength and low water absorption properties. These factors make it a durable and visually pleasing building material. Granite is often used for both interior and exterior walls, floors and stair treads. Granite is divided into three groups based on its intended use.

■ **Standard building granite** is used as an external structural material.

■ **Granite veneer** is used as a protective and decorative material and is not intended to perform any structural function.

■ **Masonry granite** is used when great amounts of strength and durability are required. This is the thickest of the granite sizes and is most commonly used in block form.

Slate ■ Slate has a natural tendency to split into tough, thin sheets called slates. Colors are usually black or gray and occasionally red, green and purple. Slate is usually available in three grades of finish:

■ **Natural cleft** is not mechanically smoothed; its flat surface is a result of its natural stratification.

- **Sand rubbed** or **semirubbed** finish is partially smoothed but not completely even.

- **Honed** slate is mechanically smoothed to a very even texture.

Uses of slate include slate roofs, countertops, walls, flooring, paving or walkways. Early classroom chalkboards were made of sheets of slate.

Limestone ■ Limestone, when unearthed, is usually relatively soft and workable. With prolonged exposure to air, the stone develops a hard, durable surface. One of the most commonly used stones in construction, limestone is available in all four forms: rubble, crushed, dimensional and flagstone. It is also commonly used for sculptures. Limestone sheathing panels are produced in lengths of up to 16 feet with widths of up to six feet.

Egyptian builders used limestone blocks (some weighing over 2½ tons) to construct the great Sphinx and the Pyramid of Cheops, ca. 2530 B.C. The Pyramid was originally faced with polished limestone to reflect the sun. The stones were cut so that even today it is difficult to force a knife blade between two surfaces. (Courtesy of Gerald Brommer)

Sleek marble blocks form a smooth exterior on the East Wing of the National of Art, Washington, D.C., designed by I.M. Pei. (Courtesy of George Barford)

The South Texas Museum, Corpus Christi, appears as a white marble sculpture when viewed from this side.

Marble ■ Marble, although once used as a structural material, is now used almost exclusively as a protective or decorative material. Even more so than with granite, there is a huge diversity of colors, grains applications and qualities of marble. Some types of marble are extremely durable, while others will quickly disintegrate if exposed to precipitation or other adverse weather conditions. One interesting application of marble is its use in thin sheets to form a translucent wall. These walls filter sunlight into a soft, pleasant glow.

Marble is graded into four quality grades by the Marble Institute of America.

- **Grade A,** the premium grade, is uniformly highly workable and sound with few, if any, flaws.

- **Grade B** is similar to grade A, but is not as uniform in its workability and has a limited amount of repaired voids (lines of separation and faults).

- **Grade C** is marble of uncertain variations in its workability and relatively frequent repaired flaws.

- **Grade D** is the lowest grade; marble in this category has numerous flaws and the greatest variation in workability.

Sandstone, a comparatively soft stone, has long been carved into architectural ornaments. This carving, entitled *Toothache*, was sculptured in 1250 A.D. It adorns the Wells Cathedral in England. (Courtesy of Gerald Brommer)

STRUCTURAL STEEL SHAPES

Shape	Descriptive Name
I	American Standard Beams
[	American Standard Channels
L	Angles-Equal Legs
⌣	Bulb Angles
T	Tees
⊥	Elevator Tees
T	Wall Tees
⌐	Zees

Sandstone ■ Sandstone is the most porous of the commonly used stone types. Because of its porous nature, sandstone can absorb up to six percent of its weight in water. This high water content makes sandstone very susceptible to damage from freezing-thawing cycles. If water absorbed into the stone is allowed to freeze, it expands, causing the stone to crumble or break apart. Some forms of sandstone are much more durable than others. Sandstone may be used in its natural state or processed into wall panels, flagstones and paving.

■ Steel

Steel is an extremely strong, hard and easily formed metal consisting primarily of iron, carbon and manganese. The use of steel as a primary structural material is a relatively new process. The Home Insurance Building in Chicago, the first building using a steel skeleton frame, was built in 1885. Since that time **skeleton construction,** the use of steel framing, has become the predominant means of building large-scale buildings and structures.

There is an infinite number of steel alloys available for use in construction systems today. By slightly altering the manufacturing process and materials, steel can be made to fulfill almost any given criteria. The major classifications of steel are carbon, alloy, high-strength low-alloy and stainless.

Carbon Steel has carbon added to the steel, but not substantial amounts of any other alloys except manganese. The hardness of carbon steel is controlled, primarily by the amount of carbon content. A very mild (soft) steel (containing 0.05–0.15 percent carbon) is very tough and workable. A medium-carbon steel with a carbon content of between 0.25 and 0.35 percent is commonly used in structural construction. Tool-grade carbon steel, the hardest and most brittle, has between 1.05 and 1.20 percent carbon content.

Alloy steel is designated by the alloy being added. A copper-alloy steel has greater resistance to corrosion. Using a nickel alloy improves the strength of the steel, while chromium added as an alloy not only increases strength but also acts as a hardener.

High-strength low-alloy steel is a fairly recent development. This steel can be up to 40 percent stronger than the same weight of structural carbon steel. This allows steel structures to use significantly less steel, or to support more weight with the same amount of steel.

Another notable advantage of this steel is that it forms its own protective oxide covering. This film acts as a barrier between the steel and environmental conditions that may cause corrosion and rust. Although this film is not adequate protection in extremely corrosive applications, such as when exposed to large amounts of salt spray or industrial fumes, it does eliminate the need for periodic painting and greatly reduces the probability of structural elements corroding to unsafe degrees.

The high strength of steel allows architects and builders to reach for the sky. The structural steel frame of Chicago's Sears Tower was made beforehand (prefabricated) in sections and bolted into place on site. The tower is clad in black-coatred aluminum and bronze-tinted glass. (Skidmore, Owings and Merrill, architects. Courtesy of George Barford)

Stainless Steel is broken into almost forty standard types with many more varieties available under different trade names. The main alloy in stainless steel is chromium, which increases its corrosion and heat resistance. Available finishes range from nonreflective to one comparable to a plate glass mirror.

Reinforcement bar, commonly called "re bar" is used to increase the strength of concrete. These bars are available in a variety of thicknesses, both standard and metric. Although special, high-strength reinforcement bar is available by special order, most of the bar used is available in three grades. Grade 40, grade 50 and 60 have minimum yield strengths of 40,000, 50,000 and 60,000 psi respectfully. Reinforcement bar intended to be used in more corrosive environments is coated with an epoxy or galvanized.

Mirror glass makes the PPG Place in Pittsburgh shine like a crystal palace. (John Burgee and Philip Johnson, architects. Photo by Richard Payne, AIA)

Protective Materials

■ Glass

Glass provides a structure with a firm protective layer against precipitation, wind and undesirable temperatures. Unlike other protective materials, glass provides this protection while allowing natural light, solar heat and, when movable, ventilation. Whether used in windows or as sheathing, glass improves the appearance of a room by providing a view to the outside and by creating the perception that the room is larger than it really is.

Glass is usually bought in prefabricated units, such as windows, and doors. Unassembled sheet glass is available, but is usually used for custom designs or replacing broken or damaged prefabricated units.

There are six grades of glass: mirror select, mirror, glazing select, glazing A, glazing B and greenhouse. Greenhouse grade has the greatest amount of irregularities and imperfections. Normal residential windows and glass panes are produced in thicknesses ranging from 1/16 to 1/4 in. The desired thickness is dependent on the size and placement of the window or door. Thicker glass provides the strength needed for larger panels or for windy conditions.

Friends, Romans, Countrymen, Lend Me Your . . . Windex

Ancient Roman public baths and homes of wealthier citizens used basic forms of passive solar heating—large rooms constructed with large, open portals in the wall facing south. Although these openings created drafts, they provided enough heat and light to make them a high-status feature in buildings.

During the first century A.D. clear glass (or sometimes mica) began to be used as a covering for these openings. These windows prevented drafts and held the heat inside, greatly improving the comfort of these dwellings.

Flat sheets of glass were formed by pouring molten glass on a smooth surface and flattening it with rollers. Smaller sheets were formed by blowing glass into a bubble and spinning this bubble until it formed a cylinder. This cylinder was then cut and flattened on an iron plate covered with sand. Despite these rather primitive means of manufacturing, window making was a thriving industry in ancient Rome. This industry was also fairly advanced. Ruins of the city of Pompeii indicate south-facing, bath-house windows almost ten feet tall and over six feet wide.

Large glass windows and skylights provide a good view to the outside, making the room appear larger than it is. (Courtesy of Andersen Corp.)

Tempered glass is heat treated to produce glass that is three to five times stronger than ordinary glass. This material is often used in such applications as patio doors and swinging glass doors where there is a danger of breakage.

Laminated glass has a thin layer of polyvinyl butyral sandwiched between tightly fitting layers of glass. If the glass breaks, the polyvinyl layer hold the shards in place, reducing the potential for injury. Automobile windshields use laminated glass.

Low E (Emissivity) glass is a sandwich of two glass panes with a microscopically thin metallic layer, usually silver and zinc oxides, between them. This metallic layer reflects radiant heat and ultraviolet radiation. Ultraviolet radiation is the part of the light spectrum responsible for skin cancer as well as the fading of drapes, curtains and other fabrics. By blocking radiant heat flow, Low E glass helps keep the building cooler in the summer and warmer in the winter.

Reflective glass is often used in office buildings or other large structures. It has a thin metallic coating that gives this glass its mirror-like appearance. Reflective glass reduces the amount of solar heat, glare and visible light entering a building, as well as providing a greater degree of privacy.

■ Insulation

Insulation is used to protect the interior of a structure, its contents and inhabitants from adverse temperatures. Insulation is a relatively new addition to building technology. Only a few decades ago its use was considered to be optional. With increased energy costs and understandings of structures of today, adequate insulation is now considered to be a necessity.

Insulation is somewhat unique in the field of construction materials. It is one of the few elements of a structure that actually pays for itself in a given amount of time. The cost of insulating materials and installation is eventually offset by reducing heating and cooling costs.

R value is the measure used for insulation. It refers to a material's resistance to heat flow. The higher the R value, the more thermally efficient the material is.

Many insulating materials are not fireproof. Some, such as polystyrene (styrofoam), burn rapidly and emit toxic fumes when heated. Therefore, some insulating materials must be kept away from possible sources of fire and/or be covered by non-flammable materials such as gypsum board. Insulating materials are available in a number of different forms.

Batts and **Blankets** come in a variety of thicknesses and 16 and 24-inch widths to fit between framing members. Batts may be faced with a paper or reflective-foil layer; non-faced batts are also known as friction-fit insulation. Batts and blankets are similar in every way except for length. Batts are shorter, while blankets are designed for longer areas, such as between joists.

Loose-fill insulation is bulky and sold by the bag. On the job site, the bags are opened and the material is either blown or poured into place.

Rigid Board is usually available in $4' \times 8'$, $4' \times 4'$, and $2' \times 8'$ sizes. Rigid-board insulation may be used as a sheathing material, an underlayment beneath and/or around foundations or for interior purposes.

Reflective Foil uses thin metallic layers to reflect radiant heat. Although available as a separate material, its most common application is as a facing for batt or blanket insulation.

Foamed-in-place insulation is usually a polyurethane product. As the name implies, it is pumped or poured directly into an existing cavity where it expands into a solid foam.

Sprayed-on insulation is applied directly to exposed walls or ceilings. Although now illegal, asbestos was often applied in this manner.

Just as there are a variety of forms of insulates, there is also a large number of materials used for insulating a structure.

Rock Wool. One of the older insulating materials, it is produced from a variety of materials, including limestone, lead, slag, old firebrick and furnace slag. Its appearance resembles that of dirty cotton or wool, hence its name. Rock wool is usually installed in loose fills, blown or hand spread around an area.

Fiberglass. One of the most common forms of insulation in use today, fiberglass can be used in blankets, batts, loose fill and rigid boards. Fiberglass is relatively inexpensive, does not emit fumes, is non-combustible, noncorrosive and is very resilient. Fiberglass can, however, lose its insulating properties if allowed to become wet.

Cellulose is produced from wood products, usually wood waste or byproducts such as newspaper or other paper materials. Because of its high degree of flammability, chemical flame retardants must be added. Many bands are also treated for rodent and pest resistance. Although cellulose

Fiberglass insulation can be installed as batts *(above)* or loose fill (below). (Courtesy of Owens Corning, Inc.)

The Urea Formaldehyde Controversy

While the development of new construction materials can be very rewarding to its developers, installers and consumers, it can also become a disaster. One product, urea formaldehyde foam insulation (UFFI), indicates some of the dangers of product development.

When it was first promoted in the early 1970's, UFFI showed great promise for both its developers and consumers. In less than a decade, over 600,000 homes and 50,000 businesses used this product. As an insulant UFFI was believed to be little short of a miracle material. Besides being inexpensive and possessing high thermal resistance (R value = 3.5 — 5.5 per inch thickness), UFFI can be blown into existing walls through small holes drilled into the interior or exterior walls. Once blown into a wall cavity it quickly expands and hardens into a solid foam. This eliminates the expense of removing existing walls to install batts or the formation of uninsulated gaps or pockets commonly formed by poured insulation.

The initial financial success and consumer satisfaction soon turned sour. It became very apparent that UFFI has some significant disadvantages. The most disturbing of these is its health effects. Over time UFFI releases, through a process known as outgassing, formaldehyde vapors into the air. In extremely high concentrations formaldehyde is fatal, but only in concentrations many times greater than those released by UFF.

However, a percentage of the population is extremely sensitive to even low levels of formaldehyde. These people sometimes experience headaches, dizziness, nausea and irration of the skin, eyes, throat, nose and gastrointestinal tract. At least one report also suggested formaldehyde as a possible cancer-causing agent. Although this report remains controversial, it was enough to effectively kill the growing UFFI business.

As if the health effects alone were not bad enough, it also appears that UFFI is not as good an insulant as was once believed. One problem is shrinkage. When UFFI is fresh, it completely fills the wall cavity. Over a period of time, the foam shrinks. Tests results have shown shrinkage of as much as 7.3 percent over only 20 months of normal use. Because of this shrinkage the United States and Canadian governments have reduced their estimates of UFFI's expected R value down to 2.5 per inch thickness, a substantial decrease.

It also appear that UFFI rapidly degrades when exposed to high temperatures and humidity. One test indicated disintegration in as little as 7 weeks, when exposed to 122° temperatures and 92 percent relative humidity. These conditions may sound excessive, but are commonly encountered even in temperate regions.

Public health concerns and poor thermal performance can obviously mean financial ruin for manufacturers and distributors of UFFI, but the economic hardship does not end there. Some people owning UFFI-treated homes are finding that they cannot sell their homes, or if they can, they must take thousands of dollars off the sale price.

At least one state and the Consumer Product Safety Commission have unsuccessfully attempted to ban the use and sale of UFFI. Many states are now requiring homeowners to notify perspective buyers of the presence of UFFI. Regardless of individual state regulations, UFFI remains a terrible investment for residential homes and, at best, a highly questionable choice for other applications.

The material that was believed to be a dream come true in the '70s has reappeared as a nightmare in the '90s.

"R" Values of Selected Building Materials

Material	R value, per inch of thickness
Plywood (Douglas fir)	1.25
Particleboard	
low density	1.85
medium density	1.06
high density	0.85
Cellular Glass	2.63
Expanded polystyrene	
molded beads	3.57
Extruded polystyrene	
smooth skin	5.0
cut cell	4.0
Expanded polyurethane	6.25
Perlite, expanded	2.70
Vermiculite, exfoliated	2.27
Sand, gravel and	
stone aggregate	0.08
Brick	
Common	0.20
Face	0.11
Hardboard siding (.437 in.)	0.67
Hardwoods (oak, maple	
and similar species)	0.91
Softwoods (pine, fir)	1.25
Blankets and Batts	
(fiberglass, rock wool	
and cellulose)	3.70*
Loose fill	
(fiberglass, rock wool	
and cellulose)	3.33*
Single-pane glass window	1.0**
Double-pane glass window	2.0**

*Varies considerably with the amount of compaction.

**Rough approximations only.

offers a high R value at a relatively inexpensive price, the presence of water, either from leaks or from water vapor, can quickly change this insulation into a soggy mass that offers little, if any, thermal protection.

Polystyrene is available in two forms, extruded and expanded. Extruded polystyrene is more commonly known by its trade name, styrofoam. Expanded polystyrene is known as beadboard. Both forms are usually used in sheets up to 4' × 8' and in thicknesses up to several inches. Some relatively uncommon applications use polystyrene as either a custom-molded or loose-fill insulation.

Polyurethane and Polyisocyanurate Foams are some of the most efficient thermal barriers in use today. These foams are usually formed into sheets and covered with a reflective metallic foil coverings. They are extremely popular as a sheathing material for residential construction. Sheets are available in thicknesses starting at 1/2 inch and widths of 2 or 4 feet by lengths of 8 to 12 feet.

Urea-formaldehyde foam (commonly referred to as UFFI) is designed to be pumped, in liquid form, into wall cavities where it rapidly expands and hardens into a solid foam. Urea-formaldehyde foam is most commonly sold to professional installers premixed in 50 gallon drums. Although not as common in the United States, it is also sold as a dry powder or concentrated liquid that are prepared at the job site.

Perlite is a naturally occurring volcanic glass that is crushed and rapidly heated to form small, light, closed cell granules. Its use in residential construction is relatively rare, but is occasionally poured to fill small spaces or cracks. Its most common uses are to produce relatively lightweight roofing boards for commercial and industrial buildings or to fill the hollow cores of concrete or cinder block. It is also used as an aggregate mixed with portland cement to make lightweight insulating concrete.

Vermiculite, although produced from a different material, has many of the same qualities and applications as does perlite.

Cellular glass foam is not a commonly used or available insulation at this time. Composed entirely of extremely small, closed glass cells, this material has several advantages over other insulates. The most notable of these advantages is in its strength, particularly its compressive strength and its durability. Cellular glass foam is most commonly sold in block form, usually either 1' × 2' or 1-1/2' × 2' with thicknesses from 2 to 5 inches.

■ Siding

Siding is used to provide a protective shield over the external walls of a structure. Some structural materials, such as stone or logs, do not require any form of siding. Although the primary purpose of siding is protective, the final decision as to the type and style of siding is often a matter of appearances. All siding materials must provide protection from precipitation, but some also provide the additional benefit of increased insulation.

Plywood siding is usually bought in standard 4 × 8 sheets. There are over a dozen different surface grades available, from smooth to rough-sawn.

The tree species used for plywood siding are usually Douglas Fir, Redwood, Cedar or Southern Pine, although a large variety of other woods, including exotic hardwoods, may be special ordered. Different species produce plywood of varying strengths. This strength is indicated by a number from one to five, one being the hardest from such trees as Loblobby Pine and Western Larch, number five, the weakest grade, is made from Basswood or Balsam Fir.

Grading is based on the number of, and composition of, patches on a 4 × 8 sheet. Special Series 303, the premium grade, allows only natural defects and no patches. 306-6 allows up to six patches per sheet, 303-18 up to 18 patches per sheet. The material used to form these patches is indicated by the letter following the grade number. 303-6W indicates the presence of up to six wood patches, 303-30S indicates as many as thirty synthetic patches.

Wood siding is milled into five different forms. Clapboard and bevel remain the most popular of these forms. Green wood that is milled for siding is cut to 1 inch thicknesses. Widths range from 4 to 12 inches. It is important to remember that significant shrinkage occurs during the drying process resulting in siding somewhat smaller than its original size. Wood siding is sold in random lengths. Bevel siding is often sold with one side smooth and the other rough sawn. The side exposed is dependent upon the finish used, rough side out for staining, smooth for painting.

Redwood clapboards provide a striking exterior sheathing. Wood siding, when properly installed and maintained, can last for centuries. (Courtesy of Andersen Corp.)

Wood Shingles and Shakes are among the oldest known siding and roofing materials still used today. Shakes are fashioned by hand forming a straight flat surface. Often these shakes are sawed diagonally across their length producing tapered forms. Manufactured wood shingles are almost always tapered.

The size of wooden shingles and shakes are expressed by two numbers such as 16 X 5/2 or 18 X 4/2. The first number refers to the length of the individual shakes. The second set of numbers (5/2 on the first example above) is the thickness, in inches, of the given number of shingles stacked together. The designation of 16″ X 5/2 would indicate shakes that are 16 inches long and five stacked together are 2 inches thick.

Aluminum Siding is available with a wide variety of textures and colors. Aluminum siding is available with an insulating backing attached. Although this slightly increases the R value of the wall section, the total energy saving is minimal due to the gaps between the insulating strips. Uninsulated siding is manufactured in .024 inch thicknesses; insulated siding is somewhat thinner (.019 inch).

Aluminum siding is sold in squares. Each square is designed to cover 100 square feet of surface. It is available in widths of 8″, 10″, 12″ and double 4″ simulated lap siding. Lengths are usually 12′ or 12-1/2′.

Steel Siding is considered to be more durable than aluminum siding. Sizes available are similar to aluminum, except that steel is sold in shorter lengths (9′4″). For maximum durability, steel siding should be coated with vinyl at least 4 mils in thickness.

Vinyl Siding is often warranted for as long as 50 to 60 years, indicating a durability greater than aluminum and similar to a good quality steel siding. Vinyl is available in a great variety of textures and colors. During normal weather conditions it is exceptionally resilient and holds colors and gloss well. Extreme cold temperatures cause vinyl to become very brittle and susceptible to damage. Panels are usually 8 or 10 inches wide and 12′6″ in length.

■ Roofing Materials

All roofing materials must protect structures from precipitation and other adverse weather conditions. The selection of roofing material for a particular structure is based on four main criteria.

Durability. The life expectancy of roofing materials varies greatly. Roll roofing, for example, might last only five years under normal conditions while slate or clay tile roofs, given maintenance as needed, will outlast most buildings.

Building design. Some materials are only appropriate on roofs with a given pitch (steepness of the roof). The structural strength of the building must be examined before selecting a roofing since there is a tremendous difference in the weight of roofing materials. Heavier materials could cause a building that is not adequately supported to collapse.

Clay roofing tiles are expensive, but durable and attractive. (Courtesy of Vande Hey Roofing Tile, Inc.)

Style. The appearance of the roof is a major selling point for roofing materials. Not only must the material be pleasing to the eye, it must blend in with the rest of the building. For example, clay tile roofing would look very much out of place on a contemporary home with aluminum siding.

Cost plays an important role in the selection process. The adage "you only get what you pay for" is particularly true with roofing materials. The more durable and attractive materials usually demand a much higher price.

Asphalt Shingles. Until the 1960's, asphalt shingles had a felt backing that allowed water to be absorbed into the shingle. By substituting fiberglass for the felt, asphalt shingles are now completely water resistant, lighter, more durable and fire resistant. The mineral granules that form the top layer of the shingles provide fire protection and shelter the waterproof asphalt layer from direct sunlight.

Like most roofing materials, asphalt shingles are measured by the **square.** A square is enough material to cover 100 square feet of roof. A **bundle** is a subunit of a square. Asphalt shingles usually contain three or four bundles per square.

Traditional asphalt shingles measure 12″ × 36″ (1 × 3 feet) although metric sized shingles that are a full meter long (39-3/8 inches) are sometimes used. The most common asphalt shingle is the three-tab shingle. When installed, notches cut into an individual shingle give it the appearance of three separate panels (tabs). Asphalt shingles are also available in two or four tab square shingles as well as random tab styles that have three to five tabs of varying widths on each shingle. Shingles without any cutouts (single tab), interlocking "T" shaped and hexagonal shingles are also available.

Available Roofing Tiles

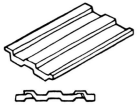

French tile

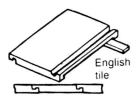

English tile

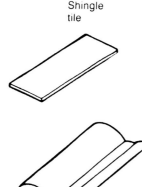

Mission tile

Shingle tile

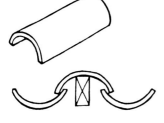

Spanish tile

Wood Shingles and Shakes mentioned under siding, are also used as a roofing material. Wooden shingles can beautify or complement a variety of building styles. Properly installed and maintained, wood shingles and shakes, particularly those fashioned from cedar, are extremely durable and require relatively little maintenance. The primary disadvantages of wood shingles are their high purchase price and fire hazard, if not treated with a flame retardant.

Shingle and Shake Panels have two courses of wooden shingles attached to exterior-grade plywood sheathing. Each panel is between 9 and 18 inches wide; all are manufactured in eight-foot lengths. The primary advantage of panels over individual shingles is reduced time and labor, and therefore, cost of installation.

Slate is the most expensive roofing material in common use today. Slate is formed when layers of sedimentary clay are subjected to high pressure and temperatures under the earth's surface. When mined, slate is easily split into desired thicknesses.

Slate is completely fireproof, pleasing to the eye and will outlast any building. The heavy weight of slate roofing requires a building to be constructed soundly and include strong rafters.

Slate is available in thickness from 3/16 to 1-1/2 inch. Thicker slate is installed towards the eaves of the roof, thinner towards the peak. Widths and lengths range from 10 × 6 inches to 24 × 16 inches with 12 × 8 inches being the most common. Larger sizes require less time and labor for installation. Slate arrives at the job site with two prepunched nail holes for easier installation.

Clay tiles are among the oldest known roofing materials. The classic half circle form of clay tile is believed to have been originated by workers sitting forming these tile over their thighs. Clay tile is durable, particularly in dryer, warmer climates. Clay is somewhat similar to slate roofing in that it is attractive, long lasting, requires significant amounts of time and labor to install and is relatively expensive.

Metal roofing uses three main types of metal. The most common of these is **terne.** This material is formed by dipping copper-bearing steel sheets into a terne metal, 80% lead and 20% tin. This process produces a roofing that is highly weather resistant.

Grading for terne metal is based on the weight of the coating for 436 square feet of sheeting. A grading of 40 pounds is considered to be optimal for roofing applications. This material is available in various sizes of sheets or in 50-foot rolls of various widths.

Heavy zinc coatings produce a **galvanized** sheet roofing material. For permanent structures this coating should be at least two ounces per square foot. The most commonly available thicknesses are 26 and 28 gauge.

Aluminum roofing is available in either corrugated sheets or shingle forms. A baked-on vinyl coating provides both nonfading color and increased weather resistance.

Asphalt is used on flat, or nearly flat roofed commercial or industrial buildings. Asphalt is graded by its softening point (the temperature in which the material becomes somewhat fluid). Asphalts with a lower softening point will tend to resist cracking and be self healing. However, the selection of the correct asphalt is not as simple as merely selecting the lowest soften point. If an asphalt with a low softening point is used in a hot climate or on a roof with slightly too much pitch, it will tend to run and thereby reduce its protective capabilities. For correct selection, the local climate, steepness of the roof and expected roof temperatures must be considered.

Asphalt is generally applied between asphalt impregnated felt and an outer layer of gravel, pebbles or slag. This outer layer acts much like the granules on asphalt shingles, protecting from direct sunlight, adding fire protection and sealing in the volatile oils.

Sod is normally associated with the homes of early American prairie pioneers. Surprisingly, sod roofing is still in limited use today. Sod is the uppermost layer of topsoil, held in place by thick webs of grass roots. Its primary advantages include good thermal protection, fire resistance and cost (it is usually free for the taking). Because of its low resistance to precipitation, sod can only be used in dry climates. Other disadvantages include heavy weight and limited availability. (Sod roofs require thicker sod layers usually found only in some prairie areas).

Thatch consists of bundles of reeds, leaves or straw layered over a wooden framework. As with sod roofs, its use is uncommon in industrialized countries. Thatch also shares other characteristics with sod: it is a free and readily available resource in some areas and it needs periodic replacement. Unlike sod, it is lightweight, more water resistant (if properly constructed) but presents a significant fire hazard.

European villages, such as this one in Italy, have used clay tiles for centuries.

SUMMARY

Proper selection of construction materials should be based on:

- Cost
- Geographic location
- Architectural styles
- Environmental patterns
- Availability of resources

Materials can be classified as structural, protective or decorative, although these categories overlap somewhat. Wood, concrete, brick, stone and steel are common structural materials. Protective materials such as glass, fiberglass, and various types of siding and shingles are used for windows, insulation, siding and roofing.

• •

Study Questions

1. Identify at least three materials that are protective, structural or decorative.

2. What are the best and the lowest grade of glass commercially available?

3. What is the advantage of tempered glass? Laminated glass? Low E Glass?

4. How does adequate insulation "earn" money for the occupants of a shelter?

5. What is R value and why is it important?

6. What does the plywood grading 303-30S indicate?

7. Why are boards and lumber smaller than their given dimensions?

8. What are the dimensions of wooden shakes labeled 20 × 6/2?

9. How does the local weather influence the appropriate choice of siding material?

• •

10. A roof has a total surface area that measures 40 by 60 feet. How many squares of shingles must be purchased to cover this roof?

11. If the above roof were covered with asphalt shingles, how much would the shingles weigh? 3/4 inch slate? Spanish clay tiles?

12. What are the advantages and disadvantages of wood shake or shingle roofing or siding?

13. Is wood used in the following dimensions classified as being timber, dimension lumber or as a board?
a. 2 × 4 inches; b. 1 × 4 inches; c. 5 × 8 inches; d. 4 × 4 inches; e. 2 × 2 inches; f. 6 × 6 inches.

14. If the above wood was designated as structural light framing, what term would be used to describe each of the above sizes?

15. Why is wood pressure-treated?

16. What are some of the benefits of using an indigenous material?

17. What commonly used building materials are indigenous to your area?

18. What factors influence the selection of construction materials in your area?

· ·

Suggested Activities

1. Conduct an inspection of the building you are in right now. For each of the major materials used in the construction of that building, answer each of the following questions.
a. Is it primarily structural, protective, decorative or a mixture of the above?
b. What possible substitute materials could have been used?
c. How durable is the material?
d. How must the material be protected to maintain this durability?

2. Select several members from the class to act the role of material sales representatives. Other members of the class or the instructor should specify a list of factors concerning the design and application of an imaginary structure. This list should include function, size, expected service time, location, design and environmental conditions. Each of the groups will select a different building material that can be used to form the exterior surface of this structure. Groups should be given ample time to "sell" their product to the "consumers" (the remainder of the class). At the end of these presentations, the consumers will vote as to which of the materials they consider to be the most appropriate for the given application.

· ·

Glossary

Admixture   Special material added to concrete to meet a specific requirement of the site or application.

Aggregate   Material in concrete that does not react with water or cement and adds strength and volume.

Alloy steel   Steel composed of various other metals such as carbon, copper or nickel to improve strength or hardness.

Brick   Earthen material formed and dried into rectangular blocks.

Decorative material   Materials that add to the visual appeal of a structure.

Dimensional lumber   Lumber with both sides at least 2″ thick.

Indigenous resource   Material locally available within a particular area.

Insulation   Material that protects a structure, its contents and inhabitants from adverse temperatures.

Particleboard   Wood panels made by heating and pressing a mixture of small wood particles and a bonding resin.

Pressure treating   Process of infusing wood with chemicals toxic to insects and fungus. This makes the wood resistant to rot.

Protective material   Materials that shelter a structure and its inhabitants from adverse environmental conditions.

R value   A measure to determine a material's resistance to heat flow and thus its insulating efficiency.

Reflective glass   Glass with a thin metallic coating giving it a mirror-like appearance.

Retarders   Materials that slow down the setting time of concrete.

Rock wool   Spun mineral insulation.

Shake   Wooden shingles used in roofing or siding.

Skeleton construction   The common method of framing large-scale buildings using steel components.

Structural material   Materials that support the weight and/or maintain the shape of a structure.

Tempered glass   Heat-treated glass that is three to five times stronger than ordinary glass.

Terne   Composite steel roofing coated with 80% lead and 20% tin.

Thatch   Roofing composed of layered bundles of reeds, leaves or straw.

Waferboard   Wood panels similar to particleboard using larger wood particles.

Chapter 3

Material Properties

Chapter Concepts

■ Pulling and pushing forces encountered by structural materials are known as tension and compression.

■ Structural materials such as steel, concrete and wood have different tensile and compressive strengths.

■ Linear elasticity is the direct relationship between force and deformation.

■ When a structural member has been loaded past the point of elasticity and permanently deforms, the member has reached plasticity.

■ Brittle materials are usually not used as structural materials because they collapse quickly after the ultimate strength point has been surpassed.

Key Terms

compression	strain
ductility	stress
elasticity	tension
modulus of elasticity	toughness
plasticity	

Bridge builders must choose materials with the right properties for the job. Engineers draw up detailed plans showing the stresses on materials, such as steel used in the cables and concrete used in the road bed. (Courtesy of STN International)

Great piers of granite, strong in compression, join with steel wires, strong in tension, to form the Brooklyn Bridge in New York City. (Photo by Wayne Andrews)

Introduction

Each structural material has a different combination of specific mechanical, thermal and chemical properties. When building a structure, it is important to understand these properties in order to choose the right structural material for the job.

For a high-rise building, the materials used must have great compressive strength (which means they must be able to stand up under a great pushing weight). Bridge cables must have tensile strength; when pulled, they must stretch without breaking. If the structure will be exposed to extremes of temperature, you must know how much the materials used will expand and contract. Does a material rust easily? It may need a protective coating. Will it melt at high temperatures? Then it would collapse in a fire.

Lets look in detail at these properties themselves and then at how they affect common structural materials.

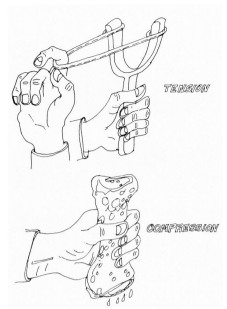

TENSION

COMPRESSION

Mechanical Properties

Mechanical properties are related to the strength of the material. This strength is determined by the ability to resist a force without breaking. There are two simple forces acting upon these materials: a pulling force called **tension,** and a pushing force called **compression.** When you pull a slingshot back, it is in tension; when you squeeze a dish sponge, it is in compression.

■ Tensile and Compressive Strength

To resist these forces, all structural materials need to have either **tensile strength** or **compressive strength.** Tensile strength may be defined as the ability of a structural material to resist stretching divided by the tensile force applied to the material. In equation form:

$$\text{Tensile strength} = \frac{\text{stretching resistance}}{\text{tensile forces}}$$

The material of both the tent and the hammock are under tension. Woven fabric has good tensile strength. (Courtesy of Moss Tent Works, Inc.)

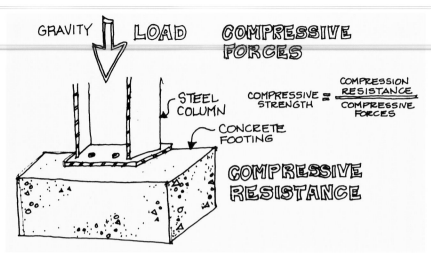

GRAVITY LOAD COMPRESSIVE FORCES

STEEL COLUMN

CONCRETE FOOTING

COMPRESSIVE STRENGTH = COMPRESSION RESISTANCE / COMPRESSIVE FORCES

COMPRESSIVE RESISTANCE

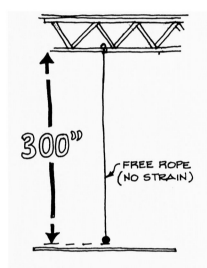

300"

FREE ROPE (NO STRAIN)

STRAIN

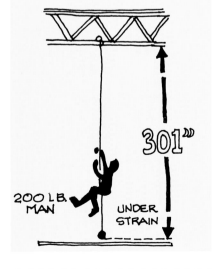

301"

200 LB. MAN

UNDER STRAIN

Similarly, compressive strength may be defined as the ability of a structural material to resist compression divided by the compressive force applied to the material. In equation form:

$$\text{Compressive strength} = \frac{\text{compression resistance}}{\text{compressive forces}}$$

Materials that are under tension (pulled) actually lengthen and materials that are compressed (pushed) become shorter. In the examples above, you would easily be able to see the slingshot stretching and the sponge getting smaller, but the changes in structural materials are usually too tiny to be seen. When a tall building is erected, the length of the concrete footing changes (shortens) with the addition of each new floor, although this change in length may be too small for the eye to detect. Likewise, as more and more cars drive onto a suspension bridge, the cables lengthen although, again, these changes are very minute.

These changes in length are strains on the material. **Strain** on structural materials may be defined as the changes in length divided by the original length of the material. In equation form:

$$\text{Strain} = \frac{\text{changes in length due to tensile or compressive forces}}{\text{original length}}$$

If for example, a climbing rope in your gymnasium 25 feet (300 inches) long becomes 1 inch longer under load (when a 200 pound person begins to climb the rope), its strain would be 1/300.

This strain on the material is caused by a force (stress) pushing or pulling the material. **Stress** may be defined as the tensile or compressive force on a structural material divided by the area it is applied to. In equation form:

$$\text{Stress} = \frac{\text{tensile or compressive force}}{\text{area}}$$

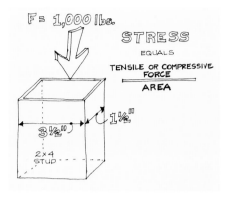

If, for example, a load of 1,000 pounds were placed on top of a 2 × 4 standing vertically (1.5″ × 3.5″ = 5.25 square inches), its stress would be calculated as: 1000/5.25 = 190.5 pounds per square inch.

All structural materials must be able to resist compression and/or tension. But, when selecting structural materials for certain applications, other mechanical properties also must be considered, in particular, elasticity and plasticity.

■ Elasticity

As mentioned earlier, all structural materials will increase or decrease in length under pulling and pushing forces. **Elasticity** refers to the material's ability to return to its original size and shape once the force has ended. There are two conditions of elasticity:

■ The material must not stretch or shorten so much that it fails under load.

■ The material must return to its original size and shape after the load is removed.

All structural materials are elastic, but there is a lot of variation in the degree of elasticity they possess.

Imagine a basketball bouncing on a wooden floor. The compressive force of the ball hitting the floor bends the floor very slightly. As the ball bounces up again, the floor returns to its original size and shape because of the elasticity of wood.

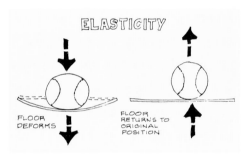

The players get a little help from the elasticity of the floor when it springs back to its original shape after being compressed by their weight. (Courtesy of Nike)

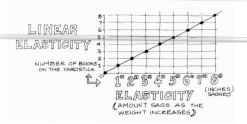

LINEAR ELASTICITY

NUMBER OF BOOKS ON THE YARDSTICK

ELASTICITY (INCHES SAGGED)
(AMOUNT SAGS AS THE WEIGHT INCREASES)

A material is said to be **linear elastic** when the degree that it deforms under load is directly related to changes in that load. A simple yardstick can be used to illustrate linear elasticity. Span the yardstick between two desks. Place a book (load) carefully in the middle of the yardstick and measure the distance the stick moves downward (deformation). Now place a second book of equal weight on top of the first book. You can follow this with a third book. If the yardstick is linear elastic, the deformations under load will be equal. For example, if one book yielded a deformation of 1/2 inch, two books should yield a deformation of 1 inch and three books should yield a deformation of 1-1/2 inches.

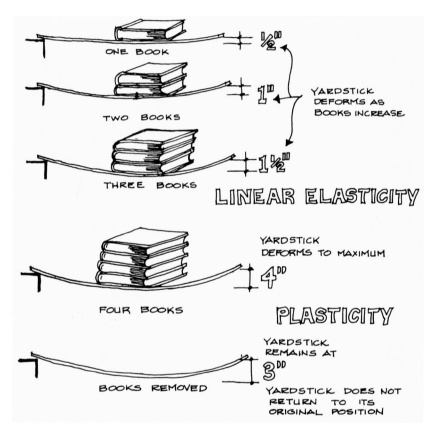

ONE BOOK — ½"

TWO BOOKS — 1"

THREE BOOKS — 1½"

YARDSTICK DEFORMS AS BOOKS INCREASE

LINEAR ELASTICITY

FOUR BOOKS

YARDSTICK DEFORMS TO MAXIMUM 4"

PLASTICITY

BOOKS REMOVED

YARDSTICK REMAINS AT 3" YARDSTICK DOES NOT RETURN TO ITS ORIGINAL POSITION

The discovery of material linear elasticity was made by an Englishman named Robert Hooke (1635–1703). He noticed that there was a connection between stress and strain up to a certain point. He tried to protect his discovery by recording his finding as an anagram: CEIIINOSSSTUU.

He later decoded the anagram into Latin to read "Ut tensio sic vis," meaning "As the elongation, so is the force." According to Mario Salvadori in *Why Buildings Stand Up,* his secrecy was motivated by the fear that someone else might patent his idea by applying it to watch springs.

Professional baseball players, such as Ellis Burke of the Boston Red Sox, rely on their trusty wood bats to send the ball over the fence. Would aluminum bats make for more homers? (Courtesy of the Worcester Telegram & Gazette)

The Bat With "Boiinngg"

To Big League fans, it is a disaster. To high school and college athletic departments, it is a needed financial break. To college baseball players, it is often what stands between them and the "show," the chance to play professional baseball. What is it?

It is the aluminum bat. The bat that has replaced the Louisville Slugger and other wooden bats in all leagues except the pros. And, say the experts, it won't be long before the *boiinngg!* of aluminum replaces the *crack!* of wood in the World Series.

The secret of the aluminum bat is the superior elasticity of aluminum. This material property, long understood by engineers and builders, has become important to baseball players.

When a ball hits a bat, the bat yields slightly. As the ball moves away again, the bat returns to its original shape, giving the ball a little push. As it returns to shape, it gives the ball more spring. This means that an aluminum bat can hit a ball more often and further than a wooden bat.

■ Plasticity

All structural materials have limits to their elasticity. As loads increase beyond those limits, material deformation will no longer be linearly proportional to the load. The material may not return to its original state.

Plasticity can be thought of as permanent deformation. In many materials, modelling clay for example, plasticity is a useful property. When you squeeze or roll the clay into some shape, you would not want it to bounce back into its original shape again. However, in structural materials, plasticity is generally considered an undesirable property.

Let's change the yardstick example. If a fourth book were placed on the yardstick and the yardstick deformed by 6 inches (instead of the expected 2 inches), the yardstick is said to be plastic. In this example the yardstick would not return to its original shape even after all the books (the load) were removed from the yardstick. It had reached its yield stress point, the point at which a material changes from elastic to plastic.

Elasticity can also be graphically illustrated. Notice in the following graph that from 0 to A we have a linear elastic condition indicated on the graph as a straight line. When the fourth book is placed on the yardstick the graph begins to curve and reaches the yield stress point at B. The yardstick begins to stretch and eventually breaks at point C.

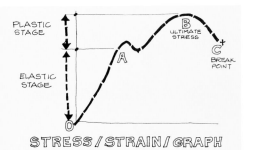

. . . .

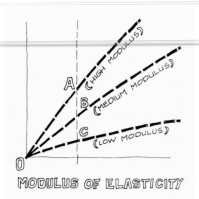

MODULUS OF ELASTICITY

Provided that only three books were ever loaded on the yardstick, it would always return to its original shape, indicating perfect elasticity. Good designers make sure that their structures are not loaded above point A or permanent deformation will occur. The elastic-plastic relationship is called the modulus of elasticity or Young's modulus (named after Englishman Thomas Young 1773–1829).

The measurement of stiffness of a material is the modulus. The stiffer the material, the higher the modulus. The following graph illustrates low, medium and high modulus materials.

Although reaching plasticity is undesirable for structural materials, it is important for materials to be able to become plastic, rather than suddenly collapse under stress. Structural materials that are plastic under high loads do not reach their breaking point quickly. As they become plastic, the materials provide warnings that they are permanently damaged. This helps us determine that a structure is overloaded or will fail in a short time. In a suspension bridge, for example, if the steel cables are pulled to such a degree that they exceed their elastic limit, they will become plastic (that is, they will permanently deform). This warns the engineers that the bridge may collapse, so they can quickly take some action.

This interstate bridge collapsed without warning. Several people died when their cars plunged into the river. Bridge engineers must inspect regularly bridges for telltale signs of stress in the materials. (Mianus River Bridge, Connecticut. July 9, 1983. Courtesy of the Greenwich Historical Society)

■ Brittleness

Brittleness is the opposite of plasticity. Brittle materials are avoided as structural materials because they give no warning of failure after they have surpassed their elastic point. Although ceramic tile is strong in tension and compression, it is rarely used as a structural load-carrying material because it is brittle and therefore can fail without warning.

■ Toughness

Toughness is another important mechanical property of structural materials. **Toughness** is a form of strength related to the amount of energy or impact a material can absorb before it breaks.

Ductility is related to elasticity and plasticity. When a material can change its shape easily under load without breaking, it is said to be **ductile.** Glass, for example, is very strong in compression, but not very ductile. A heavy compressive load may be gently placed on glass without it breaking. But a small impact such as a hammer hit may shatter the glass. Mild steel is a ductile material, while concrete, glass and cast iron are rather brittle.

. . . .

Additional Properties

Additional properties related to structural building materials include thermal and chemical properties. Structural materials behave differently under changing temperatures. Steel will reach its elastic limit in a fire if the temperature rises tof 1200° F. When the steel becomes plastic, it will deform. Steel buildings that are not fireproofed therefore will collapse more quickly during a fire than wood or concrete buildings. Concrete has a high insulating characteristic and provides an additional safety factor before the reinforcing rods within the concrete become plastic. Wooden buildings usually take a longer time to collapse than steel buildings because wood's plasticity is not greatly affected by heat. Its compressive and tensile characteristics, however, are diminished as fire reduces the size of the timbers.

Structural materials may also be processed or chemically treated to increase their fire resistance, reduce corrosion, rust and decay. Metal structural materials are sometimes combined with other metal materials to create an alloy that will resist corrosion and/or rust.

A recent development in rust prevention is a type of steel that forms a surface rust only a few hundredths of an inch and then stops. This reduces maintainace costs associated with continued painting. Such products as COR-TEN™ and Mayari R™ are examples of this weathering steel.

. . . .

As fire reduces the size of wooden timbers, structures are likely to collapse under tensile and compressive forces. (Courtesy of the Worcester Telegram & Gazette)

A Benevolent Rust

When is rusting a benefit to bridges and buildings? A type of steel called Cor-Ten, actually rusts to form its own protective corrosion barrier just by being out in ordinary weather conditions. The process takes from 18 months to 3 years. Once oxidation is complete, minimal rusting occurs. In 20 years, the rusting is maintained at approximately two to two and a half thousandths of an inch.

Cor-Ten steel works the best when complete wetting and drying occur. There are design limitations when using Cor-Ten. It should not be used when the surface will collect and retain water, as this will accelerate corrosion.

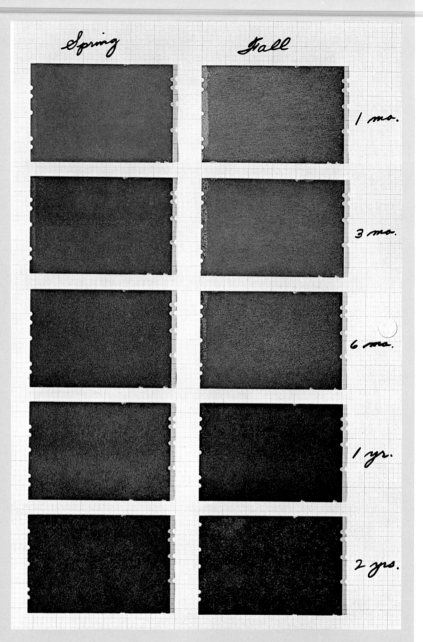

Test samples of Cor-Ten steel show how a protective layer of rust builds up over time. (Courtesy of USX Corp)

The first iron bridge still stands today, having withstood heavy floods and other natural forces for over 200 years. It is restricted to pedestrian traffic now. (Iron Bridge, Shropshire, England, 1779. Courtesy of George Barford)

· ·

Structural Materials

Structural materials fall into three main groups: metals, natural materials and synthetic materials (plastics). Common metals used in structural applications include mild steel, high tensile steel, cast iron, and aluminum. Common natural materials include stone, brick, wood and concrete. Synthetic materials are less common in construction systems, but their use is increasing. Synthetic materials used include fiberglass reinforced plastic (FRP) and other fiberous composites. Materials are also used in combination with each other. For example, reinforced concrete and prestressed concrete are often combined with steel to increase tensile strength.

■ Iron

Cast iron is iron that has been melted and poured into forms. Its great advantage is that it can be formed into just about any shape. Cast iron is very hard and brittle and is not used often because of the availability of more elastic materials, such as concrete and steel.

Because it is brittle, cast iron is more reliable in compression than in tension. When cast iron is loaded beyond its elastic capacity it will break without warning.

As a structural material, cast iron was displaced by wrought iron (a less brittle material) and steel around the middle of the nineteenth century.

· ·

Steel

Steel, as a structural material, has an advantage over iron because of its elasticity. When steel is overloaded it deforms. Unlike iron, the deformation can usually be seen, thus warning people that the structure is overloaded.

Another advantage of steel is that it can be easily fastened. Riveting and bolting, the older method of fastening, is currently being replaced by welding joints, sometimes in combination with high tensile bolts. The welding process actually fuses two structural members together, creating a structure that acts as one member.

The thermal properties of steel are a major disadvantage. It has a 1200° F melting point and becomes brittle at −30° F. This creates problems in extreme temperatures. This means that a steel structure can lose its rigidity and collapse suddenly during a fire, and elasticity will be reduced in extremely cold climates.

The ability of steel to be welded together is an important property. (Courtesy of NASA)

Aluminum

Although aluminum has excellent structural properties, it is not often used as a structural material because of its high processing cost in comparison to steel.

Aluminum's big advantage is its light weight versus strength ratio. It is actually stronger than steel per pound and offers additional protection against corrosion. It is used in special applications where small amounts are needed or where cost is not so important.

An aluminum framework, called mullions, supports the glass on the building. (One South Wacker Building, Chicago. Helmut Jahn, architect. Courtesy of George Barford)

. . . .

Stone

Many types of stone are used as structural materials. Geologically, stone falls into three categories: igneous, sedimentary and metamorphic rock.

Igneous or volcanic rock is very hard, which makes it difficult to shape into structural materials. The most commonly used igneous rock is granite.

Sedimentary rocks can be split easily, but is softer than igneous rock. Sandstone and limestone are sedimentary rocks used as structural materials.

Metamorphic rock is gradually formed when sedimentary rock is changed by heat and pressure, becoming hard and crystalline. Marble is one common metamorphic rock. Although it is very hard, it is not very durable.

Most stone has a compressive strength about ten times greater than its tensile strength. The highest strength is found in granite and the lowest in the sandstone and limestone.

Granite is a common building material in New England. It is an igneous rock with great compressive properties. (Photograph by Julia Runk Jones)

Stone is commonly used to carry compressive loads, such as columns, walls and arches. It is also used as an exterior sheathing because of its great durability and low maintenance. Some very beautiful skyscrapers have exterior sheathing made of marble.

■ Brick

The most frequently used brick for structural purposes is fired brick (brick baked in a furnace or kiln). Despite its stone-like appearance, brick differs from stone in very significant ways. Unlike stone, with specific compressive strength, the compressive strength of brick is dependent on the quality of the clay used and the conditions of firing. Also, brick cannot be fashioned in large blocks; they are usually smaller units to avoid cracking during firing. It is limited as a structural material because the compressive strength of brick is relatively low and its tensile strength is almost negligible.

However, there are some advantages to brick. Its lower density makes it lighter than stone. This low density also makes it easier to cut than stone. When compressive strength is not a consideration, brick is an excellent filler material and exterior sheathing.

· ·

Wood is a renewable material with good compressive and tensile properties. What other common construction material appears in this photograph?

■ Wood

The structural properties of wood depend on the species of tree it came from, the amount of grain and how it was processed. Two boards from the same species may vary greatly in compressive and tensile strengths if the grain of one is straight and the grain of the other is curved. The strength of wood is also related to its moisture content.

Wood is comparatively good in compression and tension depending on relation of the stress to the grain of the wood. It's compressive and tensile strength are greatest when it is stressed in the direction of the grain. It is much weaker in resisting stresses across the grain. This limitation of grain direction is overcome by using plywood, which is a series of layers of wood grain with alternating grain directions. This makes the strength of the wood the same in all directions.

There are some disadvantages to wood as a structural material. Although a wood-framed building may stand longer than a steel building during a major fire, it still catches on fire at relatively low temperatures.

■ Concrete

Concrete has great compressive strength, almost as great as the strongest stone. However, it does not have much tensile strength. Its compressive strength is about ten times greater than its tensile strength.

Reinforced Concrete ■ Reinforced concrete is one of the most popular structural materials because it combines the compressive strength of concrete and the tensile strength of steel to create a material that is very versatile.

Because of the thermal resistance of concrete, the steel reinforcing rods are protected from heat better than steel-framed buildings. This means that in a fire it would take longer for the reinforcing rods to reach their plastic point.

Prestressed and Post-Tensioned Concrete ■ Prestressed concrete is made using steel cables or tendons in palce of steel reinforcing rods. The cables are stretched before the concrete is poured into the form. After the concrete hardens, the tension on the steel cables is released and the concrete gets compressed by the tension in the steel cables.

Prestressed concrete prevents tension cracks in the bottom of reinforced concrete beams. The beam is compressed before the load in order to counter-balance the tension forces. One disadvantage of prestressed concrete is that

Prestressed and reinforced concrete allow architects and builders to create fluid, eye-pleasing form. The French architect Francois Hennebique, born 1842, was the first to use reinforced concrete on a large scale. (Courtesy of the Precast/Prestressed Concrete Institute)

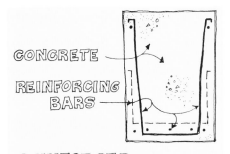

CONCRETE

REINFORCING BARS

REINFORCED CONCRETE BEAM

These workers are post-tensioning a beam on the construction site. This method permits each beam to be tensioned to a specific amount depending on the application.

PRE-TENSIONED CONCRETE BEAM

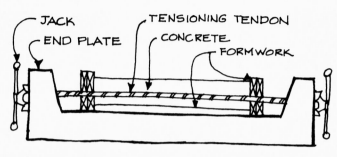

JACK
END PLATE
TENSIONING TENDON
CONCRETE
FORMWORK

POST-TENSIONED CONCRETE BEAM

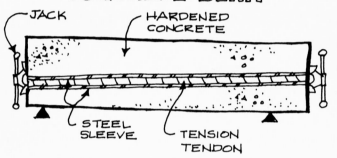

JACK
HARDENED CONCRETE
STEEL SLEEVE
TENSION TENDON

it must be manufactured in special plants and transported to the construction site.

The post-tensioning of concrete is a method of placing a stress on a reinforced concrete beam to counterbalance the tensile forces that occur when it is under load. Post tensioning occurs where the steel cables are pulled against the concrete after the concrete has set. This is accomplished by placing plastic tubes in the form before the concrete is poured so that the cables do not attach to the concrete.

Post-tensioning has some advantages over prestressed concrete. It can be done at the site after the beam or column has been made. Also, the tensioning can be controlled and adjusted after the structural member has been loaded. However, post-tensioning requires additional equipment and labor, which increases the cost.

■ Synthetic Materials

Some synthetic materials (plastics), such as new resin-fiber composites, are stronger than steel in tension and compression. However, most plastics deform easily and are very expensive to produce. Therefore are not made into large structural forms. An exception is the pneumatic roof, which uses high strength synthetic fabrics. These fabrics have excellent tensile strength.

Membrane structures can cover large areas—as large as this football field at the Detroit Lions' Stadium. (Courtesy of NASA)

SUMMARY

Structural materials used in construction systems must have certain important properties. They must be strong enough to withstand pulling forces known as tension and/or pushing forces known as compression. These two forms of mechanical strength are tensile strength and compressive strength. Elasticity is another important property of structural materials. It is the ability of a structural material to return to its original size and shape after a force is removed. When a structural material reaches its elastic limit, it becomes plastic and deforms. Brittle materials will collapse suddenly after they have passed their elastic limit. Toughness is the ability of a material to withstand impact.

Thermal and chemical properties of structural materials must also be considered. Some materials, such as steel, become plastic very quickly during a fire, causing them to collapse. Ironically, heavy wood-framed structures usually stand longer than steel structures during a fire. Some materials may be chemically treated to reduce corrosion, rust or decay.

There are three categories of structured materials: metals, natural materials and synthetic materials. All materials have their own specific properties, which affect their uses.

Study Questions

1. Describe tensile and compressive strength using examples of structural materials found in a typical playground.

2. What is the difference between strain and stress?

3. Describe how a rubber band and a bridge have similar elastic properties.

4. Describe what happens when a load is increased beyond the linear elastic point? What is this called?

5. How does fire affect the properties of steel versus wood?

6. Why is steel a better structural material than iron?

7. What advantages does brick have over stone?

8. What factors determine the structural properties of wood?

9. In what ways can the tensile properties of concrete be improved?

10. What are the advantages and disadvantages of synthetic materials?

Suggested Activities

1. Survey the types of materials used in your school as compared with your home. Make a list and describe the properties of each material and why it was used.

2. Use stiff wire and clay to make a reinforced beam. Try using rubber bands and clay to make a post-tensioned beam.

3. Talk to your local fire department about the comparative properties of various structural materials to withstand fire.

4. Look for examples of CORTEN™ steel used in your community. List some possible applications for such a product. Write to USX Corporation for more information on the properties of CORTEN steel (USX, Public Affairs Dept., 600 Grant St., Pittsburgh, PA 15219-4776).

5. Find two boards of equal length: one made of softwood, the other of hardwood. Think of different ways to test the compressive and tensile strength of these boards.

Glossary

Compression   A pushing load that contracts or shortens a material.

Elasticity   The ability of a material to return to its original shape and dimensions after a force is removed.

Modulus of elasticity   The measurement of stiffness in a material.

Plasticity   The opposite of elasticity; the permanent deformation of a material after the force has been removed.

Strain   A proportional deformation of a material under a force per unit length.

Stress   Tensile or compressive force on a material divided by the area it is applied to.

Tension   A pulling load that lengthens a material.

Toughness   The ability of a material to withstand shock.

Chapter 4

Structural Elements

Chapter Objectives

■ Structures are systems composed of a combination of a few basic structural elements.

■ The two types of structural elements are rigid and nonrigid.

■ Many structural elements can be made with a variety of construction materials.

■ Each structural element has basic characteristics that describe how the element functions in a structure.

Key Terms

arch
beam
bearing walls
cable-stayed
cables
column
dome
frame
geodesic dome
gusset
icosahedron
lift-slab
mass structures

membranes
plates
pneumatic structures
post and lintel
slabs
space frame system
structural element
thrust
truss
truss frame system
trussing
vault
voussoirs

Although structures may seem complex, they are actually composed of a few basic elements used in combination. The beam is one of the most common elements used. This large beam, or girder, is being used to support a bridge. (Courtesy of Blount, Inc.)

Structural Elements

Most structures seem very complex and confusing at first glance. In reality, they are systems composed of combinations of a few structural elements. A **structural element** is a basic component, feature, or basic part of a structure. Structural elements are not walls, floors, and roofs. These larger parts of a structure are made from a combination of smaller parts, namely elements such as beams, columns, arches, and trusses.

Elements serve two purposes:

- giving form to the structure and
- supporting the structure.

Every structure must work against gravity, which pulls everything to the ground. A well designed structure will be a combination of the best structural elements made of the best materials to create a balance between gravity and other forces and the form and shape of the structure. Each element has its own unique characteristics, including the materials it can be made from, its size limitation, and how it can be applied. Understanding these characteristics is essential for architects, designers, builders, and engineers in construction.

It can take years of education and experience to develop a thorough understanding of structural elements. After reading this chapter you should be able to identify the basic structural elements and explain their characteristics.

Structural elements may be classified by a number of different factors. In this book, structural elements are classified based on the amount of flexibility they display. Basically, elements are viewed as rigid (relatively non-flexible), and nonrigid (fairly flexible).

Rigid Structural Elements

No structural element is completely rigid. The amount of flexibility in each element varies, depending on the materials used and the size and cross-sectional shape of the element. Nevertheless, rigid structural elements must remain relatively firm and non-flexible in order for a structure to be stable against gravity and other forces.

Beams are often used in wood-frame construction. (Courtesy of Forest Products Lab)

Rigid structural elements compose the larger of the two classification groups and include beams, columns, arches, geodesic domes, plates, trusses, mass, bearing walls, and frames.

Beams are defined by their means of support.

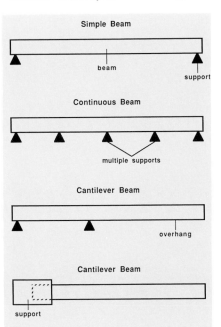

Beams

Beam is the generic name for linear elements used to span a gap between two supports. There are numerous names for beams, such as girder, joist, rafter, header, and lintel. A girder is a large beam used in heavy construction projects, such as bridges and skyscrapers. Joists are beams placed side-by-side in an assembly to create a surface for floors or ceilings in wood-frame construction. Beams are usually horizontal, but they may be inclined. Rafters are inclined beams used in wood-frame construction to create a shell for a roof. Headers, also used in wood-frame construction, are short beams placed above openings for doors or windows. A lintel is the masonry equivalent of a header.

Types of Beams ■ There are many beam variations based on their means of support. Simple beams have two supports located close to their ends, thus spanning the maximum amount of open space. Continuous beams have a series of equally spaced supports along their length, which reduces the usable spanned space. Cantilever beams are anchored to, and extend from, only one support and span less distance than simple or continuous beams. In structures, cantilever beams usually exist as overhangs of simple or continuous beams that extend beyond their last support.

. . . .

Beam Materials ■ Beams are made from a variety of materials. The ancient Romans and Greeks made extensive use of masonry beams in their temples. However, masonry has limited spanning abilities. If you look at the ruins of their temples, you will see that the ancient builders were forced to use numerous closely spaced supports. Today, masonry is rarely used as a beam material.

Concrete by itself also has limited spanning abilities. However, when reinforced with steel rods it is used quite often as a beam material, especially for short-span highway bridges.

Wood is the most commonly used beam material in house construction for floor and ceiling joists, rafters, and headers. Dimension softwood lumber ranging from 2 × 4s to 2 × 12s are used, depending on the specific application.

Steel is one of the most important beam materials. Structural steel shapes, especially the I, and T are used extensively as skyscraper and bridge girders. Structural steel is available in sizes from 3 inches to 3 feet in depth.

Beam Characteristics ■ Beams tend to bend or sag when supporting a weight. Sagging beams can cause a structure to collapse. To avoid this, it is important to understand the depth-to-span ratio of the beam. In general, as span between supports increases, depth of the beam must also increase to prevent sagging.

Structural steel shapes, especially the I and T, are used extensively as bridge girders. (Courtesy of Beazer Materials and Services, Inc.)

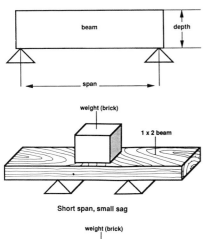

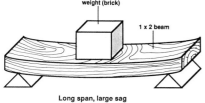

beam / depth / span

weight (brick) / 1 x 2 beam

Short span, small sag

weight (brick) / 1 x 2 beam

Long span, large sag

1 x 2 beam on edge, increased depth

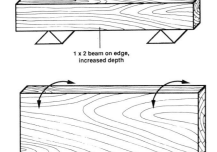

top heavy,

The depth-span relationship can be demonstrated by spanning short and long distances with a beam made from 1 × 2 lumber. A 1 × 2 beam simply supported at both ends will not sag noticeably under a weight when spanning a short distance. However, as the span increases, the weight on the beam will cause a much larger sag. However, placing the 1 × 2 beam on edge (increasing its depth) gives it increased depth and also increases its strength.

There are two options for limiting this sag: adding additional supports or increasing beam depth. By adding supports, a continuous beam is created with increased strength.

One negative side effect of increasing beam depth is a decrease in stability. When the 1 × 2 beam is on edge, it tends to be top heavy and less stable, thus toppling easily. This toppling can lead to minor problems or major failures in a structure. To improve stability, the width of the beam is increased. Two examples of this are laminated wood headers and the flanges on steel I-beams, both of which achieve stability with increased depth and width. Another option is to use a built-up beam, such as the plywood box beam.

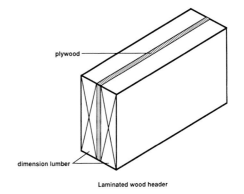

steel I-beam

plywood / dimension lumber / Laminated wood header

Plywood Box Beam

Beams are an important structural element and structural engineers are always looking for more efficient beams. The plywood box beam is an important innovation in beam efficiency. A plywood box beam is built in the form of a long hollow box. The top and bottom flanges and stiffeners are made from dimension lumber, usually 2 × 4s, and the web is made from plywood. An alter-

top flange / web (plywood) / stiffeners / bottom flange
Plywood Box Beam

native design for lighter applications is shown. Plywood box beams can be assembled using nails, screws, or bolts, but gluing is the preferred technique.

Plywood box beams have the increased depth needed for long

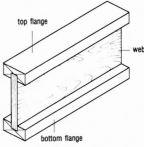

top flange / web / bottom flange
Modified Plywood Box Beam

spans without the added weight from a laminated wood beam or steel I-beam. The increased depth creates superior spanning capabilities. Plywood box beams have been used in spans of over 100 feet.

The Capitol Building, Washington, D.C. Many government buildings use columns because they give a sense of size and importance to structures.

Columns

Column is the generic name given to linear, vertical elements used to support beams and other elements. The column is probably the most important element, creating height in a structure. As with beams, there are a number of different types of columns, including piers, piles, and pillars. Piers are short, stout, massive columns used as the main vertical supports in bridges. Piles are foundation supports made of steel that are driven deep into the ground using specialized pile-driving equipment. Pillars are columns with cross-sectional shapes other than circular, such as square, rectangular, I-shaped, or H-shaped. (In the strictest definition, columns have circular cross-sectional shapes.)

Column Materials ■ The columns in ancient Greek and Roman temples were made by stacking large individual round stones. Today masonry continues to be a popular column material because of its superior resistance to crushing. Many impressive structures in our society use stone columns very similar to those used by ancient builders. Manufactured masonry products, such as concrete block and brick, are also popular as column materials.

Reinforced concrete that is cast in place or prefabricated is used extensively for large structures requiring piers or pillars. Using concrete rather than stone for columns saves construction time and still provides superior resistance to crushing. Many medium-sized skyscrapers use concrete columns.

Wood is not easily crushed, but it does have a tendency to buckle (or bend). To prevent this buckling, wooden wall studs (a type of column) are closely spaced in a series and reinforced with top and sole plates.

Steel and aluminum are two metals commonly used for columns. Steel is the main column material for all skyscrapers. Structural shapes like the I, H, and square (pillars) are used. Aluminum is popular as a material for the fluted columns supporting roofs over porches on many homes.

Column Characteristics ■ Columns create height in structures by supporting beams and other elements. Two main problems facing columns are crushing and buckling. If a column crushes or buckles, a dangerous collapse of at least part of the structure results, particularly in multi-story structures. To avoid this engineers always "over-design" columns; that is, they design columns stronger than needed for the job.

One important characteristic of columns is the diameter-to-length (height) ratio. In general, short, large-diameter columns tend to crush without buckling first, and long, slender columns tend to buckle before crushing. Also, as the length of a column increases, it loses its ability to support weight (assuming that the column material remains constant). The mathematical

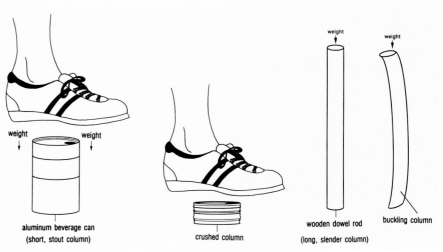

Diameter-to-length ratio of columns can be demonstrated with an empty aluminum beverage can and a long, thin wooden dowel rod. If you place the can (a short, stout column) in an upright position and push down with your foot, the can will support only so much weight and will then crush. The dowel rod (a long, slender column) will buckle before it crushes.

weight | weight
aluminum beverage can
(short, stout column)

crushed column

weight | weight
wooden dowel rod
(long, slender column)

buckling column

The length-weight relationship can be demonstrated using a 5″ × 10″ piece of cardboard (similar to that found on the back of writing tablets) as a simulated column. In this experiment, the long column length (L), ten inches, is twice as long as the short column (1/2L), five inches.

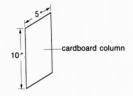
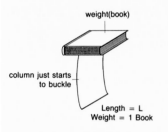
cardboard column

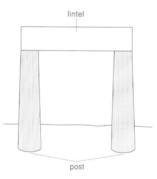
weight(book)

column just starts to buckle

Length = L
Weight = 1 Book

Hold the cardboard column in an upright position with the long dimension (L) vertical. Experiment with weights (small books) to determine the maximum weight that can be held by the column before it begins to buckle. Now, reposition the column with the short dimension (1/2L) vertical, and repeat the procedure. You should find that the short column (1/2L) will hold four times the weight of the long column (L).

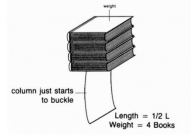
weight

column just starts to buckle

Length = 1/2 L
Weight = 4 Books

relationship can be summarized as follows: If the length of a column is doubled, it will be able to support only one-fourth the weight. And it follows that if the length of a column is reduced by half, then it will be able to support four times the weight.

Another important consideration is the stiffness of the column material. In general, columns made from stiffer materials will support more weight. Compare the weight-supporting abilities of a wooden dowel and a metal welding rod of similar lengths and diameters.

■ The Post and Lintel System

The column and beam cannot work independently to form a structure. Usually, the column and beam are combined to form the **post and lintel** system. In the basic post and lintel system, two upright elements (posts or columns) hold a third element (lintel or beam) laid horizontally across their top surfaces. Most ancient structures were built this way using stone as a primary material for both components. Over the ages, the post and lintel system has evolved due to changes in technology (tools, materials, and processes), but the system remains basically the same as it was thousands of years ago.

lintel

post

The lion gate at Mycenae, Greece, is a good example of an ancient post and lintel system.

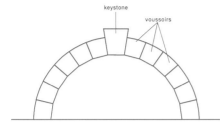

keystone
voussoirs

■ Arches

An **arch** is a curved structural element that spans an open space, providing height. The arch was developed thousands of years ago as an improvement over masonry beams. Arches, built by stacking a series of wedge-shaped masonry blocks called **voussoirs** in a curve, are capable of spanning much longer distances than straight beams. In fact, the ancient Romans, who made extensive use of this building element, could span distances of up to 100 feet with their masonry arches.

Before an arch can be built, a curved form must be erected to support the voussoirs as they are being stacked. Once the top voussoirs are in place, the form can be removed and the wedge-shaped blocks hold each other in place. The keystone (the center stone) is really unimportant in structural terms, but is often enlarged or emphasized for ornamental purposes.

Arches can be built in many different curved shapes, such as semicircular (half circles), segmental, pointed, and flat. The pointed arch, which does not have a keystone, is usually associated with tall Gothic cathedrals. The flat arch is quite unusual and may not look like an arch at all, but the distribution of weight through its voussoirs makes it an arch all the same.

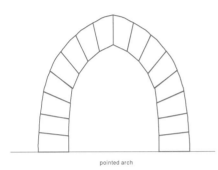

pointed arch

Types of Arches ■ There are two types of arches: fixed and hinged. Fixed arches are stiffer than hinged arches and are therefore more sensitive to thermal expansion and contraction and to foundation movements. Fixed arches are best suited for short spans, such as window and door headers, or short bridges, and tunnels, where large movements are not expected.

Hinged arches are more flexible; they can accommodate movements created by thermal effects and foundation shifts. Two-hinge arches are usually used for long spans, such as bridges, with the hinges located at the abutments. Three-hinge arches are popular for medium roof spans, such as those found on metal industrial buildings. The three hinges give this type of arch the maximum amount of flexibility and freedom to move when subjected to thermal or foundation stresses.

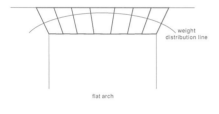

weight distribution line

flat arch

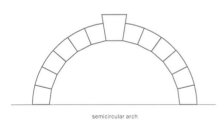

semicircular arch

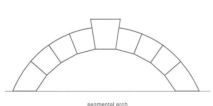

segmental arch

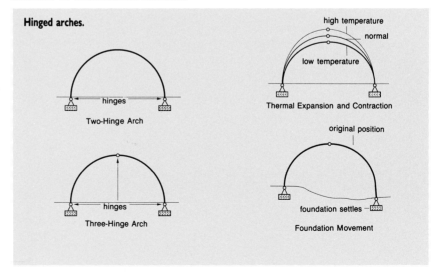

Hinged arches.

Two-Hinge Arch

Three-Hinge Arch

high temperature
normal
low temperature

Thermal Expansion and Contraction

original position

foundation settles

Foundation Movement

"Gateway Arch"

One of the most famous arches in the world is the Gateway Arch in St. Louis. With a span and rise both over 600 feet, it is also one of the largest.

The designer of the arch, Eero Saarinen, developed the curved shape by suspending a chain, tracing the curve onto paper, and inverting the paper to view an arch. He experimented with the chain suspended in different positions until he liked the arch shape.

suspended chain

arch curve

The unique structure of the arch can be examined by imagining a slice taken from the arch and viewed in cross-section. The arch cross-section is an equilateral triangle with a hollow interior surrounded by a steel inner skin. Visitors can ride to an observation platform at the top of the arch in elevator-type cars that operate through the hollow interior. The outer skin is made of polished stainless steel, which gives the arch its glimmering appearance. Between the inner and outer skins the arch is stiffened with reinforced concrete extending about half way up both legs. To resist thrust, the base of each leg is anchored into reinforced concrete foundations, which act as buttresses.

Photo by George Barford.

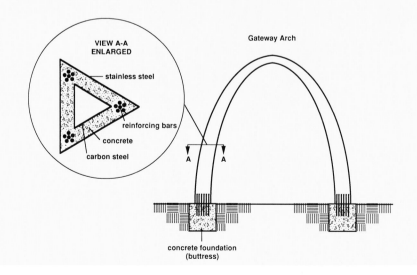
VIEW A-A ENLARGED
stainless steel
reinforcing bars
concrete
carbon steel
Gateway Arch
A   A
concrete foundation (buttress)

Laminated wood arches are still used for bridges today. (Courtesy Forest Products Laboratory)

Arch Materials ■ The oldest arch material, masonry is still important today, but only for limited spans, such as above doorways and windows.

Reinforced concrete is a popular material for medium-span arch bridges. Individual components can be precast and then assembled on-site, or the arch may be cast in place.

Wood may not seem like a potential arch material at first, but laminated wood arches are used. Wood arches are used for the beauty of the grain and can be highly ornamented. They are prefabricated in a shop and then shipped to the building site. Special forms and clamping systems are required to bend individual pieces of dimension lumber into the arch form. Laminations are secured with glues and other adhesives.

Steel is the most popular arch material for long spans, especially bridges. However, long-span steel arches are not pure arches like masonry, concrete, and wood. Rather, they are made by building up a frame with curved top and bottom pieces and short, straight trussing between. (Trusses will be explained in detail later.) Long-span steel truss arches are usually hinged.

Arch Characteristics ■ Arches have a tendency to push outward at their bottoms. This outward push is called **thrust.** In general, as the span of an arch increases in relation to the rise (span-to-rise ratio), thrust increases. If not contained, it can cause the arch to collapse. Three techniques are used to control thrust: ties, buttresses, and modifying the span-to-rise ratio.

Ties are steel cables or rods secured from leg to leg of an arch at its base or foundation. Ties help the base of the arch resist thrust forces. Buttresses are heavy supports placed against the outside of the arch foundation to resist thrust. In modifying the span-to-rise ratio, the key to controlling thrust is to have a rise as high as is economically possible in relation to the span.

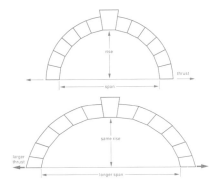

As the span of an arch increases in relation to the rise, thrust increases.

Arch characteristics and thrust-control techniques can be demonstrated using thin metal rods (coat hangers or welding rods) bent in the curve of an arch. Start with two rods of equal length curved with different span-to-rise ratios. Make one arch semicircular (half circle) and the other segmental (less than a half circle). Hold each arch in an upright position and press down on their tops. More pressure will be required to cause the semicircular arch to thrust outward. String or fishing line fastened

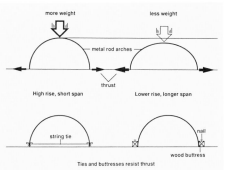

between the bases on each arch demonstrates the ability of ties to resist thrust. With the ties removed, buttresses can be simulated by securing two small blocks of wood outside the bases of each arch.

The West Virginia University Coliseum, Morgantown, WV, has a concrete vault roof. (Photo by Stan Komacek)

The Vault and Dome: Variations of the Arch ■ Two structural systems that evolved from the arch design are the vault and dome. A **vault** is created by placing a series of arches together face to face to form a long, uninterrupted internal span. Common examples of vaults include concrete tunnels, corrugated steel sheds, and other structures with rigid, barrel-type roofs. A **dome** is created by revolving a series of arches about a common crown or center point. Domes are primarily used as ornamental devices on important governmental buildings, or roofs for churches and sports arenas.

Domes and vaults have characteristics similar to arches in terms of thrust and span-to-rise ratio, and use most of the same materials.

■ Geodesic Domes

The domes that evolved from the arch should not be confused with geodesic domes, which are a much different structural element. A **geodesic dome** has a spherical form similar to arch domes, but is composed of lightweight, linear struts connected in the form of triangles over the entire surface area of the sphere.

Most structural elements have ancient origins and cannot be traced to one individual. The geodesic dome, however, is a 20th century invention of engineer R. Buckminster Fuller.

R. Buckminster Fuller—Inventive Engineer

R. Buckminster Fuller (1895–1983), called "Bucky" by his friends and followers, was an inventive American engineer years ahead of his time. In addition to the geodesic dome, Bucky created many futuristic inventions, including a structure called the Dymaxion house. Built in 1929, the Dymaxion house, which Fuller called a "dwelling machine," was designed to be fully automated, solar-powered, low-priced, and lightweight. Fuller planned to use stamped, lightweight materials to keep the weight of the Dymaxion around three tons. A typical one-family wood-frame house weighs about 150 tons! The entire structure, when disassembled, fit into a tube sixteen feet long and four feet in diameter.

Bucky also designed the Dymaxion car. Built in 1934, the Dymaxion car had three wheels, carried eleven people, was capable of speeds over 110 miles per hour, got a terrific 40 miles per gallon, and could move into a parking space sideways!

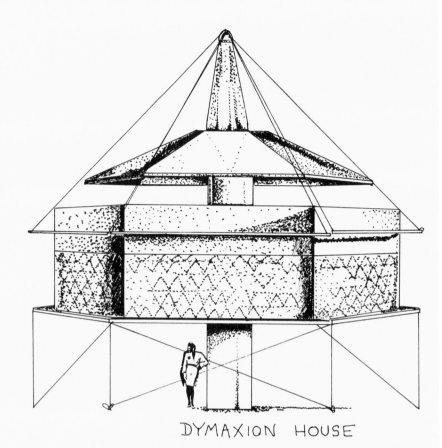

DYMAXION HOUSE

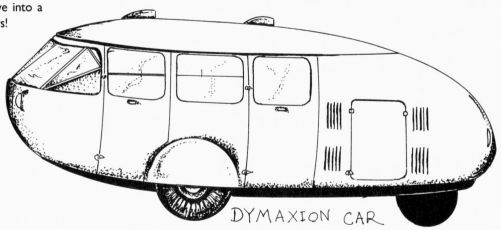

DYMAXION CAR

This house is a two-frequency geodesic dome.
(Photo by Stan Komacek)

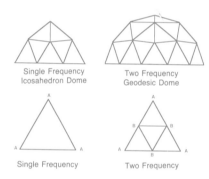

Single Frequency
Icosahedron Dome

Two Frequency
Geodesic Dome

Single Frequency

Two Frequency

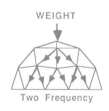

WEIGHT

Two Frequency

Weight is are distributed
more in two frequency
geodesic domes

WEIGHT

Single Frequency

Types of Geodesic Domes ■ Geodesic domes are categorized by the number of different strut lengths they have. The simplest geodesic dome, the **icosahedron,** is a single-frequency dome. In an icosahedron dome, all the struts are the same length or frequency. More complex domes have more frequencies. A two-frequency dome has two frequencies (two lengths of struts). Large geodesic domes that span hundreds of feet may have up to a dozen or more frequencies.

Geodesic Dome Materials ■ Geodesic domes can be constructed from a variety of materials, including wood, aluminum, steel, plastic, and plywood. The biggest advantage of a geodesic dome for most applications is its light weight relative to the space it covers. For this reason, aluminum is the preferred material for larger structures, while lumber may be used for smaller structures, such as greenhouses and storage sheds.

Geodesic Dome Characteristics ■ Geodesic domes are lightweight and look fragile. However, they are very strong structures. This combination of light weight and strength is best demonstrated by the weather station geodesic domes designed and built by Fuller for the Air Force in the 1950s.

The Air Force was looking for a structure that could shelter fragile radar equipment from arctic winds and snow in northern Canada. Fuller designed a 49-foot diameter dome that weighed only 1,140 pounds. The entire structure could be moved by helicopter to the building site. Many engineers thought Fuller's dome would collapse in any wind over 20 miles per hour, but the structures withstood freezing arctic winds of 200 miles per hour.

The frequency of a geodesic dome determines its overall strength. Basically, the more frequencies, the more stable and strong the dome will be. Each strut on a geodesic dome distributes a part of the weight above it. More struts mean more distribution of the weight and a stronger dome.

The U.S. Pavilion at the Expo 67, Montreal, Canada, designed by Buckminster Fuller. The outer grid of aluminum struts in this complex geodesic dome support the weight of 2,000 acrylic caps.

◼ Plates

Plates, also called **slabs,** are relatively thin structural elements used to span areas between beams, columns, and other elements. Plates are used to enclose framed structures and create a surface for flooring, roofing, and walls.

Plate Materials ◼ The two most common examples of plates are plywood and concrete slabs. In light construction projects, plywood, or other similar manufactured wood sheets, are used for subflooring, wall sheathing, and roof decking. In many heavy construction projects, reinforced concrete slabs are used to create floors and flat roofs. Concrete slabs, which may be precast or cast in place, often have hollow or T-shaped cross-sections.

Plates can also be steel or plastic, in the form of corrugated sheets. These sheets are generally used to cover commercial buildings. Corrugated steel plates are also used to create forms for cast-in-place concrete slabs.

Plate Characteristics ◼ Two factors that must be considered when using plates are the means of support and the depth-to-span ratio. Plates may be supported by one-way or two-way supporting methods. Plates supported by the one-way method have a tendency to sag between the supports. Two-way support reduces this sagging tendency.

The performance of plates using one-way and two-way supporting systems can be demonstrated by adding a weight to a supported sheet of cardboard or thin plywood. When supported by the one-way method, the plate will sag noticeably. The two-way supporting system provides dramatic improvements.

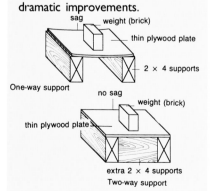

sag   weight (brick)

thin plywood plate

2 × 4 supports

One-way support

no sag   weight (brick)

thin plywood plate

extra 2 × 4 supports

Two-way support

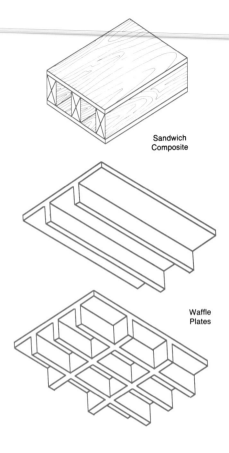

Sandwich
Composite

Waffle
Plates

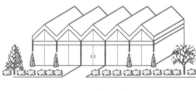

Folded Concrete
Roofing

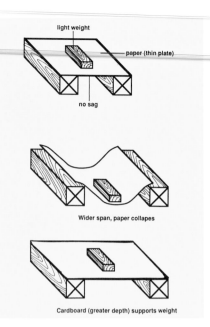

light weight

paper (thin plate)

no sag

Wider span, paper collapes

Cardboard (greater depth) supports weight

The depth-to-span relationship in plates can be demonstrated by placing a small weight on a piece of paper (plate) that is supported using the one-way method. A weight of a few ounces can be held if the supports are spaced close enough. However, as the span increases, the paper will not be able to support the weight. If a piece of cardboard (a plate with more depth) is substituted for the sheet of paper, it will be able to support the weight.

The depth-to-span ratio of plates is similar to that of beams. Basically, as the span increases, depth must also increase to support the same weight. Plate depth may be increased by a number of techniques. The depth of plywood plates may be increased with sandwich composites, which are similar to the plywood box beams described earlier. In sandwich composites, small wooden beams are sandwiched between two sheets of thin plywood.

Increased depth does not have to cover the entire surface area of a plate. The depth of concrete plates is often increased with integral ribs placed at regular intervals. The ribs increase the weight supporting ability of the concrete without dramatically increasing weight or costs. For even more weight-supporting capacity, additional ribs may be added at right angles, creating what is known as a waffle plate.

Plate depth can also be achieved by folding or corrugating the plate material. Folded concrete plates are popular as a roofing element. Thin steel and plastic plates are usually corrugated to improve their strength. Combining corrugated plates to create a composite results in an even stronger plate.

The strength of a folded plate can be demonstrated with a sheet of paper. A flat sheet of paper doesn't have the strength to support its own weight. However, if the paper is folded along its length, it may be able to hold the weight of a few pencils.

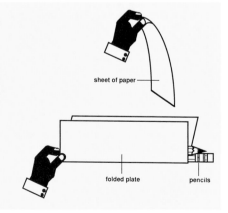

sheet of paper

folded plate

pencils

Inputs

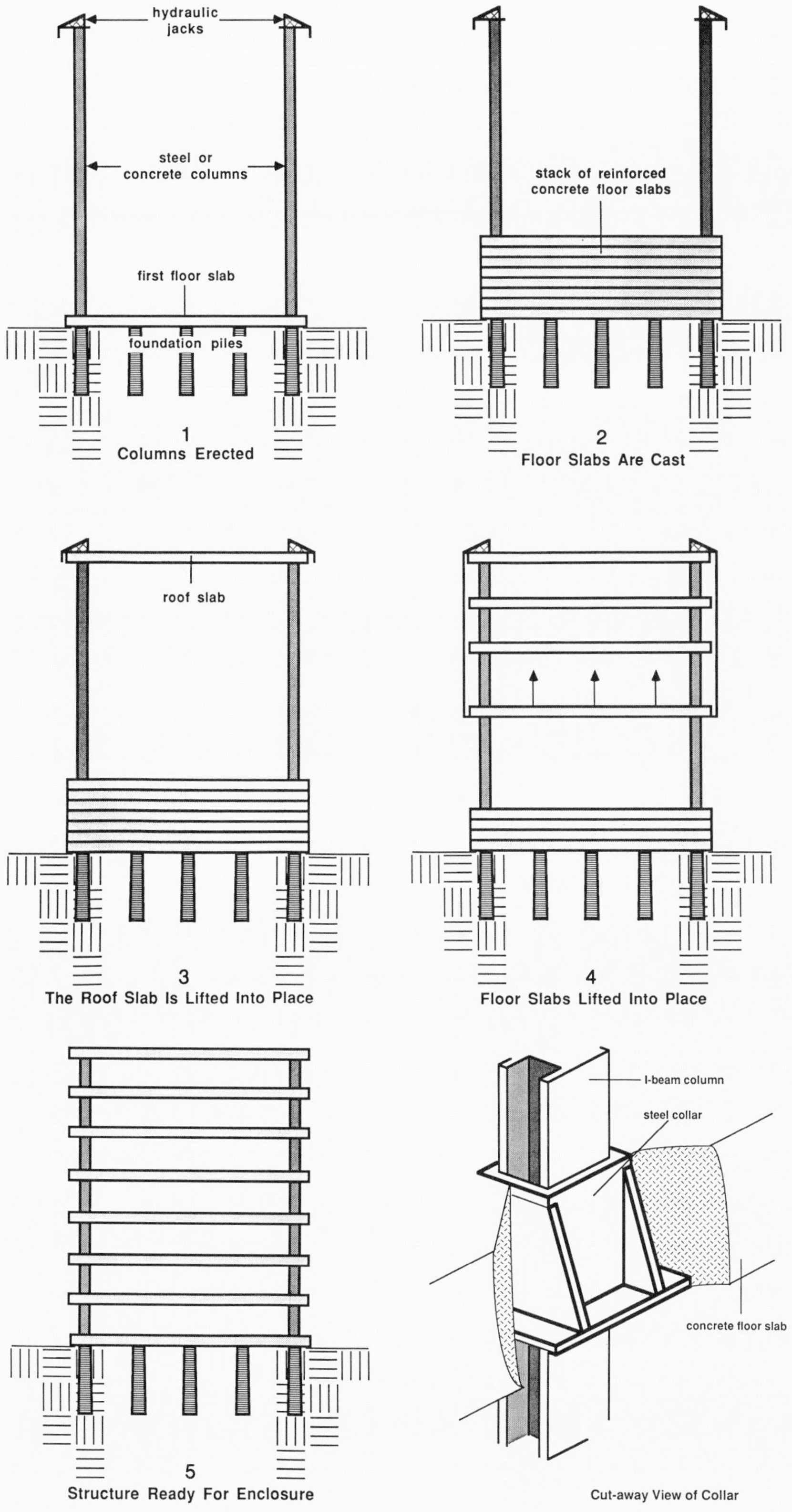

Lift-Slab Construction of Skyscrapers

An interesting technology that uses concrete slabs as a major structural element is the **lift-slab** method of constructing shorter skyscrapers. After the foundation is in place, the first-floor slab is cast. Then, steel or reinforced concrete columns are erected to their full height and secured to the first-floor slab. Next, a series of reinforced concrete slabs are cast and stacked one at a time on top of the first floor slab. Each of these slabs will be used for one floor of the skyscraper. The slab for the roof is the last to be cast.

During casting, a membrane of melted paraffin or other material is placed between each floor slab to facilitate separation of the slabs later. Also, steel collars are cast into each slab around each column.

Once all the slabs have been cast and allowed to cure, they are lifted vertically one at a time using hydraulic jacks mounted on top of each column. Lifting is slow, with slabs moving about seven to ten feet per hour. The roof slab is lifted first and subsequent floors in order. As each slab reaches its destination, it is welded or attached to the columns by fastening the steel collars at each column.

After all the floors are in place, the structure is enclosed and finished for use. Skyscrapers of over twelve stories have been economically constructed using the lift-slab method.

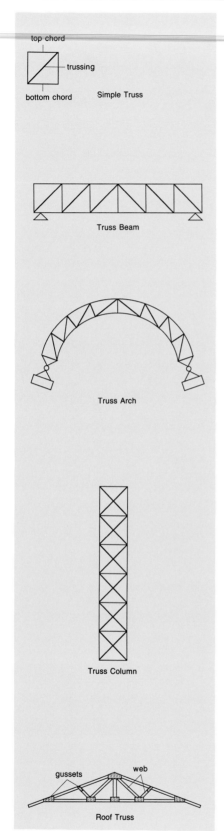

top chord

trussing

bottom chord   Simple Truss

Truss Beam

Truss Arch

Truss Column

gussets   web

Roof Truss

■ Truss

A **truss** is an arrangement of linear members connected together to form a series of triangles lying in a straight plane. The simplest truss is a box frame with a diagonal brace called **trussing.** Structural trusses are created by extending this simple truss. Trusses are capable of supporting considerable weight over relatively long spans. They are used for bridges, floors, roofs, and towers.

Types of Trusses ■ Trusses can be used to reinforce the basic structural elements, such as beams, columns, and arches, or used as components to a structure, such as roof trusses. These configurations are all two-dimensional (length and width), but trusses can also be formed into three-dimensional shapes for added stability and strength.

Trusses are usually named for their inventor or basic geometry. Some of the more common trusses are illustrated. The Pratt and Warren trusses are the most common used.

Truss Materials ■ Trusses are primarily made from wood or steel, depending on the size of the structure and the weight it must support. Floor and roof trusses for wood-frame construction are usually prefabricated in a factory and then shipped to the building site. Because of their superior strength and stability, trusses can be made of lighter weight dimension lumber. Usually, 2 × 4 lumber can be used for all the truss members rather than the larger sizes normally used for joists and rafters. Wooden floor and roof trusses are usually assembled with gussets. A **gusset** is a plywood or metal plate that is nailed or glued over the joints of the truss.

Steel trusses are used for large structures, such as bridges and commercial buildings. The steel used in trusses usually has some formed cross-sectional shape, such as Ts and Ls. Steel truss members are assembled by welding, riveting, or bolting. Steel gussets may be added in structures that will support larger weights.

Two famous structures built with steel trusses are the Statue of Liberty and the Eiffel Tower. The trusses of the Eiffel Tower are easily seen, but the metal skin on the Statue of Liberty covers her inner truss structure.

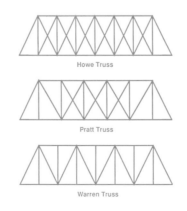

Howe Truss

Pratt Truss

Warren Truss

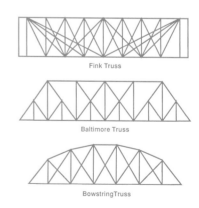

Fink Truss

Baltimore Truss

BowstringTruss

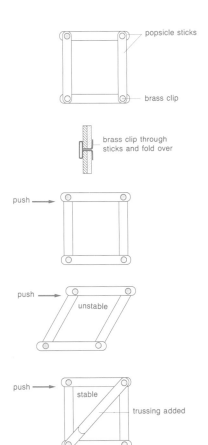

popsicle sticks

brass clip

brass clip through sticks and fold over

push

push

unstable

push

stable

trussing added

Truss Characteristics ■ The basic truss design is built on the principle that the triangle is a rigid configuration that will not change shape or collapse unless the length of one of its members is changed or its joints are disconnected. This principle, which makes trusses strong and stable, can be demonstrated with a popsicle stick frame.

Note that the truss joints are pinned, allowing the members to pivot. When actually constructed, the joints would be solidly assembled, probably with gussets, but for most structural analysis, trusses are assumed to have pinned joints. This is because simple trusses react to stress with a hinge-type action. They act as though they *were* pinned.

This frame is not very stable and changes shape easily. However, if trussing is added diagonally across the frame, the resulting truss has tremendous stability and is strong in resisting shape-changing forces.

The trussing principle also applies to other structural elements, such as the beam. The original frame, extended to create a beam, is unstable; when trussing is added, it becomes very strong and stable.

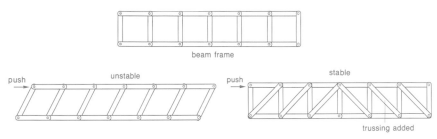

beam frame

push   unstable

push   stable

trussing added

Truss Frame System

The **truss frame system** (TFS) was developed in the late 1970s by the United States Forest Products Laboratory in Madison, Wisconsin. It is a building system that incorporates a roof truss, stud walls, and floor truss into one unit. Structures are built by erecting equally spaced TFS units on a foundation and covering the walls and roof with sheathing.

TFS was developed after the Forest Products Lab investigated structural failures due to tornadoes, earthquakes, and other natural disasters. They found that most failures occurred because of

poor connections at the joints between the walls, the floors, and the roof. In stick-built wood-framed structures, the walls are nailed on top of the floors and the roof is nailed on top of the walls. In the prefabricated TFS units the wall studs run from the bottom of the floor truss to the top chord of the roof truss, thus providing superior strength.

Not only is strength improved; TFS structures can be erected quickly. An entire structure can be built in the time normally required to erect roof trusses on top of conventional floors and

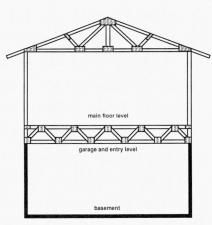

main floor level

garage and entry level

basement

Cross-section view of truss frame system on foundation

walls. Because the entire TFS is made using only 2 × 4s, instead of larger dimensioned lumber, total cost also can be reduced.

■ Space Frame System

The space frame system is a variation of the truss. The name "space frame" is often confusing. People tend to assume that this system will be used to build structures in outer space. While NASA does plan to use structural elements similar to trusses and space frames for their proposed space station, the space frame system got its name because it is used to cover large open spaces with relatively few support columns.

Space frame systems are created when a three-dimensional truss beam is extended to cover a large area. The space frame system is one of the most economical methods available for covering exhibition halls, airport terminals, and other structures where wide open space is required. Not only are space frames economical, they are also strong and lightweight. The largest space frame roofs can cover over 850 square feet with relatively few supporting columns.

Space frames are constructed with the same materials (wood and steel) and have basically the same characteristics (strong and stable) as trusses.

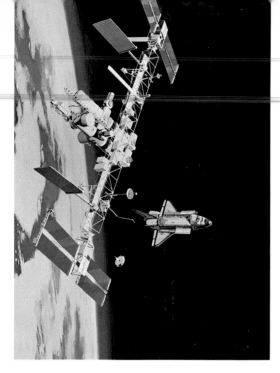

The twin boom Space Station design uses the space frame system. (Courtesy of NASA)

■ Mass

The simplest structural element is mass. Mass is defined as a large quantity of material having an indefinite size and shape. Structures can be built by giving mass a definite size and shape. **Mass structures,** also called solid

A dam is a common example of a mass structure.

This cut-away model shows how the ancient Egyptians built the pyramids as mass structures. The only usable internal spaces were the burial chambers and related passageways.

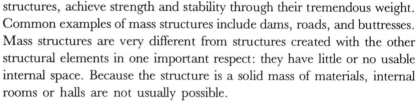

Concrete blocks are commonly used to build bearing walls.

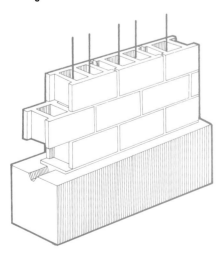

structures, achieve strength and stability through their tremendous weight. Common examples of mass structures include dams, roads, and buttresses. Mass structures are very different from structures created with the other structural elements in one important respect: they have little or no usable internal space. Because the structure is a solid mass of materials, internal rooms or halls are not usually possible.

Mass Materials ■ The primary materials used for mass structures today are earth, rock and concrete. Building mass structures with these materials is fairly easy using heavy equipment such as bulldozers, road-paving equipment, and concrete-casting machinery. To build roads and highways, highly specialized paving equipment has been developed that lays out long ribbons of concrete or asphalt.

The buttress, a mass structure developed to strengthen the tall Gothic arch, has limited use today. It is primarily used in concrete buttress dams and as concrete abutments in arch bridges and dams.

■ Bearing Walls

Bearing walls are similar to plates or slabs, except that they are in a vertical position rather than horizontal. Bearing walls serve the same function as columns by supporting floors and roofs to produce height in a structure. Unlike columns, however, bearing walls enclose space, thus creating rooms. Of course, openings may be built into bearing walls for doors and windows, if needed. The concrete block walls used for the foundation of wood-frame structures are the most common example of bearing walls.

Bearing Wall Materials ■ Concrete and masonry materials are the primary materials used in bearing walls. Building bearing walls with masonry materials (concrete block and brick) is time consuming and requires skilled masons. Pre-cast or cast-in-place concrete bearing walls can be constructed rather quickly with less skilled workers.

. . . .

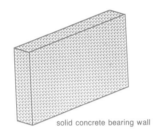

concrete block bearing wall

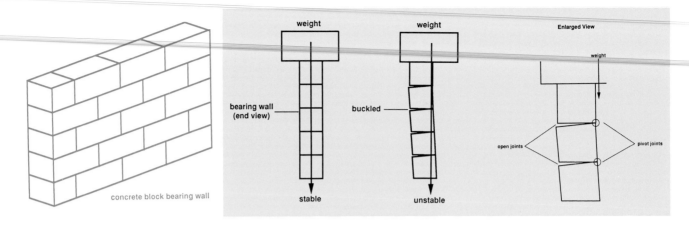

weight   weight   Enlarged View

bearing wall (end view)   buckled   weight

open joints   pivot joints

stable   unstable

solid concrete bearing wall

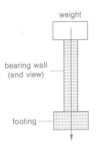

weight

bearing wall (end view)

footing

Bearing Wall Characteristics ■

Bearing walls have characteristics similar to columns. The primary structural consideration is buckling of the wall from uneven loads. A bearing wall constructed of concrete block is very strong and stable, if the supported weight is directed through the center of the vertical wall.

If the direction of the weight is off center or the wall is tilted from vertical, the wall will have a tendency to buckle and collapse. The buckling begins when the joints between the blocks open, resulting in a series of very small pivot points that must bear the entire load. This problem can be overcome by constructing the wall of solid concrete rather than blocks. The solid wall doesn't have joints that can open. As long as the solid wall is securely anchored to a footing, it will be able to withstand a much larger off-center load.

A similar reaction occurs when an underground concrete block foundation wall is exposed to side forces from water or ground movement. Bearing walls are not designed to withstand these side forces and the joints open, which can result in a disastrous collapse of the entire structure. This is why adequate drainage must be provided outside underground foundations.

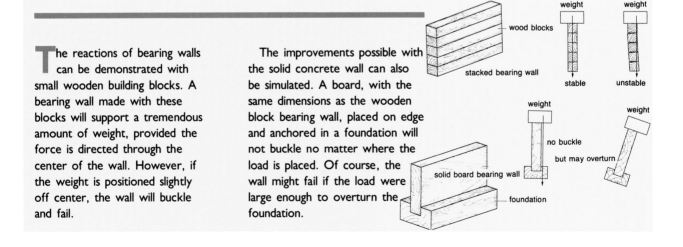

The reactions of bearing walls can be demonstrated with small wooden building blocks. A bearing wall made with these blocks will support a tremendous amount of weight, provided the force is directed through the center of the wall. However, if the weight is positioned slightly off center, the wall will buckle and fail.

The improvements possible with the solid concrete wall can also be simulated. A board, with the same dimensions as the wooden block bearing wall, placed on edge and anchored in a foundation will not buckle no matter where the load is placed. Of course, the wall might fail if the load were large enough to overturn the foundation.

wood blocks

stacked bearing wall

weight   weight

stable   unstable

weight

no buckle

but may overturn

weight

solid board bearing wall

foundation

Wood and steel are the two most common materials for framing. What are the benefits and drawbacks of each?

■ Frame

A **frame** is a three-dimensional network of assembled components used to create the skeleton of a structure. This skeleton, which is composed of post and lintel elements, supports the weight of the structure and creates the outlines for rooms. A covering or skin is added to the skeleton to enclose the rooms. The skin may also serve to stiffen or brace the frame.

Framed structures use less material to enclose a given space than bearing walls and are thus lighter. For this reason, framed structures can be much taller than bearing-wall structures.

Frame Materials ■ For smaller structures, wood is the primary frame building material. Wood is relatively inexpensive and easily worked using hand tools, so it is a natural choice for residential construction. The floor, wall, ceiling, and roof assemblies for most houses are all built using wood framed construction.

The skeleton frames for tall skyscrapers are made of steel. Steel is a heavy material but, due to its great strength, very little steel is used to build a frame. Therefore, it produces a relatively light structure, even in a skyscraper with a height of several hundred feet or more. The largest skyscrapers in the world are all built using steel skeleton frames.

· ·

Frame Characteristics ■ Framed structures exhibit characteristics similar to the truss frame. The basic frame, whether in wood or steel, can be very unstable. It has a tendency to twist and bend. Three techniques are used to stabilize framed structures: reinforced joints, trussing, and rigid plates.

The joints where individual frame members connect can be stiffened with reinforcement, such as plates or angles. These techniques are not used with wood frames, but rather with steel frames, which tend to have fewer joints. Trussing, diagonal braces between frame members, can be installed more quickly than reinforced joints. Thin rigid plates, such as plywood sheets and concrete panels, installed on the outside of a frame, are the most effective means of reinforcement, but also the most costly. Trussing and rigid plates are used to stabilize both wood and steel frames.

. . . .

Nonrigid Structural Elements

Nonrigid structural elements are flexible. The two basic nonrigid structural elements are, cables and membranes. Neither of these structural elements has a definite shape that can be used to form a structure. They must be combined with rigid elements to create structural systems.

Suspension bridges rely on woven steel cables as one of their main structural elements. The Golden Gate Bridge is one of the longest suspension bridges. (Courtesy of George Barford)

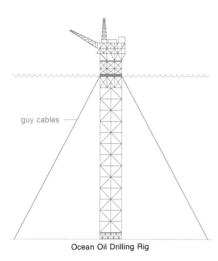

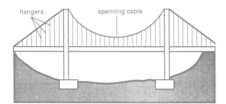

Ocean Oil Drilling Rig

Three types of cables: *(above)* guy cables anchor oil drilling rigs to the ocean floor; *(below)* hangars and spanning cables are both used by suspension bridges.

■ Cables

Cables, long, slender, rope-like elements, have been used for centuries to span long distances. Primitive societies built foot bridges spanning 100 feet or more using vines and rope as cables. Today, woven steel cables are the long-span champion. The longest spans in the world, suspension bridges, use cables as one of the main structural elements.

Types of Cables ■ There are three different types of cables: hangers, guys, and spanning cables. Hangers, also called suspenders, are suspended vertically to support a weight. The two most common examples of hangers are the wires used to support a suspended ceiling and the vertical cables that support the road surface in a suspension bridge. Guys are cables used to brace rigid vertical structures, such as towers and antennas. Spanning cables are the draped steel cables used in suspension bridges and cable-stayed bridged.

Cable Characteristics ■ Cables, being nonrigid elements, are subject to changes in shape. The most critical of these changes is the sag experienced by spanning cables. The relationship between sag, span, and thrust is an important consideration in the design of spanning cable. In a spanning cable, as the span increases in relation to sag, thrust (the force that pulls on both ends of the cable) increases. (This is similar to the span, rise, thrust relationship of arches.)

The span for a given bridge usually cannot be changed. Therefore, the task of architects and structural engineers is to find the optimum cable sag

You can demonstrate the span, sag, and thrust of cables by draping a spanning cable (rope) with a large sag between two supports (your hands) and adding a weight to the cable. Notice the amount of thrust (outward pull by your hands) required to support the cable and weight. Now, spread your hands to increase the span, thus reducing the sag of the cable. Notice the change in the amount of thrust you must exert to support the weight. The cable

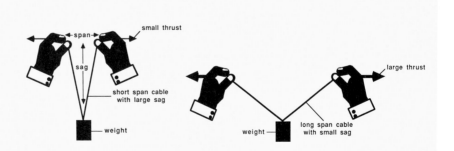

strains to support the weight, which seems heavier when there is less sag. Because of this characteristic, long spans with

small sags require fairly thick cables. On the other hand, shorter spans with larger sags can be made with thinner cables.

• •

Cable-Stayed Bridges

One of the most recent innovations in bridge construction is the **cable-stayed** bridge. Cable-stayed bridges are supported by relatively thin cables that radiate from towers to the road deck, unlike traditional suspension bridges with thicker cables draped in a gentle curve between towers. Cable-stayed bridges are less costly than suspension bridges, but normally best suited for spans of less than 1500 feet. Suspension bridges have been built with spans of over 4500 feet.

European architects and engineers developed the cable-stay design. The Pasco-Kennewick Bridge in Washington State, finished in 1978, was the first cable-stayed bridge built in the United States.

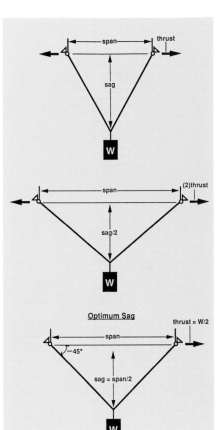

(the sag that uses the least volume of cable material). Small sags require thicker cables than the longer-cabled large sags. In either case, the total volume of cable required is approximately the same. When the span is constant, the mathematical description of the sag-thrust relationship is:

As the sag is reduced by half, the thrust will increase by a factor of 2. Conversely, as the sag doubles, thrust is halved.

Suspension bridge cables support a series of weights (road deck) along their span, rather that one centrally located weight. In these situations, the optimal cable sag is approximately one third the span.

Another important characteristic is the means of anchoring suspended cables. In the experiment on the previous page, your hands were the anchors. In a suspension bridge, huge concrete anchors are built to provide the needed thrust. Inside the anchors, the woven cables are divided into separate strands to distribute the thrust.

The African Tropical Forest Pavilion: A "Non-Building"

Visit a tropical forest in the middle of a New England winter? You can at the African Tropical Forest Pavilion at the Franklin Park Zoo, in Boston, MA, thanks to an amazing pneumatic structure.

Basically the Pavilion is a giant tent with a circular base. The African Tropical Forest Pavilion really has no internal support. Three flexible steel girders or "bents" meet at the top similar to the way poles of a tent bend to connect. The fabric roof is made of teflon coated glass yarn. Steel cables extending from the base to the bents support this fabric roof.

The fabric is on the outside of the structure. Inside of the pavilion, air pressure is kept lower than outside. This slightly lower pressure forces the roof to hug the steel cables.

Furthermore, because the roof is made of a translucent material, light easily enters. The fabric roof with light entering, looks similar to the way the sky over the tropical rainforest looks. Architects and designers worked hard to establish a naturalist appearance to the zoo.

In fact, hand crafted rocks are placed in strategic locations so that viewers do not see other visitors in the distance. Animals and their prey are placed next to each other separated only by glass barriers and moats.

Membranes

Membranes are thin, flexible materials used to enclose or cover an area. They are one of the oldest structural elements. The tent, the most common example of the membrane, was used as early as 8000 BC by nomadic cultures.

Today, membranes are becoming popular as a roofing material. In the United States membranes are used to roof large sports stadiums, including the largest, the Louisiana Superdome, which is capable of seating over 95,000 fans. The largest membrane roof in the world, over the Haj Terminal at the Jeddah International Airport in Saudia Arabia, covers an area the size of 80 football fields.

Types of Membrane Support ■ Membranes, being nonrigid elements, must be supported in order to create a structural form. Two methods are used to support membranes: stretching and pneumatic pressure.

Membrane can be stretched between other structural elements, such as columns, beams, arches, domes, and cables. The basic tent uses the most common form of stretching, a combination of columns and cables.

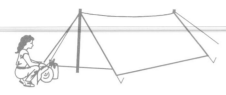

The distinctive saddle shape of a stretched membrane can be clearly seen in the tent *(above)* and the Saddledome sports arena in Calgary, Alberta, Canada *(below)* . (Courtesy of Alberta Travel)

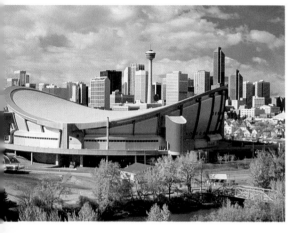

Notice the curvature at the top of the tent shown at left. This curve, which is typical of a stretched membrane, is called a saddle. The basic saddle shape is reproduced in the Saddledome, built for the 1988 Olympic Winter Games in Calgary, Alberta, Canada. The saddle-shaped membrane roof is stretched between two arches inclined in opposite directions. The saddle shape may be produced in a membrane in many other ways, including stretching over crossed arches, suspending from A-framed trusses, draping over columns, or stretching over or hanging inside a geodesic dome.

Pneumatic Structures ■ Using pneumatic (air) pressure to support membranes creates an interesting type of structure called a **pneumatic structure.** There are two types of pneumatic structure: air-inflated and air-supported. Air-inflated structures are supported by pressurizing the air contained within enclosed membrane layers. Air-supported structures consist of a single membrane layer anchored in place and supported by a small internal pressure.

The figures below show both types of pneumatic structure in the form of an arch. Air-supported structures are usually a variation of the arch when viewed in cross-section, but air-inflated membranes can be shaped into columns, beams, arches, trusses, or even building components, such as walls and roofs. One interesting variation of the air-inflated structure is the ribbed structure which consist of a series of arch-shaped inflated tubes (like long balloons) fastened together to create a vault. The tubes, which are anchored to the ground, form the walls and roof for a structure. The Fuji Pavilion at Expo 70 in Osaka, Japan was constructed in this manner. The 75-foot-high structure consisted of sixteen tubes, each twelve feet in diameter.

Pneumatic structures are lightweight and can be used to span large distances and areas without internal supports. This makes them ideal for sports stadiums, such as football and baseball fields. The roof of the Superdome is pneumatically supported. Other stadiums with pneumatic roofs include the Pontiac Silverdome in Michigan and the Hubert H. Humphrey Metrodome in Minnesota.

Membrane Materials ■ For thousands of years, membranes were made of natural materials, such as animal skins and cotton yarns woven into

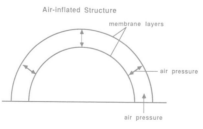

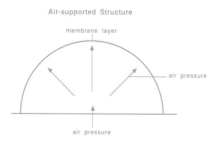

Methods of supporting membranes include a rigid superstructure, such as the a-frame truss system or steel arch frame, and the pneumatic structure, which can be air-inflated or air-supported.

This air-inflated membrane structure is being used to protect a building site from inclement weather. The small photo at right shows the exterior of the membrane structure. Notice how large it is compared to the neighboring house.

The tent, a membrane structure used 10,000 years ago, is still popular today. (Courtesy Cabella, Inc.)

Teflon-coated fiberglass provides a strong material for membrane roofs.

canvas. However, they burned easily and deteriorated quickly. Today, synthetic materials, primarily nylon, polyester, and fiberglass, are used for membranes.

Small, lightweight, temporary structures, such as camping tents, are usually made from nylon and polyester plastics. Larger, more permanent structures, such as sports stadiums, use fiberglass as a membrane material. The fiberglass is coated with Teflon, vinyl, or silicon, with Teflon being the most popular coating. Teflon-coated fiberglass, which is airtight, waterproof, noncombustible, and unaffected by chemicals and pollutants, can be made stronger, yet more flexible, than steel. The material has the added advantages of rejecting dirt, resisting abrasions, and reflecting heat from sunlight while being translucent enough to provide natural lighting.

Membrane Characteristics ■ To achieve maximum strength, membranes must be stretched and curved into the saddle shape. Of course, the overall strength of a membrane structure depends upon a number of factors, including the strength of the cables, anchors, and supports, and the technique used to assemble the membranes.

Many people do not trust what appears to be a weak, flimsy material. Doubts about the strength of membranes relate to collapse from cutting, winds, snow, and escaping air, and to the reliability of the internal air pressure under air-supported roofs.

However, these doubts are unfounded. The fiberglass fabric used on large structures cannot be cut with a knife or even a hatchet. In fact, electric saws with carborundum disks are required to cut the materials. Strong winds and heavy snow have caused tears in membrane fabrics, but the roofs did not collapse. In fact, repairing a torn membrane roof is relatively easy. Often, the membrane panels are zippered together. When a tornado blew out panels in the roof of the Pontiac Silverdome, the torn ones were zippered out and new ones were zippered in.

Many people think air-supported roofs will collapse when the doors are opened. Usually, double doors are installed to create air locks that reduce air escape. Also, since the internal air pressure used is slight, if the doors were left opened, the air would escape very slowly. In fact, it would take a hole several hundred square feet to cause the pneumatic roof over a sports stadium to deflate quickly. Even if that were to happen, most large membrane roofs are designed with cables that suspend from the walls to prevent the roof from falling on people in the event of a major air release.

Doubts also surround the internal air pressure inside an air-supported structure. Many people assume that the internal air pressure is so high it would be uncomfortable to be inside these structures. In reality, the air pressure required to support the membrane roof only needs to be slightly higher than the surrounding air pressure. This slight pressure increase, which is about the same as going from the top floors of a skyscraper to the ground, is not even noticeable. Internal pressures of less than 5 pounds per square foot are common in most large air-supported structures.

Most strucures are systems created by combining several basic structural elements. The architect, engineer, and builder must be aware of the various structural elements, the materials they are made of, and their basic characteristics, in order to design and construct safe structures.

Structural elements may be categorized as rigid and nonrigid elements. Rigid elements must remain relatively stiff in a structure, while nonrigid elements are usually fairly flexible. There are a number of variations for each rigid and nonrigid element and most elements can be created from a variety of materials, including wood, masonry, concrete, steel, and plastics.

Each structural element has special characteristics and structural functions that determine which materials should be used, how the element will be designed, and where the element may be applied.

Study Questions

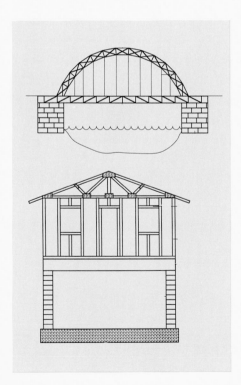

1. What are the two purposes of structural elements in constructing structures?

2. What are the two types of structural elements? How are they different?

3. Why is it important to study structural elements, the materials they are made from, and their basic characteristics?

4. What is the difference between a structural element and a structural system?

5. Make a list of the structural elements and identify common materials used for each. Describe why you think certain materials are or are not used for particular elements. Also, describe the basic characteristics for each element.

6. How many structural elements can you identify in the two drawings at left?

Suggested Activities

1. Look at structures in your community and identify the structural elements and structural systems used to construct them.
2. Perform the experiments described in this chapter for each element to verify their basic characteristics.
3. Build models of the structural elements using available materials, or build models of interesting structures that exemplify certain elements, such as the Golden Gate or Brooklyn bridges.

Glossary

Arch   Curved rigid structural element that spans an open space and provides height in a structure.

Beam   Linear, horizontal, rigid structural elements used to span a gap between two supports; also called girder, joist, rafter, header, and lintel.

Bearing walls   Vertical rigid structural elements composed of a stack of blocks, such as concrete block walls.

Cables   Long, slender, rope-like nonrigid structural elements used as hangers, guys, or for spanning; most commonly used in suspension bridges.

Cable-stayed   A type of bridge in which the deck is supported by relatively thin cables that radiate from towers.

Column   Linear, vertical, rigid structural elements used to support beams and other elements; also called pier, pile, and pillar.

Dome   Rigid structural element created by revolving a series of arches about a common crown or center point.

Frame   A three-dimensional network of assembled components used to create a skeleton of a structure.

Geodesic dome   Rigid structural element with a spherical form, similar to arch domes, but composed of lightweight, linear struts connected in the form of triangles over the entire surface area of the sphere.

Gusset   A plywood or metal plate nailed or glued over the joints of the truss.

Icosahedron   The simplest geodesic dome; a single frequency dome with all its struts the same length.

Lift-slab   Method of constructing shorter skyscrapers in which all the reinforced concrete floor slabs are cast on the ground and lifted and secured on columns.

Mass structures   Structures composed of large quantities of material, such as concrete, earth, or rock, also called solid structures.

Membranes   Thin, flexible materials used to enclose or cover an area.

Plates   Thin, rigid structural elements used to span areas between beams, columns, and other elements: also called slabs.

Pneumatic structures   Structures in which membranes are supported by pressurized air.

Post and lintel   Structural system that is a combination of column (post) and beam (lintel) elements.

Slabs   Thin, rigid structural elements used to span areas between beams, columns, and other elements; also called plates.

Space frame system   A three-dimensional truss beam extended to cover a large area; one of the most economical flat roofing methods.

Structural element   A basic component, feature, or basic part of a structure; two types are rigid (beam, column, arch, etc.) and nonrigid (membranes and cables).

Thrust   The outward push at the bottom of an arch and the force required to anchor a spanning cable.

Truss   Rigid structural element; an arrangement of linear members connected together to form a series of triangles lying in a straight plane.

Truss frame system   Building system that incorporates a roof truss, stud walls, and floor truss into one unit.

Trussing   The diagonal bracing component used in trusses.

Vault   Rigid structural element created by placing arches in a series to form a long, uninterrupted internal span.

Voussoirs   Wedge-shaped masonry blocks used to build an arch.

Chapter 5

Loads on Structures

Chapter Objectives

- In order to resist loads, structures must possess stability (equilibrium), strength, and rigidity.

- Loads on structures come from three main sources: weight of the structure, occupants or users, and natural elements.

- Loads are classified as static (motionless) or dynamic (moving) and dead (structure weight) or live (all loads except structure weight).

- Building codes, which are regulations established to guide the design of structures, have built-in safety factors.

- Structures must be designed to resist loads from water, wind, earthquakes, thermal conditions, foundation settlement, and snow.

- Designers must make tradeoffs between structural efficiency and the security of the structure's occupants.

Key Terms

base isolation	live load
building codes	load
concentrated load	moment
dead load	occupant load
design live load	resonant load
downwash	rotational equilibrium
dynamic load	safety factor
efficiency rating	static load
equilibrium	tuned dynamic damper
factor of safety	uniform equilibrium
impact load	venturi effect
linear equilibrium	wind drift

Winds loads on the Tacoma Narrows bridge caused its total collapse. Understanding the loads on structures is important both in design and construction.

load —
occupant —
structure

A person sitting in a chair being pushed by another person illustrates the basic reactions of a structure to loads.

Loads on Structures

People construct structures for a purpose, such as shelter or support. In order for a structure to fulfill that purpose, it must first meet the requirement of resisting loads. A **load** is any effect that creates a need for a resistive force to prevent collapse or failure of a structure. Loads come from three main sources: structure weight, (weight of the materials in the structure), occupants or users (people or traffic), and natural elements (wind, rain, earthquake). Structures must resist these loads and transmit them safely to the ground.

To envision the basic reactions of a structure to loads, think of a person sitting on a chair. The chair (structure) supports its own weight and the weight of a seated person (occupant) by transmitting these loads safely to the floor. Natural element loads (a gust of wind) can be simulated by a second person pushing the chair from the side or back. The chair structure must also resist this load.

Structures obey basic principles of physical science related to gravity, the transmission of loads, and motion. In physics the "law of least work" says structures transmit loads to the ground by the path of least work or least resistance. If a weakness exists in a structure, the load will find this path of least work and may cause total collapse of the structure.

Structures must not fail. People trust structural engineers to design safe structures. This chapter will help you understand the effect of various loads on structures.

Structures transmit loads to the ground by the path of least resistance.

■ Stability, Strength, and Rigidity

To resist loads, a structure must possess three characteristics: stability, strength, and rigidity. We can see examples of these characteristics by looking at the structure of the human body. A football player must resist loads from opposing players. To improve his stability, he will assume a low center of gravity stance with his body weight spread out over three points. He gets rigidity from his bones, which provide the main structural support for the human body. Strength may be the most important. A football player may be rigid and stable, but if he is weak, he can still be knocked over by the loads from a stronger opposing player.

bones (rigidity)

3 point stance (stability)

Like good athletes, structures must have rigidity, stability and strength.

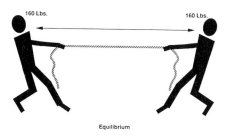

160 Lbs.   160 Lbs.

Equilibrium

If two people pull with equal weight in a tug of war, equilibrium results and neither moves. What would happen if one let go?

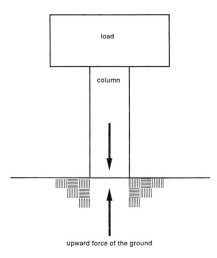

load

column

upward force of the ground

The column and load are in vertical linear equilibrium with the ground.

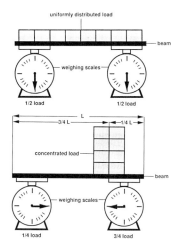

uniformly distributed load

beam

weighing scales

1/2 load   1/2 load

L

3/4 L   1/4 L

concentrated load

beam

weighing scales

1/4 load   3/4 load

Uniformly distributed and concentrated loads. The resistance force in each support is proportional to the distribution of the load along the beam.

■ Stability

Stability, a measure of the integrity of the entire structure in resisting loads, depends on the size and shape of the structural elements. Remember that deep, wide beams and short, squat columns are stable, while deep, narrow beams and tall, slender columns tend to be unstable. Like the three-point stance of the football player, triangular elements, such as the truss, geodesic dome, and space frame, tend to create very stable structures.

Equilibrium ■ Stable structures are balanced; structural engineers call this equilibrium. **Equilibrium,** which means balance, can be demonstrated by two people of equal weight pulling against each other in a tug of war. The structure they create is in equilibrium and stable since the loads they exert balance each other. If one person lets go, equilibrium will be lost. If equilibrium is lost in a constructed structure, failure or collapse results.

There are two types of equilibrium:

Linear Equilibrium The two people pulling in opposite directions demonstrate horizontal **linear equilibrium.** The orientation of their forces is in a horizontal plane, but most structures must resist vertical forces due to gravity. A column supporting a load demonstrates vertical linear equilibrium. The combined weight of the load and the column pushes down on the ground. The ground develops a resistance force upward to prevent the column from sinking. When the resistance force of the ground is equal to the combined weights of the column and load, they are in vertical linear equilibrium.

Vertical structural elements must also adapt to varying loading conditions. Consider a simple beam with a **uniform load,** one spread evenly over the span of the beam. If the beam has two supports, each will develop a resistance force equal to one half the combined weight of the beam and the load. If the load is shifted to create a **concentrated load,** the resistance force in each support will be in proportion to the distribution of the load along the beam. The closer the load is to one support, the more resistance force that support must develop. Vertical equilibrium will be maintained, provided the material in each support has sufficient rigidity and strength.

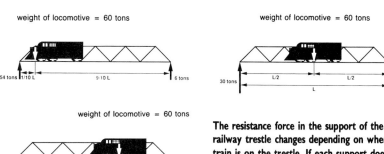

weight of locomotive = 60 tons

54 tons 1/10 L   9·10 L   6 tons

weight of locomotive = 60 tons

30 tons   L/2   L/2   30 tons
L

weight of locomotive = 60 tons

20 tons   2/3 L   1/3 L   40 tons

The resistance force in the support of the railway trestle changes depending on where the train is on the trestle. If each support does not have the strength to hold the concentrated load, vertical equilibrium would be lost and the trestle would collapse.

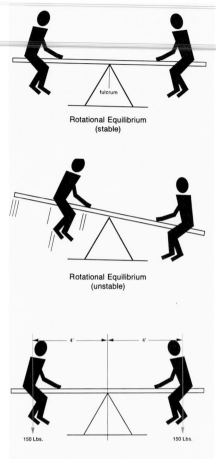

Rotational Equilibrium
(stable)

Rotational Equilibrium
(unstable)

Rotational Equilibrium Formula - Wt. × Dist. = Wt. × Dist.
150 Lbs. × 4' = 150 Lbs. × 4'
Moments - 600 Ft.-Lbs. = 600 Ft.-Lbs.

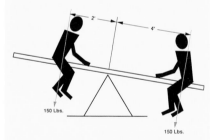

Rotational Equilibrium Formula - Wt. × Dist. = Wt. × Dist.
150 Lbs. × 2' = 150 Lbs. × 4'
Moments - 300 Ft.-Lbs. = 600 Ft.-Lbs.

See-saw rotates in direction of larger moment

The see-saw illustrates rotational equilibrium. It rotates in the direction of the larger moment. When the moments on each side of the fulcrum are equal, rotational equilibrium exists.

Rotational Equilibrium The most common example of rotational equilibrium is the seesaw. **Rotational equilibrium** (balance) is achieved by two people of equal weight on the seesaw. However, if one person is heavier or moves closer to the fulcrum (pivot point), the seesaw rotates in that direction and equilibrium is lost. The seesaw no longer balances. A simple mathematical procedure can be used to help us restore equilibrium to the seesaw. The product of the weight times the distance from the fulcrum is called **moment** or torque. When the moment on one side is equal to the moment on the other side, then rotational equilibrium results. If the moment is larger on one side, the seeasaw will rotate in that direction. As we shall see later, rotational equilibrium is important in helping skyscrapers resist wind loads.

■ Strength

Strength depends on the stress limits of materials and the connections and joints between structural elements and components. Structures are only as strong as the weakest material or joint in a critical location. For example, a chair is only as strong as the weakest material or joint in the seat, back, and legs. The law of least work is important when strength is considered.

■ Rigidity

Three factors affect rigidity: choice of structural element, materials used in elements, and connections and joints in the structure. The beam and arch are examples of rigid structural elements; cables and membranes are nonrigid (flexible) structural elements. Construction techniques such as

The 1987 collapse of the L'Ambiance Plaza in Bridgeport, Connecticut, illustrates the importance of the least work law. The thirteen-story building was being constructed by the lift-slab method. Several lower floors were lifted and safely secured to the columns. Three concrete slabs for upper floors, each weighing 320 tons, were being lifted when, for unknown reasons, the stress limits of a collar in one of the slabs were exceeded. The collar twisted and failed suddenly. The three upper slabs cracked and fell, taking the floors below with them. A domino effect resulted in the collapse of the entire structure and the deaths of twenty-eight workers. This tragic accident points out the importance of the weakest element. (See diagram on opposite page.)

finishing nails - diameter too thin

correct diameter - too short

correct diameter & length

Correct nailing techniques are important to the rigidity of a structure.

stretching or suspending in particular configurations, can increase the rigidity of flexible elements. Rigid elements can be made more rigid, particularly through the use of trussing.

The elastic nature of materials is important to rigidity. The more elastic a material, the less rigid. Aluminum is three times as elastic as steel, and is thus considerably less rigid. Engineers must consider the eleastic nature of materials when designing structures for particular loads.

There are a variety of fasteners and fastening techniques used in construction, including nails, screws, bolts, welds, and adhesives. To create proper rigidity, it is important to select the correct type and size of fasteners. In addition, workers must properly install and apply fasteners. A nailed 2 × 4 wood joint will fail just as easily when the correct nail is installed improperly (driven in partially and bent over) as when the nail selected is too short or intended for another purpose (using finishing nails in 2 × 4 wall stud joints).

. . . .

Classification of Loads

Loads come from three main sources:

- structure weight
- occupants or users
- natural elements.

There are a number of different ways of classifying these loads. They are divided into two main classification systems: 1) the effect of the load on a structure (static or dynamic) and 2) the permanence of the load (dead or live). Each of these classification systems serves a different purpose for the structural designer and engineer. But remember: each system classifies loads from structure weight, occupants and users, and natural element sources.

L'Ambiance Plaza failure.

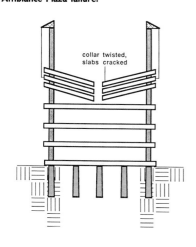

collar twisted, slabs cracked

■ Static and Dynamic Loads

Static Loads ■ Static means motionless or slowly changing. Examples of static loads on a structure are the weight of the structure, its occupants or users, and any furniture or equipment it contains.

. . . .

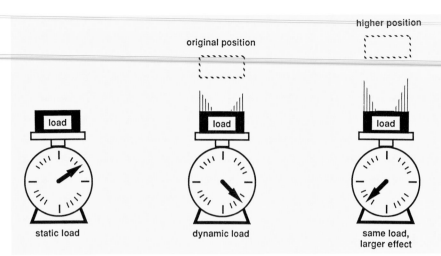

original position

load

load

load

static load

dynamic load

same load,
larger effect

**The same load applied statically and
dynamically have very different effects.**

Engineers can more easily predict the effects of static loads than those resulting from dynamic loads. Calculating the weight of a structure, predicting the weight of occupants, or estimating furniture weights is routine.

Dynamic Loads ■ Dynamic means moving or changing rapidly. Dynamic loads come from the natural elements (wind, waves, earthquake), heavy moving traffic (loaded trucks over a bridge), or accidents (a boat crashing into a bridge pier).

Predicting the effects of dynamic loads is difficult. The difference between the effects of static and dynamic loads can be demonstrated with a scale and a small object. When the object is resting on the scale (motionless load), the reading indicates the static load, which equals the weight of the object. However, when the object is dropped on the scale from a few inches (moving load), the initial reading (when the object hits) indicates a dynamic load, which is greater than the weight of the object. If the object is dropped from a higher point, the dynamic effect is even larger.

Dynamic loads can have dramatic and dangerous impacts on structures. Imagine the effect of a brick resting on your foot (static load) versus the same brick being dropped on your foot (dynamic load). The structure in your foot could probably withstand the stress of the static load with no problems, but the dynamic load could cause failure of the structure. (A broken foot!)

There are two types of dynamic loads: impact and resonant.

Impact loads, like the object dropped on the scale and the brick falling on your foot, hit a structure quickly with a magnified force. Heavy gusts of wind or a truck crashing into a building are examples of impact loads. They hit quickly and with a force that is magnified by their dynamic movement.

Resonant loads hit a structure with a small force that continues over a longer time period. Steadily blowing winds and traffic moving continually over a bridge are examples of resonant loads. At first, resonant loads may seem to be relatively harmless to structures, but they can have dramatic effects over time. Some of the most dangerous and powerful forces on structures are resonant loads. Let's look more closely at them.

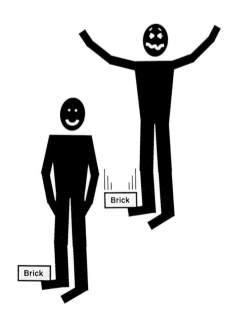

Brick

Brick

Tacoma Narrows Bridge Collapse

The most dangerous situation for a structure is when the wind blows in rhythm with oscillations (or vibrations) from wind drift. The wind begins to blow in resonance with the oscillations, which creates magnified loads.

You can demonstrate these oscillations by holding a thin strip of paper loosely between your hands and blowing on an edge. The paper will vibrate up and down. The wind alternates blowing over the top and then under the bottom of the paper which bends both ways trying to resist.

The most dramatic example of this was the collapse of the Tacoma Narrows Bridge in Washington. The suspension bridge, which was 2800 feet long and unusually flexible, had been called "Galloping Gertie" because of its continued wave-like motion. In 1940, it was demolished by the aerodynamic forces of a steady 42 mile-per-hour wind.

In the Tacoma Narrows Bridge, the wind blew like this over a period of several hours, causing the bridge deck to begin oscillating wildly up and down. The wind stayed constant, but the oscillations got larger, until the elastic properties of the materials (steel and concrete) were exceeded and the entire bridge fell. Today, scale models for most long bridges and tall skyscrapers are subjected to wind tunnel testing before the structure is built.

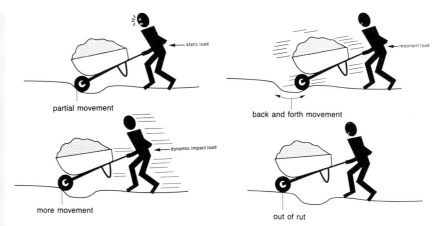

partial movement — static load

back and forth movement — resonant load

more movement — dynamic impact load

out of rut

Another example will help us understand the dramatic effects resonant loads can have. Imagine you have just finished loading a large wheelbarrow with dirt and now you want to haul it away. As you begin to push the wheelbarrow, you realize that the wheel is in a small rut in the soil. With a hard, steady push (a static load), you are only able to move the wheelbarrow part way up the side of the rut. The wheelbarrow drifts back. You try a quick, hard push (a dynamic impact load). The wheel moves further up the side of the rut, but drifts back unsuccessfully. Then you push the wheelbarrow as far forward as you can and let it drift back into the rut, but this time, when it reaches the end of its drift, you apply another force to the wheelbarrow. It moves further up the side of the rut and you seem to be making progress. You continue to push in rhythm with the back and forth movements of the wheelbarrow, each time moving further up the side of the rut. The forces you are applying seem to increase in strength and finally you are able to move out of the rut.

What you just experienced was the power of resonant loads. The successive loads (force) you applied were in resonance, that is in rhythm, with the oscillations (back and forth movements) of the wheelbarrow. By applying a resonant load, you were able to combine your load with the load of the moving wheelbarrow. The combined loads moved the heavy wheelbarrow out of the rut.

Resonant loads applied to structures can have the same dramatic effects. There is a story about a battalion of soldiers marching across a small bridge. The soldiers were well trained; every man was in step. Unfortunately, their precise marching created loads that were in resonance with the bridge, which collapsed without warning! The most important consideration of resonant loads concerns wind loads on skyscrapers. This will be examined later.

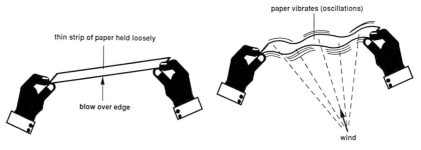

thin strip of paper held loosely

blow over edge

paper vibrates (oscillations)

wind

Material	Density (Lbs./Ft.^{3})
Wood, pine	27
Wood, oak	45
Concrete	145
Concrete, steel reinforced	150
Aluminum	170
Steel	500

Density of various construction materials.

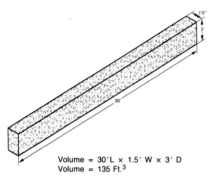

Volume = 30'L × 1.5' W × 3' D
Volume = 135 Ft.^{3}

Dead Load = Volume × Density
Dead Load = 135 Ft.^{3} × 150 Lbs./Ft.^{3}
Dead Load = 20,250 Lbs. or 10.125 Tons

Calculating the dead load of a reinforced concrete bridge beam.

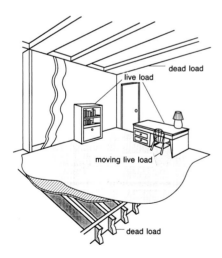

Dead loads are a permanent part of the structure. Live loads can be moved or changed over time.

Dead and Live Loads

The second classification system is based on the permanence of the load on a structure. Dead loads are a permanent part of the structure, while live loads change over time. As with static and dynamic loads, the sources of loads are still structure weight, occupants and users, and natural elements.

Dead Loads ■ Dead loads come from the weight of structural elements and components, such as the roof, walls, floors, and foundation. They are the weight of the structure itself. Normally, dead loads are the largest of any loads on a structure.

The size of individual structural elements and the materials used determine the dead load. Different materials have different densities. Density is a measure of the weight of a specified amount of a material, usually a cubic foot (ft^3). The densities of several common construction materials are listed here in pounds per square foot (psf). Because of the variations possible in the actual make-up of a material (concrete mixtures, steel alloys, presence of knots in wood, etc.) these densities are averages for comparison only.

Engineers calculate the dead load for an element by multiplying its volume by its density. For example, a reinforced concrete bridge beam measuring 30'L × 1.5'W × 3'D would have a volume of 135 ft^3. The approximate density of reinforced concrete is 150 lbs/ft^3 (pounds per cubic foot). Multiplying the volume by the density, the dead load of the beam would be 20,250 pounds or 10.125 tons. To determine the total dead load for the entire bridge, the engineer would add together the weights of each element and component in the bridge.

To calculate dead loads for conventional wood frame structures, special tables can be used. These simplify the job of calculating dead loads by giving the weights of various structural components in psf.

Dead load calculation is important to the total cost of a structure, since it includes all the materials used in construction. If material and labor costs were added to dead load calculations, the total cost of the structure could be computed.

Live Loads ■ Live loads are technically anything not permanently attached to the structure. Live loads, which can be moved or changed over time, come from two sources: People, furniture, machines, and traffic are considered live **occupant loads;** snow, winds, earthquakes, and water are examples of live loads from **natural elements.**

You may find it hard to think of machines and furniture as live loads, since they are not "alive." But remember, live loads can be changed over time. Since furniture and machines can be moved or replaced, they are considered live loads.

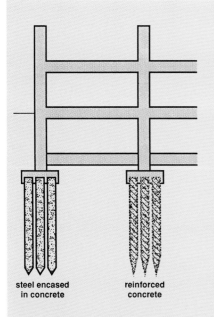

steel encased   reinforced
in concrete   concrete

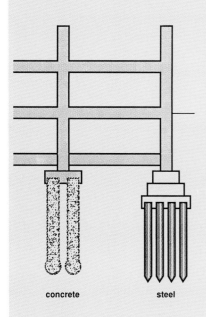

concrete   steel

The tremendous dead loads of a skyscraper require steel or concrete pile foundations.

Calculating Dead Loads for a Small Skyscraper One of the most important considerations is the ability of the foundation to support the dead load without excessive settling (sinking). Large structures can exert tremendous dead loads on their foundations. If you were a structural engineer it would be your job to calculate dead loads. Here is a simplified example of those calculations for a small skyscraper:

PROBLEM:

A skyscraper 100 stories high has 12" thick reinforced concrete floors measuring 30' square. The design calls for 36 foundation columns. What is the dead load exerted on each foundation column?

SOLUTION:

First, find the volume of the floors:

FLOOR VOLUME = 30' × 30' × 1'
FLOOR VOLUME = 900 ft^3

Next, multiply the floor volume by the density of reinforced concrete to get the dead load of each floor:

FLOOR DEAD LOAD = 900 ft^3 × 150 lbs/ft^3
FLOOR DEAD LOAD = 135,000 lbs/floor

To convert this figure to tons divide by 2000 lbs/ton:

FLOOR DEAD LOAD = 135,000 lbs/floor / 2000 lbs/ton
FLOOR DEAD LOAD = 67.5 tons

Next, multiply the dead load for one floor by the number of stories to get the total dead load:

TOTAL DEAD LOAD = 67.5 tons × 100 stories
TOTAL DEAD LOAD = 6750 tons

Divide the total dead load by the number of foundation columns to find the load on each column:

LOAD PER COLUMN = 6750 tons / 36 foundation columns
LOAD PER COLUMN = 187.5 tons

Even good, solid soil can support only about four tons/ft^2. This is why most skyscrapers have concrete or steel pile foundations sunk through the soil into solid bedrock, which has a much larger load-bearing capacity than soil.

Of course, this example is simplified. We did not take into consideration the dead load for external and internal walls, the roof, and other dead load items. Still, it illustrates the importance of accurately calculating dead loads.

Weights of Building Components and Materials

Component/Material	psf	Component/Material	psf
ROOFS		**FLOORS**	
3 - ply roll roofing	1	Hardwood, 1/2"	2.5
3 - ply felt and gravel	5.5	Vinyl tile, 1/8"	1.5
5 - ply felt and gravel	6.5	Asphalt mastic	12/inch
Shingles -		Ceramic tile, 3/4"	10
Wood	2	Fiberboard underlay, 5/8"	3
Asphalt	2 -3	Carpet and pad (average)	3
Clay tile	9 - 12	Timber deck	2.5/inch
Concrete tile	8 - 12	Concrete deck	12.5/inch
Slate, 1/4"	10	Wood joists -	
Fiberglass	2 - 3	2 x 8 @ 16"	2.1
Aluminum	1	2 x 10 @ 16"	2.6
Steel	2	2 x 12 @ 16"	3.2
Insulation -			
Fiberglass batts	0.5	**WALLS**	
Rigid foam	1.5	2 x 4 studs @ 16"	2
Wood rafters -		Steel studs @ 16"	4
2 x 6 @ 24"	1	Lath, plaster	see Ceilings
2 x 8 @ 24"	1.4	Gypsum drywall, 5/8"	2.5
2 x 10 @ 24"	1.7	Stucco, 7/8" on wire	10
2 x 12 @ 24	2.1	Windows, glazing and frame -	
Skylight -		Small pane, single glazing,	
Glass, steel frame	6 - 10	wood or metal frame	5
Plastic, aluminum frame	3 - 6	Large pane, single glazing,	
Plywood sheathing	3/inch	wood or metal frame	8
		For double glazing add ->	2 - 3
CEILINGS		Brick veneer -	
Suspended steel channel	1	4", mortar joints	40
Lath -		1/2", mastic	10
Steel mesh	0.5	Concrete block -	
Gypsum board, 1/2"	2	Lightweight, unreinforced, 4"	20
Fiber tile	1	Lightweight, unreinforced, 6"	25
Drywall, 1/2"	2.5	Lightweight, unreinforced, 8"	30
Plaster -		Heavy, reinforced, grouted - 6"	45
Gypsum, acoustic	5	Heavy, reinforced, grouted - 8"	60
Cement	8.5	Heavy, reinforced, grouted - 12"	85
Suspended lighting (average)	3		

NOTE: Weights for variable thickness materials, such as plywood, are given for an assumed 1" thickness (/inch in table).

Calculating Live Loads. Calculating live loads is a simple matter of adding together the weights of all the loads that are not a permanent part of a structure. The example below shows how live loads would be calculated for a construction technology classroom.

		LBS.
30	students x 160 Lbs. (average each)	4800
30	desk chairs x 40 Lbs. each	1200
1	teacher	185
1	teacher's desk and chair	125
2	cabinets x 225 Lbs. each	450
1	bookcase and books	285
1	overhead projector	25
1	VCR, monitor and stand	100
3	computer stations	330

Total Live Load =   7500 Lbs.

Floor Size   =   20' x 30'

Floor Size   =   600 Ft.^{2}

$$\text{Uniformly Distributed Load} = \frac{7500 \text{ Lbs.}}{600 \text{ Ft.}^2}$$

$$= 12.5 \text{ psf}$$

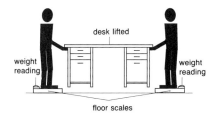

To determine the weight of the desk, add the readings on each scale and subtract the students' weights.

Determining the weights of most items is fairly easy. The weight of the teacher and students was determined with floor scales. Two scales could be used to find the weight of desks.

(SAFETY NOTE: Using this technique to weigh larger objects, like cabinets, can be dangerous for the people involved (and the cabinet too) and should not be tried. Instead, estimate weights or obtain weight information from furniture catalogs.)

Live loads are often assumed to be uniformly distributed over a floor. If the classroom above measured $20' \times 30'$ (600 ft^2), the uniformly distributed load would be 12.5 psf (7500 lbs/600 ft^2 = 12.5 psf).

The expected live loads are important to the total dead load of a structure. Usually, the larger the live load, the larger the dead load required. Designing structures for live and dead loads may seem like a difficult problem, but it has been simplified by the use of building codes.

Building Codes

Building codes are laws or ordinances that specify minimum standards for structural support. Codes are designed for the protection of the occupants and users of structures. There are no nationally accepted building codes, but there are a number of unofficial model building codes written by construction organizations. Often, states, counties, and cities adopt and/or modify these model codes.

Two examples of model building codes are the *Uniform Building Code* published by the International Conference of Building Officials in Whittier, California and *The Basic Building Code* published by the Building Officials and Code Administrators International in Chicago, Illinois.

There are also codes written by organizations that specialize in one aspect of construction. The following is a partial list of organizations that publish specialized codes:

American Concrete Institute
American Institute of Steel Construction
American Iron & Steel Institute
Aluminum Association
National Fire Protection Association
American Institute of Lumber Construction
American Plywood Association

There are also a number of regional lumber associations across the United States that publish building codes.

■ Building Codes, Design Loads, and Safety Factors

The live loads specified in building codes are called **design live loads.** This means the structure must be designed for the live loads specified. The table at the left lists typical uniformly distributed design live loads in psf for floors. Live loads vary for different applications. Notice the 40 psf live load specified for school classrooms and the 125 psf load for libraries. In each case, the floor must be designed to support the load specified.

Under normal situations, a classroom floor will never be loaded to 40 psf. The design loads specified in codes are always much larger than the normal expected loads; they have a built in safety factor. A **safety factor** or **factor of safety** means the structure is designed to support a load much larger than would normally be expected.

Live Loads for Floors

Application	psf
Armories	150
Assembly areas[1], auditoriums-	
Fixed seating areas	50
Movable seating areas	100
Stage areas	125
Balconies, residential use	60
Exit facilites[2]	100
Garages -	
General storage and repair	100
Private vehicle storage	50
Hospitals	40
Libraries -	
Reading rooms	60
Stack rooms	125
Manufacturing -	
Light	75
Heavy	125
Offices	50
Printing plants	150
Residences[3]	40
Reviewing stands, bleachers	120
Schools	40
Sidewalks, driveways	250
Storage -	
Light	125
Heavy	250
Stores -	
Retail	75
Wholesale	100

[1] Includes dance halls, playgrounds, gymnasiums
[2] Includes hallways, stairways, fire escapes
[3] Includes homes, apartments, hotels

Consider the live loads of 12.5 psf calculated above for the classroom. The classroom would seem to be quite crowded with thirty desks, thirty students, and the other contents. But to reach the 40 psf code load for classrooms, there would have to be three times the present contents in the room. The design live load specified in the code is much larger than the normal loads the engineers expected for the classroom. In this particular case, it is over three times as much.

Determining the actual factor of safety built into a code is difficult. Many variables are considered when the codes are developed, including the ultimate stress of materials, the uniformity of materials, and whether the expected loads will have static or dynamic effects. The primary consideration is the ultimate stress of materials. The factor of safety can be defined as the ultimate stress divided by an allowable or acceptable stress (a stress that will not cause the material to fail or deform).

$$\text{Factor of Safety} = \frac{\text{Ultimate Stress}}{\text{Allowable Stress}}$$

On average, a safety factor of two is typical for most building codes. That means the code load is only half the size of the load that would cause failure or deformation of the materials used. Obviously, the classroom example calculated above with a live load of 12.5 is quite safe, being less than one third the code design load of 40 psf.

Although two may be typical, safety factors of four and five are not uncommon in some structures, especially when dynamic loads with unpredictable effects are expected. The saying "better safe than sorry" applies to safety factors. The ancient Egyptians definitely used this principle in their construction. Their pyramids were built with a safety factor of at least 24!

Building codes and safety factors are continually reviewed and revised based on innovations in construction materials, techniques, and our understanding of loads and their effects on structures.

· ·

Live Loads from Natural Elements

Nature creates many of the most powerful live loads on structures. Engineers must consider the impacts of water, wind, earthquakes, and other natural elements on the design and construction of structures.

■ Water Loads

There are two types of water loads: standing water (as in a reservoir) and moving water. The water in a reservoir can exert a tremendous static load on a dam. In fact, the deeper the reservoir is, the larger the load. Static water loads are measured as pressure. The pressure water exerts on the

· ·

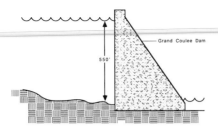

Water Pressure = Water Depth × Water Density
Water Pressure = 550′ × 62.4 Lbs./foot³
Water Pressure = 34,320 psf

Calculasting the water pressure exerted on the face of the Grand Coulee dam.

face of a dam can be calculated by multiplying the depth by the density of water, which is 62.4 lbs/ft³. The Grand Coulee Dam, the largest concrete gravity dam in the world, is 550′ high. If the reservoir were completely filled to the top of the dam, the water would exert a pressure of 34,320 psf. The dam resists this pressure with its tremendous weight of over 21.26 million tons of concrete. The water creates a static load on the dam and engineers can easily predict its effects. Factors of safety built into the design insure that the dam will not collapse, be overturned or pushed off its foundation by the reservoir.

Moving water on the other hand, creates unpredictable effects because of its dynamic nature. Ocean waves and rivers are examples of moving water. Waves hitting an offshore oil rig can cause tremendous loads that can not be accurately calculated. Oil-drilling platforms anchored to the sea floor must be designed for many unusual situations, including impacts loads from 100′ high waves, static and dynamic loads from sea ice and moving icebergs, and resonant loads from millions of rhythmic, repeating waves.

The turbulence created by water flowing around the piers of bridges and flooding houses are two more examples of the dynamic loads possible from moving water. Flooding water can lift a house right off its foundation and turn it into an unwilling boat. Whole towns can be washed away in large floods.

Offshore oil drilling platforms must resist dynamic wave loads. (Courtesy of Amoco)

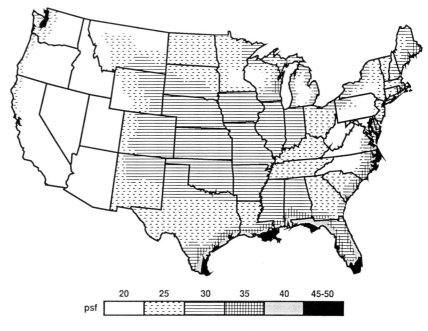

Wind Map of U.S.

■ Wind Loads

Building codes include structural specifications for resisting wind loads. The codes are based on historical wind speed studies conducted by meteorologists in various parts of the country. Every day, wind speeds are measured in various areas across the country. An average wind speed is calculated for each area based on the history of these measurements. This average wind speed is recorded on a wind map. Shown above is a wind map for the United States. The speeds shown are for measurements taken at about 30 feet above ground level. Wind maps are continually updated.

Strong winds are rated on the statistical possibility of their occurring over a given time period: commonly 30, 50, or 100 years. Historical records are used to determine the strongest wind that might be expected in one of these time frames. These strongest expected winds are called 30-year winds, 50-year winds, or 100-year winds.

Structures are commonly designed for a 50-year wind. A 50-year wind design would protect the structure and its occupants in a 50-year wind, but allows minor structural damage from a 100-year wind. Building structures for 100-year winds would be extremely costly. It would be cost prohibitive except in areas where a 100-year wind could cause the structure to collapse and lead to the death of occupants. In these areas, construction techniques are employed to brace the structure against such a wind.

Many areas are exposed to the possibility of tremendously strong winds from hurricanes or tornadoes. Building structures to withstand such extreme loads is economically impractical.

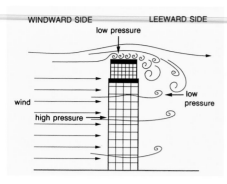

WINDWARD SIDE   LEEWARD SIDE

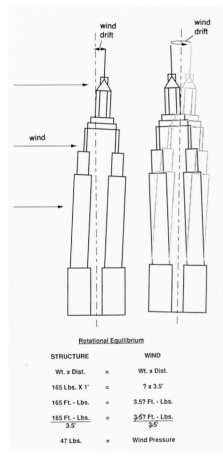

Rotational Equilibrium

STRUCTURE		WIND
Wt. x Dist.	=	Wt. x Dist.
165 Lbs. X 1'	=	? x 3.5'
165 Ft. - Lbs.	=	3.5? Ft. - Lbs.
$\frac{165 \text{ Ft. - Lbs.}}{3.5'}$	=	$\frac{3.5? \text{ Ft. - Lbs.}}{3.5'}$
47 Lbs.	=	Wind Pressure

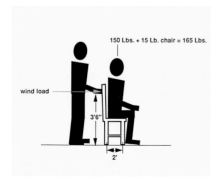

150 Lbs. + 15 Lb. chair = 165 Lbs.

wind load

Structural Reactions to Wind Loads
■ Wind loads are measured in pressure. Wind blowing around a structure creates high and low pressure zones. The windward side (facing the wind) receives the direct high pressure of wind loads and surfaces on this side can be pushed in. The leeward side (opposite the wind), and the top (roof), are exposed to swirling winds and a low pressure system. This low pressure creates suction on windows and roofing materials.

The Venturi Effect
This low and high pressure is the result of the **venturi effect.** The venturi effect (the person who discovered this effect was named Venturi) states that when a moving fluid (wind is a fluid) is restricted in its flow, its speed increases and its pressure decreases.

Airplane wings use the venturi effect. As the wing cuts through the air, the air flow is restricted and forced over the top of the wing. The air moves faster over the top of the wing and creates a low pressure, called lift, which keeps the plane aloft.

Wind Drift
Tall structures react to winds by rocking back and forth. This rocking is called **wind drift.** During wind drift, the structural elements on the windward side are placed in tension, while leeward side elements are in compression. The 1352′ tall World Trade Center has a wind drift of six feet. The six-foot movement takes almost 10 seconds. The materials in the structure are strong enough to withstand this movement, but people inside the top floors sometimes get airsick.

Wind Loads and Rotational Equilibrium
Rotational equilibrium is an important consideration when wind loads are concerned. Consider the example illustrated to the right. A 200′ tall building measuring 50′ square at the base weighs 100 tons. It is exposed to a 4 psf wind pressure. The total wind load, found by multiplying the wind pressure by the area of the windward face, equals 20 tons. Wind tries to tip over the building by rotating it around its bottom leeward corner (the fulcrum point). Wind is assumed to act as a force directed half way up the side, so the wind pressure has a lever arm of 100′. The weight of the building is assumed to act downward on the center line, so it has a lever arm of 25′. The moment of the structure must be greater than the moment of the wind if the structure is to resist overturning. Calculating for rotational equilibrium, the moment of the building is 2500 ft-tons and the wind moment is 2000 ft-tons. The building moment is larger and it is thus able to resist the wind pressure.

You can perform two experiments to demonstrate this principle. In the first, a 150 lb. student sits in a 15 lb. chair that has legs 2′ apart. The top of the chair is 3′–6″ above the floor. (Student and chair are the structure.) Another student pushes on the back of the chair simulating a wind load. The calculations show that the wind (student pushing) would have to exert 47 pounds of pressure to overturn the structure.

· ·

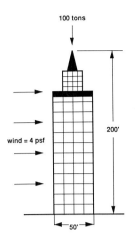

100 tons

wind = 4 psf

200'

50'

Total Wind Load	=	Wind Pressure x Windward Area
Total Wind Load	=	4 psf x 200' x 50'
Total Wind Load	=	40,000 Lbs or 20 Tons

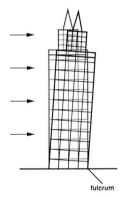

fulcrum

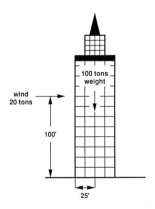

100 tons
weight

wind
20 tons

100'

25'

Rotational Equilibrium

BUILDING		WIND
Wt. x Dist.	=	Wt. x Dist.
100 Tons x 25'	=	20 Tons x 100'
2500 Ft.-Tons	>	2000 Ft.-Tons
	Building Wins!	

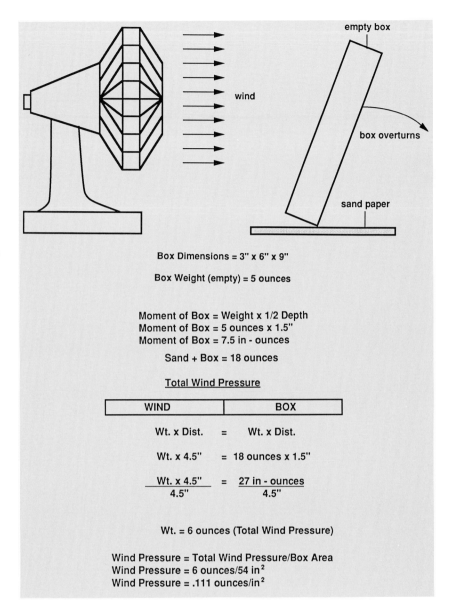

wind

empty box

box overturns

sand paper

Box Dimensions = 3" x 6" x 9"

Box Weight (empty) = 5 ounces

Moment of Box = Weight x 1/2 Depth
Moment of Box = 5 ounces x 1.5"
Moment of Box = 7.5 in - ounces

Sand + Box = 18 ounces

Total Wind Pressure

WIND	BOX
Wt. x Dist. = Wt. x Dist.	
Wt. x 4.5" = 18 ounces x 1.5"	
$\dfrac{\text{Wt. x 4.5"}}{4.5"}$ = $\dfrac{27 \text{ in - ounces}}{4.5"}$	

Wt. = 6 ounces (Total Wind Pressure)

Wind Pressure = Total Wind Pressure/Box Area
Wind Pressure = 6 ounces/54 in^2
Wind Pressure = .111 ounces/in^2

The second experiment uses an empty cereal box to simulate a skyscraper and a fan for wind loads. Wind loads from the fan will blow the empty box over. We don't know the actual wind pressure, but we do know its moment is larger than the moment of the box. The moment of the box, calculated by multiplying its weight by one-half its depth, is 7.5 inch-ounces. Add small amounts of sand to the box until it just drifts back and forth slightly from the wind. If more sand is added now, the box will resist the wind and stand upright. If a little sand is removed, the box will overturn. At this point we can closely approximate the total wind pressure exerted on the box with the rotational equilibrium equation. Dividing the total pressure by the area of the box gives us the pressure of the wind, which is a little more than one-tenth of an ounce per inch squared.

• •

Wind Design Considerations ■ Structures must have additional rigidity and weight built into their designs to resist wind loads. The stiffer and heavier a structure is, the less wind drift it will experience and less susceptible it will be to overturning. Concrete plates or x-bracing are usually installed over an inner core to stiffen skyscrapers from the inside. The designer of the John Hancock Building in Chicago placed the x-bracing on the outside of the structure for added rigidity as well as aesthetic reasons. Bridges often have x-bracing under their road deck and wood frames are reinforced with diagonal wind bracing.

Wind Engineering ■ Wind engineering is a relatively new technology and science that aims to predict, prevent, and control excessive winds on city streets. Wind engineers build scale models of skyscrapers and entire cities, which they place in wind tunnels to study the venturi effect and other air flow phenomena are illustrated below. Some of the problems associated with winds and structures.

When wind hits the side of a building it is often directed down the side to the streets. This effect, called **downwash,** can hit the street with tremendous force. In one instance, downwash knocked over a half-ton mail truck! Wind engineers have found the stepped design of old skyscrapers deflects downwash and prevents some of it from reaching the streets below, while modern straight-sided buildings direct the full pressure of the wind directly on traffic and pedestrians.

Wind flow restricted to a narrow street increases speed due to the venturi effect. Unsuspecting pedestrians can be knocked over by these winds.

The venturi effect also comes into play when wind moves under a building with an opening, such as a parking garage. The venturi effect, which speeds the wind through the garage, can be aided by the low-pressure system present on the leeward side of the building (air always moves from high to low-pressure areas). A 20 mph wind hitting the windward side of the garage can be transformed into a 60 mph wind by these combined effects.

The John Hancock Building, Chicago. The external x-bracing is both a design element and a source of added rigidity.

Structures need additional rigidity to resist wind loads.

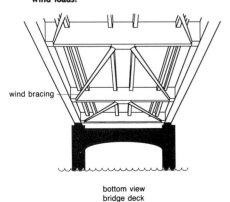

bottom view
bridge deck

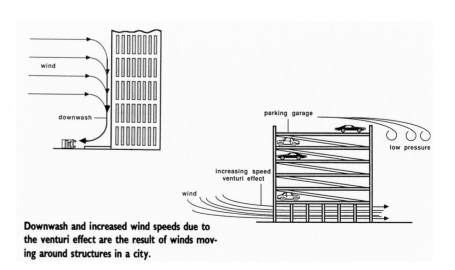

Downwash and increased wind speeds due to the venturi effect are the result of winds moving around structures in a city.

Tuned Dynamic Damper

Adding plates or x-bracing to skyscrapers is time consuming and expensive. For years, engineers have been looking for cheaper alternatives. One interesting innovation designed to help skyscrapers resist wind loads is the **tuned dynamic damper.** The 960' tall Citicorp Center in New York (8th tallest skyscraper in the world) has a mass concrete tuned dynamic damper that weighs over 400 tons and is about the size of a two-car garage. When the building starts to drift, computer-controlled sensors detect the movements and activate shock absorbers, which move the mass in tune (in rhythm) with the drift, but in the opposite direction. This damps out or absorbs the wind energy from the building, thus reducing drift. Tuned dynamic dampers have been successfully applied in other skyscrapers as well.

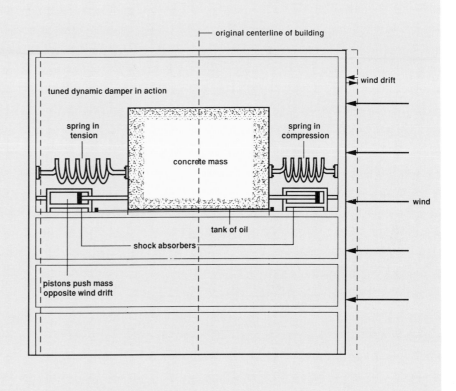

■ Earthquake Loads

Earthquakes, which are the result of the earth's crust moving and shifting, can exert a tremendous load on structures. The magnitude of energy in an earthquake is measured exponentially on the Richter scale. A Richter scale reading of 4 to 5 will probably create little damage, while an 8 reading may cause structural collapse. Strong earthquakes can cause devastating structural failures and great loss of life. The strongest earthquake in recent years (1988) killed close to 100,000 people in Soviet Armenia. The most disastrous earthquake in North American history struck Mexico City in 1985, killing 20,000 people. The San Francisco earthquake, 1989, killed 45 people.

The dynamic loads exerted on structures during an earthquake are in a horizontal direction, similar to wind loads, but the load is directed to the foundation rather than the superstructure. In an earthquake the inertia of the structural mass tends to remain stationary while the foundation moves

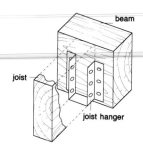

beam

joist

joist hanger

Metal straps, hangers, clips, and plates have been developed to increase joint rigidity in wood frame structures.

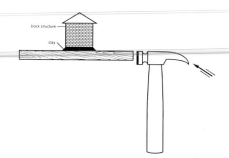

block structure

clay

Demonstrating the reactions of a structure to earthquake loads.

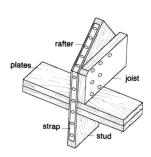

rafter

plates

joist

strap

stud

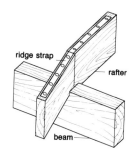

ridge strap

rafter

beam

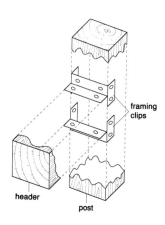

framing clips

header

post

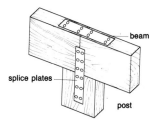

beam

splice plates

post

horizontally. You can demonstrate this principle with a model structure made of building blocks. Build the structure on a board and simulate an earthquake by hitting the board on the end with a horizontal load. The board (foundation) will move, but the structure will tend to remain stationary. Stresses build at the joints between the blocks in the model and, if you make the quake large enough, the structure will collapse.

It is not economically practical to design and construct structures to resist the greatest possible earthquake loads with no damage. Building codes specify techniques designed to protect occupants and to minimize building damage. Earthquake-resistant designs are relatively lightweight and rigid. The lighter mass will produce less resistance to movement by inertia and the rigidity will keep joints and connections from failing.

Earthquake Resistant Design Considerations ■ Four techniques are employed to help a structure resist earthquake loads. The first two, x-bracing and plates, are similar to the techniques used to resist wind loads. Of course, holes cut in plates for windows and doors will reduce rigidity.

The third technique is to improve rigid connections at joints. In an earthquake, the beams, columns, and other structural elements don't fail, the connections and joints between them do. If the joints between building blocks in the experiment above were rigid and reinforced, the structure could probably withstand the simulated earthquake. The truss frame system explained in the previous chapter was originally developed for earthquake-resistant wood frames. Another set of innovations are the metal joist hangers, straps, and plates designed to improve the rigidity and strength of joints in wood frame construction. These add a little to the cost of the structure, but serve the valuable purpose of preventing or reducing nail pull out in an earthquake.

The fourth earthquake resistance technique is called **base isolation.** With this technique, the base of a structure is isolated from the ground by a grid of bearings. The bearings, measuring 17″ high by 30″ in diameter and weighing close to a ton each, are composed of alternating layers of steel plate and thick rubber sheets. The rubber allows the bearing to stretch as much as 15″ horizontally in an earthquake and still support the structure. Base isolation is primarily used on large structures, such as skyscrapers.

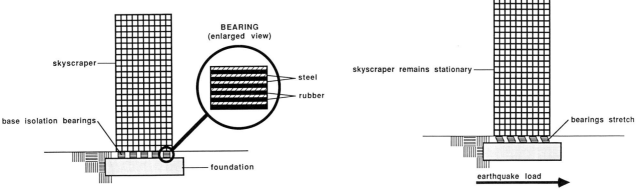

The base isolation system is being used to help skyscrapers resist earthquake loads.

The Smart Skyscraper

Engineers are always studying new ways to make structures resistant to earthquake loads. For years, they have been constructing structural models and testing them on a shake table. The base of a shake table is supported on a cushion of air. Hydraulic cylinders shove, shake, and vibrate the base to simulate earthquake loads. Scale model structures on the table register effects similar to those of full-sized structures in similar situations. This type of experimentation has lead to many innovations in earthquake-resistance design. The most recent innovation is the smart skyscraper developed by Professor Tsu Soong at the State University of New York at Buffalo.

Also called active control, the smart skyscraper would look similar to other conventional skeleton frame structures with x-bracing. However, the bracing in Soong's design would be made of stretched steel tendons (cables) attached to the corners by hydraulic pistons. During an earthquake, sensors located throughout the structure would detect movements and tighten the tendons to add increased rigidity to the frame. At the present time, the smart skyscraper is only in the model stage, but shake table tests make Soong confident his design will someday help protect structures from earthquake loads.

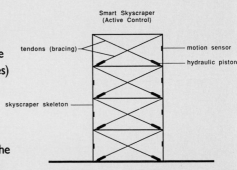

The smart skyscraper would increase its rigidity by tightening tendons with hydraulic pistons.

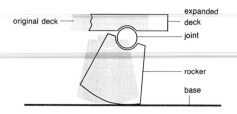

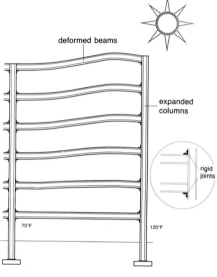

■ Thermal Loads

All materials expand and contract when exposed to changing thermal conditions. The coefficient of expansion for steel is .0000067 inches per degree Fahrenheit. That means a 100 degree temperature change will cause each inch of steel to expand or contract .00067 inches. This may not seem like very much, but consider the effect in a 200' high building or 200' long bridge. At 200 feet the .00067 inch change equals 1-1/2″ of total variation. Structures must be designed to retain their strength and integrity when such changes occur.

The expansion of a steel bridge girder could be restricted between two solid abutments, but the compressive forces generated would actually reduce the strength of the steel by as much as one half. Also, the restricted girder would buckle, causing cracks and bumps in the road surface. A better solution is to allow the girder to expand and contract. Moveable joints, such as a rocker joint, allow for thermal loads and protect the strength of the structure.

Another example of movable joints are the hinged joints used in steel frames and arches. Hinged arches were discussed in the previous chapter. Vertical thermal loads on columns in skyscrapers pose special problems. Temperatures inside most skyscrapers are maintained around 70° F with air-conditioning equipment. In certain areas, outside temperatures can range from 0° F in the winter to 120° F in the summer. In the heat, the columns expand, which is acceptable, but beams can be buckled and deformed by this movement. Hinged connections must be used to permit bending at the beam and column joints.

Control joints, also called expansion joints, are used in concrete sidewalks and roads. A gap between slabs allows for thermal expansion and contraction. Building complexes composed of several long structures jointed together also employ expansion joints. Halls running through these structures are several inches apart where they join and have separate foundations, which allows for different expansion rates and foundation settlements. You may have noticed these joints, which are usually covered by plates, in long hallways at your school or in a hospital.

(Above) Bridges must have movable joints, like this rocker joint, that permit structural elements to expand and contract from thermal loads.

(Below) Reactions of columns and beams due to thermal loads.

(Right) Long hallways often have expansion joints for thermal load reactions.

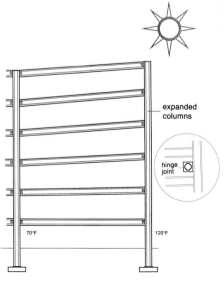

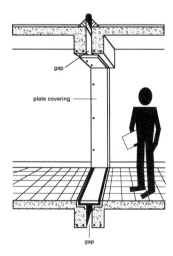

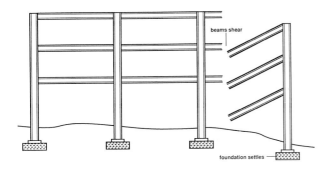

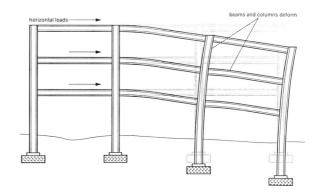

Foundation settlement loads can cause beams to shear off or create horizontal loads on columns and beams.

◼ Foundation Settlement Loads

Problems from foundation settlement loads are the most common cause of damage to structures. This damage can range from minor cracks to total collapse. Settlement loads occur when the dead load of the structure causes uneven settling of the foundation. Two extreme cases of ground settlement are illustrated above. In the first, one end of a structure drops and the beams shear off, leading to the collapse of several floors. In the other case, the foundation drops, but the beams do not shear off. In this instance, the beams and columns sitting on the higher part of the foundation are forced to bear horizontal loads pulling the structure to the right. Beams and columns are designed to resist vertical loads, not horizontal ones. This type of loading can cause buckling or shear in elements, or the total collapse of the structure.

◼ Snow Loads

Building codes for snow loads vary by locale. For example, codes in high mountain regions may require roofs to support snow loads of 100 psf. Northern Maine and Canada have snow load codes of around 80 psf, while Florida has a zero snow load. Snow is a static live load (changes slowly, not a permanent part of the structure) that must be resisted by the strength of the roof system.

Snow can be quite heavy and has been known to collapse large roofs. A 80 psf snow load on a 24′ × 56′ roof can exert a force of over 53 tons. In addition, melting snow sliding off a pitched roof turns into a dynamic load capable of tearing off gutters and downspouts.

The Leaning Tower of Pisa

Probably the most famous example of foundation settlement loads is the Leaning Tower of Pisa, in Italy. The foundation under the 191′ high tower began to settle unevenly during construction, which began in 1174. The builders tried to correct the settlement, but were unsuccessful. Today, the tower continues to fall over at a rate of about 1″ every eight years. The top of the tower is now out of plumb by 16′!

Various techniques have been studied to prevent total collapse of the structure, but Pisans only want to stabilize the tower, not straighten it. The leaning tower is a popular tourist attraction and the Pisans are afraid nobody would come to their town to see a straight tower.

(Courtesy of The Italian Cultural Institute)

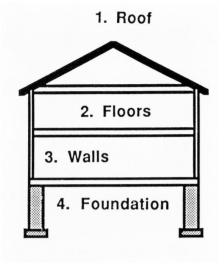

1. Roof

2. Floors

3. Walls

4. Foundation

Engineering Structures: From the Top Down

Structures are engineered (designed to resist loads) in reverse order from the way they are built. The roof or top surfaces are designed first. The engineers must consider building codes for the effects of loads from wind, snow, ice, and traffic (for example, on a bridge deck). Next, the floors are designed for the intended live loads from occupants or users. Third, the walls or vertical supports are designed to support floors and the roof. Finally, the foundation can be designed. It must be strong enough to transfer all dead and live loads to the ground safely.

Structural Efficiency and Occupant Security

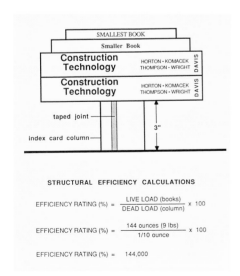

STRUCTURAL EFFICIENCY CALCULATIONS

$$\text{EFFICIENCY RATING (\%)} = \frac{\text{LIVE LOAD (books)}}{\text{DEAD LOAD (column)}} \times 100$$

$$\text{EFFICIENCY RATING (\%)} = \frac{144 \text{ ounces (9 lbs)}}{1/10 \text{ ounce}} \times 100$$

$$\text{EFFICIENCY RATING (\%)} = 144{,}000$$

The most efficient structure, in load-bearing terms, would have the least amount of dead load for a given live load. This is the live load to dead load ratio or **efficiency rating.** A simple demonstration of structural efficiency can be performed by rolling a single 3″ × 5″ index card into the shape of a round column 3″ tall. The dead load of this structure is able to carry a tremendous amount of weight. Several large books stacked carefully and kept aligned with the center line of the column will be required to cause failure. If the card weighs 1/10 of an ounce and the column can support 9 pounds of books, the efficiency rating for the structure would be 144,000 percent. The index card column is capable of supporting 1440 times its own weight. That is a very efficient column.

Notice that this demonstration is done with a static load. The unpredictable and potentially disastrous effects of dynamic loads on structural efficiency become apparent when one book dropped on the column causes total collapse.

Of course, tradeoffs must be made to insure structural safety as well as safety and security for occupants. Technology is available to construct structures with high efficiency ratings, but the needs of people for security must be considered. For example, a lightweight skyscraper may be able to withstand wind loads structurally, but the drift may cause its occupants to feel like they are on an amusement park ride. The same is true of a floor sheathing that is structurally sound and efficient, but gives slightly when people walk over it. This bouncing effect may prove upsetting to people, even though the structure is strong. Some people are very uneasy about traveling over bridges that have a screen-type deck, the kind where you can see through the road deck to the river, lake, or ravine below, even though this type of decking is obviously very strong and efficient.

The Importance of Proper Building Practices

Structural failures occur for a number of different reasons, including substandard construction materials, miscalculations about the effects of various loads, and miscommunication between the architect, engineer, contractor, and worker. Another area that causes problems is building practices. Many structures have fallen during construction because workers did not follow proper building practices.

A disastrous example of this was the failure that occurred many years ago to a half built steel-frame high-rise. The steel frame was to be covered and reinforced by concrete plates. One particularly cold and windy day, the work crew decided to install the plates up the windward side of the building first to protect them from the wind. Unknowingly, they created a huge sail area on the windward side. The frame, which was not reinforced on the other three sides, was not designed for this lateral load. Beams and columns deflected and the structure became dynamically unstable. It collapsed, killing several workers.

After this accident, closer attention was paid to the proper sequence of erecting structures and the use of temporary bracing. Today, the frame, main reinforcement, and temporary bracing go up with the structure.

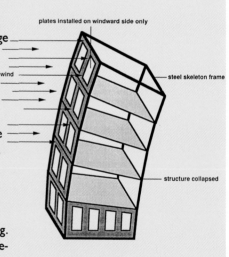

plates installed on windward side only

wind

steel skeleton frame

structure collapsed

SUMMARY

Structures are important products of construction technology that serve human needs. In order for a structure to serve its intended function properly and efficiently, it must first resist the various loads that try to knock it down. Structures must possess a combination of stability, strength, and rigidity in order to resist loads.

Loads are classified on the basis of their effects on a structure (static or dynamic) and the permanence of the load (dead or live). All loads come from three main soruces: structure weight, occupants, and natural elements. The effects of static loads come from motionless or slowly changing sources, such as furniture, occupants, snow, and thermal conditions. Dynamic loads come from moving sources, such as wind, earthquakes, and moving traffic. Dead loads come from the weight of the structure itself, while live loads come from all nonpermanent sources, such as occupants, and the natural elements (wind, snow, earthquake, etc.)

Engineers must consider the effects of various loads on structures. Their efforts are often simplified by the use of construction laws and regulations called building codes. In cases where unexpected loads occur, the possibility of structural failure always exists.

. . . .

Study Questions

1. What are the three main sources of all loads?

2. What are the differences between static and dynamic loads? Can you identify three examples of each? Which specific loads do you think have the most dramatic effects on structures? Why?

3. Explain the differences between dead and live loads and identify three examples of each. Describe the example you think is the most dramatic.

4. What three characteristics must a structure possess in order to resist loads? Which of these is most important for wind loads? Earthquake loads? Water loads?

5. Describe resonant loads. Give one example of the effects of resonant loads on structures.

6. Why do structural engineers design structures from the top down?

. . . .

Suggested Activities

1. Conduct the various experiments explained in this chapter to verify the effects of loads on structures.

2. Investigate the specific building codes for your local community. See what special codes have been established for snow, wind, water, or earthquake loads.

3. Write to the specialized code writing organizations for information on building codes specific to certain materials, such as concrete or timber frames.

4. Construct models of interesting load resistant construction techniques described in this chapter, such as the tuned dynamic damper, x-bracing skeleton frame or bridges, bridge rocker joint, etc.

5. Research one particular load of interest to you, write to organizations or schools who study the load, write a short paper, and construct a model to explain how engineers design structures to resist that load.

Glossary

Base isolation   Earthquake resistance technique that uses a stack of steel and rubber to isolate a structure from its foundation.

Building codes   Laws or ordinances that specify minimum standards for structural support.

Concentrated load   Load that is not uniformly distributed, but rather focused on one point.

Dead loads   Loads from permanent parts of a structure, such as the weight of structural elements or components.

Design live loads   Live loads specified in building codes.

Downwash   Wind that is deflected down the side of a tall building into the street below.

Dynamic loads   Loads that come from moving sources, such as the natural elements, moving traffic or accidents.

Efficiency rating   A ratio of the live load to dead load of a structure; a measure of structural efficiency.

Equilibrium   Means balance; stable structures have equilibrium. Linear and rotational are the two types.

Factor of safety   Over-designing structures to resist loads much larger than those expected, also called safety factor.

Impact load   Type of dynamic load that hits a structure quickly with a magnified force.

Linear equilibrium   When opposing loads are balanced in a horizontal or vertical orientation, such as in a tug of war.

Live load   Load that can be moved or changed over time; anything not a permanent part of the structure.

Load   Any effect that creates a need for a resistive force to prevent collapse or failure of a structure.

Moment   In rotational equilibrium, the product of a load times its distance from the fulcrum; also called torque.

Occupant loads   Loads on a structure from occupants, such as people, furniture, machines, and traffic.

Resonant load   Type of dynamic load caused by a small force that continues over a long time period.

Rotational equilibrium   When two loads are in balance over a fulcrum or pivot point, as in a seesaw.

Safety factor   Over-designing structures to resist loads much larger than those expected, also called factor of safety.

Static loads   Loads that result from motionless or slowly changing bodies, such as the weight of the structure, its occupants or users, and any accessories, such as furniture or equipment.

Tuned dynamic damper   Heavy mass of concrete attached to the top of a skyscraper by springs and shock absorbers, used to damp out or absorb wind energy and reduce wind drift.

Uniform load   Load spread evenly over a structure or one of its elements.

Venturi effect   Scientific principle that says when a moving fluid (wind is a fluid) is restricted in its flow, its speed increases and its pressure decreases.

Wind drift   The rocking back and forth of structures due to wind loads.

About the Activities

Construction is all around you, but how does it really work? What can you do to make such things as materials, structures, wind dynamics and safety considerations seem more real? How can you bring the outside world into your classroom?

Try the activities that appear here and at the end of the other parts of this book. These activities will:

- Reinforce ideas and concepts you've learned in this book

- Exercise your math and geometry skills

- Integrate concepts from science

- Introduce you to problem-solving through the "design brief" approach

Use these activities to explore the constructed world and your own imagination. Solve problems. Work with a construction team of your peers to design a bridge or tower, or site a waste treatment plant. Extend your knowledge of construction by making bricks, testing the strength of index cards, designing a cantilever beam. Exercise your creative thinking skills. Invent variations on these activities, and see how well they work. *And don't be afraid to make mistakes!* You can learn from mistakes, and you'll be better able to anticipate them once you've experienced a few.

Above all, have fun!

ACTIVITY 1

Building Materials

Reference Chapter 2: Construction Materials

Concept

Building Materials
A variety of building materials are used in construction. Each material has applications for which it is best suited.

Objective

In this activity you will work with two building materials: brick and wood.

Introduction

Building materials are an important part of our world. Look at your home, apartment or school. What materials can you find there and name? Windows, doors, flooring, walls, etc. are all used in the buildings around you. These are usually made from wood or masonry materials. Quite different materials are used in building roads and bridges.

Over the past 2000 years a variety of building materials has been developed to build shelters for human use. These shelters protect us from the environment. The log cabin, for example, was built from trees cut from the forest. But the prairies of the midwestern United States had no forests. Houses were built from sod, the thick layer of grass and soil that covered the area. Sod was plentiful and when cut into blocks, could be stacked to provide protection from the weather.

Wood in the form of trees and earth in the form of clay are the two most used building materials. Let's look at these two building materials to see how they are used in constructing houses today.

The brick has been in use for a very long time. Early Egyptians mixed straw with clay from the earth and formed it into a basic building block. These blocks were baked in the hot sun to turn them into porous, hard blocks. These blocks were good for building because they insulated and protected the people from the heat and cold. Clay and wheat straw were plentiful. Wood was more valuable as a fuel to heat and cook with.

Today, bricks are a common building material. Mortar made from cement, sand and water bonds the bricks together. The Romans were the first to discover how to make cement from finely ground volcanic material. When mixed with water, the powdered cement turns back into a stone-like material. Today we use cement to make concrete, a common building material. Sidewalks, roads, tunnels, backyard patios, housing foundations and football stadiums are made of concrete. This material is in a liquid form when it comes to the construction site. It includes a mixture of sand, stone, cement and water. Once poured into a form and finished, it hardens into a stone-hard mass. Iron bars are often added to increase the strength of concrete structures.

Materials

Brick Making

wet clay (about 2 lb.)	mixing bowl or bucket
straw: cut into short pieces	oven
apron	brick mold
water	scissors
plastic sheet to cover table	

Log Cabin
architect's scale or ruler
handsaw
backsaw
sketching paper
scale logs (sections of tree limbs about 3/8″ in diameter, 8″ and 10″ long)
plywood baseboard—approximately 14″ square
roofing material such as a cedar shingle or a piece of thin plywood
white glue

Procedure

Several activities are suggested here to provide experiences with different materials used in building. The brick making activity shows a primitive method for making a building brick. When building the log cabin model, construction techniques with this type of construction can be simulated.

Brick Making

1. Construct the brick mold of available material; plywood, sheet metal or scrap wood. Cut the materials to size as shown in the drawing.

Brick Mold

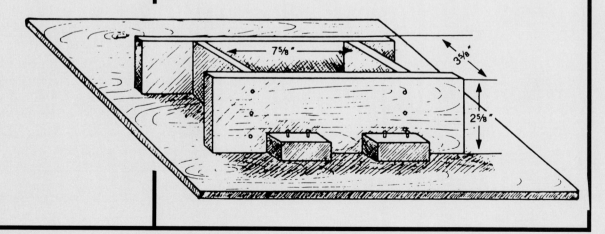

2. Cover the work table with plastic sheet and put on an apron or protective clothing.

3. Cut the straw to short lengths of about 1/2″ to 1″.

4. Add water to the clay and knead it by hand until the clay is soft and pliable. Add the water slowly, a small amount at a time. You want a clay that is soft and moldable, not liquid.

5. Add straw to the clay mixture.

6. Pack the clay/straw mixture into the mold. Strike off any extra with a straight-edged piece of wood.

7. Let the brick set overnight. Leave the top uncovered to allow moisture to escape.

8. Remove the mold slowly. If the brick is dry enough to hold its shape, the mold can be removed and the brick put in the sun to dry.

9. Set the oven temperature at 200 degrees F.

10. Place the partially dry brick on a piece of sheet metal and put in the oven.

11. Bake the brick overnight. If the oven has a circulating fan, leave the fan on to help draw out the moisture. If the oven in a household stove is used, leave the door slightly open to allow moisture to escape.

Log Cabin Building

1. Sketch plans for a cabin. Make your drawing to a scale of 1/4″ = 1′. This should produce a model about 8″ × 10″.

2. Select and cut the scale logs to size. Note: All of the scale logs made from sections of tree limbs should be straight.

3. Cut a "V" notch 3/4″ from the end of each log. The notch should be cut on the top and bottom on each end using the backsaw.

4. Place the first row of logs using pieces for the front, back and side walls. Check for squareness after the first row is complete. When placing the second row of logs, a space must be left for the door of the cabin. Place small amounts of glue in the notches to hold the pieces together.

5. Continue placing the rows of logs until the bottoms of the window openings are reached. At this point begin leaving spaces for the windows.

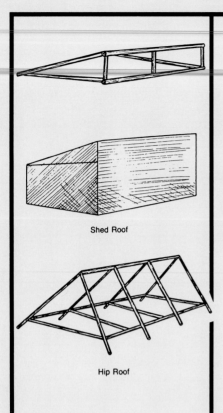

Shed Roof

Hip Roof

6. At least one full row of logs should be placed above the window openings.

7. Build one more row of logs but don't glue it to the rest of the cabin. This will be used as the roof frame.

8. The roof should be made separately and added to the cabin later. Logs smaller in diameter can be used to frame the roof shape. Choose either a shed-style or a gable roof design.

9. Cover the roof frame with a roofing material. Glue and/or nail the roofing material to the frame. Place the roof on the cabin.

10. Finish the cabin by adding your own touch of creativity.

Suggestions for Further Study

Visit the reference section of your city or county library. Ask the librarian for information on testing standards of construction materials. **A.S.T.M.** (American Society of Testing Materials) publishes books on the standards for building materials. Find the standards for bricks. Record the information and report to your class.

Other class members might select other materials such as framing lumber or plywood siding. Is there a standard for log constructed homes? Log homes are popular in some areas of the United States.

If there is a log home in your community, it might be possible to visit the home to discover how it was constructed. Is there a log home manufacturer in your community? If so, a trip there to see how the parts for log homes are manufactured should be very interesting.

ACTIVITY 2

Popsicle Bridge Design Brief

Reference   Chapter 3: Material Properties

Design Brief   In this activity teams of four or five people will design a bridge
                     made of popsicle sticks and chart the ultimate strength or elasticity
                     point using destructive testing.

Procedure   1. Form teams of four or five.

2. Each team will be given ten sticks to span a distance of one foot.
   (Additional materials include five rubber bands and wood glue.)

3. Weights must be used in the center of the bridge to calculate and
   chart the linear elasticity of the bridge.

4. The chart should contain:
   linear elasticity line
   ultimate strength
   point of plasticity (point of deformation)
   collapse point

5. Compare findings from each group.

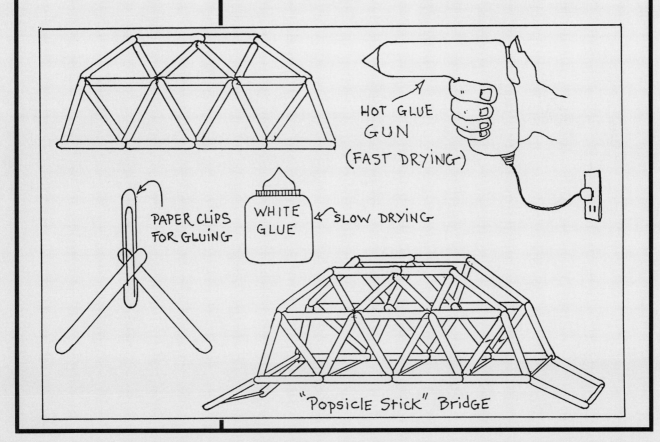

HOT GLUE GUN (FAST DRYING)

PAPER CLIPS FOR GLUING

WHITE GLUE ← SLOW DRYING

"Popsicle Stick" Bridge

ACTIVITY 3

Cantilever Beam Design Brief

Reference

Chapter 4: Structural Elements

Introduction

Beams are one of the most important structural elements. They are linear, rigid elements used to span a gap between two supports. One type of beam is the cantilever, which extends from one support. (Most beams have two or more supports.) In this activity, you will compete with other members of your class to design an efficient cantilever beam.

Design Brief

Design and construct a cantilever beam to achieve the maximum possible span.

Cantilever Beam

Parameters

The following parameters must be met in the design, construction, and testing of your cantilever beam. Your teacher may want to change certain parameters.

1. Students will work in small groups of two or three to design and construct their cantilever beam. (Students in small classes may work alone; in large classes, larger groups may be used.)

2. A drawing (dimensioned sketch with important notes) is required for each beam design.

3. The materials used will be determined by your teacher, but may include some of the following:

   Structural Materials: (Your teacher will probably set limitations on the maximum amount of material you may use.)

   - 1/8″ × 1/8″ balsa or other wood

   - small diameter steel rods

   - popsicle sticks/tongue depressors

   - paper or plastic straws

   Fasteners: (limits may be set)

   - wood glues

   - hot glue stick

   - brazing/welding rods

Miscellaneous (at teacher's discretion)

- string (kite string, limited quantity)
- 8-1/2″ × 11″ paper (limited quantity)

4. A time limit will be set for the design and construction of the beam. Your teacher will decide on the completion date for the beams.

5. The total costs associated with constructing the beam must be tabulated by each group. Each material used will be assigned a dollar value.

6. Length of span will be measured on the central horizontal axis of the beam from the anchor (support) to the furthest extending point.

7. There are no limitations on the width of the beam.

8. The anchor will be a concrete block 4 cubic inches in size. You must construct a form for casting the anchor. All anchors will be poured from the same batch of concrete. This anchor must be the only support for the cantilever.

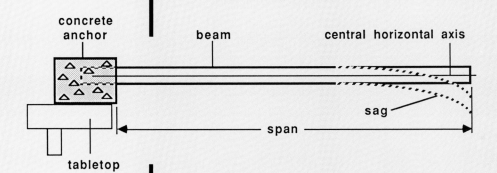

9. You also will be responsible for designing a method of securing your beam to the anchor.

10. Maximum sag for your beam must not exceed 10 percent of its overall length. Beams that sag beyond the maximum will be disqualified from the competition.

Research & Development

Consider the following suggestions when designing and constructing your beam:

- As a group, brainstorm ideas for your design—consider all ideas no matter how "weird".

- Review the information in this chapter related to the span, depth, and sag characteristics of beams.

	■ Go to the library and conduct research on cantilevers, study their design and construction.
	■ Consider the limitations of the materials that will be used to construct the beam.
	■ Study efficient cantilever beam designs you have seen.
	■ Consider some of the structural elements and systems you have seen or read about that can be used to reinforce and stabilize beams.
	■ Each group member should sketch their best ideas. As a group, review each design; combine, refine, and improve until you have a design the group wants to try.
	■ Make a scale mock-up of your design using toothpicks or plastic coffee stirrers/straws for materials.
Evaluation	1. Each beam will be inspected to insure adherence to the parameters.
	2. Each beam must be weighed (grams or ounces).
	3. Beam drawings and Cantilever Beam Costs Worksheets must be submitted to the teacher.
	4. The span of each beam will be measured by the teacher as described in the parameters above.
	5. The following categories will be used to determine the "winners" of the competition:

■ Maximum Span (overall winner)

■ Structural Efficiency (inches per gram or ounce)

$$\frac{\text{Beam span (inches)}}{\text{Beam weight (grams or ounces)}}$$

■ Economic Efficiency (cost ($) per inch of span)

$$\frac{\text{Beam costs (dollars)}}{\text{Beam span (inches)}}$$

■ Innovative Design (student vote)

Beam Building Material Costs

Structural material (wood, etc.)	$_____ / linear inch
Fasteners (glue, etc.)	$_____ (for all)
Paper	$_____ / half sheet
String	$_____ / linear inch
Time (+ / - if < / > time limits)	$_____ / minute

Cantilever Beam Costs Worksheet

Names:_____

	Amount Used	Costs
Structural Materials		
Fasteners		
String		
Paper		
Total Costs		

Cantilever Beam Test Data

Span = _____

$$\text{Structural Efficiency} = \frac{\text{Span (in.)}}{\text{Beam Weight}} = \underline{\qquad}$$

$$\text{Economic Efficiency} = \frac{\text{Beam Costs}}{\text{Span (in.)}} = \underline{\qquad}$$

ACTIVITY 4

Geodesic Dome Design Brief

Reference   Chapter 4: Structural Elements.

Introduction   Geodesic domes are a relatively new invention in the field of construction technology. While most structural elements, such as the beam, column and arch have been around for thousands of years, geodesic domes were patented in 1954 by R. Buckminster Fuller. In the past 35 years, some of the most spectacular structures built have been geodesic domes, including the Expo Dome constructed for the 1967 world's fair in Montreal (see page 107) and Epcot Center in Disney World. In this activity, you will design and construct a geodesic dome.

Design Brief   Design and construct a geodesic dome structure.

Research & Development   There are many problems to be solved in designing and constructing a geodesic dome. Here are a few of the problems you will have to solve:

1. **Strut Materials.** You can build a geodesic dome from a number of different strut materials, including 1 × 2 lumber, steel pipe, conduit, dowel rods, plastic pipe and other materials. Deciding which material to use will be based on the intended use of the dome, tools and machines available, materials available, and the time your teacher wants to devote to the activity.

2. **Frequency.** The frequency of the dome poses interesting problems. In general, the more frequencies, the more stable the dome. Of course, more frequencies means more struts to keep track of and install. For most smaller domes, single- or two-frequency domes are very strong and stable. As the size of a dome increases, the frequency should also increase. If not, the struts would become very long and subject to buckling. Consider building a small single-frequency dome first and a larger two-frequency dome later.

3. **Dome Size & Strut Length.** The size (diameter) of your dome is related to strut length. Strut length is calculated by multiplying math constants by the desired radius.

Calculating Strut Length-Single Frequency Dome

Procedure	Sample Problem
1. Decide dome diameter wanted. 2. Divide diameter to get radius. 3. Multiply radius by constant 1.05. 4. Answer is strut length.	Diameter wanted = 10 feet Radius = 5 feet 5 feet x 1.05 = 5.25 feet or 63 inches

Calculating Strut Length-Two Frequency Dome

Procedure	Sample Problem

1. Decide dome diameter wanted.
2. Divide diameter to get radius.
3. Multiply radius by constant .618.
4. Answer is long strut length.
5. Multiply radius by constant .546.
6. Answer is short strut length.
	Diameter wanted = 10 feet
	Radius = 5 feet
	Long strut -
	    5 feet x .618 = 3.09 feet
	Short strut -
	    5 feet x .546 = 2.73 feet

Vertex
(point of intersection of struts)

NOTE: These calculations are from vertex to vertex. If your connector system does not permit the struts to reach the vertex, your dome will be slightly larger than planned. Adjust sizes, if desired.

ADDITIONAL NOTE: Dome size and strut length are also related to strut materials. As strut length increases, the buckling tendency of some strut materials must be considered. For example, a 1 × 2 wood strut 3 feet long is fairly strong and stable, but likely to buckle if extended to 6 feet.

4. **Connector System.** A quality connector system is critical in successful geodesic dome construction. There are several possibilities,

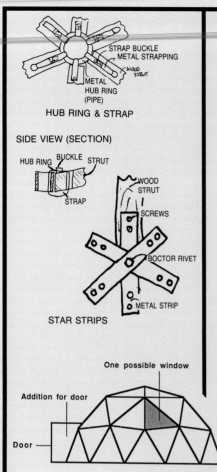

HUB RING & STRAP

SIDE VIEW (SECTION)

STAR STRIPS

One possible window

Addition for door

Door

Procedure

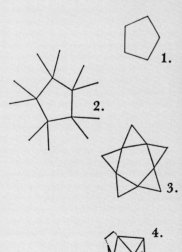

1.

2.

3.

4.

depending on the strut material you use. You might be able to purchase connectors, or fabricate your own. One possibility is stamped metal disks, used in pairs to sandwich struts for bolting.

The connector system used in the 1 × 2 dome above is made of strips of metal riveted together in the center and drilled for screws that fasten to the struts. This type of connector is recommended for the first-time dome builder because it is flexible and can be adjusted during assembly by bending and twisting to match angles on the struts. It also produces a strong dome.

Smaller tabletop domes or tent-sized domes made with wooden dowel or metal rod struts can be connected with flexible plastic tubing. Short sections of tubing bolted or glued together will be strong enough for smaller domes and still provide flexibility.

Another solution, possibly the simplest, can be applied to domes having plastic tubing or metal conduit struts. The ends of each strut are flattened and drilled with a hole for a large bolt, which can be passed through several struts for fastening.

5. **Covering.** If you decide to cover your dome, consider using membranes (plastic sheet) or plates (plywood, hardboard). If the dome will serve as a permanent shelter, preventing leaks will be a major concern.

6. **Doors and Windows.** The odd angles on a geodesic dome make it difficult to install standard doors and windows. An addition may be needed to install a door. If your dome is covered with plywood, install a plastic covered frame in one triangle to create a window.

Single Frequency Domes
You will need 25 struts for this dome.
1. Join 5 struts to form a 5-sided pentagon on the ground or floor. This is the base for the dome.

2. Attach two struts at each vertex to create "Vs" extending away from the pentagon as shown in the drawing.

3. Connect the "V" struts to create triangles that extend from each side of the pentagon.

4. Raise each of the triangles and place a strut between the top points of triangles. This will keep the triangles in an upright position.

5.

6.

5. Separately from the dome base you have been working on, connect 5 struts at a single vertex to create a star shape. This will be the top of the dome.

6. Attach the five open ends on the top you just created on the five points on top of the base you worked on earlier. Congratulations, you have just constructed a single frequency icosahedron geodesic dome!

    This procedure may be used to build any size single frequency geodesic dome. Whether you are planning to build a tabletop model with four-inch struts or a greenhouse-sized dome made from pipe or lumber, this procedure will work. When building larger domes you will need to add temporary internal supports to keep the dome in an upright position during steps 4–6.

Two Frequency Domes

1. Join 10 long struts using 4-point connectors to form a 10-sided decagon. This is the base for the dome.

2. At each connector joint on the decagon, attach 1 long and 1 short strut as shown. Pattern is 2 short struts, then 2 long struts, then 2 short struts, etc. as you go around the decagon.

3. Form triangles around the base by connecting adjacent pairs of short struts and long struts. Three more struts will be added to the point of the triangles made with short struts. Four more struts will be added to the point of the triangles made with long struts.

4. Place the triangles in an upright position and connect the tops of adjacent triangles with short struts.

5. At the top of each triangle made with short struts, add 1 short strut. At the top of each triangle made with 2 long struts, add 2 long struts.

6. Connect the struts you just added to form pairs of adjacent triangles as shown in the illustration. Be sure to join 1 short strut between 2 long struts.

7. Connect the points of the pairs of triangles you just formed using long struts. These 5 struts are extra dark on the illustration to reduce confusion.

1.

2.

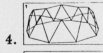

3.

4.

5.

6.

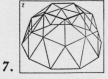

7.

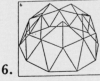

ACTIVITY 5

Pneumatic Structures Design Brief

Reference   Chapter 4: Structural Elements

Introduction   Pneumatic structures consist of membrane materials supported by air pressure. Roofs over sports stadiums are the most popular application of pneumatic structures. Some of the largest sports stadiums in the world have pneumatically supported roofs, including the Louisiana Superdome in New Orleans, the Pontiac Silverdome in Michigan, and the Hubert H. Humphrey Metrodome in Minnesota.

In this activity, you will design and construct a pneumatic structure.

Design Brief   Design and construct a pneumatic structure.

Research & Development   Constructing real-life, full-sized pneumatic structures like those used in sports stadiums poses many technical difficulties. In this activity, it may be a good idea to make scale models. Tabletop models or larger models are easy to make and help you understand how real pneumatic structures are constructed.

Here are some of the problems you must solve in this activity:

1. **Means of Support.** Pneumatic structures can be air-supported or air-inflated. Air-inflated structures are more difficult to make

(Photo by Stan Komacek)

because the membrane must be enclosed and inflated. Air-supported structures are easier to make. A sheet of plastic secured to the floor or walls can be supported to create a roof.

Tabletop models can be supported very easily with a hair dryer. Larger structures can be supported with a box fan or vacuum cleaner. Notice the box fan in the lower left of the color photograph.

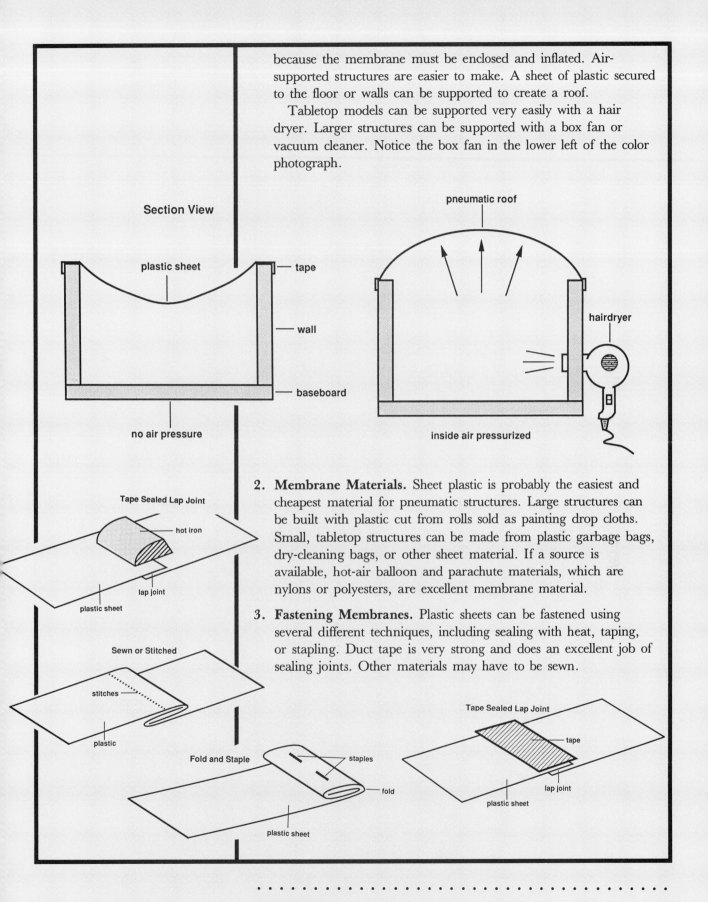

Section View

plastic sheet

tape

wall

baseboard

no air pressure

pneumatic roof

hairdryer

inside air pressurized

Tape Sealed Lap Joint

hot iron

lap joint

plastic sheet

Sewn or Stitched

stitches

plastic

Fold and Staple

staples

fold

plastic sheet

Tape Sealed Lap Joint

tape

lap joint

plastic sheet

2. **Membrane Materials.** Sheet plastic is probably the easiest and cheapest material for pneumatic structures. Large structures can be built with plastic cut from rolls sold as painting drop cloths. Small, tabletop structures can be made from plastic garbage bags, dry-cleaning bags, or other sheet material. If a source is available, hot-air balloon and parachute materials, which are nylons or polyesters, are excellent membrane material.

3. **Fastening Membranes.** Plastic sheets can be fastened using several different techniques, including sealing with heat, taping, or stapling. Duct tape is very strong and does an excellent job of sealing joints. Other materials may have to be sewn.

4. Structural Form. Pneumatic structures can take many different forms. Some design ideas are illustrated here. The easiest designs are based on geometric shapes. Once you pick a form for the entire structure, make patterns that can be used for consistent cutting of individual panels.

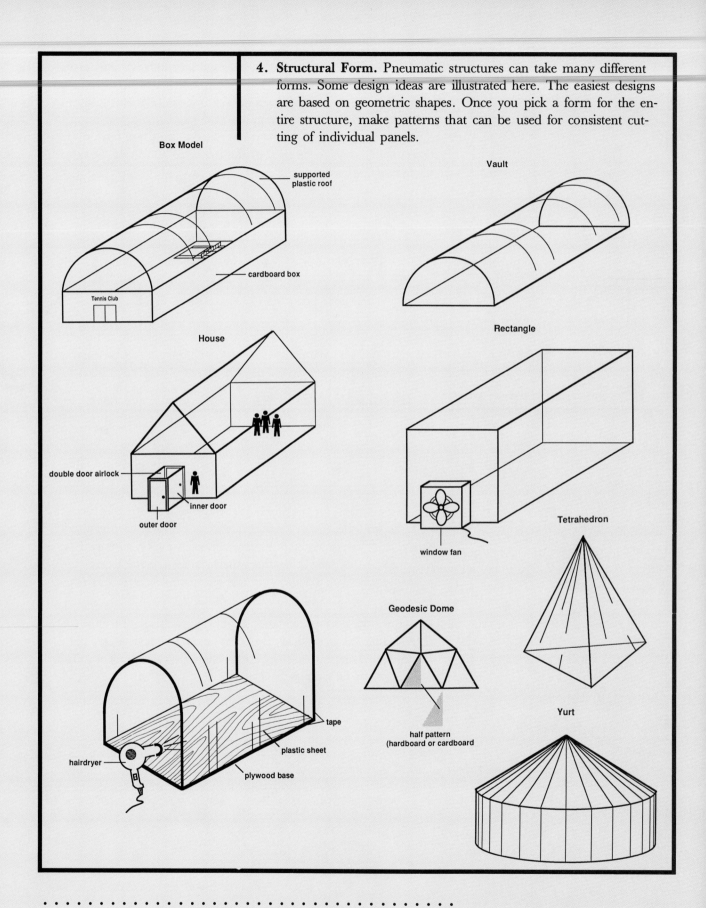

Box Model

supported plastic roof

cardboard box

Tennis Club

Vault

House

double door airlock

inner door

outer door

Rectangle

window fan

Tetrahedron

Geodesic Dome

half pattern (hardboard or cardboard)

Yurt

tape

plastic sheet

plywood base

hairdryer

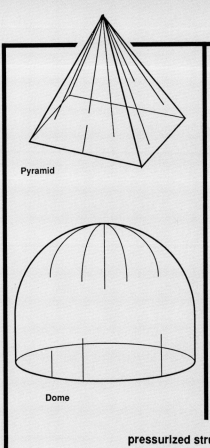

Pyramid

Dome

5. Controlling Air Pressure. You may be surprised how strong the air pressure created by a hair dryer or fan can be. Continuous air flow into a sealed membrane can cause joints and seams to burst. Full-sized pneumatic structures have sensors that detect the internal pressure in an air-supported structure and control fan operations, shutting fans off when the optimum pressure is reached.

You can make a barometer-like device to monitor air pressure in your structure. With some experimentation, you can use this device to determine the optimum air pressure for your pneumatic structure.

6. Doors. The simplest door for your larger models would be overlapping plastic that created a slit through which you can enter and exit. Of course, full-sized doors can be used, but you may want to consider double doors or revolving doors to create an air-lock and prevent rapid loss of air pressure.

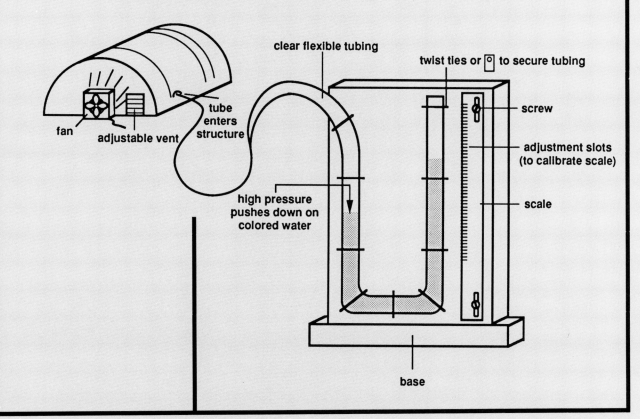

pressurized structure

clear flexible tubing

twist ties or 🔘 to secure tubing

fan

adjustable vent

tube enters structure

high pressure pushes down on colored water

screw

adjustment slots (to calibrate scale)

scale

base

Enrichment Topics

Vacuum Structures

Consider experimenting with vacuum structures. These structures are created by covering a frame with membrane materials and sucking out the air inside, thus creating a vacuum. This building technique was employed in the design and construction of the African Tropical Foust Building at the Franklin Park Zoo in Boston (see page 119). Notice how the fabric in the tents takes on the saddle shape so important to membrane structures. You can make structures like this, too. Some design ideas are illustrated.

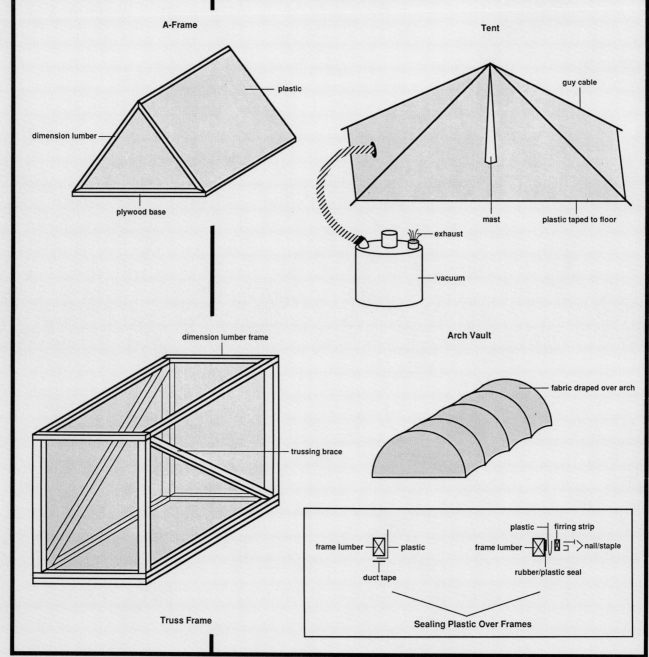

A-Frame

plastic

dimension lumber

plywood base

Tent

guy cable

mast

plastic taped to floor

exhaust

vacuum

Arch Vault

fabric draped over arch

dimension lumber frame

trussing brace

Truss Frame

frame lumber — plastic

duct tape

plastic — firring strip

frame lumber — nail/staple

rubber/plastic seal

Sealing Plastic Over Frames

Inputs

Testing Structural Collapse

If you build an air-supported structure, conduct experiments to determine collapse time and weight-supporting properties. Stop the air flow, open the doors, and time the collapse of the structure. You may be surprised how long it takes! You may also be surprised how much weight an air-supported membrane can support. Deflate a structure, place varying amounts of weight on top, and try to raise the structure to its full height.

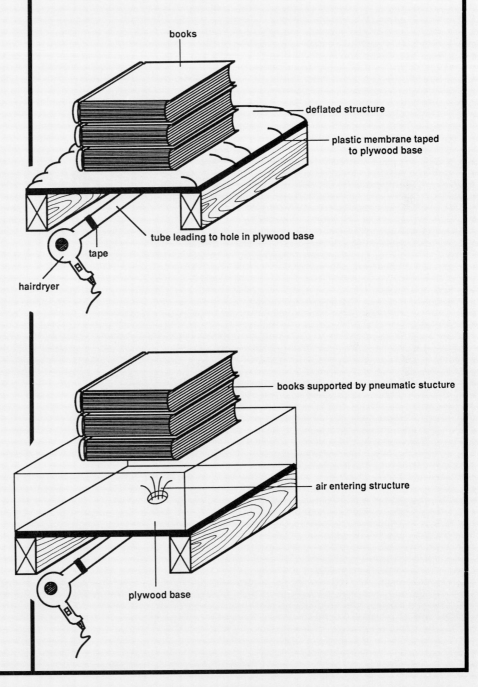

books

deflated structure

plastic membrane taped to plywood base

tube leading to hole in plywood base

tape

hairdryer

books supported by pneumatic stucture

air entering structure

plywood base

ACTIVITY 6

Building Truss Structures

Reference

Chapter 5: Loads on Structures

Concept

Hinged Joint. Structures that use hinged joints require some form of bracing. The most common brace is the truss. Other structures that use rigid frames (joints) may be strengthened with the addition of trusses.

    Related Concepts: hinged structure, rigid structure, compression, tension, stability.

Objectives

On completion of this activity you will have built several different truss structures and will be able to (1) describe how trusses replace flexible supports (guy wires), (2) describe how the truss works on the principle of the triangle and (3) identify why it is necessary to use trusses in hinged structures.

Considerations

1. Why is the triangle used so often in buildings and other structures?

2. How does a structure with hinged joints differ from one that has rigid joints?

3. Can an oil derrick, a bridge and an airplane be built using similar structures?

Materials and Supplies

tongue depressors
cardboard
round toothpicks
glue
staples
assorted small nails, pins and bolts
string or light cord
turnbuckle

Procedure

1. Drill and pin four pieces of wood together as shown in figure 1. (Tongue depressors are a good size for this activity.)

2. Apply pressure on the top and on the corner of the square wooden frame as shown above. What do you observe in the strength and stability of the wooden frame? Do the corners bend as though they were hinged?

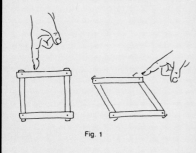

Fig. 1

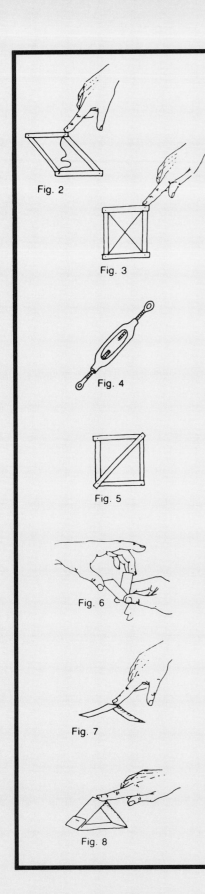

Fig. 2

Fig. 3

Fig. 4

Fig. 5

Fig. 6

Fig. 7

Fig. 8

3. Tie a string between two opposite corners of the frame and try the same tests for strength and stability. What do you now observe? Is the frame strong in one direction and weak in another? (See figure 2)

4. Attach a second thread between the other corners and try the same test. What do you find when you apply force? (See figure 3)

5. If you are building a larger frame, you may want to use a turnbuckle (figure 4) to take up any slack in the cables. Are the cables and turnbuckles examples of compression or tension?

6. Construct another frame by repeating step 1. Place a wooden support across the frame between two opposite corners (figure 5). When you test this frame what do you discover? Is it necessary to have two supports to make the frame stable and strong? Is the support an example of compression or tension? What shape is formed by the frame and the cross support?

7. Construct a third frame (see step 1). Glue each corner. After the glue has set, test the frame as before. Does this frame need a truss? How does this rigid frame differ from the hinged frame?

8. Cut a 4″ × 1″ strip of cardboard. Fold the strip in the middle to form a "V".

9. Hold the V upright and pull down on the point (figure 6), pulling on the point to close the opening of the V.

10. Place the V on the table and push down on the point (figure 7). Pushing on the V spreads the open side.

11. Cut another piece of cardboard, about 3″ long and fold it back 1/2″ from the ends to form two tabs. Fasten this piece across the open end of the V to form a triangle—using glue, staples or paper clips. Repeat the tests you made previously on the V. (See figure 8)

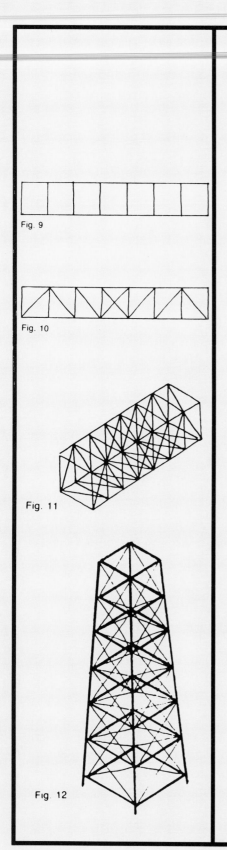

Fig. 9

Fig. 10

Fig. 11

Fig. 12

12. Push on one corner, the opposite side still tries to spread, but it can't unless the tension force is strong enough to break the fastening. If you pull on one corner, the opposite side compresses. This rigid frame resists a change of shape when forces are applied to it.

13. Assemble two frames with dimensions as shown here. First cut the top and bottom beams to length. Then cut 2″ posts and glue them to the beams (See figure 9).

14. Cut diagonal braces to fit and glue them in place on one truss. When the glue has dried, compare the two trusses by pushing and twisting them gently. The braced truss will be much more rigid. Then complete the second truss (figure 10).

15. Connect the two trusses with 2″ crossbeams at top and bottom. Pins can be used again to hold the parts to be joined. Be sure that the sides are perpendicular to the top and bottom (figure 11).

16. By pushing and twisting gently on the truss sides, you can see that the bridge framework is still not very rigid. The two sides can easily move parallel to one another.

17. Now that the model truss structure is completed stand it up on one end (figure 12). Have you seen any structures similar to this? If you were going to build a truss structure to be used in this manner, how do you think you would improve it? Could you build the structure with a wider base, like a trussed pyramid? Would you add any trusses to the inside of this structure? Have you seen such structures? Could you run guy wires from the structure down to the ground to make it more stable? Have you seen structures like this?

18. Lay the structure down with a block supporting each end (see figure 13). Place a flat piece of cardboard inside the structure on the bottom. Have you seen structures like this?

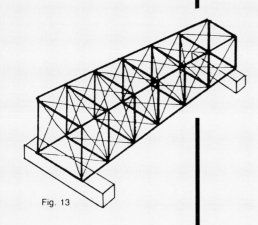

Fig. 13

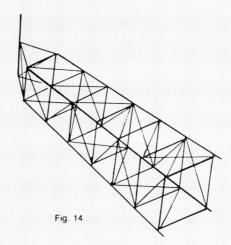

Fig. 14

19. Compare the truss structure you built with the airplane structure (figure 14). How are they similar?

Assessment Activities

In each orientation of the truss structure (standing up, lying down or moving about) which parts can support the larger compression load? What parts will hold the larger tension load? Can any of the tension members be replaced with cables to make the structure lighter? If truss structures get their strength from the triangles that are formed, where do rigid structures get their strength?

Student Analysis

1. Identify the minimum number of flexible braces needed to support a square. The minimum rigid braces needed?

2. Determine which members change from tension to compression and compression to tension when a truss bridge is turned into a tower.

Suggested Indepth Study

1. Collect pictures and photographs of unusual truss structures.

2. Secure a picture of a bridge and identify the compression and tension.

3. Design and build a model truss rafter that could be built and then lifted into place.

4. Build a trussed tower of toothpicks 24″ tall that will support a brick. (Limit yourself to 124 toothpicks.)

House of Cards

Reference

Chapter 5: Loads on Structures

Introduction

The weight of a structure is called its dead load; nonpermanent loads on the structure are called live loads. Structures must have the characteristics of stability, rigidity and strength to efficiently transmit both dead and live loads safely to the ground. There are many techniques that can be used to improve and reinforce structures, including bracing, laminating materials, and adding support members. When structural engineers and designers want to test a technique, they often build and destructively test model structures. In this activity, you will build and destructively test a house of cards. An efficiency rating and factor of safety will be calculated.

Design Brief

Design a reinforcing technique for a house of cards that will produce the most efficient structure in your class.

Parameters

The following parameters will be followed:

1. Students will work in groups of two or three to design and test their house of cards.

2. Each group will receive the following materials:

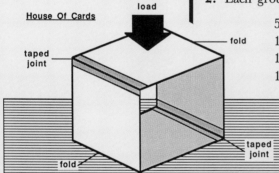

House Of Cards

> 5 index cards, $3'' \times 5''$
> 1 sheet of tablet or notebook paper, $8\frac{1}{2}'' \times 11''$
> 18'' tape (any kind available)
> 12'' string (kite string or similar)

3. The total costs of your design will be calculated using the material costs assigned below:

> Index cards—$1500 each or $100/in^2
> Paper—$935 total or $10/in^2
> Tape—$450 total or $25/in
> String—$120 total or $10/in

4. Costs will also be added or subtracted for time. A time limit will be established by your teacher. Exceeding the time limit will result in $5/minute being added to total costs. Coming in under the time limit will result in a subtraction of $5/minute.

Inputs

5. Two of the index cards will be folded across their long dimension and taped together to form the box. Use your tape wisely!

6. The remaining materials may be used to reinforce the card house to resist a live load applied across its side.

7. All structures will be destructively tested using a static, live load of sand to identify the strongest and most efficient designs.

Evaluation

1. The total costs of each structure will be calculated. Unused materials will be measured in the basic cost units described above. The smallest acceptable unused unit of each material is listed below.

> Index cards—square inch
> Paper—square inch
> Tape—linear inch
> String—linear inch

2. Each finished structure will be weighed in grams or ounces.

3. Each structure will be destructively tested and the live load weighed in pounds.

4. The following calculations will be performed to determine winners in the competition:

- Structural Efficiency Rating (overall winner)

- Maximum Live Load

- Economic Efficiency Rating

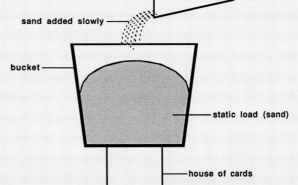

House of Cards
Data Collection Sheet

Team Members _____ Date _____

1. Material Costs. Calulate the total costs for your design.

Material	Quantity Used	Unit Costs	Total Costs
Index Cards	2	$1500 each	$3000
Index Cards (in2)		$1500 each $100/in2	
Paper (in2)		$10/in2	
Tape (linear in)		$25/in	
String (linear in)		$10/in	
Time (minutes)		>Limit, +$5/min <Limit, -$5/min	

TOTAL MATERIAL COSTS

2. Weigh your design to determine its DEAD LOAD. Destructively test the structure to determine its maximum LIVE LOAD and caluclate a Structural EFFICIENCY RATING using the formula below.

Dead Load	Live Load	Efficiency Rating

$$\frac{\text{Efficiency}}{\text{Rating}} = \frac{\text{Live Load}}{\text{Dead Load}} \times 100$$

3. Calculate ECONOMIC EFFICIENCY ($lb) using the formula below.

Economic Efficiency

$$\frac{\text{Economic}}{\text{Efficiency}} = \frac{\text{Total Material Costs}}{\text{Live Load}}$$

ACTIVITY 8

Tallest Tower

Introduction

Building tall towers requires an understanding of the importance of several factors, including dead and live loads, stability, rigidity and strength, and following proper building practices.

In this activity, you will design and construct a tall tower structure.

Design Brief

Design and construct a tower that is taller than any other tower in the class using available materials.

Parameters

The following guidelines must be followed:

1. **Design Teams.** Teams of 3 or 4 students will work together to design and construct the tower.

2. **Materials.** You will be limited to the type and quantity of material specified by your teacher. The following materials will work:

   - drinking straws (plastic or paper)
   - balsa wood (1/8″ × 1/8″)
   - wood strips (1/8″ × 1/8″)

3. **Tools.** The cutting and fastening tools you use will be deterined by the materials specified by your teacher. Straws can be cut with scissors and fastened with straight pins; balsa, other wood strips, or toothpicks can be cut with utility knives and fastened with hot glue. **Always cut safely when using uitility knives.**

4. **Design.** The base of the tower must fit inside a 8″ diameter circle. The tower must be free standing—no guy wires may be used.

5. **Testing/Evaluation.** Your tower must support a tennis ball (live load) on its pinnacle for 60 seconds without collapsing.

6. **Time Limit.** The time limit will be determined by your teacher. Typical time limits would be one class period for design and experiment and one class period for construction and testing the tower.

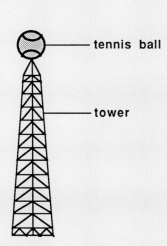

tennis ball

tower

Research & Development	Consider the following:

1. Think of other tall towers you have seen. Try to identify how they maintain stability, rigidity, and strength.

2. Brainstorm as many ideas as you can in a short period of time. Write or illustrate your ideas, select the best ideas, and begin to construct your tower.

3. Your tower must be free standing. Create a design that is not top heavy and unstable.

4. Remember, the tower must support a tennis ball on its pinnacle. Be sure to design a method for attaching or supporting the ball to prevent it from rolling off.

5. Consider constructing the tower using modules. Each person in the group could work on one module, then all the modules could be connected to assemble the tower.

Gettysburg, Pennsylvania. (Photo by Stan Komacek)

ACTIVITY 9

Floors and Safety Factors

Reference

Chapter 5: Loads on Structures

Introduction

Floors must support their own dead load, plus any live loads from people, furniture, and accessories. The design of floors is controlled by building codes. Building codes specify the live load for which floors must be designed. A safety factor or factor of safety is built into building codes.

In this activity, you will calculate the dead load, total live load, live load per square foot, and factor of safety for a room in your home or school.

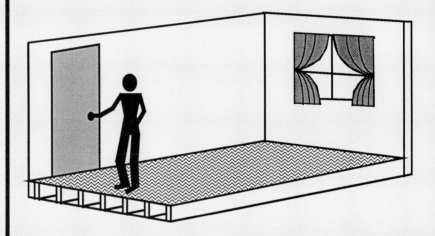

Materials

tape measure
calculator & pencils
Chart: Weights of Building Materials and Components (**page 136.**)
Floors and Safety Factors Data Collection Sheet.

Procedure

1. Pick a room in your home or school. Measure the room to the nearest inch. Calculate the total FLOOR AREA and record it on the Data Collection Sheet.

2. Determine what materials and techniques were used to construct the floor of the room. Identify and list the permanent materials used (not carpeting or other floor coverings).

3. Calculate the DEAD LOAD for the floor. Record on Data Sheet.

4. List all the items being supported by the floor. Weigh or estimate the weight of each item. Add these together to determine the TOTAL LIVE LOAD on the floor. Record totals.

5. Divide the TOTAL LIVE LOAD by the FLOOR AREA to get the UNIFORM LIVE LOAD.

6. Assume a code live load of 40 psf. Divide this by the UNIFORM LIVE LOAD to determine the FACTOR OF SAFETY.

7. Determine how much more total weight would have to be added to the room to reach the 40 psf specified in the building code.

Floors and Safety Factors Data Collection Sheet

Name:_____ Date_____

Room chosen	
Room size	
Floor area	
Dead load	
Total live load	
Uniform live load	
Factor of safety	

ACTIVITY 10

Simulating Wind Dynamics with a Flow Table

Introduction

Wind moving around, between, and under buildings can cause dramatic increases in wind speed due to a physical phenomenon called the venturi effect. Wind engineers test model structures in wind tunnels to learn more about the venturi effect. If you don't have a wind tunnel, you can construct a flow table to simulate wind dynamics.

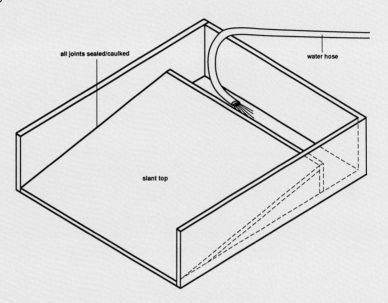

A flow table can be constructed using exterior plywood. The size and dimensions of the table are up to you, but dimensions that have worked before are 2′ long × 1′6″ wide × 8″ deep. Two important factors must be included in the design: well sealed joints (use caulking) and a gradual incline on the slant top. An angle of 30° or less works best.

Section View

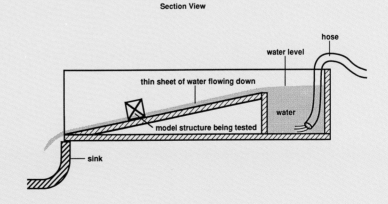

How The Flow Table Works

The figure shows a section view of the flow table being used. Model structures (plexiglass, sealed plywood or lumber, etc.) are cut out and secured to the table with a temporary adhesive or tape. Water can be used, because water and air have similar flow characteristics. Water flows through a hose to fill up the tray on the right side. As the tray overflows, a thin sheet of water flows down the slant top around the model structures and into a sink. Food coloring is added to the water flow using an eye dropper. The food coloring gives visibility to any swirling eddies and increases in flow speed.

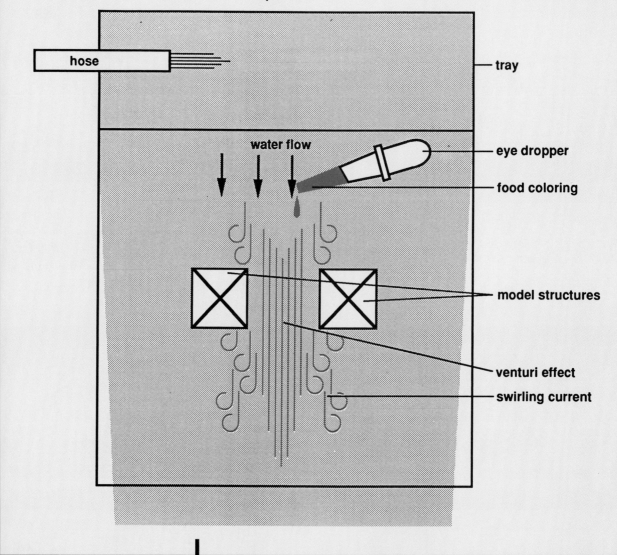

Top View

hose

water flow

tray

eye dropper

food coloring

model structures

venturi effect

swirling current

Suggestions/Considerations

1. Since the water must flow down the slant table in a uniform thin sheet, the slant top must be level across its width.

2. The rate at which water flows into the tray will determine the depth of the thin sheet and its speed. Experiment with different flow rates.

3. Since the eddies and swirls will develop and disappear quickly, a video camera can be used to record the effects. The tape can then be played back at slow or stop motion for detailed analysis.

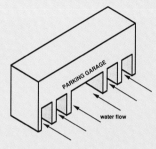

water flow

Cross-sectional geometric shapes - try different sizes and directions of water flow.

Downwash Tester

sidewalk

skyscraper

water flow

Part II

Process

Chapter 6

Design Guidelines and Process

Chapter Concepts

■ Before construction systems are built, there is a detailed and extensive design process based on six interactive stages: motivation, preparation, ideation, incubation, illumination, and verification.

■ Socially relevant and culturally sensitive design considerations should be of utmost importance in the design of all construction systems.

■ Technical design guidelines that must be considered in the design of construction systems are durability, construction ease, maintainability, function and aesthetics.

■ Soil erosion and sedimentation can be minimized by using environmental design guidelines with control techniques.

■ Designing with nature includes the use of renewable energy associated with the climatology of an area and the use of materials indigenous to the region.

■ Renewable energy systems reduce dependence on fossil fuels and help reduce the environmental impact associated with the burning of fossil fuels.

Key Terms

aesthetics
creativity
durability
ideation
illumination
incubation

maintainability
motivation
preparation
sedimentation
verification

(Preceding page:) **Construction workers ready the top of a concrete foundation for framing. This is part of the process stage of construction. (Courtesy of the United Brotherhood of Carpenters)**

This airport terminal successfully combines function and aesthetics. A complex solar collection systems helps to heat the large open space while allowing the skylights to brighten the interior. The careful use of color heightens the effect. (Photo by Norman McGrath, courtesy of Einhorn Yaffee Prescott, P.C.)

I. DESIGN GUIDELINES

Design guidelines fall into three categories: social, technical and environmental. These three categories are interrelated, and deal with the questions and concerns that arise whenever a structure is built.

For examples of the social, technical and environmental concerns involved in design, let's look at the design of a resource recovery plant (a plant that sorts recyclables from mixed wastes).

Social concerns might include: Who will pay for the facility? Where is the most socially acceptable location for the plant? Is there really a need for such a facility or are there other options available, such as separating recyclable materials before they enter the waste stream? Who will construct the facility? Will the labor force come from outside the community? Will it be union or non-union? These are all important social concerns that should be considered early in the design process.

Technical concerns are the most obvious: What is the most economical way to construct and maintain the facility? What type of materials will be used in its construction? How long will the facility last before it needs repair? How can the plant be designed so that it is aesthetically pleasing in its surroundings? Are the necessary tools, materials and skilled labor force available locally?

Environmental concerns are becoming increasingly important: Will the facility have a negative effect on the local ecology? What noise levels can be expected from normal operations? Are local streams or rivers likely to be affected by soil erosion during construction? Will the site be located in environmentally fragile areas, such as wetlands or marshes?

This incinerator turns trash into energy. It seems like a good idea, but how will it affect the community? Does it produce toxins that impact the local environment? Does it have a high noise level? Are the local roads adequate for the continual stream of trucks carrying the refuse? Questions such as these must be considered before the facility is built. (Courtesy of Wheelabrator Frye)

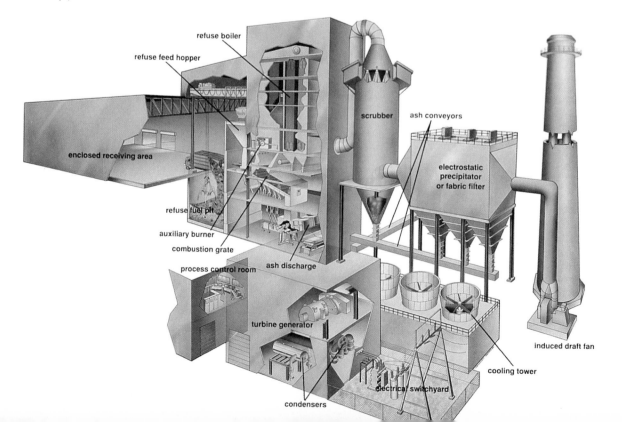

refuse boiler

refuse feed hopper

scrubber

ash conveyors

enclosed receiving area

electrostatic precipitator or fabric filter

refuse fuel pit

auxiliary burner

combustion grate

process control room

ash discharge

turbine generator

induced draft fan

cooling tower

electrical switchyard

condensers

Once the social, technical and environmental concerns have been recognized, the final design decisions must balance their relative importance. The most socially appropriate site may have environmental problems associated with it. Technical design decisions may require that outside labor be hired to construct the facility, although social concerns would favor hiring local workers. Having a clear set of guidelines helps the designer make these difficult decisions.

. . . .

Social Guidelines

Social guidelines are the most elusive. It is not easy to measure the importance of a social impact, because it is not something that can be easily seen. In addition, many social concerns are culturally based. What is socially appropriate in a rural township in the midwest may not be socially appropriate in a city on the west coast.

Nevertheless, there are some basic social guidelines that should be considered in the design process: (1) social impact, (2) cultural sensitivity, and (3) appropriate social siting.

It is important to consider the needs of the handicapped when designing public buildings, such as the inclusion of automatic doors. (Courtesy of Frank C. Nahser, Inc.)

Social Precept 1: Design should have a positive social impact.

In order to assess the social impact, the following questions should be addressed:

1. Is this construction project needed in the community?

2. What short- and long-term effect will this new construction project have on local community members?

3. What long-term effect will this project have on the economic stability of the region?

4. What impact will the construction project have on the institutions of society (family, community, state, religion, trade, education, and recreation)?

5. How will this project benefit the community in the long run (in say, 20 years)?

Social Precept 2: Design should be culturally sensitive.

Cultural sensitivity design relates to the history of the region. If, for example, an area of a city has a rich heritage in stone masonry, it would be culturally insensitive to place a high-rise glass-exterior building in this neighborhood. Questions that rise out of social precept 2 are:

1. Does this construction project threaten any aspect of the local history of the area?

2. Does this construction project enhance the cultural heritage of the area?

3. Does this construction project blend aesthetically with the architectural history of the region?

Social Precept 3: Design should be sited appropriately according to the intended use.

Many areas have zoning ordinances concerning appropriate siting of development projects based on intended use. Single-family residential districts, multi-family housing districts, commercial districts, and industrial districts are just a few examples of zones established by local governments to insure that development is socially appropriate.

Zoning ordinances often have rules governing the design of structures as well as location. Zoning ordinances should be reviewed early in the design process. If zoning ordinances are not available, the siting of a construction project must address the following questions:

1. How are already established neighborhoods impacted by the siting of this construction project?

A shipyard is a construction project with a long-term effect. Once in place, it often becomes linked to the economic stability of the region. (Courtesy of Conoco)

2. Which alternative sites in the region have a similar intended use (i.e. industrial areas, residential areas, commercial areas, etc.).

Technical Guidelines

There are technical guidelines relevant to all construction systems, regardless of type. These are durability, ease of construction, maintainability, functional requirements and aesthetics. That is, all structures, whether they are bridges, houses or dams, should be durable, easily constructed, maintainable, functional, and aesthetically pleasing.

■ Durability

Durability is defined as the life expectancy of a structure. The Hoover Dam, for example, has a life expectancy of 300–400 years. An average house built today may have a life expectancy of 80–200 years. Elements of a structure also have life expectancies. Asphalt roofs usually have only a 15–25 year life expectancy and need to be replaced after that time. Factors influencing durability include material choice, material application and craftsmanship.

Technical Precept 1: Materials should be chosen that have the greatest durability, while considering cost, availability, application and the quality of the work.

Material choice is directly related to durability. Some materials are clearly more durable than others. However, there is a trade-off between durability and material cost. Less expensive products are often substituted for most durable products in order to keep the total price of the project to a minimum. Locally available materials are usually less expensive and easier to replace than those from other regions. Therefore, they are used more often, even though they might not be as durable. Installation costs also affect choice of material. For example, cedar roofs may last 100 years; but the installation costs are high compared with asphalt shingles. When choosing material, it is important to consider both short- and long-term economics.

Material application requires an understanding of the advantages and disadvantages of various materials. Because structures are often made from many materials, it is also important to understand how different materials are used together. For example, high quality cedar siding does not usually need maintenance during its long life span. However, if it is applied with nails that rust, the result may be a siding that needs to be maintained or

Adobe is a material indigenous to the American southwest. Although in a wetter climate it would deteriorate easily, adobe is both durable and inexpensive in this dry region. This adobe church is still in excellent condition after 200 years. (Courtesy of Sarbo)

replaced before its life cycle is reached. Using galvanized nails would be more appropriate for a low maintenance, long-life siding.

Craftsmanship of any structure may increase or decrease its durability. High craft takes advantage of the life expectancies of materials chosen. Poor craft may reduce the overall durability of a structure. If, for example, windows and doors are not properly sealed from the rain, the wood framing members will degrade from moisture.

■ Ease of Construction

Technical Precept 2: When designing a structure, consider the technical construction processes that are needed. Use locally available tools, machines, and skilled labor, whenever possible.

Most technical construction processes require tools, machines and a skilled work force. If it is difficult to acquire the tools and machines needed in the construction process, then an alternative process may be chosen. Furthermore, if the technical skills of the local work force are not adequate for the design, then choosing another design or method may be preferable to bringing in an outside labor force.

Difficult construction processes require more time, which adds to the overall construction costs. Time overruns are sometimes greater than the cost of materials.

The complex technical process involved in the construction of this egg-shaped theatre required highly specialized equipment and knowledge. This would be an inappropriate project if cost was a critical factor of if the available labor force was relatively unskilled. (Courtesy of the Empire Performing Arts Center, Albany, New York)

Using a strong design element focuses attention on the entrance of the building. (Photo by Rhonda Fournier)

■ Maintainability

Maintainability is related to the long-term operating costs after construction has been completed. By considering operating efficiency and material depreciation, the designer can reduce the maintenance requirements of a structure.

Technical Precept 3: Design should include long-term efficiency and depreciation considerations, thus minimizing system maintenance requirements.

Operating efficiency is the cost associated with the structure after it is built. This may be related to energy efficiency. Structures that require heating and cooling, can be designed to minimize energy requirements, thus reducing overall operating costs. In some cases, the monthly cost of energy to heat and cool a structure may be higher than the monthly mortgage payments. Long-term energy efficiency is an important consideration.

• •

Depreciation costs are the costs associated with the normal degradation of components of construction systems. This is usually related to materials used. Wood siding that has been painted will require painting in just a few years. Wood siding that has never been painted will weather about 1/8–1/4 of an inch per one hundred years. Leaving natural wood siding unfinished reduces overall depreciation and maintenance costs.

■ Functional Requirements

Functional requirements are based on the overall purpose of the construction system. Whether the purpose is sheltering, supporting, containing, directing, or transporting, the structure must meet the overall functional requirements. In order to meet these requirements properly, the design must follow sound engineering principles concerning forces and loads. When these requirements are not met, structural systems can fail, sometimes with catastrophic results.

Technical Precept 4: Design must meet general functional requirements by following sound engineering principles.

For example, in Kansas City, an interior balcony in the Hyatt Regency collapsed on June, 1986 killing 28 people. In New York State, an interstate bridge collapsed killing 7 people in March, 1987.

In less catastrophic cases, when a roof leaks it fails to meet the functional requirement of sheltering people from outside natural elements. When water pipes break in cold weather the structure fails to meet the thermal functional requirement. Each construction system must meet a host of functional requirements associated with its intended purpose.

The concrete railing sections of this parking garage collapsed because of inadequate functional requirements. (Courtesy of the Worcester Telegram and Gazette)

In 1977, the collapse of an earthen dam led to a destructive flood in Johnstown, Pennsylvania. The dam did not meet functional design precepts. (Courtesy of the Johnstown Historical Society)

Although the lines of this Japanese pagoda are complex and varied, visual chaos is avoided by repetition of the design elements. This creates a pleasing harmonious balance. (Courtesy of Japan National Tourist Organization)

■ Aesthetics

Aesthetics refers to the beauty and form of construction systems. Louis Sullivan (1856-1924), the great Chicago architect stated that **form follows function.** This means that structural integrity is a precondition for aesthetically pleasing buildings. Another great architect, Frank Lloyd Wright (1869-1959) took Sullivan's concept one step further by saying that **form and function are one.**

Wright meant that beautiful buildings are a result of form and function serving the same purpose. Although aesthetics are subjective, there are certain principles and elements of design that are basic. One recurring theme of aesthetically pleasing design is simplicity.

General design elements are used in all construction systems, whether or not the architect, designer, or engineer is aware of them. Some of these are texture, pattern, unity, variety, and emphasis. More specific elements include line, space, shape, mass and color. An infinite number of combinations can be created with the general and specific design elements.

Granite may have a rough surface or it may be polished to a smooth surface. When the texture is actually as it appears it is tactile texture. (Photo by Brent Miller)

Texture and pattern are surface elements. Texture is smooth, bumpy, rough, gritty and so on. It is related to the feel or the perception of feel (how a surface looks like it would feel).

Pattern is the use of recurring motifs or themes. In many cases the structural elements themselves create the recurring themes. In other cases, pattern is added as a facade to the structural element. The structural cables used in a suspension bridge are recurring form patterns.

Technical Precept 5: Unity and variety are design elements that must be balanced in order to avoid visual chaos and visual boredom.

Unity and variety are elements that must be carefully balanced so that the design appears simple without becoming boring. If sunsets were all identical, they would soon become boring. Variety provides visual interest by breaking up unity, but too much variety creates chaos.

Technical Precept 6: Emphasize only one feature in a structure, otherwise visual chaos may be the result.

Emphasis is a highlighted visual point that attracts our attention. It is usually the first thing people look at when they approach a structure. For example, a designer can emphasize the entrance way of a building by carefully choosing elements of design that call attention to it. Most structures have some point of area of visual emphasis. When there is more than one point of emphasis in a design, the result may be visual chaos and clutter.

Specific design elements which make up the general elements include line, shape (form) and color. All constructed structures include a combination of line, space and color.

The strong use of geometric line combines the many parts of this house together into a visual whole. (Photo by Joseph W. Molitor)

Line is the most fundamental element of design. Line can be used in many ways. Geometric lines, abstract lines, symbolic lines, contour lines are just a few of the possibilities. Lines can be used as pattern, texture, or emphasis. St. Mary's Cathedral in Tokyo, Japan, uses contour lines to create an elegant visual sculptural shape. The John Hancock Building (see cover photo) in Boston, Massachusetts, uses horizontal and vertical lines to create a strong rectangular pattern that emphasizes stability.

• •

Shape is also known as form. Two types of shape are geometric and abstract (or free-form). Geometric shapes, such as the square, triangle and circle, are the most commonly used shapes for structures. Abstract, or free-form, shapes have a sculptural quality. Transporting structures often are characterized by free-form shapes. These shapes often require specialized construction techniques.

Color is a powerful element of design that can be manipulated to create many effects. Colors have a powerful psychological effect. Psychologists believe that warm colors, such as red, yellow and orange, stimulate emotion, while cool colors, such as blue and green, relax people. Many of the darker colors found in nature are referred to as earth tones. Earth tones are particularly popular in construction systems because they help structures blend harmoniously with the natural environment.

. . . .

Environmental Guidelines

There are guidelines to minimize environmental impacts and use principles from nature that apply to construction systems. Proper waste disposal, protection of wetlands and other environmentally fragile areas, noise pollution and protection of aquifers are all environmental issues that must be considered when designing construction systems. Even wildlife concerns can affect construction design. For example, because the Alaska pipeline cut across the elk migration route, the pipeline had to be revised off the ground to allow the elk to pass under. Fish ladders must be built into dams along migratory routes of fish, especially salmon.

Let's look at how one major environmental issue, soil erosion and sedimentation is affected by construction and how it can be managed.

Many dams have been built across the migratory routes of the salmon. If fish ladders were not designed into these dams, the salmon could not spawn and the entire species would be endangered. This fish ladder in Holyoke, Massachusetts, shows how the fish can swim up over the dam and continue their route to the spawning grounds. Later the young salmon will come down the ladders on their way out to sea. (Courtesy of Massachusetts Electric)

Soil erosion is a serious problem facing the construction industry. Erosion from construction projects is 2000 times greater than erosion on forested areas. The resulting sedimentation is clogging our waterways. (Courtesy of the U.S. Dept. of Interior)

■ Minimizing Soil Erosion

Soil erosion is one major environmental impact associated with most construction systems. Land is cleared and graded in the construction process and this leads to uncontrolled runoff of water and the resulting erosion and sedimentation. Each year more than a million acres of land in the United States is converted from agricultural and forested land to suburban and urban land. Houses, shopping centers, schools, industrial parks, highways, and airports are continually being built. These construction projects drastically increase runoff.

Soil erosion from construction projects is about 10 times greater than on agricultural land, 200 times greater than on pasture land and 2,000 times greater than on forested areas. Soil type, slope, rainfall, and construction methods affect the amount of this erosion and sedimentation.

Erosion and sedimentation can be economically controlled by following certain general principles when land is prepared for construction projects.

Environmental Precepts 1–5:
1) **Use soils that are suited for development.**
2) **Leave soils bare for the shortest possible time.**
3) **Reduce the velocity and control the flow of runoff.**
4) **Detail runoff on the site to trap sediment.**
5) **Release runoff safely to downstream areas.**

■ Designing with Nature

Other environmental guidelines focus on utilizing the special characteristics of the natural environment in order to make the best use of material and energy resources. The local geology and climate determine what materials are available locally for building and what energy sources are appropriate for a particular location.

Environmental Precept 6: Utilize indigenous materials when the quality and price of the materials are reasonably competitive and the renewable rate and local ecology remain healthy.

Indigenous materials should be used if the quality and price are competitive with similar imported materials. However, when local materials are cheap, there is a tendency to use them up. These materials should not be exploited beyond the regeneration capabilities of nature of it using them will harm the natural ecology of the area. For example, if trees are to be harvested and processed into building materials, the rate of harvesting should match with the rate of regeneration. A long-range forestry plan is necessary when wood is harvested and used as a building material.

When needed materials cannot be found locally at a reasonable price, it is necessary to import them from other regions. The importing of materials from great distances increases the negative environmental impact in two ways. Greater amounts of energy are consumed during the transportation process and the conversion of this energy negatively impacts the natural environment by causing air pollution.

Environmental Precept 7: Design should conserve construction materials.

The geodesic dome is an example of "doing more with less." Because the geodesic dome can carry heavy loads in comparison to other types of structures, it uses less materials to do the same job. (Photo by Stan Komacek)

By following sound engineering practices, structures can be designed to meet the forces and loads that are anticipated. Over-designing structures, beyond accepted safety margins, is a waste of construction materials. R. Buckminster Fuller, the inventor of the geodesic dome, coined the term **"doing more with less."** This means that engineers should optimize materials in order to conserve the earth's resources. The geodesic dome is a lightweight structure that can carry very heavy loads in comparison to other structures. This means that less construction materials are needed to meet the same performance standards as other sheltering structures.

Environmental Precept 8: Energy systems of structure should be based on renewable energy sources when the microclimate of the sites are appropriate.

The environmental impact of energy systems varies depending on the type of energy system used in the structure. Fossil fuels, such as coal, oil and gas are finite and produce pollutants that enter the atmosphere. In many cases, solar and indirect solar systems minimize negative environmental impacts.

Energy systems that are needed to support the construction system after construction should be found locally and be renewable if possible. Climatology of a region often helps determine what energy source is most appropriate. Solar energy systems and indirect systems (i.e. wind, hydropower) should be incorporated into building design if the **microclimate** (local climate at the site) is appropriate to such applications.

Environmental Precept 9: The energy systems of structures should follow energy conservation guidelines.

Using energy conservation techniques in building design also helps minimize environmental impact. These measures apply to most sheltering structures such as houses, apartments and commercial buildings.

• •

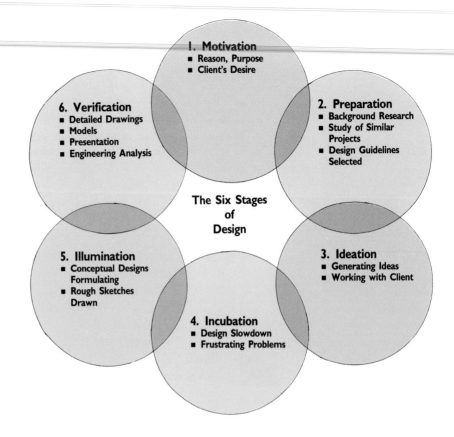

The Six Stages
of
Design

1. **Motivation**
   - Reason, Purpose
   - Client's Desire

2. **Preparation**
   - Background Research
   - Study of Similar Projects
   - Design Guidelines Selected

3. **Ideation**
   - Generating Ideas
   - Working with Client

4. **Incubation**
   - Design Slowdown
   - Frustrating Problems

5. **Illumination**
   - Conceptual Designs Formulating
   - Rough Sketches Drawn

6. **Verification**
   - Detailed Drawings
   - Models
   - Presentation
   - Engineering Analysis

II. THE DESIGN PROCESS

Most construction systems require a design process that generally consists of six stages:

- Motivation

- Preparation

- Ideation

- Incubation

- Illumination

- Verification

This process is nonlinear; it usually does not occur step by step. The stages overlap and it is possible for the designer(s) and client to be in more than one stage of the process at the same time. However, for discussion it is convenient to study the stages one at a time.

Designers must work closely with their clients, blending their creativity with the client's needs. (Photo by Brent Miller)

Motivation

Building on speculation is more risky, but can stimulate the buying process in a slow period. (Photo by Brent Miller)

Motivation provides the purpose or reason for undertaking new projects. Without it, the process would not begin.

Motivation is often a blend between the client's desire or objective and the designer's creativity. It is often said that architects or engineers are only as creative as their clients allow them to be.

In this stage the general problem is defined by the client and communicated to the engineer, architect or contractor.

When architects as famous as Louis Kahn or Frank Lloyd Wright worked on a project, their clients tended to give them "creative license," the freedom to design without interference. Most architects and designers, however, must work very closely with their clients.

Clients take many different forms. A client may be an individual, a corporation, a government agency, or a public municipality. In some cases, an architectural or engineering firm may design and build a structure first in order to attract a client during the planning or construction stages. Large office complexes, condominiums and housing developments sometimes are built in this way. This is called building on speculation. It is more common, however, to have a client before development begins.

Preparation

The preparation stage has two parts:

- Background research and
- The establishment of general guidelines.

Background research is very important for any new construction system. It is usually done by the engineering or architectural firm, not by the client. Some firms have very detailed files of completed projects that are reviewed in preparing for a similar project. Other firms must go to libraries, consultants, or out into the field in order to research a new construction project or system.

Social, technical and environmental guidelines should be established during this stage. These guidelines must be thoroughly researched at the preparation stage, because they help direct the design effort not only at this stage, but through all stages of the construction design project.

Careful preparation is critical to a successful construction project. The background research done now will guide the entire design process. (Photo by Brent Miller)

Ideation

The ideation or conceptual stage is often overlooked in the construction design process. It is the stage that promotes new and unusual ideas, when creativity is fostered. **Creativity** can be defined as the combination of things and thoughts in new ways to produce something unique. Ideation is a conscious process to produce new and useful designs that are substantially different from past construction projects.

■ Fostering Creativity

There are many formal techniques that can help the designer or design team develop creative ideas. One of the most popular ideation techniques is mindstorming. Under the title "brainstorming" this technique was developed by advertising executive Alex Osborne in an attempt to promote creativity among his employees. Two other techniques that are related to brainstorming include sketchstorming and modelstorming. The sketchstorming techniques uses rapid two dimensional sketches to help the designer(s) develop new ideas. The modelstorming technique uses rapid three dimensional prototypes to promote creativity.

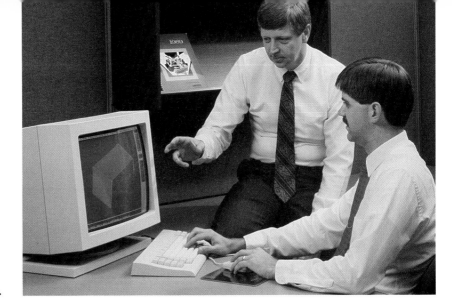

Computer-aided design (CAD) systems are becoming increasingly popular. A CAD system can not only replace the drawing board, it can also help the designer develop and refine ideas.

Guidelines for mindstorming, sketchstorming and modelstorming include:

- No criticism is allowed

- Wild ideas are encouraged

- Many ideas are needed

- Spinoff others' ideas

Although there are exceptions, mindstorming lends itself to small groups, such a design team, while sketchstorming and modelstorming are best for individuals.

Computer-aided design systems (CAD systems) have gained popularity in recent years. Although CAD systems are usually thought of as a way to replace the tedious drafting work of the traditional drawing board, their greatest potential lies in their ability to aid the designer in developing and refining ideas. They can be tools to stimulate the already creative designer.

. . . .

Incubation

Frustration often builds up during the creative process. Taking a break at this point can bring a new perspective to the problem. (Photo by Brent Miller)

In the incubation stage, design production slows down because of a high level of frustration with difficult or unforeseen problems. One way to deal with this frustration is to take a break from the design work for a predetermined period of time. After a break, it is often easier to look at the problem in a refreshed manner.

Some firms assign "fresh blood" or new designers to help out on difficult problems. Some may place a particular construction design problem "on the back burner" for a while and work on a different design. In some cases architects and engineers must abandon their direction all together and go back to the first stages of the process (the motivation and preparation stages).

. . . .

The illumination stage is often triggered by a period of relaxation. (Photo by Brent Miller)

Illumination

The illumination stage is where a possible solution to a particular problem suddenly appears in the designer's mind. When this happens, it is important to quickly transfer the idea to paper either in words or in drawings.

This is not just a one-time occurrence. In the design of most construction systems, many small ideas or solutions will suddenly appear to the designer. And, for some strange reason, these solutions often appear while the designer is relaxing.

This stage may be triggered by the ideation stage through techniques of mindstorming, sketchstorming and modelstorming. It is important to keep a sketchbook in case the solution presents itself during unusual hours. Buckminster Fuller always kept a sketchbook at hand to visualize his ideas.

Verification

Verification is also known as the detailing stage. The general solution must be detailed to (1) meet the criteria developed in the preparation stage and (2) communicate with all people involved with the construction project. This stage produces detailed drawings, models, presentations, and structural analysis.

Detailed drawings may include architectural drawings and engineering drawings. Scaled models are often used to communicate the design concept in 3-D. In some cases a design presentation accompanied with a design brief may be used to communicate with clients or client groups. Structural analysis is also part of the verification stage. If detailed structural components are not properly sized, catastrophe may be the result.

Drawings are used to communicate details of the design project to all of the groups involved with the project. Clients, engineers, contractors, and subcontractors need these details to carry out the project.

Detailed drawings are also used for bidding purposes. For example, electricians must review the electrical plan before they can estimate how much the job will cost. Without detailed drawings it would be impossible for contractors and subcontractors to place bids.

Scaled models communicate the design concept in three dimensions. Models are often used to communicate with the clients. Three-dimensional models help less technically trained person visualize how the final outcome may look. Many details, such as electricity and plumbing, are usually left out of a three-dimensional model. The two-dimensional drawings are used to build the scaled model.

Structural analysis is a very important part of the verification stage. It is the use of applied math and physics to insure that the structural com-

Detailed drawings are used to communicate the completed design to clients and construction workers.

Process

ponents of the structure will be sufficient to withstand the predicted loads, stresses and stains associated with its expected use. Sometimes structural analysis is subcontracted to a structural engineer or engineering firm.

The design presentation is usually made to the client(s). It may be accompanied by a design brief, two-dimensional drawings and sometimes three dimensional models. At this point, the client may approve the design concept as is, have the design concept slightly modified or reject the design concept altogether. If the design group has worked closely with the client throughout the entire process, the design is more likely to be approved.

Although some design briefs are quite elaborate, they tend to be short summaries of the entire project. Design briefs are used to highlight the overall nature of the design solution. Designers may also use drawings, renderings, models, structural analysis and economic analysis during the presentation to clients. The client's formal or informal approval must be obtained before construction can begin.

Scale models are often used to present designs to clients. They help less technically trained people visualize how the finished structure will look. This elaborate model was created by architect Louis Kahn. (Courtesy of the University of Pennsylvania)

These are social, technical and environmental guidelines that should be considered in the design process. Basic social criteria to be considered include social impact, cultural sensitivity, and appropriate social siting. Technical guidelines relevant to all structures are durability, ease of construction, maintainability, functional requirements and aesthetics. Environmental guidelines are intended to minimize environmental impact. This is particularly important with soil erosion and sedimentation. Other environmental guidelines focus on designing with nature, utilizing the special characteristics of the natural environment in order to make the best use of material and energy resources.

The design process unites the understanding of tools, materials and processes with creative ideas. Understanding the phases of the process can help all of us become more creative in the designing of construction systems.

Although it varies from designer to designer, there are general phases that are common. It begins with desire or **motivation.** Homework or background research is necessary to **prepare** the designer. Many creative **ideas** are needed to develop the design concept. Frustration, at some point, usually sets in and the design project slows down or **incubates** for a while. And, for some unapparent reason, the construction solution flashes or **illuminates** itself to the relaxed and well prepared designer. The illuminated idea must be communicated to others and **verified** through detailing. This detailing takes the form of architectural drawings, engineering drawings, structural analysis, the design presentation and the design brief.

. . . .

Study Questions

1. What are the major problems of balancing social, technical and environmental guidelines associated with construction systems?

2. List and describe at least three technical guidelines of construction systems and discuss how these guidelines are related to costs.

3. Describe the difference between "form follows function" and "form and function are one."

4. Find examples of texture, pattern, unity, variety and emphasis in your school building or neighborhood.

5. List three techniques that can be used to control soil erosion and sedimentation during the construction process.

6. Describe what is meant by "doing more with less."

7. Why must a designer(s) communicate closely with a client throughout the entire design process?

8. At which stage in the design process is creativity fostered the most? Explain.

9. Background research or "doing your homework" is part of which phase? Explain the importance of this phase.

10. What are some techniques to deal with the frustration that is common during the incubation phase?

11. Why are sketchbooks important, especially during the ideation and illumination phases?

12. Why is it critical to develop detailed drawings and models in the verification phase of the design process?

. . . .

Precepts Governing Design Guidelines

Social Precepts

1. Design should have a positive social impact.

2. Design should be culturally sensitive.

3. Design should be sited appropriately according to the intended use.

Technical Precepts

1. Materials should be chosen that have the greatest durability while considering cost, availability, application and the quality of the work.

2. When designing a structure, consider the technical construction processes that are needed. Use locally available tools, machines and workers, whenever possible.

3. Design should include long-term efficiency and depreciation considerations, thus minimizing system maintenance requirements.

. . . .

4. Design must meet general functional requirfements by following sound engineering principles.

5. Unity and variety are design elements that must be balanced in order to avoid visual chaos and visual boredom.

6. Emphasize only one feature in a structure, otherwise visual chaos may be the result.

Environmental Precepts 1–5

a) Use soils that are suited for development.
b) Leave soils bare for the shortest possible time.
c) Reduce the velocity and control the flow of runoff.
d) Detain runoff on the site to trap sediments.
e) Release runoff safely to downstream areas.

6. Utilize indigenous materials when the quality and price of the materials are reasonably competitive and the renewable rate and ecology remain healthy.

7. Design should conserve construction materials.

8. Energy systems of structures should be based on renewable energy sources when the microclimate of the sites are appropriate.

9. The energy systems of structures should follow energy conservation guidelines.

. . . .

Glossary

Aesthetic Of a beautiful quality.

Creativity A process in which people combine ideas, tools and materials in new ways to produce something unique.

Durability Lasting in spite of hard wear or frequent use.

Ideation Developing new and unique ideas.

Illumination A phenomenon where the answer or solution to a problem seems to jump into the investigator's mind without warning.

Incubation A phenomenon where frustration blocks problem solving and creativity for a period of time.

Maintainability Easy to keep in good working order.

Motivation A strong desire to do something.

. . . .

Preparation Gaining background knowledge and/or skill.

Sedimentation In environmental use, it means a result of soil erosion in which particles settle in rivers and lakes.

Verification The answer or solution to a problem is tested and analyzed.

Chapter 7

Construction Processes and Tools

Chapter Objectives

■ There are basic measuring, separating, combining, and forming processes that construction workers should be able to perform.

■ Construction workers must understand and follow all safety rules when using tools, machines, and processes.

■ Construction workers use hand tools, power hand tools, and machines to process information and materials.

■ Separating processes involve using tools to reduce the size and shape of a material by cutting or removing part of the material.

■ Combining processes involve using tools to add one piece of a material to another to build structures or protect materials.

■ Forming processes involve using tools to change the contour or shape of a material.

Key Terms

abrading
adhesive fastening
brick set
builder's level
circular saw
combining processes
crosscut saw
darbying
edging
floating
forming processes
framing square
laser level
mechanical fastening

mortar
pigment
power hammer
power miter box
power plane
primer
rip saw
screeding
separating processes
snips
troweling
vehicle
zigzag rule

Tools and processes have changed a lot since Colonial times in the 16th and 17th centuries. The "pit saw" shown here was used to saw boards using a rip saw: back-breaking work. (Courtesy of the Plimoth Plantation)

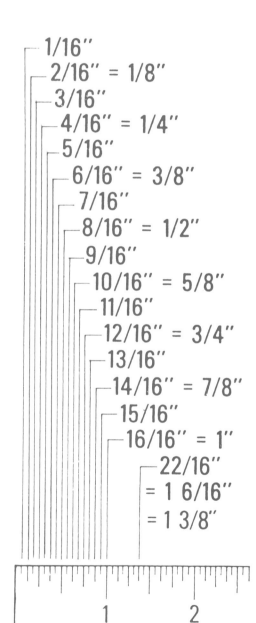

1/16"
2/16" = 1/8"
3/16"
4/16" = 1/4"
5/16"
6/16" = 3/8"
7/16"
8/16" = 1/2"
9/16"
10/16" = 5/8"
11/16"
12/16" = 3/4"
13/16"
14/16" = 7/8"
15/16"
16/16" = 1"
22/16"
= 1 6/16"
= 1 3/8"

1   2

n every field of technology, there are basic tools and processes that are a vital part of how that technology works. No matter how sophisticated our technology may be, workers in technological fields must still be able to use tools to perform basic processes safely and efficiently. This is true in construction technology as well. Construction workers must understand and be able to perform such basic processes as measuring, sawing, drilling, and nailing, to name a few. These basic processes are the important skills that construction workers employ to build the structures in our world.

Competent construction workers must know the tools of their trade— their uses, applications, limitations, and safety considerations. Construction workers become craftspeople through years of studying these processes and developing their tool-use skills. As a student of construction technology you should also know about and be able to perform some of these basic processes using the correct tools safely, properly, and efficiently.

A detailed description of all the processes and tools of construction would be impossible in this text, but a few of the more important and basic ones will be described in this chapter. Four categories of processes and tools will be examined: measuring, separating, forming, and combining.

Measuring Processes

Measuring is a basic process in any field of technology. Workers must be able to measure accurately. In construction, accurate measurement skills are critical to a safe, pleasing, and well-built structure.

■ The English Measurement System

The English system of measurement is used most often in the construction field for linear (length) measurements. The basic unit of measurement in the English system, the inch, is divided into fractional parts, such as 1/2", 1/4", 1/8", 1/16", 1/32", or halves, quarters, eighths, sixteenths, and thirty secondths. The fractional inch measurement system coincides with the common sizes of many standard construction materials: 2 × 4s measure 1-1/2" by 3-1/2", plywood is sold in thicknesses from 1/4" to 3/4", and concrete blocks measure 7-5/8" square by 15-5/8" long.

The Importance of Safety

Construction workers must be able to select the best or correct tool for the job, know how to operate their tools and, above all, they must know and perform the proper safety rules when using tools. Standards of safety in the construction industry are established by OSHA, the Occupational Safety and Health Administration. OSHA, which is a branch of our federal government, is responsible for insuring that workers and the companies they work for maintain safe and healthy working conditions.

Students studying technical fields, such as construction, must also know and follow the safety rules that apply to the tools and processes they are learning. Your teacher will establish the safety rules that apply to the tools and machines you will be using in your construction technology lab. In addition, the following rules are provided as general guidelines for safety in construction technology:

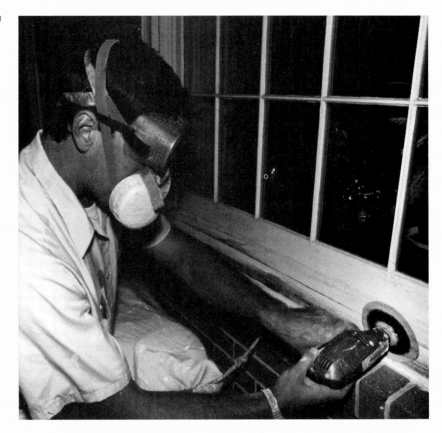

- Learn all the safety rules that apply to the construction lab in your school and to each of the tools and machines you will be using.
- Always obtain permission from your teacher before using any tool or machine.
- Always use proper safety equipment, such as tool and machine guards, safety glasses, hard hats, and gloves.
- Use proper lifting techniques, get assistance or use proper lifting equipment when moving heavy materials. Nearly one-fourth of all construction-related accidents occur during material handling and lifting operations.
- Avoid horseplay in the construction lab and on the building site.
- Always obtain first aid for any injury, no matter how minor it may seem.
- Keep the lab and all work sites clear of all potential hazards; good housekeeping is important to safety.
- Keep all tools in good working condition; replace or repair any damaged tools.
- Provide adequate ventilation for all painting, finishing, gluing, or other processes that create dust, fumes, or vapors.

- Always follow established safety precautions when working on the installation or repair of electrical systems.
- Use the right tool for the job; tools should only be used for the purpose for which they were designed. Tools are for work; do not play with tools.
- Respect the power and dangers involved in using tools and machines; do not take short cuts to save time.

Every year, thousands of people are injured when working with tools. Following these general safety rules and the other specific guidelines established by your teacher will help you avoid injuries.

The fractional divisions of an inch are an indication of the number of these parts found in one inch. For example, there are two halves, four quarters, eight eighths, sixteen sixteenths and thirty-two thirty-secondths in one inch. Each of these divisions is identified on scales and rulers with vertical markings. The longest markings are for inches, the next longest for halves, then quarters, eighths, etc. with each marking being progressively shorter. In addition, the divisions are multiples of each other. As an example, 1/8″ is equal to 2/16″ and 4/32″; 3/4″ is equal to 6/8″, 12/16″, and 24/32″. In these cases, the fraction is always reduced to its smallest multiple until it can not be reduced further.

■ Measuring Tools

Construction workers use a variety of measuring tools. The type of measuring tool used and its number of divisions will vary depending upon the accuracy and detail required on the job. As an example, rough framing carpentry may require accurate measurement to one-eighth or one-quarter inch, while finish carpentry requires accuracy to one thirty-secondth inch.

Pocket Tape Measure ■ One of the most important measuring tools is the pocket tape or tape measure. The tape measure consists of a flexible steel tape that retracts into a metal or plastic case. The tape has a concave shape which allows it to remain rather firm and rigid when extended. Tape measures come in a variety of lengths, with 6′ to 25′ being commonly used. For larger construction jobs, lengths up to 100 feet are also available.

The pocket measure is the constant companion of the carpenter. Carpenters building a house may start out using 50′ tape measures in the framing stage. In the later finishing stages where working dimensions are smaller, shorter tape measures suffice. (*Right:* Courtesy of the United Brotherhood of Carpenters. *Above:* Courtesy of Lufkin)

Tape measures have a loose hook on the end of the tape. The hook is loose to permit accurate measurement of inside and outside measurements. The amount of play in the hook is equal to the thickness of the metal material used to make the hook itself. By moving back and forth, the hook adjusts for its own thickness. Tape measures with square cases often have the size of the case printed on them. This allows a worker to make accurate inside measurements, such as between a doorway, by adding the case size to the measurement read off the tape. Some cases also include a locking mechanism to prevent the tape from retracting while a measurement is being taken.

Zigzag Rule ■ The **zigzag rule** is another common measuring tool for construction. The zigzag rule is made from hardwood and folds into 6″ lengths. The rigidity of the zigzag (or folding) rule makes it suitable when the flexibility of steel tapes is undesirable. Measurement divisions are printed on both sides of folding rules and run in opposite directions. This permits measurement from one direction to be checked quickly from the other direction without turning the tape around. Six feet is the most common length of the folding rule.

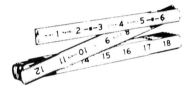

Folding zigzag rule.

■ Layout and Checking Tools

Being able to measure length accurately is often only one half the job. Workers must also be able to use other tools for layout and checking activities, such as laying out cutting lines, identifying the placement of structural members and drilling locations and checking for square, plumb, and level. These are measurement processes that require special tools.

Framing Square ■ Squares are used to measure angles, most often 90° angles, or square. The **framing square,** also called a rafter square, is the most commonly used layout and checking tool in construction. Framing squares have a multitude of uses, such as laying out roof rafters, marking angular cuts on boards, laying out stair stringers, and checking corner joints for square. The most common framing square has a 24″ long by 2″ wide blade with a 16″ long by 1-1/2″ wide tongue.

The framing square is one of the most versatile measuring tools available to construction workers. A quality framing square can be used not only for measuring length and squareness, but the many tables printed on the square can be used to calculate the hypotenuse of a right triangle (the brace table), board feet (the essex board measure table) and a number of different rafter angles (the rafter table).

Framing square.

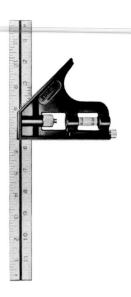

Combination Square ■ The combination square has a 12″ long steel blade that can be moved along a handle. The handle has 45° and 90° angles that can be used for marking cutting lines on boards. The handle also incorporates a small spirit level and scribing tool.

Try Square ■ Try squares commonly have a 6″ or 12″ blade fixed to a handle at a 90° angle. Like the combination square, the try square is used to mark cutting lines across boards.

All squares are precision instruments. Construction workers need to be confident that their square is measuring angles accurately. Squares should not be dropped or abused because they may become distorted and give inaccurate measurements.

Hand Level ■ The hand level is used to check level and plumb in building members. An aluminum or hardwood frame, usually 24″ or 28″ in length, contains several spirit level vials. The vials contain a bubble that, when aligned with markings on the vial, indicate level or plumb. Special purpose levels come in 4′ and 6′ sizes with additional vials for larger surfaces and more accurate measurement checks. Like squares, levels are precision instruments that should not be dropped. The glass vials can be shattered or become distorted. Fortunately, levels have several vials so that if one becomes broken the level is still usable. The vials are also located in different positions and orientations so that no matter how the level is picked up it can be used to check level or plumb.

Line Level ■ The line level is a small, single vial level that can be suspended on a tightly stretched string or line. Line levels are used to establish or check level between two horizontal points that cannot be reached by a hand level. Masons often use line levels to check the levelness of brick or concrete block walls.

Parts of the Builder's Level

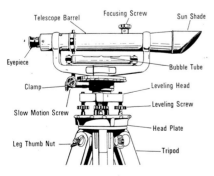

Telescope Barrel
Focusing Screw
Sun Shade
Eyepiece
Bubble Tube
Clamp
Leveling Head
Slow Motion Screw
Leveling Screw
Head Plate
Leg Thumb Nut
Tripod

Builder's Level ■ The **builder's level** is a tool used for identifying the corners and boundaries of a structure, checking the depth and levelness of excavations, and laying out the position of footers, frames, and concrete forms. It consists of a telescope mounted on a tripod. Workers site a target rod through the telescope to make their measurements.

Plumb Rod ■ A plumb rod is a weighted tool attached to the end of a string, it is used to measure plumb or vertical trueness. When suspended from a given point, the plumb bob can be used to check the vertical alignment of two points. The plumb bob is also used in conjunction with the builder's level.

One of the most recent innovations in the construction field is the application of the laser for measurement processes. **Laser levels** are now common in construction.

The laser level used in construction should not be confused with those used in manufacturing. In manufacturing, high-energy lasers are used to cut and drill steel, plastic, and other materials. These lasers can be very dangerous and require extreme safety precautions. Construction laser levels have a low energy output that is comparatively safe and cannot cut materials. However, the small red light beam of even a low energy laser can cause damage if the light is directed into the eye.

The laser beam is created when electric energy excites electrons in a helium neon gas. The beam has the characteristic of being perfectly straight. This characteristic makes it applicable for level measurement in excavations and pipeline installation. Some laser levels can be rotated about a center point to project a beam around the inside of a room to locate a level drop ceiling.

■ Material Processing Tools

Measurement tools are used to process information. Workers read information off a scale to determine size, distance, height, depth and other measurements. Most other construction tools are used to process materials. Cutting a steel I-beam, nailing two boards together, drilling a hole, and painting a house are examples of processes that change the size, shape, or characteristics of a material.

Most material processing tools give the worker a mechanical advantage over the materials being processed. Mechanical advantage is a physical phenomenon that occurs when a small force is used to move a larger force. Humans can generate only rather small forces on their own. You can't cut a piece of lumber in half with your bare hands, but with a saw, you can. The saw gives you a mechanical advantage over the board. It extends and amplifies your strength and permits you to perform the important process of sawing. Combining an electric motor with a saw blade to create a power tool, such as a portable circular saw, creates an even greater mechanical advantage for the worker.

HAND TOOL

POWER HAND TOOL

MACHINE

■ Hand Tools, Power Hand Tools, and Machines

There are three classifications of tools: hand tools, power hand tools, and machines. Hand tools, the simplest and smallest tools, are held in the hand to perform work and are powered only by the muscles of the worker. Hammers, hand saws, screwdrivers, and pliers are common examples of hand tools.

Power hand tools are also held in the hand of the worker, but they are powered by another source of power, such as an electric or pneumatic motor.

• •

Construction Jobs Ranked in Order of Risk

Job	Deaths/ 100,000
1. Asbestos and Insulation Workers	78.7
2. Structural Metal Workers	72
3. Bulldozer Operators	39.3
4. Carpenters	33.5
5. Surveyors' Helpers	33.3
6. Roofers	31.9
7. Crane Operators	19.3
8. Plasterers	14.2
9. Construction Inspectors	7.6
10. Engineers	7.3
11. Surveyors	6.1
12. Architects	4.3

Both hand tools and power hand tools must be moved to perform work. Hammers are swung in an arc, screwdrivers rotated, and portable circular saws moved in a straight line.

Machines, on the other hand, remain stationary while work is being performed. Machines incorporate a stationary base or legs that support a powerized tool. Machines are more complex than hand and power hand tools and usually include finer adjustments that can be used to perform more accurate material processing. Common examples of machines used in construction include the radial arm saw, power miter box, and saw buck.

Safety Factors ■ All tools pose certain safety hazards. Some people may think hand tools are very safe, while power hand tools and machines are dangerous to operate. However, every year, more people are actually hurt in accidents with hand tools like hammers, screwdrivers, and chisels, than with power tools. Of course, because of the increased power of machines and power hand tools, the potential for more serious and even potentially fatal injuries exists. No matter what tool you are working with, always respect the potential dangers and follow safe working practices.

· ·

Classifying Material Processes and Tools in Construction

Processes and tools used to change materials can be categorized into three general groups: separating, combining, and forming.

Separating processes involve reducing material size and shape by cutting or removing part of the material. Common examples of separating include sawing boards to length, drilling holes in a wall, and cutting glass to fit a window.

Combining processes involve adding one piece of material to another to build a structure. In construction, materials are commonly combined by nailing, screwing, welding, and gluing. Materials may also be combined to protect one material with another. For example, many construction materials are painted or covered with other finishes for protection from the elements.

Forming processes involve changing the contour or shape of a material. Pouring wet concrete into a form and smoothing the edges of a new sidewalk as it cures are two common examples.

· ·

Separating Processes and Tools

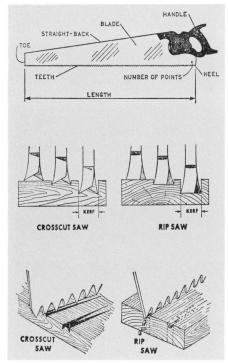

Four separating processes will be examined in this section: sawing, shearing, drilling, and abrading. Each of these processes is basic to construction technology.

■ Sawing Processes

The two main types of saws used for cutting wood are the **crosscut saw** and **rip saw.** Crosscut sawing involves separating a board by cutting across the grain in the wood. Ripping is done by cutting with the wood grain. Because of the difference in these processes, crosscut and rip saws have different types of teeth. Close inspection of a crosscut saw will reveal teeth that look like small pointed knives alternately bent in opposite directions. This bend is called the set. The knife points cut the width of the kerf and the wood chips between are pushed out by the rest of the teeth. As the saw cuts into the board, the set prevents the saw blade from binding.

The rip saw, on the other hand, has flat-bottomed teeth, which are also set in alternating directions. The flat bottoms of the individual teeth remove wood along the grain in chunk-sized pieces, much like a wood chisel.

Because of the difference in the shape of the teeth and the sawing processes, the cutting angles are different for crosscut and rip saws. A rip saw should be held at a 60° angle to the wood, while a crosscut saw works best at a 45° angle.

Crosscut saw. Notice the characteristic 45° angle. (Courtesy of the United Brotherhood of Carpenters)

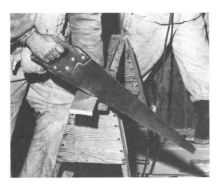

■ Hand Saws

Hand saws, which are made from spring steel, are identified by their length and pitch. Pitch is the coarseness or the number of teeth points in each linear inch of a saw blade. This information is usually stamped on the heel of the saw. Two popular crosscut saws are the 8 point 26″ and the 12 point 26″ models. The 8 point model is used for fast sawing, but produces rather rough cuts. The 12 point cuts slower and produces a smoother cut. The 6 point, 26″ rip saw is commonly used by carpenters. When sawing thin wood materials or when smoother finished cuts are required, a saw with more teeth points should be used. Coarser saws should be used for rough cutting and on heavier lumber.

Two other important saws are the hacksaw and compass saw. Hacksaws are used to cut metal materials. Fine hacksaw blades, such as the 32 pitch (32 teeth per inch), should be used when cutting thin materials, while coarser blades like the 18 pitch should be used for heavier metals. The compass or keyhole saw, with its long, tapered blade, is used to cut curves in plywood and other sheet materials. One important use is for sawing holes in gypsum wall board so electrical outlets and switches can be installed.

■ Power Hand Saws and Machines

Portable Circular Saw ■ One of the most popular power hand saws is the portable **circular saw.** A circular saw, which is used to make straight cuts, has a round saw blade rotated by an electric motor. A trigger switch is built into the handle for easy access by the operator. The base of the saw can be adjusted for the depth and angle of cut.

Various styles and sizes of blades for the circular saw, including rip, crosscut, and combination blades, are available from 6″ to 10″ in diameter. Some blades are carbide tipped to improve their wear characteristics and reduce the need for sharpening. There are also special purpose blades for cutting plywood, plastics, and even masonry materials.

Saber Saw ■ The saber saw, also called a portable jigsaw, has a reciprocating blade. As with the circular saw, there are many different styles of blades based on the particular material being cut, the thickness of the material, and the type of cut being made. Saber saws are most often used to make curved cuttings, but they can also be used for straight cuts. The base can also be adjusted to make bevel cuts.

Power Miter Box ■ The **power miter box,** also called a motorized miter box, consists of a portable circular saw mounted on a stationary stand. The saw pivots on a point and is held in a position above the cutting table by a spring. Straight crosscutting and mitering cuts can be made by positioning a board on the table, adjusting the angle of cut, pulling the trigger control, and pulling the handle down against the spring to bring the blade into contact with the board. Power miter boxes are popular for quick cutting of smaller dimension lumber, such as 2 × 4s.

Radial Arm Saw ■ The radial arm saw, also called an overarm saw, is a machine with a blade and electric motor assembly attached to a yoke that slides forward and backward on an overhead arm. This is one of the most versatile sawing machines. Its multiple adjustments permit the radial arm saw to be used for straight and beveled ripping, as well as straight, mitered, compound mitered, and beveled crosscutting. The blade of a radial arm saw can be replaced with special attachments for shaper cutters, router bits, and dado heads.

The portable circular saw has revolutionized the construction industry. (Courtesy of the United Brotherhood of Carpenters)

The cordless saber saw enables work without availability of electrical outlets. (Courtesy of Black & Decker)

Process

An auger bit is usually used to make a counterbored hole because it makes a relatively flat bottom for the bolt head. The counterbore is made before the shank hole is drilled with a twist drill.

A special tool called a *countersink* is used to make the angled sides of the shank hole. This is done after the hole is drilled.

Saw Buck ■ A saw buck, which is similar to a radial arm saw in operation, is used primarily for frame and trim work. The blade and motor assembly, which travels forward and backward on a pair of overhead guides, can be adjusted for most of the straight and mitered cuts made by the radial arm saw, except for ripping operations.

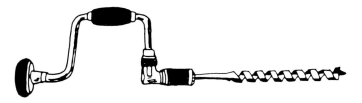

Brace And Bit

■ Drilling Processes and Tools

Drilling is a separating process used to create round holes in materials. In construction, drilled holes can be used for assembling materials with screws or bolts or for running electrical, plumbing, or other utility systems through the frame of a structure.

Drill Bits ■ There are a number of different types of drills and bits. The auger bit, which has a small feed screw centered on the cutting end and a tapered square shank on the other end, is used in a hand brace for drilling processes. The square shank does not fit the auger bits in regular hand and electric drills. Auger bits range in size from 1/4″ to 1-1/4″ in diameter. The size of an auger bit is stamped on the shank end in a whole number that represents the bit size in sixteenths of an inch. As an example, a number 8 auger bit will drill holes 8/16″ or 1/2″ in diameter, a number 16 bit is used for 1″ (16/16″) holes. The feed screw on an auger bit serves to center the bit and also pulls the drill through the wood. A damaged feed screw will probably cause the bit to be useless.

Other types of drill bits include the twist drill, Forstner bit, and expansive bit. Twist drills, which have a continuous diameter and straight shank

Drill bits. *Back* (from left): brad point adjustable counter bore bit, twist drill, boring auger, brad point drill, spade bit, power bore bit, Forstner bit, multi-spur bit. *Front:* countersink bit, counterbore bit, countersink bit with stop collar for setting depth, chamfer bit.

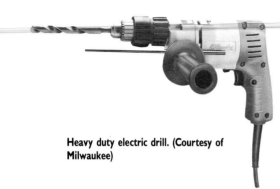

Heavy duty electric drill. (Courtesy of Milwaukee)

The cordless electric drill has become an indispensable tool in construction. This man is using it to drill a high-rise frame. (Courtesy of NASA)

that will fit any collet or chuck of the correct size, are general purpose drill bits used most often to drill holes of 1/2" or less in diameter. Forstner bits don't have a feed screw or a twist. Drilling is done by two lips and a circular steel rim. Forstner bits are used to make relatively smooth, flat-bottomed holes from 1/4" to 2" in diameter. The expansive bit can be adjusted to drill holes larger than one inch in diameter.

The countersink is another important drilling tool. It is used to widen the tops of drilled holes to permit flush mounting of screws with flat heads.

Portable Electric Drill ■ The portable electric drill is a popular power hand tool for performing drilling processes in construction. Three common models, 1/4", 3/8", and 1/2", are rated by the size of the largest shank that can be fitted into the chuck. Most electric drills have a trigger switch and one or more special features, such as continuous or variable speed, reversibility, or rechargeable batteries for cordless operation. Accessories can also be purchased for driving screws and drilling in masonry materials.

■ Abrading Processes and Tools

Abrading, also called sanding, is a separating process that uses abrasives to remove small bits of materials to create a smooth surface for painting or other finishing operations. Finishing operations, such as painting or varnishing, magnify any blemishes like scratches, dents, or machining marks that are on the surface of materials. These blemishes cannot be covered over and hidden by paint, no matter how many coats are applied. They must first be smoothed with abrasives.

Structural frames are not often sanded, unless they will be visible and exposed to the elements. More often, the interior and exterior finish carpentry work, such as window and door trim, wooden baseboards, and door jams, are sanded to prepare them for finishing.

Coated Abrasives ■ Coated abrasives consist of a paper or cloth backing with tiny abrasive particles glued to one surface. The abrasive particles, called grit, are crushed synthetic or natural mineral particles. The grit particles are graded to a particular size for uniform cutting and abrading. The tiny grit particles cut with an action similar to a chisel.

There are a variety of coated abrasives for sanding and smoothing wood, metal, and plastics. The most popular abrasive materials are flint, garnet, and aluminum oxide. Flint is a natural mineral abrasive with a light tan color. Flint is the common inexpensive household sandpaper and is used primarily for sanding wood. Garnet is also a natural mineral abrasive used on wood. It is reddish orange in color and is one of the best and most expensive abrasives. Aluminum oxide is a synthetic abrasive, brownish gray in color, and used primarily for abrading metal materials.

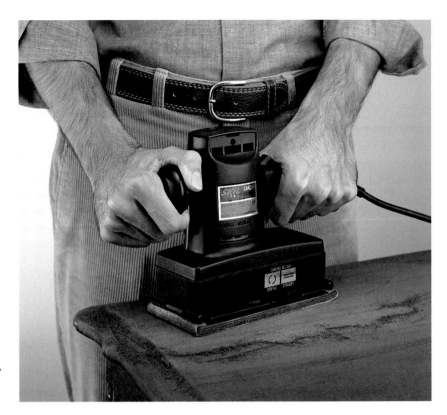

An electric vibrating hand sander. Although more "forgiving" than the belt sander, it nevertheless must be used with care to avoid damage to the wood. (Courtesy of Skil)

A number printed on the back of coated abrasives specifies its coarseness. The range of coarseness is very wide with 40 to 600 being common grit numbers. The smaller the number, the coarser the grit. Flint does not have a grit number; instead, designations such as very fine, fine, medium, and coarse are used.

Hand sanding processes are often sufficient for small jobs, but most often power hand tools, such as oscillating, vibrating, or belt sanders are used. Each of these tools is hand held and uses electric or pneumatic power to enhance the cutting action of the abrasive. Belt sanders must be kept in motion constantly because they cut quickly and can cause unsightly depressions or even ruin a wooden piece.

■ Shearing Processes and Tools

Shearing involves one or two cutting edges being forced through the material being separated. A simple example of shearing is the common household scissors. Unlike sawing, shearing processes create no chips (small bits of material). Saws remove small bits of wood from the kerf, but shearing tools make a clean cut without creating wasted chips at the point of separation. Shearing tools commonly used in construction include chisels, planes, snips, and knives.

· ·

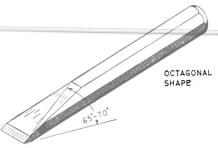

Cold chisel

Wood chisel

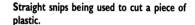

Hand plane

Straight snips being used to cut a piece of plastic.

Chisels ■ There are a number of different types of chisels, each with special uses. Chisels have a single steel cutting edge beveled on one or both sides that is used to trim small pieces of material from wood, metal and masonry. Wood chisels usually have a wood or plastic handle and sharp steel blades beveled on one side that range in size from 1/8″ to 2-1/2″ wide. Hand pressure or a soft faced mallet is used to apply the force needed to cut joints, grooves, or holes in wood.

Cold chisels are made from a solid piece of steel. Since cold chisels are used to cut metal and masonry materials, the cutting edge, which is blunter than a wood chisel and beveled on both sides, is hardened and tempered. Cold chisels must be struck with a hammer to supply the necessary cutting force.

The **brick set** looks similar to a cold chisel, but has a wider cutting edge that matches the width of the bricks it is used to cut. Cutting masonry bricks and concrete blocks involves lightly scoring a cut line on the material with the brick set, then breaking off the unwanted parts with sharp blows from a mason's hammer.

Planes ■ Planes are used to shave small bits of material from wood members to create plane (flat) surfaces. One of the most popular uses of the plane is for shaving down doors to fit a doorway. A plane consists of a sharp chisel-like blade, called a plane iron, that protrudes from the bottom of the assembly. There are adjustments on a plane for the depth of cut, positioning of the plane iron, and size of the opening in the bottom. A plane is usually held with two hands and positioned so that its bottom rests flat on the wood being cut. When the plane is moved with the grain, the protruding plane iron cuts shavings from the wood.

There are a wide variety of sizes and styles of planes, but the more common hand tool models are the jointer, block, and jack plane. The jointer plane is the largest, ranging in size from 18″ to 24″ long. The block plane, the smallest model (5″ to 7″ long), can be used with one hand to shave end grain and small pieces of wood. The mid-sized model (12″–15″ long), the popular jack plane, is considered an all-purpose plane and can be used for most jobs.

As with other construction tools, planes have also been powerized. **Power planes** often replace hand planes because of the advantages of increased speed, which reduces time and costs, improved accuracy in removing materials, and the production of smoother surfaces. Wood surfaces up to 2-1/2″ wide can be cut to a depth of 3/16″ quickly and accurately with a power plane.

Jointers and planers, common woodworking machines, are also used in construction to produce flat faces and edges on wooden members, such as hardwood flooring or siding. Often, these machines are used in a manufacturing shop and the finished materials are transported to the construction site.

Snips ■ Snips which are similar to scissors in operation, are used to cut thin sheet materials, such as sheet metal and plastics. Sheet metal flashing

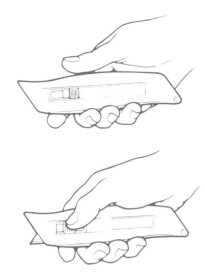

used to seal joints between a chimney and roof is cut with snips, as are aluminum and vinyl plastic siding and other exterior trim materials. Three popular models of snips are straight snips, used for straight cuts, duckbill or trojan shears, used for curved cuts, and aviation snips, which are double hinged for easier cutting of irregular curves.

Utility Knife ■ A very popular construction tool is the utility knife, which consists of a fixed or retractable razor blade mounted in a handle. This multi-purpose, razor-sharp tool is used to cut gypsum wallboard, paper roof coverings, styrofoam insulation boards, sheet plastic, vinyl flooring and carpeting, to name a few. Special blades can even be purchased to cut asphalt roofing shingles. This popular tool is also very dangerous and should be used with extreme caution.

· ·

Combining Processes and Tools

Combining processes add one material to another. These are probably the most important processes for building a structure. Posts and beams are combined to create the structural frame in wood-frame or steel skeleton-frame construction. Sheathing materials are installed to enclose the frame using combining processes. Paint, siding, shingles, and flooring materials are added for the final finishing touches. All processes that involve adding materials to the structure are examples of combining processes. In this chapter, five types of combining processes will be examined: mechanical fastening, adhesive fastening, welding, mortar bonding, and coating.

Nailing one piece of wood to another is perhaps the most familiar type of combining process. (Courtesy of the United Brotherhood of Carpenters)

· ·

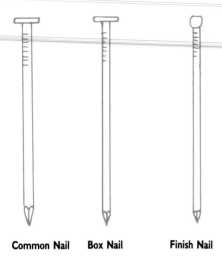

Common Nail   Box Nail   Finish Nail

■ Mechanical Fastening Processes

Mechanical fastening involves combining two or more materials using mechanical fasteners, such as nails, screws, or bolts.

Nails ■ There are three main types of nails: common nails, box nails, and finish nails. Both the common and box nails are used for fastening structural elements during the rough carpentry phase of wood-frame construction. Common nails have round, flat heads and smooth shanks. Box nails are similar in appearance to common nails, but have thinner shanks. The thinner shanks make box nails easier to drive and reduce the likelihood of the wood being split during nailing processes. However, the thinner shanks also produce a lower load-supporting capability when compared to common nails. Finish nails are thin, with small heads that can be driven below the surface of a piece of finish carpentry woodwork, such as baseboards or door and window trim. A nail set is used to drive the head below the surface. The recessed head can then be hidden with putty.

Nail size is designated by a number called a penny size, abbreviated d. Figure 8-24 illustrates the penny sizes and their corresponding lengths. Notice that the penny sizes vary by 1/4″.

Special-Purpose Nails ■ There are a number of special-purpose nails for construction that have added features.

The scaffold nail has a double head. Scaffold nails are used to build scaffolds and concrete forms and for temporary layout. The double head makes removal of the nail and disassembly of these temporary structures easier.

There are several different types of deformed shank nails. Two common deformed shank nails are the screw shank and ring shank. Deformed shank nails have improved holding power and increased resistance to being pulled out. Screw shank nails are used to install wood flooring and ring shank nails are used for subflooring and plywood.

For external applications where nails will be exposed to rain and snow, galvanized nails should be used. The galvanized coating is created by dipping the nails in zinc, which is noncorrosive, thus preventing the nails from rusting.

Dry wall nails and roofing nails both have extra large heads. This helps prevent the drywall and roofing materials they fasten from being pulled over the head of the nail. Cement coated nails, which are usually used for roofing, have a resinous coating that improves the bond between nail and wood and helps prevent pull out.

An unusual mechanical fastening system which is similar to a group of nails is the toothed plate. These plates are primarily used in factories where roof and floor trusses are manufactured. The metal plates are stamped to create nail-like protrusions on one side. After the parts of a truss have been

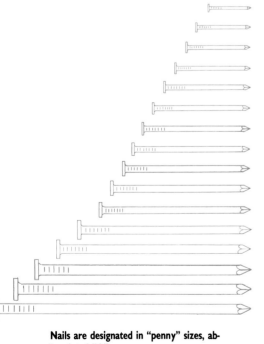

Nails are designated in "penny" sizes, abbreviated "d."

This detail of a floor truss system shows the toothed plates used in their construction.

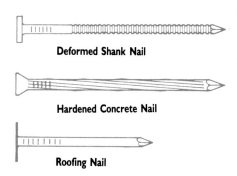

Deformed Shank Nail

Hardened Concrete Nail

Roofing Nail

assembled, toothed plates are positioned over each joint and hydraulic presses force the nail protrusions into the wooden members to create very strong joints.

Nailing Processes ■ Nails are usually installed using a hammer. The nail must go completely through the first board and penetrate the second piece as much as possible for maximum holding power. There are four main types of nailing techniques: face nailing, end-grain nailing, toe nailing, and clinching.

In face nailing, two wooden members lap over each other and are nailed together face to face or face to edge. Face nailing provides the maximum holding power, provided the nail penetrates the second member sufficiently.

In end grain nailing, the joint is formed when the end grain of the second member rests on the face or edge of the first member. The nail is driven through the first member and into the end grain of the second. Because of the lower holding power of end grain, joints nailed in this manner are not as strong as face nailed.

The toe-nailed joint has the same configuration as end-grain nailing, but because of space limitations, the nails are driven through both sides of one member at an angle into the second member.

Clinching is actually an improved method of face nailing. The nails are driven completely through both members and clinched (bent) over using the hammer. Clinching provides increased resistance to the nails being pulled out.

In each of the nailing techniques described the holding power can be improved by adding glue to the joint. The nail essentially clamps the pieces together until the glue dries. The combination of the glue and nail produces superior holding power. However, adding glue to every joint can be time consuming and expensive. One type of joint that is usually glued and nailed is the joint between floor joists and the plywood floor sheathing. The glue helps the joints remain rigid and prevents a spongy, squeaking floor.

Four Types of Nailing Processes

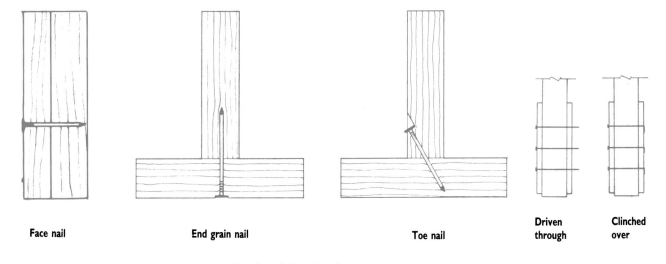

Face nail   End grain nail   Toe nail   **Driven through**   **Clinched over**

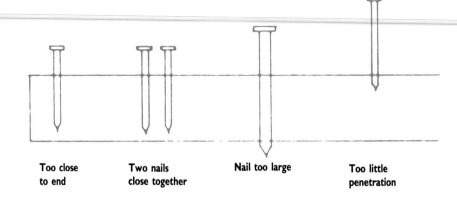

Four Common Nailing Problems

Too close
to end

Two nails
close together

Nail too large

Too little
penetration

Poor Nailing Practices ■ Poor nailing practices mean a weak joint and can lead to failure of the structure. Four common nailing problems include installing a nail too close to the end of a board, putting two nails too close together, and using nails that are too large for the wooden member. These lead to splitting of the wood and greatly reduce holding power. The fourth problem, too little penetration into the second member, does not cause splitting, but it will definitely mean reduced holding power and possible pull out of the nail. All of these practices should be avoided.

Claw hammer.

The power hammer uses compressed air to drive nails or large staples. It can be a lethal weapon if used carelessly. (Courtesy of Duo-Fast Corp.)

Hammers ■ The claw hammer is the main combining tool of the carpenter. There are a variety of styles and shapes available. Hammers are identified by the weight, in ounces, of the head. A popular weight is the 16 ounce model. There are both heavier and lighter models available. Hammer handles are usually made from wood, steel, or fiberglass and may be covered with a rubber-type material to improve the grip.

Hammering nails accurately is a skill that takes practice to develop. Hammering is also a rather slow process. This adds to the cost of construction when you consider the fact that thousands of nails are used in each structure.

Power hammers have been developed to reduce nailing time and the need for practice nailing. A power hammer uses compressed air to drive nails. Special nail designs are used, which are prepackaged in self-feed strips containing several dozen nails. When loaded into a power hammer, the nails can be driven one by one as fast as the operator can pull the trigger.

Straight blade

Flat Head   Round Head   Oval Head

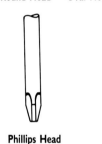

Phillips Head

The "Yankee" screwdriver is driven with a pumping motion.

Wood screws come in different gauges.

Screws ■ The threads on a screw provide a positive anchorage and increased tightening of joints that is not possible with nails. Under dynamic loads such as seismic loads, screws have improved holding properties over nails, but it takes longer to install screws than nails, which can be costly. When nails are used for fastening, no hole is needed. The nail is just driven through both pieces of wood. With screws, holes are predrilled in both wooden members before the screws are driven in with a screwdriver or wrench.

Screws can be made from steel, brass, or bronze. They can be natural metal or coated for protection from corrosion, and they can have flat, oval, or round heads.

Screw size is designated by its length and gauge. Screws are available in lengths from 1/4″ to 6″. Gauge, which is a measure of the diameter of the screw, is designated with a number, from 0 to 24. The smaller the number, the thinner gauge the screw. There are several screw gauges for each length, but all the gauges are not available in each length. For example, the 3/4″ length comes in gauges from 4 to 12 only.

When purchasing screws, the designations are written to include the gauge, length, head type, and application. A #10 × 1″ OHWS designation means a number 10 gauge, 1″ long, oval head, wood screw. The length and gauge of screw selected depends on the thickness of the materials being fastened and the load applied to the materials.

For structural fastening and for the heaviest loads, large screws called lag screws or lag bolts are used. Lag screws are similar to round-head screws, but have a head designed to be turned with a wrench instead of a screwdriver.

Screwdrivers or wrenches are needed to drive screws. The two types of screwdrivers are the straight or flat-blade and the Phillips. Flat-blade screwdrivers are used with screws that have straight slots in their heads, while the Phillips screwdriver is used with plus sign-type Phillips head slots. Like hammers, screwdrivers have been powerized. There are screwdriving attachments for electric drills and dedicated power screwdrivers.

(A)
Pilot hole is drilled through both pieces.

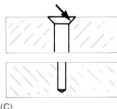

(C)
The countersink is drilled for the flathead screw.

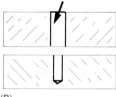

(B)
The shank hole is drilled through the pilot hole in the top piece.

(D)
Both pieces attached with the screw sliding through the shank hole and making its own threads as it is turned into the pilot hole.

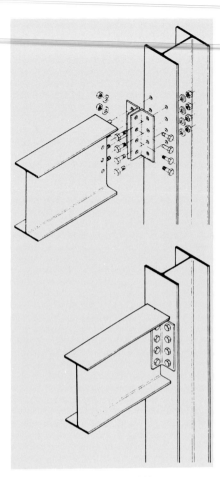

Exploded view of a bolted steel I-beam.

Bolts ■ Bolts are threaded fasteners that are put loosely through two or more pieces of material for fastening. A hole is drilled through each piece being fastened. The hole is slightly larger than the diameter of the bolt, usually by 1/16″. The bolt is inserted through the members, and a nut is tightened onto the threaded end using a wrench to tightly squeeze the members together.

Because of the time involved in drilling and aligning holes and tightening the nuts, bolts have limited use in wood-frame construction. However, they are very popular for steel framework, such as in bridges or skyscrapers. Fastening structural steel requires the use of bolting angles and several bolts, nuts, and washers.

■ Adhesive Fastening

Adhesive fastening involves the use of adhesives (glues) to combine materials. At one time only wood, paper, leather, and cloth could be fastened with adhesives. Today, there are adhesives for steel, concrete, glass, and ceramic materials as well.

Provided the materials being fastened have well matched mating surfaces, adhesive fastening has the advantage of producing a uniform distribution of loads across a joint, versus nails, screws, and bolts, which tend to create load-bearing stress only in the small areas around the mechanical fastener. Adhesive fastening also has the advantages of lower weight than threaded fasteners and an absence of nail, screw, and bolt heads on the surface of the fastened materials.

One of the main disadvantages of using adhesives is the need for pressure application at the time of fastening. This can be accomplished easily in prefabrication shops, but is rather difficult to achieve on a construction site. Another disadvantage is the time it takes for an adhesive to dry. During that time, the joint will not support very large loads. Nailed, screwed, and bolted joints can support loads immediately. The use of adhesives and mechanical fasteners together, as described earlier, helps overcome the pressure and drying disadvantages of using adhesives alone.

Glues ■ Three of the more common glues are polyvinyl resin emulsion glue, urea formaldehyde resin glue, and caesin glue.

Polyvinyl resin emulsion glue, also called polyvinyl or white glue, is purchased ready-to-use in plastic squeeze bottles. The moisture in the glue is absorbed into the wooden members being fastened, the moisture dries, and the glue hardens.

Urea formaldehyde resin glue, also called urea resin, is purchased as a dry powder that must be mixed with water to create a creamy paste. Once the paste is mixed, a chemical reaction begins between the water and a catalyst in the powder. This chemical reaction causes the glue to harden. Urea resin glue is moisture resistant and used in applications where wooden members will be exposed to moisture.

Casein glue, which is also purchased in a powder form and mixed with water, has the advantage of filling small voids in the joints and still maintaining a good connection.

▇ Welding

On the construction site, welding is a fastening option in place of bolts for steel-frame construction. When pipelines are constructed, welding is often used to fasten together the various sections of pipe. Welding is also used to combine metal frame sections in prefabrication shops.

Welding has several advantages over bolting. First, welding produces a direct connection between the two members being combined. This eliminates the need for bolting angles and the bolts themselves. Holes don't have to be drilled, thus saving time and money. Bolt holes also reduce the surface contact between the two members, which reduces the strength of the joint. Welding provides a continuous, uniform distribution of loads across the joint. Finally, welds don't normally loosen, which is a minor possibility with bolts.

One disadvantage of welding when compared to bolts is permanence. Welding produces permanent joint connections, while bolts can be removed and the joint disassembled if desired.

Electric Arc Welding ■ Electric arc welding is the most used form of welding in construction. Arc welding works by using an electric current to form an arc in a gap between the end of an electrode (the welding rod) and the joint between the two members being connected. The intense heat of the arc, which can reach temperatures of 6,000° Fahrenheit, melts the rod and portions of both members being connected. All three metals fuse when the metals cool and solidify. During the welding process, the thick coating on the electrode creates an atmosphere of ionized gas.

Electric arc welding is the most common form used in construction.

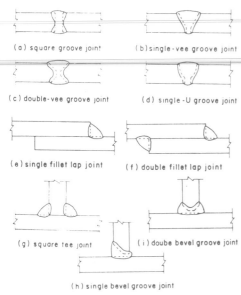

(a) square groove joint

(b) single-vee groove joint

(c) double-vee groove joint

(d) single-U groove joint

(e) single fillet lap joint

(f) double fillet lap joint

(g) square tee joint

(i) doube bevel groove joint

(h) single bevel groove joint

Types of Welded Joints

There are three classes of welded joints: butt, tee, and lap. The corners between welded members are filled with built-up welding rod called fillets. Fillets, which have a triangular shape in cross-section, are made by overlapping welds until sufficient metal has been built up. Often, the edges of thick metal members are shaped before welding to facilitate complete penetration of the weld and to provide additional surface contact for fillets. Welders must be highly skilled to maintain the proper arc gap and move the electrode to create dense, smooth fillets.

Arc Welding Safety ■ Arc welding poses special safety problems for construction workers. The arc flashes can cause blindness if viewed directly for long periods of time. Welders use special helmets with dark colored vision lenses to protect their eyes. In addition, molten metal splatters during the welding process and can burn through clothes and skin. Heavy leather gloves and special leather coverings for arms and legs are often worn for further protection of the welder.

Mortar is the cement bond between bricks. This brick wall is only as strong as the mortar bonding it together.

■ Mortar Bonding

Mortar is the cement that bonds together masonry units, such as bricks, concrete blocks, and stones. Laying masonry units is a hand process requiring years of experience and practice to develop the high degree of skill necessary to do a quality job. No mechanized or automated processes have been invented to replace the bricklayer. For thousands of years, masons have been laying bricks one by one.

Mortar is composed of one or more kinds of cement, such as portland cement, lime, sand, and water, or masonry cement, sand, and water. Masonry cement is a preblended mixture of portland cement and lime. Masonry cement also contains air-entraining agents that cause tiny bubbles in the mortar. These bubbles make the mortar more plastic and workable and slows the absorption of water from the mortar into the masonry units. The amount of water in the mixture is critical to achieving the correct plasticity and bonding since it acts as a catalyst to cause the other materials to harden. The strength of a masonry structure is dependent on the strength of the mortar, not the bricks or blocks. Remember, a structure is only as strong as its weakest element; mortar is weaker than brick.

Laying Masonry Units (bricks and concrete blocks) ■ Construction of a masonry wall begins at the corners. A line is stretched tightly around the foundation of the wall to act as a guide when the first units are laid. A bed of mortar is laid on top of the foundation to bond the first course (layer) of masonry units. The corner units are laid up first, usually three or four courses high. At the corner, the first course consists of several units laid in each direction. The units in the second course are then laid one-half unit shorter in each direction from the corner so they cover the joints in the first course. Each successive course is staggered in this manner to create an interlocking pattern up the wall.

Mortar is applied with a trowel to the tops and ends of each unit as it is added to the wall and to the tops of previously laid units. With solid units, such as bricks, all the space between units is completely filled with mortar. For hollow units, such as concrete blocks, mortar is applied only to the inside and outside faces. The mason must have the skill to quickly and consistently apply the correct amount of mortar for each joint. Mortar joints for concrete block walls are approximately 3/8″ thick; 1/2″ mortar joints are used for bricks.

After the mortar has been applied to the surfaces that will be in contact, the unit is shoved and tapped in place. When several units have been installed, they are checked for level and plumb using a hand level. A line level is attached to the stretched line to insure levelness along the length of each course. Before the mortar sets and hardens completely, the joints are finished with a forming tool to give them a finished appearance and to prevent rain, snow, or ice from entering joints and causing cracks or other damage. Concave and V-shaped are two popular shapes for finished mortar joints.

Laying a Brick Wall with Mortar

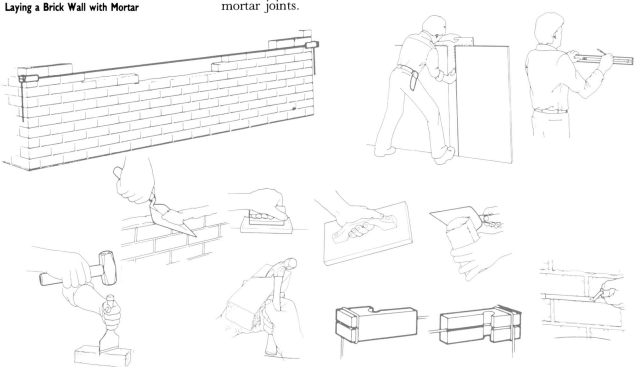

Coating materials, such as the paint on this house, protect materials from the environment, make the materials easier to clean, and add visual appeal.

(Below): Paint must be properly maintained. Otherwise the protective seal will be broken, allowing rust, rot and corrosion to enter the materials underneath. (Photos by Julia Runk Jones)

■ Coating Processes

The combining processes discussed up to this point all involved adding structural materials to a building. The final combining process, coating, doesn't add structural materials, but rather protective materials, namely paints and other finishes.

Coating Materials ■ Paint and clear finishes, such as varnish, are commonly used in construction. Both these materials are applied as coatings over other materials in a thin film. This serves as a protective shield between the materials and the environmental elements that can cause them to deteriorate. Two common construction materials, woods and metals, are susceptible to rot, rust, and corrosion from exposure to sunlight, rain, snow, and wind. Paint and varnish are used to seal wood and metal from these environmental enemies. As a secondary purpose, coatings decorate construction materials, making them more aesthetically pleasing. Coatings also make it easier to clean certain materials.

Paint ■ Paint is a mixture of tiny solid particles called **pigments** suspended in a liquid medium called a **vehicle.** The vehicle contains the solvent or thinner for the paint and serves to keep the desired consistency for brushing, rolling, or spraying paint.

The two types of paint are latex and oil-based. The vehicle for latex paints is acrylic latex, a water-soluble synthetic resin. Water is the thinner for latex paints, which makes them very popular with do-it-yourselfers. Another synthetic material, alkyd resin, is the vehicle for oil-based paint. Turpentine or mineral spirits are common solvents for oil-based paints. The vehicle in both types of paint also contains a binder, which serves to bond the pigment particles into a consistent film after drying. Latex paints tend to dry quickly, usually in thirty minutes. Oil-based paints have much longer drying times.

Selecting Paint ■ All paint is not created equal. Before paint is purchased, certain decisions must be made about the type of paint needed. Paint selection decisions are made based on three factors: the type of exposure expected, the materials being covered, and the type of service the paint must provide.

Interior and exterior are the two types of exposures. Obviously, interior paints do not have the weather and water resistance needed for exterior paints. There are special paints for a number of different materials, including wood, metal, masonry, concrete, and plaster. Paints should be matched to the materials they will be covering. Finally, the location of the surfaces being covered determines the type of service expected from the paint. Bathroom walls will be exposed to more moisture than livingrooms or bedrooms. Kitchen walls will be exposed to grease from cooking, and walls and trim near doorways, stairways, and light switches will need to be cleaned often because of marks from fingers and hands.

Interior paints provide three different types of surface finishes to match the service needed. Flat paint produces no reflections or glare and is the most susceptible to dirt and finger marks, which are difficult to remove. Flat paint has the advantage of being able to hide minor imperfections and blemishes on a surface. Gloss paint produces a glass-like finish that tends to magnify any surface imperfections, but is easy to clean. Semi-gloss is a compromise between flat and gloss. It produces a moderate sheen and thus less glare. It is also easier to clean than flat paint and has limited abilities to hide surface imperfections.

Reputable paint dealers are best informed to help you make a decision about the type of paint needed. Ultimately, however, a fourth factor is always considered when paint is being purchased: cost. As a rule of thumb, more expensive paints are easier to use, give better coverage, and last longer than cheap paints.

Preparing to Paint ■ Before any paint is applied, the surface must be properly prepared. Any cracks, dents, or nail holes should be filled. Rough materials should be sanded smooth. All dust should be wiped or vacuumed away, and the surface should be dry. The best quality paint will not perform adequately if applied over a poorly prepared surface. As another preparation when painting inside, adequate ventilation must be provided. Some paints give off toxic fumes.

On new materials, a coat of **primer** must be applied first to seal the surface and prepare a good base for the paint. Primer prevents the paint from being absorbed into the material and insures good bonding of the paint to

Sanding is an essential part of preparation for painting. A respirator should always be worn when sanding. (Courtesy of the National Paint and Coatings Association)

Painting a steel I-beam with a roller. Like brushes, rollers come in many sizes. (Courtesy of Amoco)

the surface. Just like paint, there are special primers for wood, metal, masonry, and gypsum materials and for interior or exterior use.

Painting Processes and Tools ■ Applying paint with a brush is the oldest painting technique, and still the most used. Rollers are very popular since they are quicker than brushes at covering large areas and they are very easy to use for the novice. Good paint results can be achieved using a roller even if you have minimal painting skills. Achieving quality results with spray painting equipment is the most difficult for the novice, but it is the fastest process and can give the most professional results once skills have been developed. Spraying is also the most expensive process because of the cost of the equipment.

Novice painters often make the mistake of applying heavy coats of paint in the belief that they will save time. However, no matter what painting tools are used, it should be remembered that three thin coats of paint will last longer, use less materials, and give better results than two thick coats.

Paint Brushes ■ Paint brushes, like any other construction tools, should be maintained in good working condition at all times and used properly. Two common paint brushes are the wall brush and the sash and trim brush. Wall brushes have flat, square ends and are available in sizes from 3″ to 6″ wide. Wall brushes are used for large flat surfaces. Sash and trim brushes have an angled edge, range in size from 1-1/2″ to 3″ wide, and are used for window frames and other wooden trim work.

The bristles on a brush must be matched to the type of paint being used. Bristles are made from natural or synthetic materials. For latex paints, nylon or polyester bristles should be used, while oil-based paints require natural bristles.

When applying paint to the bristles, less than two thirds of their length should be dipped into the paint. Excess paint should be removed from the bristles by tapping the brush sideways on the inside of the paint container. Paint should be applied to surfaces in long, even strokes to smooth out the paint and prevent heavy applications that could cause runs or an uneven surface texture. When painting for long periods of time, brushes should be cleaned periodically to remove any drying paint.

Rollers ■ Rollers have a replaceable synthetic fiber cover that revolves on a cylindrical cage attached to the roller handle. The most popular roller covers for general consumer use are 9″ long. The length of the fiber nap on a roller should be matched to the texture of the surface being painted. Long nap rollers are available for painting rough materials, like masonry materials, while short fibers are available for smooth materials like gypsum wall board.

Paint should be loaded evenly into the nap of a roller using a roller tray. The paint should be rolled onto the surface being covered in a "W" pattern measuring approximately three or four rollers square. Overlapping strokes should be used to cover the unpainted areas in the W pattern. Once the entire area is covered, long, light rolls should be used to even out the paint.

When adjacent areas are painted, the roller should be rolled and lifted gradually from the surface where the paint overlaps; stopping the roller and lifting abruptly will cause visible paint marks. Rollers have the disadvantage of not readily reaching into corners or areas around trim. Trim brushes must be used to paint these areas.

Spray Painting Equipment ■ Spray painting is the fastest and most efficient painting method and it can also produce the highest quality paint job. The most popular type of spray equipment in use today is the airless sprayer. Airless spray paint equipment includes a spray gun containing a motor that derives a small pump. This pump sucks paint from a container and forces it through a nozzle at pressures up to 3000 psi. The nozzle forces the paint into a fine fan-shaped spray pattern.

Spray painting can be used on any texture surface since the fine spray will adhere to smooth surfaces and reach tiny voids in rough surfaces. Caution should be used with this type of painting, however, since the high pressure of the fine spray leaving the nozzle can penetrate skin like a knife.

As mentioned earlier, using spray painting equipment requires the most practice and skill of the three methods, but once mastered it can produce professional painting results. Two key factors in achieving a quality paint job using spray equipment are how the gun is held in relation to the surface being painted and the motion of the spray gun. Spray guns should be held 6″ to 10″ from the surface. Holding the gun closer will result in excess paint build up and runs; holding the gun further away could cause the fine spray to begin drying before it reaches the surface. For a uniform depositing of paint, the gun should also be held perpendicular to the surface. Tilting the gun will result in a heavy application of paint in one part of the spray pattern.

The gun should be moved in a straight line parallel to the surface, not swung in an arc. In addition, the gun trigger should be pulled to start the spray pattern after the stroke is begun and released to stop spraying paint before the stroke is finished. These techniques reduce the likelihood of excess paint build-up in certain areas.

. . . .

Forming Processes and Tools

Forming processes involved changing the contour or shape of a construction material. The most common example of forming in construction is forming concrete. When wet, concrete is a shapeless semi-liquid material that

. . . .

Elaborate wooden formwork. Notice the steel reinforcing bars already laid in the form. Forms allow concrete to be made into many different shapes. (Courtesy of the National Plywood Association)

will take on practically any contour or shape once formed and cured. Forms or formwork are needed to contain the concrete in the desired shape while it cures. Forming concrete is similar to putting water in an ice cube tray in the freezer. The tray is a form and the curing occurs when the water freezes.

■ Form Materials

Forms are temporary structures used to contain and form concrete. They can be made from lumber, plywood, metal or cardboard. Lumber and plywood forms are usually fabricated on site, while metal forms are prefabricated in shops and then shipped to the construction site for assembly. For on-site construction of forms, plywood has the advantage of being able to bend to create curved concrete shapes. Cardboard tubes are a convenient type of form for casting round reinforced concrete columns. The tubes are erected, filled with reinforcement and concrete, and then stripped from the column once the concrete cures.

Form Qualities

Forms must be strong enough to withstand the pressure that concrete can exert on them and still maintain the desired shape without bending, sagging, deforming, or rupturing. Concrete can be very heavy. Typically, concrete weighs between 145 and 150 lbs/ft^3, but special concrete mixtures can weigh up to 600 lbs/ft^3. To contain this weight, concrete forms are usually reinforced with lumber and other anchors staked into the ground. Forms must also be tight enough to prevent leakage, especially at the joints between boards or panels. These are also reinforced with extra materials.

Forms should be easy to build, erect, and disassemble. Forms are temporary structures that must be built and then torn down when the concrete is dry. Building forms is a costly process since they do not add directly to the structure being built. For this reason, construction managers don't want workers spending long hours building and disassembling forms. Removal of the form must also take place without damaging the cured concrete.

As a third important quality, forms should not interfere with the concrete curing process. Forms made from kiln-dried lumber should be wetted before the wet concrete is cast. Concrete cures by the chemical reaction between the water and other ingredients in its mixture. Kiln-dried lumber can absorb water from wet concrete and disrupt the curing process. This can lead to incomplete curing, a finished concrete that doesn't last as long as intended or one that will not withstand loads as expected. Forms are often oiled or greased before casting. This facilitates removal of forms from concrete and makes the forms more readily usable for future jobs.

A form should be strong enough to withstand the pressure of wet concrete. It should also be easy to build and dissemble.

Concrete Finishing Processes

After concrete has been cast in the form, it must be finished to smooth the concrete and produce the desired surface texture and edge treatments. Timing is important in finishing processes. If the concrete is allowed to dry too much, it will be too hard for finishing, if too soft it will not retain textures and treatments. Experience and skill of the worker are required to make decisions about the timing of the finishing processes.

Screeding ■ The first finishing process is **screeding.** Screeding involves moving a piece of lumber, called a screed, back and forth in a sawlike motion across the top of the form to strike off any high points in the concrete. A small amount of concrete is kept in front of the screed to help workers identify and fill any low spots. Screeding leaves the surface very rough and several successive smoothing processes are required.

Darbying ■ The first smoothing after screeding is called **darbying.** A darby is moved across the concrete to produce a smoother, more level and even surface. Large floats can be used in place of a darby.

Smoothing the edges of concrete helps prevent chipping. (Courtesy of Portland Cement Association)

A bull float is used to smooth the concrete surface on large jobs. Floating requires a lot of experience. (Courtesy of Portland Cement Association)

Texturing the final surface of the concrete. Smooth concrete can be very slippery when wet.

Edging ■ When the concrete has reached the required stiffness, the corners are rounded with an edger tool. The edger has a handle attached to a piece of flat metal with one edge rounded over. The edger is moved back and forth along the edges of the concrete with the rounded edge of the edger between the concrete and the form. **Edging** produces a rounded edge that helps prevent chipping and other damage that can occur to sharp edges.

Grooving ■ Another process that helps protect the concrete from damage is grooving. A groover tool is used to cut one inch deep grooves at intervals in long concrete slabs, such as sidewalks. These grooves create a weak spot in the concrete where cracks will occur when the slab moves from ground settlements, the freeze and thaw cycle, or when tree roots expand under the slab. This controls random cracking.

Floating ■ Floating is the next surface smoothing process and is usually performed after edging. Many factors must be considered in determining exactly when floating should occur. Concrete workers must consider the temperature of the air and concrete, humidity, and wind. Each of these can affect the rate at which the concrete will cure. It takes experience to know the correct texture required for satisfactory floating. The purpose of floating is to embed the large aggregate below the surface of the concrete and to remove or level off any surface imperfections. Hand floats are usually made from lightweight aluminum or magnesium, but there are floats for large concrete jobs.

Troweling ■ After floating, troweling is used to produce the final surface texture. Depending on the surface smoothness desired, successive trowelings can be used with smaller trowels at various intervals until an glassy texture results. Often, concrete surfaces this smooth can be dangerous for people walking on them, especially when the surfaces are wet. A slightly rough surface is more desirable to give better footing and can be created by dragging a broom or brush over the surface instead of using final trowelings.

SUMMARY

There are basic processes in each field of technology that workers should be able to perform. In construction, there are four classifications of processes: measuring, separating, combining, and forming. The English system of fractional inches is the type of measurement used most often in construction. Separating processes involve reducing the size and shape of a material by removing part of the material. Basic separating processes include sawing, shearing, drilling, and abrading. Combining processes involved adding one material to another. Basic combining processes include mechanical fastening with nails, screws and bolts, adhesive fastening with glues, welding, mortar bonding, and coating with paint. Forming processes involve changing the contour or shape of a material. Casting concrete in forms and performing various concrete finishing processes are examples of forming. Workers must be able to perform these basic processes skillfully and safely using the basic hand tools, power hand tools, and machines of construction.

. . . .

Study Questions

1. Why is it important for construction workers and students to know and follow safety rules? List five important general safety rules for construction.

2. Why do you think the metric system of measurement isn't used in construction? What system of measurement is used?

3. What are the differences between hand tools, power hand tools, and machines?

4. What is mechanical advantage and how does it apply to construction tools?

5. Name four measuring tools described in this chapter and describe how they are used.

6. Name and describe four separating processes used in construction, including two tools or devices for each process.

7. Name and describe five combining processes used in construction, including two tools or devices for each process.

8. Name and describe two forming processes used in construction, including two tools or devices used for each process.

. . . .

Suggested Activities

1. Under the supervision of your teacher, practice using construction tools to perform the processes described in this chapter. Then, as a class, use your skills to build a structure.

2. Study the many uses of the framing square and learn how to use its tables for layout and measurement processes.

3. Pick one construction tool that interests you. Make a chart or poster that describes the tool, its safety rules, uses, costs, and processes.

4. Research recent technological innovations in construction tools, such as the laser level, power hammer, or airless spray gun. Learn the processes that can be performed with these tools.

5. Make a display of various mechanical fasteners, abrasives, or adhesives used in construction.

Glossary

Abrading   Separating process that uses abrasives to remove small bits of materials to create a smooth surface, also called sanding.

Adhesive fastening   Combining process which involves the use of adhesives (glues) to combine materials.

Brick set   Chisel, similar in looks to a cold chisel, used to cut masonry units.

Builder's level   Tool used for identifying the corners and boundaries of a structure, checking the depth and levelness of excavations, and laying out the position of footers, frames, and concrete forms.

Circular saw   Portable power hand tool used to make straight cuts in wood, has a round rotating blade.

Combining processes   Adding one piece of material to another to build a structure, examples include nailing, screwing, welding, gluing, and coating.

Crosscut saw   Saw used to separate board by cutting across the grain.

Darbying   Concrete finishing process, is the first smoothing process after screeding.

Edging   Concrete finishing process which produces a rounded edge on formed concrete to help prevent chipping and other damages.

Floating   Concrete finishing process used to embed the large aggregate below the surface of the concrete.

Forming processes   Changing the contour or shape of a material, examples include pouring wet concrete into a form and smoothing the edges of a newly poured concrete structure.

Framing square   Multiple purpose measuring, layout, and checking tool.

Grooving   Concrete finishing process where grooves are cut at intervals in long concrete slabs.

Laser levels   Level that uses the light from a low energy laser for measuring processes.

Mechanical fastening   Combining process which involves combining two or more materials using mechanical fasteners, such as nails, screws, or bolts.

Mortar   The cement that bonds together masonry units, such as bricks, concrete blocks, and stones.

Pigments   Tiny solid particles which give paint its color.

Power hammers   A power hand tool developed to reduce nailing time and the need for practice nailing, uses compressed air to drive nails.

Power miter box   Machine consisting of a portable circular saw mounted on a stationary stand, also called a motorized miter box.

Power planes   Power hand tool used to cut smooth, flat surfaces on boards.

Primer   Preparation material that seals the surface and creates a good base for paint.

Rip saw   Saw used to separate boards by cutting along the grain.

Screeding   Concrete finishing process involving moving a piece of lumber, called a screed, back and forth in a sawlike motion across the top of the form to strike off any high points in the concrete.

Separating processes   Reducing material size and shape by cutting or removing part of the material, examples include sawing, drilling, shearing, and abrading.

Snips   Shearing tool, similar to scissors in operation, used to cut sheet metal and plastics.

Troweling   Concrete finishing process used to produce the final surface texture.

Vehicle   The liquid medium in which paint pigments are suspended.

Zigzag rule   Rigid hardwood measuring tool which folds into 6″ lengths.

• •

Chapter 8

How Structures Are Constructed

Chapter Concepts

■ Preconstruction, construction and postconstruction are the three phases of the construction process.

■ Estimates, bids, financing and permits are important elements of the preconstruction phase.

■ Scheduling, managing, safety and inspections are essential to a good construction project.

■ Elements of the construction process include site preparation, foundations, framing, closing in the structure and installation of utilities.

■ Postconstruction includes finish work, landscaping and closing out the construction process.

Key Terms

Bearing wall structure
Bitumen
Bond beams
Breach of contract
Breaking ground
Bridge financing
Building permit
Built-up roofs
Caissons
Certificate of occupancy
Closing in
Cofferdam
Compact
Computer-Aided Design (CAD)
Construction financing
Construction phase
Contingency
Contractor

Corporation
Cost estimating
Cost-plus contracts
Critical path
Critical Path Method (CPM)
Curtain wall
Finish work
Fixed price contract
Flashing
Frame structure
Furring
Grout
Liability
Load-bearing capacity
Mass structure
Municipal bonds
OSHA

Overhead costs
Piles
Plumb bob
Postconstruction phase
Preconstruction phase
Production workers
Release
Roof decking
Site preparation
Skilled trades
Sole proprietorship
Stabilizing an excavation
Subcontract
Surface bonding
Tap
Time clauses
Zoning

Putting structures together in a precise manner requires careful planning and careful execution. This carpenter measures to ensure that the beam is exactly in place. (Courtesy of Deck House)

(1686 sq. ft. house,
528 sq. ft. garage)

First Floor
Crawl Space/Slab

Turning the plans for this house into the actual structure involves coordination between a large number of people. (Courtesy of Crestway Homes)

Introduction

It is easy to assume that once a structure has been designed and construction begins that the time for planning is over. This is not true. Planning is also critical in the actual construction process. In the design process, planning is oriented to the use of the structure, its site and how much it will cost. The purpose of construction planning is to decide how a series of ideas carefully drawn on paper will be translated into a complex three-dimensional structure.

Many people, materials, and processes must be coordinated in a precise arrangement over time under varied weather conditions in order to complete a structure. Every job in construction is challenging because the work is always changing and the place of work changes every time a new piece is added to the structure. Managing such a process is extremely complicated and requires the use of specialized coordination and scheduling systems. In fact, detailed planning charts and sophisticated computer programs are widely used to coordinate all but the simplest construction projects.

The Role of Contractors

Structures are not usually constructed by the person who owns them. A contractor is the person or company who agrees to build a structure for a given price.

Contractors usually obtain construction jobs by submitting bids to construct given structures. Usually more than one contractor bids on a given job and the owner of the project selects the contractor with the lowest bid or the low bidder who seems to be the most capable.

Price estimating is an important part of construction. There is no guarantee that the structure can be completed for the price that was bid. A contractor must bid low enough to obtain the job, but high enough to guarantee that the construction can be completed for the price quoted, preferably with some profit.

The construction process can be divided into three phases:

■ Preconstruction—Design, bidding, contracting, financing, and the obtaining of required permits take place at this stage.

- Construction—When the structure actually is being built. Usually, it includes site preparation, foundations, framing, closing in the structure and the installation of utilities.

- Postconstruction—This stage includes finish work, landscaping and other site completion work, legal closure of the construction contracts, and maintenance of the structure.

· ·

Preconstruction Phase

Traditionally, the construction of buildings is a three-way cooperative effort between the owner, the architects and engineers, and the contractor. During the preconstruction phase, the owner arranges the design, financing, and construction contract for the structure. The architect designs the structure in consultation with engineers and in accordance with local zoning, building codes, and city planning. The contractor arranges for subcontractors, workers, and materials to actually build the structure.

■ Estimating Costs and Preparing Bids

Cost estimation is complicated and critical for all contractors. People preparing cost estimates must know construction processes and materials,

Subcontractors do specific parts of a construction project. Framing is a common subcontractor role. (Courtesy of Deck House)

· ·

Cabinet and windows making are usually "farmed" out to specialists by the main contractor. (Courtesy of Deck House)

be able to read plans and specifications, know building codes and laws, and know how to use reference materials.

The first step in the cost estimation process is to estimate the cost of all materials that will be used in the structure. The amount of the labor needed by the contractor's employees is calculated next.

A contractor will **subcontract** specialized portions of the structure to the proper professionals. A subcontract is a contract between the general contractor and people who will perform parts of the work specified in the overall construction contract. Typical subcontracted areas include electrical work, plumbing, and masonry. The subcontractors utilize their specialized knowledge and the plans for the structure to develop bids for their parts of the project. These bids are then included as parts of the general contractor's bid for the overall project.

After the costs for labor, materials, and subcontractors have been obtained, the cost estimator must add estimates of the costs of construction insurance, security, and **overhead costs.** Overhead costs represent the normal costs of doing business. They include rent, telephones, legal services, and other general expenses.

Finally, a factor is added for unexpected problems and extra costs. This **contingency** amount can equal up to 10% of a project's cost. A percentage of expected profit is also added at this time. Contingency and profit amounts can also be calculated together.

■ Financing the Project

Large public construction projects such as schools, sewage treatment plants, and highways are often partly financed by issuing **municipal bonds.** Bonds are sold to the public by municipalities, self-governing bodies that can be anything from a small town to a city. The municipality then pays a set amount of interest every year to each holder of the bonds. The bonds can be paid off either on a set date or, often, whenever the town or state has the money to buy them back.

Owners of private construction projects cannot issue bonds and usually cannot gain income from selling or renting a structure until after it is completed. To pay for the construction, they must arrange financing, usually, from a bank. This is called **construction financing** or **bridge financing.**

These loans are risky, because the bank risks repossessing a half-finished building if the contractor proves incompetent or unlucky or if the real estate market collapses. Banks carefully research construction loans and require high and variable interest rates for their money. After a structure is completed, a standard loan similar to a mortgage can be obtained at a lower interest rate because the structure is no longer such a risk.

The contractor also obtains a regular business loan from the bank, using a copy of the contract and the schedule for progress payments from the owner.

Bridge-builders are responsible for the safety of the structures they build. They can be held liable if the structure fails. (George Washington Bridge. Courtesy of the New York Convention and Visitors Bureau)

This pays for materials and labor needed between, or in addition to, the progress payments from the owner. These loans also carry high and variable interest rates.

Both the owner and the contractor, therefore, are eager to complete the structure as quickly as possible. If interest rates rise, or the real estate market gets weaker, the pressure to quickly complete the structure can become extreme. This pressure is felt by every contractor, subcontractor and worker on the job.

■ Contracts and Subcontracts

Given the time pressures and costs, it is not surprising that most construction contracts between owners and contractors, and between contractors and subcontractors, contain **time clauses.** These time clauses establish penalties for the contractor if the project is not completed by specified dates. Similarly, there are often bonus payments if the contract or subcontract is completed early.

The insurance company for the contractor will look over all of the subcontracts signed by the contractor to determine his or her **liability** in various situations. Liability refers to the legal responsibilities which the contractor assumes in the construction process.

If one subcontractor does substandard work, the whole project can be delayed, creating huge costs. If this happens, the contractor will usually file

Arcosanti is an experimental city being built in Arizona. Since financing is unsteady, and most of the labor voluntary, construction has progressed slowly since it began in 1970.

a **breach of contract** lawsuit against the subcontractor. Such lawsuits can be filed any time a person who signs a construction contract fails to meet the specifications of that contract. Some of the most common reasons for these lawsuits are:

- the use of inferior materials
- use of improper methods
- failure to meet standards and
- time delays.

Most contractors organize their businesses as **corporations,** rather than owning them directly. If the corporation goes out of business or is sued for more than it is worth, the owner is not personally responsible for all the debts. Only the property of the corporation can be seized, not that of the owner. If a private business, or **sole proprietorship,** has financial problems, the owner is personally responsible for all debts of the business and can be personally bankrupted.

There are many types of construction contracts. The most common are **fixed-price contracts** and **cost-plus contracts.** As the name implies, fixed-price contracts set a fixed price for a job, which includes the contractor's amounts for contingencies and profits. A contractor's profit on a fixed-price contract is limited, but the potential loss (or liability) on any given job is unlimited. This is because the contractor must spend whatever is necessary to complete the structure in the manner agreed to in the original contract.

A cost-plus contract is more desirable because it pays the contractor the actual costs of labor and materials that the project requires plus money to cover profit and overhead. The amount of profit is usually set as a percentage of the estimated building cost. With a cost-plus contract, the contractor's profit is limited, but so is the risk of financial loss.

■ The Role of the Government

The various branches of government have a large, and growing, role in the construction industry. The major areas of government involvement are in building permits; safety regulations and procedures; and worker employment laws.

Building Permits ■ In order to begin actual construction on any project in a town or city, it is necessary to obtain a **building permit** from the municipal authorities. Many factors are involved in obtaining a permit for a large project. On large public projects such as dams and highways, it is often necessary to write an Environmental Protection Agency (EPA) plan

Environmental impact reports must be filed for large projects such as this oil refinery. (Courtesy of Chevron)

discussing all of the impacts that the project is expected to have on the environment. These plans must be approved before construction can begin.

Most cities have carefully developed **zoning** and **land-use plans** in effect. Under these plans, certain parts of the cities are set aside for certain uses. In particular, the plans are usually designed to separate commercial and industrial development from residential areas.

Land-use plans can contain hundreds of pages and many details that must be investigated before a building permit can be issued. Sometimes, whole projects must be delayed or redesigned in order to meet the conditions of these plans.

Building plans must meet the local building codes and all local fire regulations. For example, some communities require new commercial buildings to have sprinkler systems as a fire safety measure.

All of the regulations discussed above are designed to protect the public's interest in a safe, organized community. However, they serve to increase

Developers often submit land use plans as part of their initial proposals. (Courtesy of Herbert J. Siegel Management)

This view of San Francisco shows the older residential area in the foreground and the newer building of the business district in the background. Why is it a good idea to separate business and residential areas? (Courtesy of San Francisco Convention and Visitors Bureau)

the time and cost that must be invested in a building before a penny is spent on actual materials or construction.

If it seems that much of the preconstruction phase involves paperwork, then you have the right idea. Plans are drawn on paper, books of codes and regulations are read, and contracts must be written and negotiated. By the time actual construction begins, everyone is eager to start.

· ·

Construction Phase

The construction phase begins when the ground is broken for a construction project. Dirt is moved, materials are ordered and delivered, and workers are hired. Once construction begins, it is easy to forget the hundreds of hours of work that come before the actual building process. However, it is during construction that we see the results of all the previous designs, decisions and agreements.

■ Types of Construction Jobs

In the United States, over 200 billion dollars are spent each year on construction activities. There are many different types of jobs available in the construction industry. Major job areas include design, constructing, financing, and inspection. The positions range from unskilled labor on construction sites to the presidencies of multimillion dollar construction companies.

The most noticeable job in construction is that of the **production workers** working on construction sites to build structures. These workers include both unskilled laborers and skilled tradespeople, such as carpenters, masons, electricians, welders, plumbers, glaziers and many others. These jobs are very demanding for a number of reasons.

The construction worksite is constantly changing as construction progresses. The weather is changing, too. Large objects are being handled and many activities are occurring at the same time. Every worker is under pressure to complete the job as quickly as possible and yet make no mistakes. In addition, when the job is done, there is no guarantee that another job needing that worker's specific skills will be starting right away.

As a worker becomes more experienced in **skilled trades,** they can expect more regular work and higher wages. In order to be considered a **skilled tradesperson,** it is usually necessary to complete an apprenticeship. Apprenticeship programs are often arranged by cooperative agreement between employers and unions.

· ·

(Above) Heavy equipment operators are skilled tradespeople within the construction industry. (Courtesy of John Deere & Co.)

(Right) Electricians are essential tradespeople in the construction industry. (Courtesy of EDCH)

To join a formal apprenticeship program, generally you must have a high school diploma with certain math and reading skills. In addition, you must be physically fit and have some aptitude with tools. In some trades, it is possible to shorten the required apprenticeship period by studying the trade in approved vocational and technical courses.

Each of the crafts has a union to which many of its practitioners belong. On unionized job sites, the employer agrees to hire members of the various skilled trade unions. In return for paying negotiated wages and agreeing to abide by union regulations, the employer is assured that each person hired has proven skills and experience in the specified trade. Construction craft unions are the direct descendants of the craft guilds of medieval Europe.

. . . .

Computers can help managers and planners in construction projects. "Spread sheet" programs, a software with many business applications, are used to keep track of costs and schedules. Notice the scale models in the background, above the architects at the drawing table. (Courtesy of IBM)

Another large class of construction workers are the **managers and planners** of construction. This group includes architects, engineers, community planners, contractors, and work supervisors.

Many of these jobs require people with professional academic training and some even require certification by the government. In particular, architects and engineers must complete specified college degree programs and be certified in order to approve plans for construction. These requirements help insure that a designed structure can be safely and legally constructed.

A contractor does not need an advanced degree, but must have the knowledge and ability to win construction contracts and complete them successfully. Much of this necessary knowledge is obtained on the job. Work supervisors, or foremen, are often experienced construction workers who obtain additional training and then move up to supervisory jobs.

■ Scheduling and Coordinating Construction

The construction of a large building or public project, such as a dam or bridge, requires the coordination of hundreds of people and thousands of different materials. During World War II, the Navy developed a system of planning and tracking the steps in large complicated projects. This system has evolved into what is called the **Critical Path Method (CPM).**

In the critical path method, each step to be completed is listed on a detailed chart with lines connecting it to all the steps that come before and after it. In this way, the manager of a project can track progress and plan what to do next. Time estimates for the completion of each of the steps are added to the chart and the **critical path** is calculated.

The critical path is the sum of all connected steps with the longest estimated completion times. Any delays along the critical path will probably delay the entire project, but delays in other areas are not usually serious.

Maintaining schedules depends on good planning, good luck and a good visual method tracking dates and events. This critical path method chart shows how key events must occur on time for the job to flow smoothly.

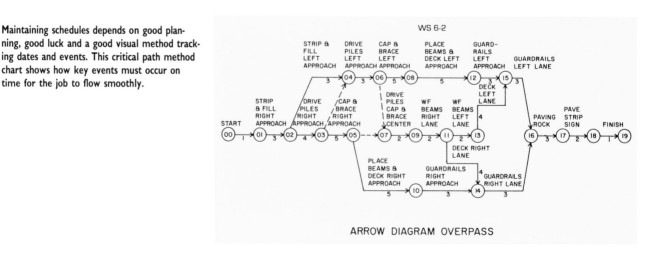

ARROW DIAGRAM OVERPASS

Of course there is far more to coordinating many different workers and materials than just designing a precise plan for construction. The hard part of the process is persuading people to follow the plan and adapting to delays, mistakes, and weather problems. The plan only serves as a guideline to keep the project managers from becoming lost in the complexity or confusion.

Architects can create the designs for an entire structure on a computer, including perspectives of what the interior will look like. (Courtesy of Mitsubishi Electronics)

■ Managing Information for Construction

Due to the complexity of construction, construction project managers have always had difficulties keeping track of all the information necessary to manage and report on their projects. The increasing role of government in construction also has added to the paperwork and record-keeping responsibilities. Today, managers of all but the smallest construction projects make extensive use of computers to store and process information.

Computers are widely used to plan the financial aspects of projects, to perform general accounting, and to inventory materials. Computers also are used to design structures, using tools such as **Computer Aided Design (CAD)** programs.

■ Safety on the Job

The government is very involved in worker safety and building safety. The Occupational Safety and Health Act **(OSHA)** or 1970 provided for the first national program for job safety and health. This act required worker safety and health standards designed to insure that everyone could work in an environment free of recognized health and safety hazards.

OSHA standards for the construction industry require that contractors follow a number of procedures and practices designed to protect the safety of workers. In addition, detailed records must be kept of the causes and results of all worker injuries that occur on the job.

Government inspectors can show up at a construction site at any time and ask to be admitted to inspect the worksite for safety violations. In fact, almost one-half of all OSHA site visits are to construction sites. This is because construction is a complicated, difficult, and often dangerous activity.

Normal **worker employment laws** affect contractors in the same ways they affect all other employers. The number of regulations concerning the employment of workers, and particularly, the vastly increased reporting and wage-withholding requirements, have affected all businesses in the United States, particularly smaller ones. The majority of construction contractors fall in this group.

Safety is particularly important in projects such as bridge building. Workers must watch their steps! (Photo by Tom and Karen Bilconish)

. . . .

◼ Inspections

Construction projects are inspected at regular intervals. A simple residential house may have its foundation, framing, electrical systems, and plumbing inspected by the local building inspector during construction. A final inspection leads to the issuance of a **certificate of occupancy,** which allows people to move into the structure.

A larger structure, such as a high-rise office building, may be subject to a number of inspections in addition to the standard visits from the local building inspectors. Federal OSHA inspectors may inspect for safety violations. The contractor will regularly inspect the work of the subcontractors to insure that they are working at the agreed upon rate and maintaining the agreed upon standards of quality. The insurance company for the contractor also may come and inspect the site at regular intervals looking for safety hazards.

Often the bank or other lender involved will hire construction experts to inspect the project to make sure the structure is being constructed properly and is meeting its planned schedule. Frequent inspections can help a lender identify problem loans early enough to take corrective action before losses become excessive.

Process of Constructing

The actual process of construction varies depending on the type of structure involved. For example, most of the work in building a large dam involves the movement of earth and the construction of a solid mass concrete structure. Dams need very little finish work. On the other hand, the construction of a bridge involves a great deal of structural and detail work but little or no landscaping.

However, there are certain basic phases that apply to most construction projects:

- site preparation;

- constructing foundations;

- framing, pouring or assembling walls;

- closing in the structure; and

- the installation of utilities.

Large-scale projects, such as construction of this railway bridge system, are a long-term process, often lasting years. The installation of this steel span required almost surgical precision, so tight was the fit. (Courtesy of Canadian Pacific)

■ Site Preparation

The preparation of the construction site involves preparing a place for the structure to be built. Generally, this means that a level and stable base must be prepared for the foundation of the structure. In addition, the site must be organized to allow for materials storage, access to materials and work spaces during the actual construction process.

There are three major steps in preparing a site for construction:

■ determination of the condition of the site;

■ layout of the site; and

■ clearing and grading of the site, as necessary.

Determination of the condition of the site is a part of the design process. However, before the site is permanently altered it must be checked by the contractor as well. Once trees are killed and thousands of dollars have been spent moving earth, it is too late to discover a physical problem affecting the entire project.

A good contractor will check the soils and grades of the site, test bore to determine the location of different subsoils and bedrock, and study the

Contractors must be sure that no pipelines or fuel tanks lie buried under the proposed construction site. (Courtesy of John Deere & Co.)

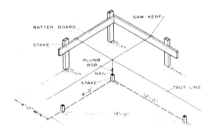

A plumb bob marks the corner of a structure.

drainage of the site before altering it. On urban sites, the contractor must be absolutely sure that there are no old fuel tanks or other toxic hazards buried under the area. If such dangers are discovered during construction, it often becomes the responsibility of the owner and contractor to remove them.

The contractor also must decide how construction materials and equipment will gain access to the site and where construction materials and tools can be safely and conveniently stored on the site.

Planning for the security of the construction site involves deciding where to establish the boundaries of the construction areas and how to protect them from typical dangers. These range from possible injuries to curious children to the loss of thousands of dollars of materials to professional thieves. Some controversial projects, such as strip mines or unpopular highways, have even experienced sabotage of their equipment while it was unattended. These dangers help explain why most major construction sites have strong fences and well-protected entrances.

The *layout of the site* involves the determination and marking of exactly where the structure will be constructed. On a simple house or garage, a transit, theodolite, or even a tape measure, is used to determine the location of the corners of the structure. Transits and theodolites are precision measuring tools with levels, optical lenses, and measuring aids.

The locations of the structure's corners are then marked by intersecting wires which run between batter boards supported by stakes. The batter boards are several feet away from the boundaries of the structure so that they will not be disturbed by the excavation of the foundation or other construction processes.

The vertical orientation of the structure is marked by having the tops of the batter boards all at the same elevation. A **plumb bob** is hung from the intersections of the wires that fall over the planned corners of the structure. The plumb bob is a small metal object with a sharp point in its center so that it marks a spot exactly under the point from which it is being hung.

Large projects are marked in much the same way, only the process is far more complicated and time-consuming. Teams of surveyors work from plans of the property and structure to mark many exact points from the structure plans onto the site. This work is checked and rechecked because a mistake would be very costly.

When the site for a road project is surveyed, the markers show not only where the road will be constructed but also exactly where soil must be cut and where it must be filled. As this work is performed, the contours of the earth change and the site must be remeasured again and again. A large project can keep a team of surveyors busy continuously for months at a time.

The *clearing of vegetation and the moving of earth* on a site are the final phases of site preparation. The amount of disruption necessary varies greatly from project to project. Building a mile of a major highway can easily involve the clearing of hundreds of acres of woodlands and the movement of thousands of tons of earth. On the other hand, the construction of a simple vacation cottage may require only the clearing of a few trees and the level-

(Above, left) Trees must be cleared as part of site preparation. Mechanized tree cutters are useful when large areas are involved. (Courtesy of Georgia-Pacific)

(Above, right) Earth-moving equipment, such as bulldozers, are now essential to construction projects. Previously, the same work was done with human and animal power. (Courtesy of John Deere & Co.)

ling of a foundation site. Some construction requires no earth moving or clearing at all.

There are many different types of heavy earth-moving equipment. The one used depends on the type and amount of earth to be moved and on the characteristics of the site and project. Bulldozers are commonly used for small projects, such as excavating the hole for a house foundation.

On large projects, many different types of equipment are used. Power shovels perform a variety of operations, including digging above and below grade, and loading dump trucks. A backhoe is similar to a power shovel except that a backhoe pulls the load to it rather than pushing it away. The dump truck is the equipment of choice for transport of large amounts of material over relatively long distances.

Draglines can pull huge quantities of earth up a slope or out of holes in front of them. They are then pulled back from the edge and can dig more. Scrapers can load, haul and unload materials by themselves. They are very useful for moving large quantities of earth over short distances. Explosives are often used to blast earth or rock loose so that it can be easily moved.

It is often necessary to **stabilize** excavations to keep the sides from collapsing. Such stabilization is usually a constructed system of walls and supports. Sometimes the soil is so stable it does not need external support. But it is important to know if stabilization is necessary, because many people have been injured by the collapse of excavations. Stabilization is particularly important if construction is occurring near existing structures such as in an urban area.

· ·

Constructing Foundations

A foundation is a structure built solely to support another structure. Every structure constructed on a site has some form of foundation. The purpose of the foundation is to provide a stable, level, unmoving platform on which to build a structure. Earth expands, contracts, and moves in other ways. That is why structures are built on foundations rather than directly on the ground.

Foundations range from a pile of concrete blocks under a mobile home to hundreds of tons of reinforced concrete under a high-rise building. Dams, towers and bridges also have foundations, which are usually made of reinforced concrete. Wood and steel are used in some foundation systems.

A foundation for a residential house can be of many different types. Typically, house foundations are made of masonry, which is either poured concrete or concrete block. If there is to be a basement, a large hole is dug in the intended location. Next a **footing** is poured to support the foundation and the rest of the structure. The size of the base of the footing is determined by the load-bearing capacity of the soil. The footing is designed so that it will not settle over time.

Drain tile is laid around a full foundation to permit drainage. The drain tile should be connected to a pipe which has an opening downhill from the bottom of the foundation. Otherwise, expensive, and often unreliable, pumps must be added to assist drainage. If there is to be a crawl space, then the site of the crawl space is cleared, levelled and covered with gravel and a waterproof layer. In either case, the foundation wall is then constructed on top of the footing.

If concrete blocks are used, they are laid carefully and checked for levelness after each **course,** or layer. Concrete blocks can be permanently joined in the traditional manner with mortar, or by **surface bonding.** This is a new technique in which you stack the concrete blocks without mortar and then join them by applying a layer of surface bonding cement to the exposed surfaces. Both methods create equally strong bonds.

To construct poured concrete foundation walls, it is first necessary to construct forms for the walls. These forms support the concrete and reinforcing rods until the concrete dries hard enough to support itself. Forms are often made of wood. They can be treated with a release agent that prevents the concrete from sticking to the wood. This allows the forms to be reused.

Houses can also be constructed on slabs of reinforced concrete which are set on top of the soil. These are poured into shallow forms and have a footer around the outside edge. A standard residential slab ranges from 4 to 8 inches thick. Garages typically are built on concrete slab foundations.

One of the biggest problems of using concrete foundations is that they can only be constructed at certain times of the year. If the weather is too cold, concrete will not set properly. This is one reason why there is a surge in construction activity in the spring as the weather becomes warmer.

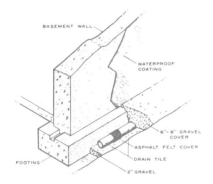

Drain tile directs water away from the foundation.

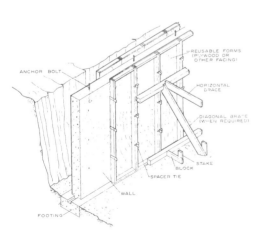

Poured concrete foundations form the base for most structures.

Generally, the construction of masonry foundations is subcontracted to specialists who have the proper forms, equipment, and expertise to produce consistently high quality foundations. Pouring tons of concrete into a 40′ × 60′ form and having it dry level within a quarter of an inch all around is not for the inexperienced or timid to try.

Another common foundation type for residential structures is the all-weather wood foundation. These foundations are framed from pressure-treated lumber in much the same way that standard houses are framed. They can be constructed under most weather conditions and they are often used for structures built during the winter.

Pole foundations are common for owner-builders to use because they rarely require heavy equipment and they cause minimal site disturbance. To build a pole foundation it is only necessary to dig the holes for the poles and then to place them in the holes so that they are level and secure. These poles are often made of poured concrete, although pressure-treated wood, such as old telephone poles is also used.

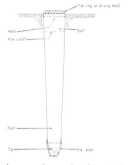

Pile foundations can be made of treated wood, steel or concrete.

High-rise buildings and other large structures are often so heavy that the amount of concrete and steel reinforcement necessary to construct an adequate and stable foundation would be extremely expensive. If bedrock lies close under the structure then caissons can be used for a foundation. However, if the soil beneath the structure has a low load-bearing capacity (that is, if it cannot bear much weight), then piles must be used.

Piles are shaped like giant spikes or rods. They can be made of wood, steel or concrete. They are usually driven into the earth by machines called pile-drivers, which act like large hammers, or by machines that vibrate the piles, causing them to settle into the earth. The diameter and length of pile used in a given situation depends on the size of the intended structure and on the load-bearing capacity of the soil.

Wood piles are cheap, but they split under the force of the pile-driver and also suffer from insect damage and decay. Concrete piles can be cast in place or precast and driven. For cast-in-place piles a steel case is driven into the ground and then filled with concrete. Precast concrete piles are lowered into drilled holes. Thin steel piles are useful if the soil is dense because they can be more easily driven. However, there is always the risk that they will hit an underground boulder and become deformed.

A **caisson** is a large cast-in-place concrete form intended to spread the load of a structure onto underlying bedrock. A caisson is essentially a shell that is forced into the ground, excavated on the inside, and then filled with concrete.

Pile driving for offshore oil platforms involves different techniques depending on the water depth, sea floor composition and other details. These piles are being driven by a steam-hammer suspended from a crane. (Courtesy of NASA)

• •

Cofferdams allow construction workers to build below sea level.

A **cofferdam** is similar to a caisson. Cofferdams are used to construct reinforced concrete foundations in areas that are wet. Bridge foundations are usually constructed by workers working inside a cofferdam on the bottom of the ocean or lake. They breathe using compressed air like divers. The cofferdams can even be submerged under the floor of the sea bed to provide a place to construct a firmer footing.

Constructing the foundation for a road or railroad bed involves the use of thousands of tons of stable material that will not settle. The earth under the road section is first **compacted.** Compacting involves applying pressure to the material to drive out the air between its particles and make it more dense and stable. Usually, gravel and other crushed rock is then spread on in a thick layer and also compacted. The surface is carefully graded and then the foundation is ready for a roadbed or railroad bed to be laid on it.

Crushed rock is used as a foundation for railbeds and roadbeds.

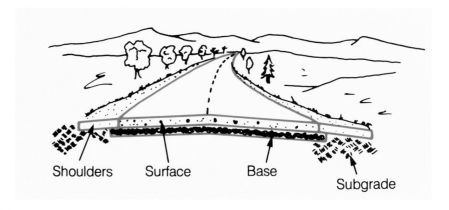

Shoulders   Surface   Base   Subgrade

Post-and-beam is one method of framing wooden structures. Standard balloon framing, using 2 × 4 studs to construct wall units is more common. (Courtesy of GSA and Jim Hatch)

■ Framing, Pouring and Assembling

Once the foundation is in place, the wall and floor systems of a structure are constructed on top of it. Most structures are of one of three types: framed, mass or bearing wall. Structures can be made up of more than one type. For example, a bridge can have piers (mass structures) supporting a bridge that is steel-framed. Traditional houses have a bearing-wall structure, the foundation, supporting a framed structure, the house itself. The majority of buildings are framed.

Framed structures are either constructed in place or assembled from components that have been previously framed.

Usually, the floor is made of joists or trusses and then covered with a subfloor of plywood or chipboard. Sections of the wall are framed on the subfloor and lifted into place. With this method it is easy to make sure the wall is square and the workers can work efficiently and safely.

When the highest floor has been completed, the roof system is installed. In earlier framing technique, frame houses had roof systems of rafters, which were constructed in place. In modern times, this method has been largely replaced by the use of roof trusses set on the wall frame and tipped into place one by one. If the job is set up properly, the trusses actually can be set in place by one person.

Small commercial buildings can be constructed with light steel frame construction. Steel studs are used to support light steel beams or trusses, which form the support for the roof structure. These buildings are usually one story and inexpensive to construct.

· ·

Large high-rise structures must be built using cranes to move equipment and materials. Notice the large mural painted on the building at right.

Large steel-frame structures must be framed in place due to the weight and size of even the smallest pre-assembled sections. A crane is used to lift each of the steel beams into place and they are then welded or bolted. The bolts used in high-rise construction are made of special high-strength steel.

Welding or bolting steel beams in place ten stories off the ground is a specialized and difficult job. Walking on a six-inch beam hundreds of feet off the ground can be complicated by water, ice, oil, or other hazards on the beam itself. The most constant danger in high-rise construction is the weather, especially wind.

Bearing walls are usually made of masonry (brick, poured concrete or concrete block). Concrete blocks are widely used in residential and light commercial structures. When properly reinforced, they also are used for multistory buildings. This reinforcement involves the use of steel reinforcing bars running vertically through the blocks and the use of reinforced concrete **bond beams.** Bond beams are reinforced concrete layers poured in horizontally around the entire structure at each floor level.

One danger in constructing tall masonry walls is that they are not very strong until after the concrete has set. There are strict requirements for bracing masonry walls under construction because a number have collapsed before the concrete was fully set. The most common cause of collapse was a severe wind load.

Bearing walls can be constructed of poured concrete also. The contractor builds forms for the walls and sets steel reinforcing bars inside the cavities

Process

in the form. The concrete is then poured into the forms and allowed to harden. After the concrete has set, the forms can be removed and reused.

Bearing walls are made of precast concrete in the form of concrete panels. As each panel is lifted into place by a crane, it is joined to the panels next to it. Many bridges are constructed of precast concrete sections connected with simple joints that lock together.

Mass structures can be made of earth, rock, or concrete. Typical examples are breakwaters, dams, and highways. The main work in constructing a mass structure is in moving the material and installing it in the form and order required. Usually, large quantities of material are required.

Most of the techniques used in building mass structures of earth or rock are the same as those used in moving earth for site preparation. Heavy equipment is used to load the material into dumptrucks or scrapers and it is then transported and unloaded where needed. Later, it can be levelled, compacted, or covered with other materials, as necessary.

Mass structures of concrete are poured in much the same way as other poured concrete construction. However, the scale of operations is much larger. When constructing a dam, it is important to keep the water away from the fresh concrete. This is done either with a large cofferdam or by rerouting the flow of the water away from the construction area.

(Below, left) Precast concrete panels are reinforced with a gridwork of steel mesh. (Courtesy of Ameron Corp.)

(Below, right) The nexagonal concrete sections of this highway overpass were made ahead of time and assembled together on site in a honey comb pattern. (Courtesy of Norton Corp.)

These workers are closing in a structure before winter. Once closed-in, finish work can continue on the inside of this house. (Courtesy of J-Deck, Inc.)

Closing in the Structure

Closing in a structure is an important step in the construction of buildings. Once buildings are closed in, they and the people working inside them are protected from the weather. Work can be completed in a more predictable and planned way.

Frame Houses ■ The walls of a frame house are covered first with a layer of sheathing and then with a layer of siding. The sheathing can be plywood or chipboard. Sometimes a new house is wrapped in a fabric, such as Tyvek, that permits water vapor to exit the house without permitting water to enter. The exterior siding of a frame house is usually made of wood, brick, aluminum or vinyl. Certain types of plywood may be used as both sheathing and siding.

Sheathing and siding are installed directly onto the frame of the house from the outside. Wood-based materials are usually nailed directly onto the house frame. Vinyl and aluminum siding are set into frames that are nailed to the house frame.

A roofing subcontractor usually installs the roof. First, **roof decking** of wood in the form of plywood, fiberboard, or boards is nailed across the top of the rafters or roof trusses to serve as a base for the roof surface and as a working platform for the roofers.

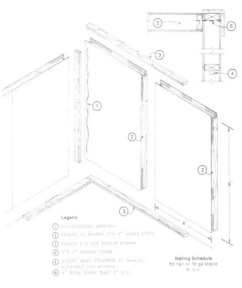

Legend
① Construction adhesive
② Single or double 2"s 4" posts (93")
③ Single top and bottom plates
④ 1"x 1" wiring chase
⑤ 3-3/8" BASF STYROFOR 1r Density
   expanded poli-styrene
⑥ 6" Ring Shank Nail 2' o/c

Nailing Schedule
6d nail or 16 ga staple
6' o.c

Stress-skin panels fit together to form a wall system.

Stress skin panels can be used for both wall and roof systems. Each panel is composed of exterior sheathing, structural lumber, insulation and an interior surface. Houses built with this system can be quickly assembled. (Courtesy of J-Deck, Inc.)

Next, roofing felt or roll roofing generally is laid across the decking to provide waterproofing. The final roof surface is often asphalt shingles set in rows and nailed into place. Other roof surfaces are wood shingles, slate, clay tiles, and metal sheets.

Roofers carefully apply aluminum **flashing** around all openings in the roof where such items as chimneys and plumbing stacks protrude. Proper installation of flashing prevents water leaks around the protruding items.

Doors and Windows ■ Typically, doors and windows are sold as units that include their own frames. Carpenters frame out rough openings in the wall; then, the units are installed and levelled in the openings.

The widespread adoption of prefabricated door and window systems is just another example of the trend in construction away from the on-site fabrication of components and toward the use of shelter component systems which are manufactured in advance. Other examples of this trend include the widespread adoption of roof and floor trusses, and the sale of prefabricated stair systems, and prefabricated plumbing stacks.

The use of prefabricated stress-skin panels for wall and roof systems illustrates the potential advantages of this trend for contractors. The wall panels are typically composed of a sheet of drywall and a sheet of plywood siding glued onto a panel of rigid foam insulation. A team of four untrained people can usually assemble all of the wall panels and add the roof system in a weekend. The doors and windows are cut into the structure after it is closed in.

The stress-skin roof panels are fitted onto normal rafters. They serve as the entire roof system including the exterior surface, insulation, and interior finish. A number of light commercial buildings are now being constructed, at least partially, with panel-based systems. This is increasingly common for roofing systems.

The site has been levelled and prepared and a footer has been poured to start construction of this owner-built single family house. Notice the pile of concrete blocks ready for wall construction.

Concrete blocks have been laid for the ground floor of the house. The gaps in the right hand end wall will become the doors of the garage intended for this level.

A steel I-Beam is used to support the floor of the walk-out basement/ground floor.

Prefabricated floor trusses are used in place of the traditional wooden joists. The trusses can span greater distances and are lighter than standard joist systems.

Roof trusses are fabricated on the second floor deck and then stacked until needed. Such fabrication is far simpler than aligning and joining rafters one by one from a precarious perch in the air.

The completion of the second floor deck permitted the easy framing of the second floor walls from studs. The wall sections were constructed flat on the deck and then lifted into place and braced.

(All photos courtesy of Gary Bolyard)

Process

Roof trusses are taken one by one from the pile and carefully set in place. Careful bracing of the load-bearing walls and the trusses themselves helps ensure the safety of the structure and of the people working on it.

Scrap boards are nailed to the trusses to brace them in place until the roof can be installed. Insulated sheathing is placed on the exterior of the wooden walls to add energy efficiency to the structure.

The roof trusses have been covered with a plywood deck. Then, a layer of asphalt impregnated fiber was rolled into place to help prevent water leakage.

A single dormer is being framed. A dormer can add a sense of variety and space to an otherwise rectangular house. The worker in the background snaps a chalk line to assure the final roofing is laid in straight rows.

The final roof shingles have been installed and the ridge cap is being set into place. The ridge cap provides critical ventilation for the roof systems.

After the structure is complete, fill dirt will be added to the uphill side. The use of a floor level which is underground on one side and ground level on the other is common in hilly areas.

The curtain wall panels that fit into the steel frame of this building bear no load. (Photo by Egons Tomsons, courtesy of George Barford)

Commercial Buildings ■ On a high-rise building, the steel or masonry frame provides the support necessary to hold up the entire structure. This has led to the development of **curtain wall** systems. These wall systems bear no structural load; their function is simply to close in and protect the building.

Light masonry is a common material used in curtain walls. Masonry curtain walls can be set in place block by block and joined to the structural building frame with metal straps, clips, or bolts. Workers usually work suspended from the top of the structure laying the block.

A faster method of hanging a masonry curtain wall is to use precast concrete panels. These panels are usually four feet square and quite thin. They are lifted into place by a crane and then anchored to the structure. It is also common for large amounts of glass to be used in curtain walls to permit the entry of light and views. These large panes are installed in the same manner as the precast concrete panels.

It does not seem logical to put a flat roof on a building and then expect it not to leak. Nevertheless, the majority of roofs on commercial buildings in the United States are flat. Flat roofs have the advantage of no wasted space under the roof and they can be conveniently coated by workers on foot.

Most flat roofs are covered with **built-up** roofs. These are constructed with alternate layers of roofing felt and **bitumen.** Bitumen is the general name for various types of tars and asphalts. Gravel or slag is usually embedded into the top coating to make it easier to walk and work on the roof.

Many commercial buildings have roofs of corrugated metal. These roofs have a gentle slope. Often, the sheets of corrugated metal are nailed directly onto the roof trusses with only a few nailing boards under them.

Other commercial roofs are sprayed directly onto the roof deck. These systems use an asphalt compound reinforced with glass fibers or a vinyl-based compound. They are particularly useful on irregular roofs where a built-up roof would be difficult to construct. Silicon rubber and synthetic rubber roof compounds are also sprayed or painted on large roof systems.

■ The Installation of Utilities

Most buildings need utilities, such as electricity, water service, sewage removal, and telephone service. The installation of utilities cannot wait until a structure is closed in. A house built on a slab foundation will have the heating ducts and plumbing installed in the slab itself before framing on the house has even begun. Utilities in high-rise buildings are installed as each floor is closed in. The electricians, plumbers and climate control technicians work on the lower floors at the same time that the metalworkers are fastening the steel components on the upper floors.

Plumbing a structure involves installing the pipes to provide water and sewage service. This job is almost always subcontracted to plumbers. Plumbing new

Installation of utilities in factory complexes includes welding large boiler units into place. (Courtesy of Riley-Stoker)

buildings requires extensive specialized knowledge of building codes, plumbing systems, and building construction. Pipes must be placed in locations where they will work properly and not freeze or interfere with the use of the structure.

Water is obtained either from a public utility or from a well on the property. If city or town water is used, the public utility company or an approved contractor will **tap** the water main to provide service to the new building. **Tapping** involves drilling a small hole in the water main and running a pipe to the structure. The water meter and shut-off valve are placed on this line.

The person plumbing a new building needs tools to cut PVC and copper pipe. He or she must carry various glues, solders, and fluxes to attach pipes to each other. In addition, a propane torch is used to heat the solder to join copper pipes. An assortment of plumbing fittings is necessary as well as fasteners to attach the plumbing to the structure.

Waste lines in the house must all be installed so that they run downhill to the main sewage pipe. Otherwise waste will collect in the pipes and eventually clog them. If the city or town provides sewage service, the public utility or an approved contractor must connect the house pipe to the public lines.

On sites where no city sewage service is available, septic systems are installed. The complexities of septic system construction and of the regulations related to it make the employment of a specialist almost mandatory.

· ·

Electrical work must meet building codes and safety regulations. Improper installation can lead to fires. (Courtesy of Miles Homes)

Gaslines criss-cross the countryside, unseen beneath our feet. Great care must be taken to insure that joints do not leak. (Courtesy of Ameron Corp.)

Electrical service is provided to a new structure by tapping onto existing power lines. This is done by the local power company. An electrical meter and a main cut-off switch are placed along the entrance line. This cut-off switch is usually inside the house to protect it from the weather. It is part of the circuit breaker box.

The electrical work on structures is almost always subcontracted to electricians. These specialists know how to safely install electrical systems which work properly and safely, and which meet all local building codes and regulations. Careful inspection of a circuit break box in a normal house will show how complicated even small electrical distribution systems are.

The initial work of wiring is done before the interior walls are finished. It involves placing all of the electrical outlets, switch locations, and outlet boxes with the wires ready to connect. After the interior drywall or other finish has been installed, then the lights, switches, and other fixtures are installed.

Telephone service is obtained by tapping into a phone cable. The local phone company is the only organization authorized to do this. Once the phone line has reached the structure, anyone can install the actual phone lines and devices in the structure.

To wire a house for telephone service is relatively simple and safe. All you need are telephone wire, standards jacks and fittings, and basic hand tools. It is preferable to run the phone wires before the interior of the structure is finished, so that the phone wires will not be exposed.

High-rise structures often have entire floors devoted to heating, cooling and utility systems. The pipes and wires for these systems usually travel up through the structure in a utility case. Fire regulations require the utility core to be sealed from the rest of the structure.

Plumbers, electricians and climate-control system specialists who work on high-rise buildings must have specialized knowledge beyond that required of people working on smaller structures. There are complex building codes and fire regulations for larger buildings. In addition, the large scale and standardized designs of larger structures place a premium on efficient repetition of correct procedures. Usually, the crews installing utilities will perform almost the same work on every floor.

The installation of gas lines in homes requires a special license due to the danger of explosion. Similarly, installing utilities on ships, dams, oil platforms, and other less common structures requires specialized knowledge and training. There are many well-paying jobs in these areas. The people who earn the most are those with a proven reputation in areas where there is a strong and steady demand for their skills.

Once the utilities have been installed, the **construction phase** of the structure is considered complete. By this time, scores of different workers with varied skills will have been involved in the construction of all but the very simplest structures. What began with a shovel full of earth has reached the point of being a closed-in structure with working utilities. Everyone can breathe a sigh of relief and commence work on the **post-construction phase** of the project.

The Post-Construction Phase

The post-construction phase is still part of the construction process. It involves completing the details of the structure, cleaning it up, and legally finishing the job. The major steps of the post-construction phase are:

■ finish work;

■ landscaping and site completion; and

■ closing out the construction process.

Of these three steps, the finish work is the most expensive and time-consuming.

The post-construction phase of this building included indoor landscaping. (Sears Tower, Chicago, courtesy of George Barford)

So-called "cathedral" ceilings leave roof rafters exposed to create a feeling of great space. (Courtesy of the U.S. Forest Service)

■ Finish Work

Finish work refers to the work that is involved in turning the completed shell of a structure with working utilities into a finished structure ready for full use. In structures other than buildings, finish work refers to the completion of all the cosmetic and other details necessary to completely fulfill the original plans for the structure.

Finish work on buildings can be divided into interior finish work and exterior finish work. The interior finish work includes completing the surface of the floors, walls, and ceilings as well as installing the lighting fixtures and any built-in appliances.

Exterior finish includes the installation of any exterior trim and painting, if necessary. It also includes railings, small stairways and other tasks that is not part of the structural framework of the building.

If this sounds like a lot of work, it is! Finish work is often complicated and it must be done carefully. After all, the finish work is the only part of the structure that most people will ever see.

Ceilings ■ When performing interior finish work, it is often wise to begin with the ceiling so that the spray or waste from completing the ceiling will fall on the uncompleted areas below.

There are many ways to apply a ceiling to the collar ties of the rafters or to the floor joists of the story above. The oldest method is to apply wooden lath across the bottoms of the joists and then to plaster over the lath. One modern method is to nail **furring strips** (1″ × 2″ boards) across the joists and then staple acoustical tile to the strips. This is faster and cleaner than plastering.

In commercial buildings the overhead ceiling is often steel or slab concrete. This surface can be left exposed or simply painted. It is also common to either put cement tile on the underside of the ceiling or to hang a suspended ceiling. Suspended ceilings are popular because they allow pipes and wires to be hidden and protected. A grid of metal pieces is suspended from the ceiling with wires and then leveled. It is then possible to drop a ceiling tile into each of the square openings in the grid.

Suspended ceiling tiles allow access to lighting and heating systems hidden above. This ceiling system also dampens sound. (Courtesy of Delta Airlines)

Process

Sculpture and murals are sometimes used to finish interior walls as shown in these rooms—one contemporary and one historical. (Courtesy of Don Drummer and Nelson Gallery of Art)

This wood finish floor has been sanded but not yet covered with a protective coat of stain or clear polyurethane. It is easily scratched or marked at this stage. (Courtesy of Deck House)

Walls ■ Traditionally, buildings of all types had walls and ceilings of plaster on lath. Now, most new hoiuses have gypsum board walls installed directly onto the studs. The sheets of drywall are then taped together at the joints and the tape is covered with drywall compound. When this dries, it is sanded smooth to hide the joints.

Drywall specialists are usually hired and paid per sheet installed. With their years of experience they can work surprisingly fast and can cut out the proper openings correctly. These openings are required to fit the sheets around electrical sockets, light fixtures, windows, and so on.

Interior walls of houses sometimes are finished with panelling. The panelling is usually made of wood or looks like it is made of wood. Panelling can be nailed directly to the studs, but it is usually better to attach furring strips first. Molding around the floors and ceiling will hide any small gaps between the drywall or panelling and the floor.

Many commercial and public structures have interior walls made of masonry. These can be left unfinished or painted. Office spaces may have drywall installed and finished as in a house.

Because of the high moisture levels, bathrooms and kitchens often have a tile finish on the floors and walls. Tiles are laid on a hard, smooth surface such as concrete or plywood, and are set with a special glue. A cement-like mixture called **grout** is used in the gaps between the tiles.

Floors ■ Framed houses usually have a **subfloor** of plywood or particle board, or sometimes concrete. A finish floor is laid over the subfloor. This finish floor can be ceramic tile, vinyl, hardwood flooring, or carpet.

Vinyl floors come in either rolls or tiles and are attached directly to the subfloor with a special glue. Wood floors are usually laid in planks directly onto a wooden subfloor. If the subfloor is concrete, strips of wood must be glued to the concrete to serve as nailers for the hardwood flooring. Carpet is laid on top of a carpet pad, which rests on the subfloor.

· ·

Most finish floor jobs are subcontracted to specialists. Thus, tile is usually set by a tile setter. Other tradespeople specialize in laying carpet. It is not impossible for a beginner to lay a tile floor or a carpet, but it is time-consuming and risky.

Commercial and high-rise buildings often have concrete floors. These may be finished with industrial-grade carpet, but they usually are just painted or even left bare. Metal flooring, usually steel, is used in some factories because it is strong and resists fire.

Finish work in kitchens can be very intricate. Cabinets and counter tops must be built and installed to fit the appliances such as stove, refrigerator and dishwasher. (Courtesy of KitchenAid)

Kitchen and Bath ■ Finishing the kitchen and bathroom involves installing all of the cabinets and any built-in fixtures. Large sums of money can be involved in this process. The cabinets are usually prefabricated and the tradesperson is responsible for installing them neatly and level in the proper location. The plumbers who installed the pipe in a house are usually called back to install the sinks, toilets, and bath units when it is time to finish these areas.

After all of the other interior finish work is done, there is one more task. The interior of the structure must be completely cleaned. People buying a new building want it to look new! They do not want a structure that looks like hordes of construction workers have been working in it all day for months, even if they know this is true.

Public Structures ■ Finishing large public structures is also important. Steel bridges and towers are almost always painted. This finishing process is not for appearance, but rather to protect the steel from the weather. Finishing a new highway can include painting the lane lines and installing traffic signs. Again, these jobs are almost always subcontracted to specialists.

Good landscaping can improve the exterior of a structure. Water, rocks and flowers provide visual interest. Some designers and contractors specialize in landscaping. (Courtesy of Beazer)

■ Landscaping and Site Completion

After a structure is built, the construction site must be transformed into the site for the intended use of the structure. This always involves cleaning up the site and it usually involves landscaping. Typically, the contractor rents a dumptruck to haul away waste from the construction process. The site then may be landscaped by the addition of walkways, plantings, and other site improvements. Sometimes, landscaping is more involved and requires the movement of large amounts of earth to improve the layout or drainage of the site. Landscaping is usually contracted out to a specialist who knows what to plant, how to plant it, and where to get it. Landscaping contractors can also construct a variety of walkways, paths, and design features, such as decorative fish ponds.

The cantilevered concrete exterior of *Falling Water*, a famous house designed by Frank Lloyd Wright, requires careful maintenance to keep it in good shape. Many visitors tour this Pennsylvania house each year. The stream and waterfall are part of the landscaping of the house.

■ Closing Out the Construction Process

After all the work on a construction project is complete, the responsibility for the structure is transferred from the contractor to the owner. At this point, many people inspect the structure carefully. These include representatives of the city, the owner, and the architect. Every part of the structure is carefully inspected and all equipment is tested to see that it operates properly.

The major and minor details of the structure are compared to the original plans and contracts. Incomplete or defective parts of the structure are noted. The contractor must then correct all these defects. If subcontractors are responsible, then the contractor calls them back to correct their work.

Once all the defects have been corrected, the owner will accept the structure. The owner and contractor must then settle on the amount of payment owed for any requested changes or justifiable extra expenses that the contractor had to spend. Negotiations can be difficult at this stage, but it is in the interest of both parties to complete the transfer of responsibility.

When agreement has been reached, the owner pays the final check owed the contractor and the contractor signs a **release.** This release is a legal document affirming that the contractor has no right to claim additional money for any reason on this project. The contractor also may sign a contract that guarantees the performance or quality of the structure for a certain period of time.

When all of these steps have been completed, the construction project is considered **closed.** The contractor can return to his or her office and calculate the total profit or loss on the project. If no job is waiting, the contractor begins investigating and bidding on other projects. The subcontractors and tradespeople begin a similar process of adding up their gain or loss and pursuing other opportunities.

. . . .

Servicing the Structure

After it is completed, a structure cannot be left and ignored. Further construction work often is necessary to maintain, rehabilitate, or add on to existing structures. Repairing and rehabilitating existing structures are major industries with significant employment opportunities. Many of the same tradespeople and subcontractors who work on new structures also service existing structures.

Expanding existing structures is another major industry. Four-lane highways are widened into six-lane highways. People add a new room on the house instead of moving. Factories need more floor space for expansion. All of these needs provide work for construction contractors and tradespeople.

As the costs of, and legal restrictions on, new construction rise, it is essential for people interested in construction careers to carefully consider the opportunities available servicing and expanding existing structures.

. . . .

Process

SUMMARY

The time for planning is not over once a structure has been designed and construction begins. Planning is also the critical part of the actual construction process. In the design process, planning is oriented to the use of the structure, its site and how much it will cost. The purpose of construction planning is to decide how a series of ideas carefully drawn on paper will be translated into a complex three dimensional structure.

Many people, materials, and processes must be coordinated in a precise arrangement over time under varied weather conditions in order to complete a structure. Every job in construction is challenging because the work is always changing and the place of work changes every time a new piece is added to the structure.

Structures are usually constructed by contractors who sign contracts with the owners of the projects. Construction projects must conform to government regulations and approvals including zoning, land use planning, building codes, and OSHA job safety standards.

Managing the construction process is extremely complicated. Contractors sub-contract aspects of the projects to specialists in such skilled trades as electrical wiring, masonry, and concrete work.

Phases of the construction process for a typical structure include:

- site preparation;
- constructing foundations;
- framing, pouring or assembling walls;
- closing in the structure; and
- the installation of utilities.

The major phases of post-construction include:

- finish work;
- landscaping and site completion;
- closing out the construction process; and
- servicing the structure.

The exact nature of the phases varies depending on the type, complexity, and location of the structure. The contractor completes his or her responsibility over the structure at the time when the construction process is closed out. Servicing and rehabilitating structures are both extremely large industries that occur after the completion of the initial construction process.

. . . .

Study Questions

1. Who are the three groups of people involved with most construction projects? How do they interact?

2. What are the three phases of a construction project?

3. What are overhead costs? How do these figure into a contractors bid?

4. What are some reasons for lawsuits in construction projects?

5. Discuss some of the ways a contractor can lose money on a fixed-price contract to build a house. How can these loses be avoided?

6. List at least four types of construction jobs. What is an apprenticeship and how is it important to job training?

7. What government agency oversees job health and safety? How does the agency ensure that safety guidelines are followed at a job site?

Suggested Activities

1. Simulate a job interview for a job in a construction company. Simulate the interview for a mason, a foreman, and an inspector. Prepare for your roles overnight. What types of questions does the employer ask? What kind of qualifications and attitudes would make you feel comfortable as an employer?

2. Obtain a syllabus for one or several college construction-related courses. Review the curriculum and determine what is being taught. What will the students be able to do at the end of the course?

3. Take a set of plans for a simple structure and try to estimate the cost of construction. Include sections for materials, labor, and overhead.

4. Invite a guest speaker from the construction industry to your class. Ask him or her to bring plans of a recent project, if available, and discuss the details of how it was constructed.

Glossary

Bearing wall structure   A structure in which a solid wall supports the weight of the structure.

Bitumen   The general name given to various types of tars and asphalts.

Bond beams   Reinforced concrete layers which are poured horizontally around an entire structure at each floor level to strengthen it.

Breach of contract   The technical name for a lawsuit against a person or company who has failed to abide by the terms of a legal contract.

Breaking ground   The moment when the construction phase of a project officially begins. Breaking ground represents a commitment by the people involved to finish a particular project.

Bridge financing   See Construction Financing.

Building permit   A written permit from the local government permitting a particular construction project to occur.

Built-up roofs   Roofs constructed by laying down alternate layers of roofing felt and bitumen.

Caissons   A cylindrical concrete foundation element which penetrates unsatisfactory soil to rest upon an underlying layer of bedrock or satisfactory soil.

Certificate of occupancy   A written statement of permission issued by local governments to allow people to move into a structure which has passed all final inspections. It which allows people to move into the structure.

Closing in   The construction step which renders a partially completed structure resistant to damage from the weather.

Cofferdam   An enclosure which protects workers underwater to permit construction work such as pouring concrete.

Compact   To apply pressure to a material to drive out the air between its particles and make it more dense and stable.

Computer-Aided Design (CAD)   The use of computers in the design and drafting of projects.

Construction financing   Temporary loans obtained to provide funds during the actual construction process.

Construction phase   Includes the activities in the construction process which occur while the structure is actually being constructed.

Contingency   A cost factor added to construction bids to cover the expense of unexpected problems and extra costs.

Contractor A person or company who agrees to build a structure under a given set of costs and conditions.

Corporation A legal entity which is created to represent ownership of a business. The owner(s) are not personally responsible for all the debts of the corporation.

Cost estimating The process of calculating how much it will cost to construct a given structure.

Cost-plus contracts A contract which sets a variable price to be payed upon completion of a specified job. The final price includes the actual costs of the contractor plus an agreed upon percentage to cover profits and overhead.

Critical path The sum of all connected steps in the plan for a project with the longest estimated total completion times. Any delays along the critical path will theoretically delay the entire project.

Critical Path Method (CPM) A planning method which is based on the calculation of the order of and relationships between all the significant steps in a project and the time required for the completion of each.

Curtain wall A wall which does not structurally support the structure. Its only structural function is to keep the elements out of the building.

Finish work The completion of all the cosmetic and other details necessary to completely fulfill the original plans for a structure.

Fixed price contract A contract which sets a fixed price to be payed upon completion of a specified job regardless of how much the work actually costs the contractor to complete.

Flashing Thin sheets of materials used to prevent the passage of water through joints in roofs or walls.

Frame structure A structure constructed by attaching many uniform building components together into structural units.

Furring The application of strips of a material to a surface to level it or provide an airspace.

Grout A cement-like mixture used to fill the gaps between tiles.

Liability The legal responsibilities for accidents and mistakes which people assume by agreeing to particular contracts and projects.

Load-bearing capacity (of soil) The amount of weight a given type of soil will support expressed in pounds, or tons, per square.

Mass structure A structure consisting of a solid unit of one or more materials. Dams are usually mass structures.

Municipal bonds Bonds which are sold to the public by various governmental bodies. A set amount of interest is paid every year to each holder of the bonds.

OSHA The Occupational Safety and Health Act of 1970 which provided for a national program for job safety and health. Also, the agency which enforces the provisions of the act.

Overhead costs The normal costs of being in business including rent, telephones, legal services, and other general expenses.

Piles A long, thin piece of a solid material driven into the ground to act as part of a foundation.

Plumb bob A small metal object with a sharp point in its center used to indicate exact vertical orientations. The plumb bob marks a spot exactly under the point from which it is being hung.

Postconstruction phase Includes the activities in the construction process which occur after the structure is closed in and largely completed.

Preconstruction phase Includes the activities in the construction process which occur before the actual construction begins.

Production workers People who work physically on construction sites to build structures.

Release A legal document by which the contractor relinquishes all claims to additional payments on a certain project.

Roof decking A material used to span across trusses or rafters to provide a surface for the application of the final roof layers.

Site preparation The preparation of the construction site to make it ready for the structure which will be placed upon it.

Skilled trades Physical jobs in construction requiring high skill levels which take years to perfect. Included are carpentry, masonry, electrical work, and so on.

Sole proprietorship A business which is directly owned by a single person. The owner is personally responsible for all debts of the business.

Stabilizing an excavation Supporting the walls of an excavation in various ways to prevent them from caving in.

Subcontract A contract between the general contractor and people who will perform specialized parts of the work detailed in the overall construction contract. Typical areas which are subcontracted include electrical work, plumbing, and masonry.

Surface bonding A method of fastening involves concrete blocks by stacking them and then applying a layer special cement to the exterior surfaces.

Tap To drill a small hole in a water or gas main to run a pipe to service a structure.

Time clauses A type of performance clause in a contract which specifies varying penalties and rewards for the contractor based on the completion date of the project.

Zoning A plan developed by the local government which sets aside certain areas for certain uses.

• •

ACTIVITY 11

Guidelines for a Waste Treatment Facility

Reference   Chapter 6: Design Guidelines and Process

Design Brief   Water supplies have grown polluted in your community from both industrial and residential waste. You have the responsibility of siting and designing a waste treatment facility in your region.

Your design team must develop a list of:

1) social guidelines
2) technical guidelines
3) environmental guidelines

relevant to the facility and your local conditions.

Parameters

1. Form design teams of four or five.

2. Social guidelines must address your choice for siting the facility. What problems might such a facility present to the surrounding neighborhoods? Is there evidence of a real social need for such a facility? How would you go about obtaining evidence? What social problems might arise from such a facility? Who should pay for the facility? Follow the three social precepts discussed in Chapter 6.

3. Technical guidelines should address the general guidelines that are listed in this chapter. A description as to how your design team will address the guidelines should follow the 5 guidelines listed.

4. Environmental guidelines are also associated with the siting of the facility. Although one site may be socially appropriate, it may be an environmentally fragile zone. How will your team make sure that the siting and use of the facility is environmentally safe?

5. Your team should develop both drawings (plans and site plans) as well as written descriptions of your design solutions.

ACTIVITY 12

The Design Process

Reference

Chapter 6: Design Guidelines and Process

Introduction

The following is a summary activity that unites all phases of the design process. This activity guides the new designer through the entire construction design process by using a checklist format. Depending upon how many of the sub-activities you choose to become involved in, this entire activity may take as long as four weeks to complete. After all, design takes time.

Procedure

MOTIVATION

1. In your sketchbooks list 5 construction design problem statements that interest you greatly. The following examples are provided as a guide. You should think of different examples.

   - *Design a house for a family of four that is compact, energy efficient, and uses passive solar energy.*

   - *Design a house that also contains a woodworking shop that can be used as a home-based cottage industry.*

   - *Design a lightweight structure that can be used by homeless persons in moderate climates.*

   - *Design a bridge that can span a 14-foot wide creek.*

   - *Design a bicycle path system that connects the neighboring towns or cities.*

2. Choose the one construction design problem statements as the design problem that you wish to work on the most. Write a short statement defining the problem on a new page in your sketchbook and circle it.

PREPARATION

1. Go to the resource center or library in your school and find 3-5 magazine articles and 3-5 books related to your design problem. Write down the names of the 3-5 articles and books in your sketchbook. Read the articles and sections of the books relevant to your particular problem.

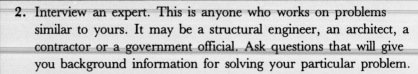

SKETCHSTORMING

FIELDSTONES

SCRIBING

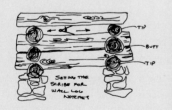

TIP

BUTT

TIP

SETTING THE
SCRIBE FOR
WALL LOG
NOTCHES

2. Interview an expert. This is anyone who works on problems similar to yours. It may be a structural engineer, an architect, a contractor or a government official. Ask questions that will give you background information for solving your particular problem.

3. Visit 3–5 structures that are related to your design problem. Sketch the unique features of the structures in your sketchbook. This will help you recall them at a later time.

4. List the social, technical and environmental guidelines (criteria) that you want your particular design problem to solve. List these guidelines on a separate page in your sketchbook under the title **Design Guidelines.**

IDEATION

1. Follow the rules for mindstorming in this chapter and conduct a mindstorming session with 3–5 persons using your design problem statement as the focus point. Use your sketchbook to record and list all of the ideas that were generated in your group.

2. Follow the rules for sketchstorming and conduct a sketchstorming session by yourself. Use your sketchbook to record your sketches.

3. Follow the rules for modelstorming and conduct a modelstorming session with others or by yourself. After the modelstorming session is over, sketch any possible ideas down in your sketchbook that resulted from the modelstorming session.

4. On the following day, choose the top three ideas that were developed from the mindstorming, sketchstorming and model-storming sessions. Use your design guidelines list to eliminate ideas that do not meet your established criteria.

INCUBATION

1. If you become frustrated, do something different from your normal routine. Try not to think of your design problem. Pursue some other projects. Exercise of some sort is also a way to relax.

2. If relaxation does not reduce your frustration, ask another person or group of persons to help you. You may wish to conduct another mindstorming session with different people in order to get new ideas. Record any mindstorming sessions in your sketchbook.

ILLUMINATION

1. Record all ideas that suddenly "pop into your head" by writing them and sketching them down in your sketchbook. Because you never know when an idea will come to you, it is important to always carry your sketchbook with you. Smaller sketchbooks fit easily into backpacks and even coat pockets.

VERIFICATION

1. Develop a set of detailed technical drawings. You may have to used additional references to develop the drawings (i.e., architectural and engineering drawing books).

2. Create a three dimensional scaled model of the design solution.

3. Using information from Chapters 3, 4 and 5, conduct a simple structural analysis on the main components of your design solution. This may also be done in your sketchbook. You may use a calculator to help with any mathematical computations.

4. Prepare a **Design Brief** that will be passed out to members of your class during your **Design Presentation.** The Brief should be no less than one page and no greater than three pages in length. Minimum components of the written Design Brief should be:

> *Design Brief Title*
> 1) Design Problem Statement
> 2) Selected Design Guidelines or Criteria
> > social guidelines
> > technical guidelines
> > environmental guidelines
> 3) The Design Concept or Solution
> 4) Future Considerations

5. Conduct a critique session by presenting your entire design solution to your class. You may use the design brief format as a guide for your presentation. The following visual aids should be used in your presentation:

> The Design Brief
> Technical Drawings
> 3-D Model

The presentation should be approximately 10 minutes long with 5 to 10 minutes for questions and answers. Classmates may also act as clients and voice their concern for weak parts of the design solution. They may also recommend changes in the design solution.

ACTIVITY 13

Measurement and Layout Maze

Reference

Chapter 7: Construction Processes and Tools

Introduction

Measuring accurately is often only one-half the job. Accurate measurements must be transferred to and laid out on materials. In this activity, you will lay out measurements to solve a maze puzzle.

Materials

- 8-1/2″ × 11″ sheet of paper
- sharp pencil and measuring device (1/16″ divisions)
- flat try square or framing square or 45° drafting triangle
- Measurement and Layout Maze Instructions

Procedure

1. Study the Measurement and Layout Maze Instructions.
2. Following the directions on the worksheet, draw the maze with the dimensions given.
3. Make sure all angles are square (90°).
4. If you make all your measurements and layouts accurately, the end of the last line you lay out should touch the beginning of the first line.
5. Give the Measurement and Layout Maze Worksheet to your teacher.

Measurement and Layout Maze Instructions

You will need a sheet of 8-1/2″ × 11″ paper, a pencil, ruler or other measuring device, and a flat square of some kind. (NOTE: Your teacher may permit you to use basic drafting tools to perform this activity.)

With the paper in a horizontal format (11″ dimension placed horizontally), identify a point 1″ down from the top and 1″ in from the upper left hand corner. From this point, measure and lay out the maze puzzle using the measurements and directions below. Every time you change directions (from horizontal to vertical as an example), make sure that the angle between directions is accurately laid out to 90°.

To reduce confusion, check each measurement twice and cross off each step as you go.

MEASUREMENT	DIRECTION
9-1/2″	horizontal to the right
7″	vertical, down
8-3/4″	horizontal, to the left
6-3/4″	vertical, up
8-1/4″	horizontal, to the right
one half foot	vertical, down
7-7/8″	horizontal, to the left
5-11/16″	vertical, up
7-5/8″	horizontal, to the right
5-1/8″	vertical, down
7-3/16″	horizontal, to the left
4-7/16″	vertical, up
6-13/16″	horizontal, to the right
one third foot	vertical, down
6-3/8″	horizontal, to the left
3-11/16″	vertical, up
5-15/16″	horizontal, to the right
3-5/16″	vertical, down
2-7/8″	horizontal, to the left
6-15/16″	slanting up to the left at 45° angle

If all your measurements and layout lines were made accurately, the end of the 6-15/16″ line should touch the starting point!

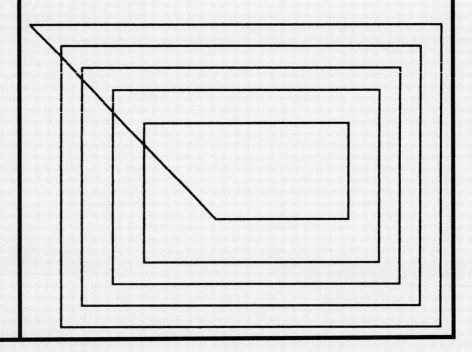

ACTIVITY 14 | Safety First

Reference

Chapter 7: Construction Processes and Tools

Introduction

Safety is a prerequisite for using tools and machines in construction. A conscientious worker knows and practices all safety rules and guidelines. Your teacher has established safety rules that you must learn before you can begin using tools to build structures. Some rules are general in natural and deal with topics such as always wearing safety glasses and hard hats, practicing good housekeeping and clean-up, and never playing or fooling around in the construction class. You must learn and follow these rules to be a successful construction student.

In this activity, you will learn the safety rules for the various tools and machines that you and your classmates will be using in the construction technology class.

Materials

- List of General Construction Safety Guidelines and Rules
- Safety Information Sheets for Tools and Machines in Construction

Procedure

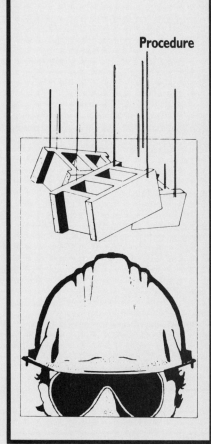

1. Obtain the general safety rules and specific tool and machine safety sheets from your teacher.

2. Study and learn the general safety rules that apply to the type of behavior and practices you are expected to perform in the construction technology lab and on the construction site.

3. For each hand tool, power hand tool, or machine you will be using, study the following information from specific safety information sheets:

   - Names of the important parts
   - Location and operation of on-off switches, adjustments, and safety features.
   - Correct operational procedures.
   - Specific safety hazards that can cause accidents.
   - Other safety rules established by your teacher.

4. Your teacher may require you to take and pass a test before you are permitted to use any tools or machines.

ACTIVITY 15

Construction Processes Practice

Reference

Chapter 7: Construction Processes and Tools

Introduction

Competent construction workers must understand and be able to perform basic processes, such as measuring, sawing materials, drilling holes, casting concrete, and applying finishes to name a few. To become a skilled craftsperson, a construction worker must spend years studying and practicing these processes. As a student of construction you will need to practice some of these same processes using the correct tools safely, properly, and efficiently.

In this activity, you will design and construct a simple structure to give you practice with basic tools and processes.

Directions

Several simple construction project ideas are illustrated to help you begin the design process. Create a set of working drawings for one of the designs and construct the structure. This activity is intended to give you the opportunity to practice using the basic tools of construction and should be completed in a relatively short time period.

Suggestions/Considerations

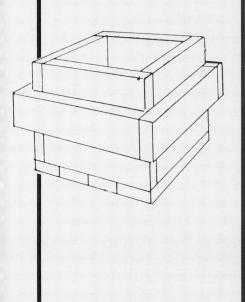

1. Before making your project selection, consider making a list of the processes and tools that will be required. (See the Sample List format.) Try to pick a project that incorporates as many processes and tools as possible.

2. At a minimum, try to make your selection include measuring, layout and checking, sawing, drilling, abrading, mechanical fastening, and coating (finishing) processes.

3. Use a copy of the chart below (provided by your teacher) to help you identify the processes required. Your teacher may help you select a project that will give you a wide variety of practice experiences.

4. Refine the designs to include any additional details that you feel will improve the appearance or functionality of the project.

5. You may have to conduct research and development activities to insure structural stability and safety. As an example, the lumber bench slats are beams that can deflect, causing the bench to collapse or buckle. Conduct experiments to identify the optimum slat length and reinforcement. As another example, the shape of the concrete ends on the other bench should not topple over backwards when people sit down. Use scale models or quick prototypes to test your designs.

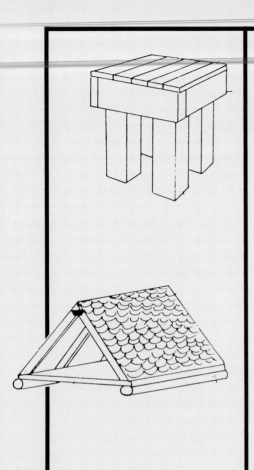

6. Make a set of working drawings for the selected project, or consider having the drafting or communication students in your school do the drawings.

7. Draw up a bill of materials for the project. On your list, be sure to include all the materials, hardware, and supplies you will need.

8. Gather the materials, supplies, and tools you will need to make the project.

9. Consider working in small groups to construct your project.

10. Be sure to follow the safety guidelines established by your teacher when using the tools and machines in your lab.

CONSTRUCTION PROCESSES PRACTICE
PROJECT EVALUATION CHECKLIST

PROCESS REQUIRED	TOOLS REQUIRED
Measuring	
Layout/checking	
Separating	
Combining	
Forming	

Outputs

ACTIVITY 16

Building a Form and Pouring Concrete

Reference

Chapter 8: How Structures Are Constructed

Concept

Building a form, mixing, pouring, and finishing concrete.

Objective

To construct a wood form and to mix, pour, and finish a concrete patio block.

Introduction

Concrete is very useful in construction. Walls, footings, sidewalks, and floors can be formed out of concrete. Concrete is a mixture of four materials: sand, coarse stone, cement, and water. Cement is the bonding material that sets up (hardens) when water is added. The result is a very strong material like stone.

To become a useful attractive floor or sidewalk the concrete must be formed and finished. Concrete is held in place on all sides by a wood frame. Steel rods (re-bar) and wire mesh are placed in the form to prevent cracking.

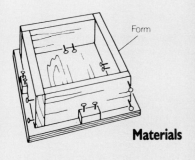

Form

Reinforcing wire mesh

Coat inside with oil

Materials

Form
1″ × 4″ × 52″ — No. 2 Pine
½″ × 14″ × 14″ — c/d Plywood
18 — 6d — common nails
1 piece wire mesh — .080, 14″ × 14″
1 50 lb. — bag of premix concrete
(or)

Concrete mixture
1 — 80 lb. bag Portland cement
Sand
Coarse stone
1 cubic yard is needed for 12 patio blocks.
Burned oil

Tools (per group)
Claw hammer
Cross cut saw
Meter stick square
Concrete edger
Concrete mixing tools/containers
1″ × 1″ × 12″ — Pine rod
Volume Measuring — 1 qt. capacity 5″ × 12″ cm long — Pine board

Procedure	A. Using a rule and pencil lay off the sides of the form.

2 pieces—1″ × 4″ × 12″

2 pieces—1″ × 4″ × 13½″

1 piece—½″ × 15″ × 16½″

C/D Plywood Bottom

B. Using a hand saw, cut on the outside of the line. Mark the length on each side. Plywood bottom should be cut with saber saw.

C. Fasten the two 12″ pieces opposite each other with 6d common nails (leave nail heads out for easy removal).

D. The form is now ready for nailing to the plywood bottom. Blocks of wood can also be nailed on the outside of the form.

E. The inside of the form should be coated with oil. The oil will act as a release between the concrete and form. Apply with a brush. Wire mesh can now be added for added strength. Place the mesh on the bottom of the form. The wire edges should be bent over 1″ to stand the mesh off the bottom.

F. The concrete should be mixed by a formula or use premix. The mixing formula is as follows:

1 part Cement

2 parts Sand

3 parts Stone

G. The form capacity is 17½ pints. Mix the correct amount of concrete for the form.

3 pts.—Cement

6 pts.—Sand

9 pts.—Stone

18 pts.—Total

Combine the sand and stone first, then add concrete until an even mixture appears.

H. The correct amount of water is important. Add water slowly to the mixture. Too much water will weaken the concrete. Add 35 oz. of water to your mixture. This will produce a 4500 P.S.I. strength after twenty-eight days.

I. Pour concrete into the form slowly. The 1″ × 1″ × 12″ rod should be used at this time. This is called *rodding*. The rod is used to push the concrete into all corners and remove air bubbles. A hammer can also be used to rap the sides. This will also help distribute the concrete. Use the rod to *screed* off the excess concrete from the top of the form.

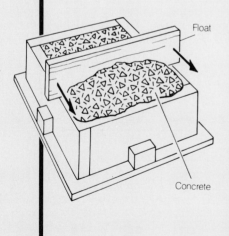

Float

Concrete

J. As the concrete begins to set-up, a finish can be applied. Draw your finger lightly across the top. If the impression remains, the concrete is ready to be floated. This term describes the finishing process. Sand is floated to the surface to give a smooth finish. A smooth piece of wood 5″ wide and 15″ long will make a good float. Draw the float across the concrete until a smooth finish appears. A concrete edger will give the edges a round-smooth appearance. Clean all tools to remove concrete.

K. The form can be removed the next day. Rough edges should be removed and the concrete block covered with plastic. This will slow down the curing process and reduce the possibility of cracks. Water should be sprinkled on the block in hot weather.

L. Remove the excess concrete from the form and store for future use.

Wood Frame Construction

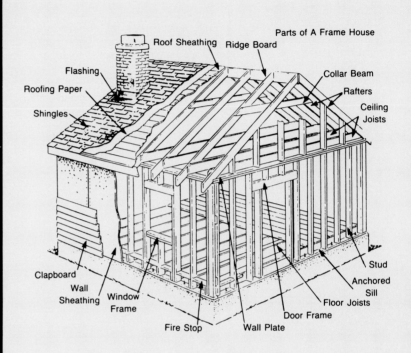

Parts of A Frame House

Roof Sheathing · Ridge Board · Collar Beam · Rafters · Ceiling Joists · Flashing · Roofing Paper · Shingles · Clapboard · Wall Sheathing · Window Frame · Fire Stop · Wall Plate · Door Frame · Floor Joists · Anchored Sill · Stud

Reference   Chapter 8: How Structures Are Constructed

Concept   Wood frame construction allows for economical use of materials.

Objective   To construct a model wall and roof section.

Introduction   Wood framed construction is the basic building method. The only exception is in parts of the world where wood is not available. Wood is an excellent material because of its strength. There are two types of wood, hard and soft. The hardwood family has a cell structure make-up different from that of soft woods. However, both types of wood cells are held together by a glue-like material. This material is *lignin*. The hardwoods are the strongest. Hardwood trees have broad leaves. Birch, maple, oak, walnut and cherry are examples of hardwoods.

Three soft woods are pine, spruce and fir. These trees have thin needles for leaves. They are often called evergreens. These soft woods are most often used in house framing. Soft woods have high strength, light weight and are most economical.

Wood is often called lumber. **Lumber** is a term used to describe wood used in the construction industry. Lumber yards are the source of different types and sizes of wood. Here is a list of some common sizes, names and uses of lumber.

Size	Name	Use
2″ × 4″ × 8′	Stud	Wall Frame/Roof Truss
2″ × 6″	Sill/Joist/ Header	Roof, Ceiling, Window, Door
2″ × 8″	Joist/Header	Floor, Ceiling, Window, Door
2″ × 10″	Joist/Header	Floor, Window, Door

Sill — a 2″ thick board bolted horizontal to the foundation wall. The sill provides a surface to nail floor framing.

Joist — a framing board that supports the main load. Used edgewise 16″ to 24″ apart, they form the floor and ceiling.

Sole Plate — a 2″ × 4″ board that rests on the floor. This sole plate is nailed to the studs in a horizontal position.

Stud — a 2″ × 4″ board used to frame the walls. Placed on end 16″ to 24″ apart.

Double Top Plate — a 2″ × 4″ board nailed to the studs in a horizontal position. A second top plate is added to overlap at the corners.

Header — a 2″ × 4″, 6″, 8″, or 10″ board used over doors and windows. They add lost strength from missing wall studs.

Bridging — a 2″ × 4″ or 2″ × 6″ board nailed diagonally between floor joists.

Rafter/Truss — a 2″ × 4″ or 2″ × 6″ nailed on 16″–24″ centers. These boards form the roof support. The slop of the roof (pitch) is measured by the roof's change in height over a one foot horizontal run.

Materials

Supply of scale lumber
   25 — 2″ × 4″ × 8′ stud
   9 — 2″ × 6″ × 8′ roof joist
   8 — 2″ × 8″ × 8′ floor header & joist
   4 — 2″ × 10″ × 8′ header for windows & doors
1/8″ plywood for sub-floor & roof sheathing

white glue
waxed paper
sketching paper
modelmaker's knife
12″ architect's scale
small framing square

The scale lumber listed above can be cut from scrap pine lumber found in the Technology Education lab. Scale size and actual size are shown below. A scale of 1″ = 1′ will be used for the model.

Scale Size	Actual Size
2″ × 4″ × 8′	3/16″ × 5/16″ × 8″
2″ × 6″ × 8′	3/16″ × 1/2″ × 8″
2″ × 8″ × 8′	3/16″ × 13/16″ × 8″

Procedure

Here is a practice exercise for you to do before starting the model. Put the letter which corresponds to the correct part of the wall section on the blank lines.

A. stud
B. top plate
C. rafter
D. sill
E. header

F. footing
G. subfloor
H. joist
I. brick veneer
J. sole plate
K. foundation

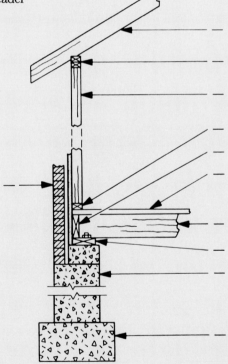

Working to a scale of 1″ = 1′ construct a wall section. The model can be made of wood cut to scale. Each piece should be measured, cut and located to scale, such as floor joist 2″ × 10″ placed on 16″ centers.

Construction of Wall Section

1. Draw the wall and floor sections on a piece of drawing paper using a scale of 1″ = 1′. Interior walls should be made 8″ high. This would be a scale height of eight feet. Wall studs are normally spaced 16″ apart on centers. In your scale model what would be the spacing between the studs? (approximately 1-5/16″) Draw each wall on a separate sheet of paper. These will be used as patterns for placing and gluing the parts together. Cover the drawing with a piece of waxed paper. This will prevent the glue from sticking to the pattern.

2. Count the number of studs needed and cut them to the proper length. Count and cut the proper number of top plates for the walls.

3. Cut the headers for the windows and doors.

4. When all pieces have been cut, they can be put in place and glued. Pins or weights can be used to hold the pieces in place while the glue is drying. Apply a small amount of glue to each end of each stud. It may be easier to dip the ends of the pieces of wood into a small puddle of glue that has been placed on a piece of waxed paper. Too much glue will cause your model frame to stick to the paper and will leave hard spots of glue on the frame.

   When the frames have dried they can be removed from the work board.

5. Roof trusses and floor sections can be made using the same procedures as the wall sections.

6. The frames can be placed vertically and then the top and sole plates and headers can be added. Place the floor section in place. Check to be certain that all parts are square. Apply a small amount of glue to the mating surfaces. Hold them in position for a few minutes until the glue begins to lose its white color. Several diagonal braces can be added to keep all the sections in position until the glue dries.

7. Add the roof section to the wall section. Be sure it is square, then add glue and hold in place until dry.

8. Your model wall section can now be placed on a base board for display.

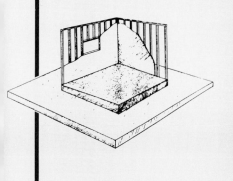

A small amount of white glue is applied to hold each member. These are laid flat on craft paper and checked for squareness. Then allow members to dry overnight. The entire floor can be glued-up together. The three sections can be built one on the other or separately.

The wall section should be framed next. A window, door and short corner must be included. The door and window sizes are scaled to $3' \times 6'8''$ and $3' \times 5'5''$ sizes. Window studs are placed on $16''$ centers.

The roof frame is built next. A truss or rafter method of framing is acceptable. The spacing is $16''$ to $24''$ between centers.

Once all three sections are complete they may be glued together or fastened with pins. A finish of stain or paint is extra. For later study, the parts can be labeled.

Suggestions for Further Study

Call a local architect and ask for a guest speaker to come to your school. This person could show drawings and models made for a building being designed. Ask the visitor to bring materials to demonstrate how the models are made.

Some questions you may want to ask the architect:

1. What does an architect do?

2. How important is the work of an architect to the design and construction of buildings?

3. What training is needed to become an architect?

4. Are there jobs in architectural firms for persons other than architects?

5. Why do architects build models?

6. Which comes first, the drawing or the model?

ACTIVITY 18

Wiring and Connecting an Electrical Fixture

Reference

Chapter 8: How Structures Are Constructed

Concept

Using electrical fixtures and wire to connect a common house circuit.

Objective

To connect an electrical circuit, inspect it, and test its operation.

Introduction

Houses are wired for electricity in three stages; rough-in, pull wire, and install fixtures. These stages are sometimes called rough-in and trim-out. Final testing and final inspection are completed last. The house plans include a drawing called the electrical worker (electrician) that includes the where and what is needed for the house.

A house has a service entrance, distribution panel, and branch circuits. Each part is found on the electrical plan drawing above.

The service entrance includes the power company's meter and the wire to the distribution panel. This meter measures the amount of electricity used by the family. The unit of electricity that we buy is the watt. The power company charges for the number of 1000 watts used in one hour. This is called a kilowatt hour.

The distribution panel sends the electricity to all parts of the house. This panel also protects the house from electrical fires. Circuit breakers or fuses are connected in the panel. A fuse cuts off the electricity during an overload or short. There may be several fuses in the panel. Larger houses need more circuits.

An electric circuit or branch circuit is a path for the electricity. The electrical path is copper or aluminum wire. Each circuit must have two wires; usually one black and one white insulated wire. A third uninsulated wire is used for added safety.

Electricity flows from the power plant through the watt meter to the circuits in the house. There are several types of circuits. Each circuit type has a purpose. Three types are lights, wall outlets, and appliances.

Materials

66″ 14-2 with ground, non-metallic sheathed cable
one male plug cap with ground
one parallel outlet with ground
one toggle switch, 15A–120V
one light fixture, porcelain
two outlet boxes
one octagonal outlet box

one screw driver — 4 inch
one wire stripping cutting tool
one voltage tester
one light bulb
one pair needle nose pliers
safety glasses

Procedure

This activity requires safety glasses. To make a good electrical connection you must follow directions.
  Practice this:
1. Strip off 6″ to 8″ of sheathing from the cable.

2. Strip ¾″ of insulation from each wire. (Careful not to nick the wire.) Should you nick the wire, cut it off and begin again.

3. Bend the wire ends in a hook shape using pliers.

4. Place the hook over the screw terminal of a switch. The hook must be placed in a clockwise direction. This will pull the end of the wire under the screw.

What to look for in a good connection:
1. Insulation touches screw terminal on switch.

2. Wire end is under screw.

Circuit Procedure:

1. Cut the 66″ of cable into three equal parts.

2. Insert the ends of two pieces of cable into each end of one outlet box. Allow 8″ of wire to be exposed.

3. Strip 6″ of sheathing from the cable.

4. Push the cable back through the clamp opening. Use a screw driver to tighten the cable clamp. Tightening the clamp too much could cause a short or open circuit.

5. Strip ¾″ of insulation from the black and white wire.

6. Form a hook, going in a clockwise direction. Connect white wire to silver colored screw. Black wire to brass colored screw. The bare ground wire is connected to the screw on the corner of the outlet (usually colored green).

7. The second cable in the outlet box should be connected the same as in procedure no. 6. Bare wire is connected to green colored screw terminal.

8. On one end of the cable, run wire through clamp of outlet box.

9. Pull 8″ of cable through clamp. Strip 6″ of sheathing.

Pigtail splice   Wire nut

10. Strip ¾ ″ of insulation from the black/white wires. Form a hook in a clockwise direction on the *black wire only*.

11. Connect the black wire to a screw terminal on your toggle switch. You should notice the switch has a top and bottom. Top is marked *off*.

12. Pull the third piece of cable through clamp in switch outlet box. Strip 6″ of sheathing and clamp at this point.

13. Strip ¾ ″ of insulation from the black wire. Form a hook in a clockwise direction.

14. Connect the black wire to unused screw on the switch.

15. Strip 1″ of insulation from each of the white wires. Twist these wires together in a clockwise direction forming a pigtail splice. Place a no. 8 wire nut over the splice, and tighten in a clockwise direction. *No bare* wire should be seen. Connect the uninsulated ground wire to the outlet box.

16. You are ready to connect the light fixture on the other end of the third wire.

17. Pull 8″ of cable through the clamp in the octagonal outlet box. Strip 6″ of sheathing and clamp at this point.

18. Strip ¾ ″ of insulation from the black and white wire. Form hooks in a clockwise direction.

19. Look at your light fixture, look for a silver and brass colored screw. Other fixtures may use silver and brass colored wires.

20. Connect the white wire to the silver screw and black wire to brass. This will prevent a possible shock hazard while changing bulbs. The bare ground wire should be connected to the outlet box.

21. You are now ready to apply a plug cap. This will be on the only end of cable not used, or the one leading from the parallel outlet. Strip 2″ of sheathing from the cable.

22. Strip ¾ ″ of insulation from both wires. Pull wires through plug cap and form hooks.

23. Place hooks under screw terminals in clockwise direction. The bare wire should be connected to green colored screw. This is another ground.

24. Once completed, your work is ready for inspection. Have someone in your class check your work for such things as loose connections or bare wire.

25. The parallel outlet, switch, and light fixture are now ready to be installed in the outlet box. Bend the wires in a "S" shape and push them inside the outlet box. The two screws in the fixture should be screwed completely into the outlet boxes.

26. Have your teacher inspect your work for *safety only*. Should you have an error that would cause a short, the teacher will point it out.

27. Install cover plates on the parallel outlet and switch.

28. Check out a light bulb and install in fixture for a test.

29. Plug your circuit into an outlet labeled by your teacher.

30. Turn the switch on. Does the light burn? Use a circuit tester to test the parallel outlet. Does this circuit work?

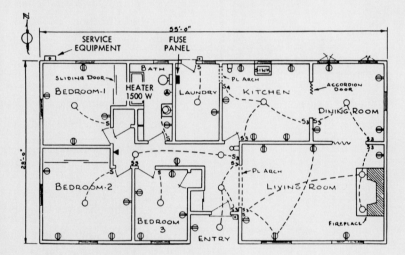

ACTIVITY 19

Land Description

Reference

Chapter 8: How Structures Are Constructed

Concept

Land description

Objective

To survey a plot of land

Introduction

Land is described for legal ownership. This process is called *surveying*. The person who does the work is called a *surveyor*. The land surveyor must study and pass a state license test.

Land is described by a drawing called a plat or land map. An important part of the surveyor's job is to read the legal description. This tells the location of the boundaries. Each boundary has a direction, north or south and a distance in feet. For example; north — 60 degrees, east — 150' (feet) 0" (inches). Land can have two, three, four, five, or more boundaries.

The boundary line begins from a known point or bench mark. Each boundary is laid out from one point to the next. The true test of the surveyor's work comes when the last point must end on the beginning point. For example: From a bench mark located on the northeast corner of Mr. Joe Johnson's property begin

south — 60 degrees, east — 150'0", then
north — 30 degrees, east — 300'0", then
north — 60 degrees, west — 150', then
south — 30 degrees, west — 300'0".

A survey instrument called a *transit* is used to measure angles. There are 360 degrees in a circle with each degree divided into 60 degree minutes. A circle marked into degrees will serve you as a transit.

The center of the circle is placed over the known point. From this point a sighting back is made to determine the direction of north. A surveyor's map will have north marked in relation to a known point. On your map the top edge of your paper will be a north direction. While you move from point to point, "always keep the north on your circle pointed to the north on your paper." You will learn in this activity how to do some surveying and how to draw a land map.

Materials	pencil circle marked in degrees map work sheet ruler

Procedure

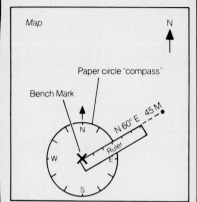

1. On the map work sheet find the bench mark and the north direction.

2. Place the circle's center over the bench mark. Line up north on the circle with north on the paper.

3. From this position mark off the direction of the first boundary. North—60 degrees, east—150'. Use the scale of 1:500, or approximately 2 mm on the map equals 41'8" distance. For example: 150' would be 90 mm scale distance on the map. Mark the direction at the edge of the circle.

4. Now use a ruler to line up the mark and the center of the circle.

5. Draw the boundary line and label its direction and length.

6. Move the circle's center to the new point. Line up north by placing south 60 degrees west over the boundary line you just drew.

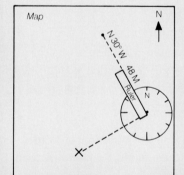

7. Now move north 30 degrees west 48 m. 48 m would be what scale distance on the map?

8. Mark the direction and draw the boundary.

9. Continue with these boundary descriptions‘
South 60 degrees—West, 45 m
South 30 degrees—East, 48 m

10. After completing the boundary, answer these questions.
    A. Did your last point end at the beginning point?

    _____Yes, _____No
    B. Does your property include the Lost Lady Mine?

    _____Yes, _____No
    C. Will your property touch the James River?

    _____Yes, _____No
    D. How far is Route 610 from the first boundary point (N 60 degrees E, 45 meters)?

    ¼" = 10' _____
    E. How far is Route 60 from the second boundary point (N 30 degrees W, 48 meters)?

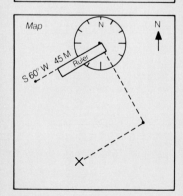

ACTIVITY 20

The Construction Enterprise

Reference

Chapter 8: How Structures Are Constructed

Introduction

The best way to maximize your understanding of the entire construction process is to perform it. In this activity, the class will be responsible for the financing, design, paperwork, marketing, and final accounting of a construction project.

    The amount of independence and assistance provided the class is up to your teacher. In some classes, the teacher will act as the head contractor and assign each task. Other classes may be advanced enough for a student to manage the whole process, permitting the teacher to act as a resource person and facilitator.

Activity Brief

The purpose of this activity is for the class to plan, build, and market a structure:

1. Research and organize
2. Select final plans

3. Obtain financing and calculate investment
4. Complete marketing of structure
5. Obtain materials and start construction
6. Close out construction process and company

Procedure

1. **Research and Organize.**
   In this phase the class will become organized into a construction enterprise. Some of the functions to be performed in this phase include:

   - organization of class by functions and project planning;

   - research of possible plans for the structure;

   - preliminary market research; and

   - research of required permissions to construct and sell a structure.

   These phases can be as simple or as complicated as you wish to make them. The plans can be obtained from a book in the library or could even be designed by the class. Similarly, the market research could just involve trying to find someone to buy a small structure of a certain type. Surveys could be performed to make market research more thorough.

   To obtain required permissions, the students (or teacher) could approach the school principal to discuss the enterprise and whether or not it is permissible to construct a structure and sell it. At the least, it should be possible to make a structure in the classroom and donate it to the school itself or charity (possibly for the materials cost). Students should participate in this process, since real world construction involves the same type of permitting process.

2. **Select Final Plans.**
   Based on the research into available plans, the preliminary marketing study, and the permissions obtained, the enterprise is ready to select the final plans of the structure to be built.

3. **Obtain Financing and Calculate Investment.**
   After final plans are selected, it is necessary to estimate the cost of the necessary materials. It is then necessary for the students to calculate how the money will be obtained to finance the construction. If existing shop supplies are used, students must calculate the replacement cost of all such materials used. The funds to cover those materials can be taken from the proceeds of the sale to reimburse the school supply budget. In other words, the enterprise should act as if it is financially separate from other activities of the class.

Cash financing may be obtained by selling shares, obtaining credit from suppliers, or from private loans. Students should wrestle with these choices even if the teacher has arranged a backup financing plan.

4. **Complete Marketing of Structure.**
It is preferable to have a sales contract signed before investing too much time and money in the project. Marketing can be performed later in the process but it is preferable to complete it now so that all students can concentrate on the actual construction process once it starts. Creating and obtaining a simple signed contract will help students understand how contracts are negotiated and fulfilled.

5. **Obtain Materials and Start Construction.**
Most students think of this as the first step and not the fifth. By the time they reach this point, students should be motivated to perform careful and efficient construction work. The plans being used should be followed carefully.

6. **Close Out Construction Process and Company.**
Once the structure is completed, the buyer should be notified to inspect the structure and close the sale. If the buyer approves, the students should then add up all the costs incurred in the construction process, pay off all of the bills, repay all of the investors (if any). Any financial surplus or deficit should be dealt with in light of previous agreements and current regulations.

Finally, the class should discuss the whole project and decide areas where they could have improved their efforts. The enterprise should then be officially dissolved.

7. **List of Possible Jobs in the Construction Enterprise.**
General contractor
Subcontractors (for roof, foundations, etc.)
Marketing Director (or Team)
Foreman/Construction Manager
Design Research Manager (or Team)
Permissions (Legal) Manager (or Team)
Bookkeeper (or Team)
Finance Director (or Team)
Materials Coordinator
Personnel Manager
Assistants to any of the above
Other titles as desired

Part III

Outputs

Chapter 9

Sheltering Structures

Chapter Objectives

■ Sheltering structures protect people, animals and things from potentially harmful aspects of the exterior environment.

■ Sheltering structures permit the creation of controlled interior environments.

■ Houses, skyscrapers, and sports arenas are examples of sheltering structures.

Key Terms

Ampitheatre
Bearing walls
Crawl space
Frame walls

Pole building
Rammed earth
Stress-skin panels
Thatch roofs

Houses, one form of sheltering structures, help keep people safe from bad weather, freezing temperatures and other hazards of nature. (Photograph by Julia Runk Jones.)

A palace, too, is a sheltering structure, in spite of its emphasis on decoration, and its atmosphere of wealth and power. (Palace of the Upper Belvedere, 1721–1724. Vienna.)

Sheltering structures protect people, animals and things from potentially harmful aspects of the exterior environment. Sheltering structures also permit the creation of controlled interior environments. A typical sheltering structure is a house. Houses are designed to protect people and their possessions from many potential exterior threats. They also provide controlled interior environments for normal human activities such as working, eating, and sleeping.

A cow shed is a sheltering structure usually designed to protect cows and their food from precipitation and wind. Because this is their only purpose, cow sheds are much cheaper to construct than homes for people. Other examples of sheltering structures include skyscrapers, warehouses, carports, offices, tents, enclosed stadiums, and forts.

How Sheltering Structures Protect

The design and construction of sheltering structures largely depends on the external threats they are intended to resist. Sheltering structures can provide protection from extreme temperatures, precipitation (rain/snow), lightning, wind (tornadoes, hurricanes), thieves, animals (insects/disease), weapons, noise, and accidents.

Thick walls and small windows give you some clues about the purpose of this building: it is a fortified castle, built in the twelfth century. Notice its position, high on a cliff, and its tall central tower. (Marksburg Castle, Branback, Germany.)

Some basic sheltering structures are shown here. How well might each protect you from the elements? How might each be heated or lit? Consider why each one is shaped as it is.

yurt

hut

igloo

wigwam

Generally, the greater the protection needed, the greater the complexity and cost of the structure. The walls of a barn can protect you from a BB gun. The military control complexes that the United States government has built inside mountains can protect their inhabitants from any weapon except a direct nuclear hit. Obviously, such a military complex costs millions more to construct than a barn.

Basic design decisions unrelated to cost also determine the degree of protection that a sheltering structure will provide. Depending on local conditions, an underground, or earth-sheltered, house can usually be built for about the same cost as a standard house of the same size. Yet, the underground house provides far more protection from noise and lightning than a standard house. Conversely, the underground house is much more likely to leak water.

Controlled Interior Environments

If sheltering structures only provided you with protection, then you could save money by living in a storm cellar and bomb shelter. Besides protecting you, sheltering structures also provide you with various kinds of control over your interior environments. The ability to control the interior environment is one of the greatest benefits of sheltering structures.

By controlling the interior environment of sheltering structures, we can create environments ideally suited to eating, sleeping, working, and storage. For example, the interior of a sheltering structure provides someone who wants to work with suitable heating, artificial light, electric power for tools, and clean, level, and dry work surfaces.

People and animals also gain psychological benefits such as feelings of security inside sheltering structures. One of the most primary human desires is to live in a sheltered space. People have a great emotional attachment to the sheltering place they call "home".

hut

tepee

isaba

Shed

Hip Roof

Gable Roof

Hip-and-Valley Roof

Mansard Roof

Sloped Turret

Helm Roof

Dome Roof

Parts of Sheltering Structures

Sheltering structures typically have three main parts: a foundation, walls or a shell, and a roof. Floors and doors are also important parts of many sheltering structures.

Foundations are supporting sub-structures that provide a stable base for sheltering structures. In a sheltering structure, the foundation serves to support the roof and walls. Some sheltering structures do not have a foundation. They just rest on the earth. Foundations are discussed in detail under Supporting Structures in the next chapter.

The walls or shell of a sheltering structure vary greatly, depending on how much protection they are intended to provide. Some shelters, such as carports, do not have walls at all, only supports for their roof structures. This is because their primary function is protection from the weather.

Generally, the most important part of a sheltering structure is the roof. The roof provides the major protection from the weather, which is the first function of most shelters. Often, the shelter structure only has to be strong enough to support its roof.

A roof must be supported over its entire area and it must have a waterproof layer. Common roof systems have trusses or rafters for support. These rest on the walls or posts of the structure and are made of wood or metal. The waterproof layer is often asphalt, which comes in either shingles or rolls.

Doors are a means of controlling the entry and exit of people and animals. Many sheltering structures do not have constructed floors. In some, the earth is the floor. In others, mats or rugs can be laid on the earth to increase comfort. In many adobe houses, a sand and clay mixture is laid onto the earth inside the structure and pounded until it is hard and flat. Sheltering structures designed for storage or work often have concrete floors. Garages have large doors that lift up out of the way so cars and trucks can enter. Houses have doors designed to admit people, animals, and normal-sized furniture. Safes and bank vaults have thick steel doors to prevent thieves from entering.

Roof styles are affected by such considerations as weather (snowfall can collapse a flat roof), building function (early church spires were intended to reach toward heaven), and architecture fashion (the dome roof of St. Paul's Cathedral in London was patterned on cathedrals in Rome).

What do these interiors say about the architets who created them? What do you think they intended to say) (*Left:* Church of Our Lady, Zwiefalten, Germany. *Right:* Marcel Breuer House I, Lincoln, Massachusetts. Photograph by Ezra Stoller, © ESTO.

Indoor stadiums allow sports events and performances to be presented, in all weathers, to large groups of people. What special features might have to be considered when building a structure such as this? (Courtesy Escambia County Civic Center)

Types of Sheltering Structures

There are three major types of sheltering structures based on what they are designed to shelter. The three major purposes of sheltering structures are to protect people, to protect animals, and to protect things. Sheltering structures can also be either temporary or permanent.

The oldest and most common type of sheltering structure is designed to protect people. People-sheltering structures can be designed for large or small groups of people.

Houses are common examples of permanent sheltering structures designed to protect small groups of people. Tents and bus stop shelters are examples of temporary sheltering structures designed to protect small groups of people.

Examples of sheltering structures protecting large groups of people include schools, churches, enclosed sports stadiums, and airport terminals. Because of the cost involved in constructing large structures, there are very few temporary structures designed to protect large groups of people. Perhaps the most familiar are the large tents used at circuses, state fairs and, occasionally, wedding receptions.

Structures designed to protect animals are another common type. Barns, chicken coops, and doghouses are all examples of these. Animals generally require less protection than people, and their shelters are therefore less expensive and easier to build. Of course, some animal shelters such as those used in modern chicken or egg farms provide total control of climate and other interior environmental variables to increase production.

Structures to protect things range in complexity from a tool shed or lean-to nuclear missile silos and Fort Knox. The cost and design of sheltering structures to protect things depends on what they must be protected from and on the level of protection required.

Theft is one of the most common threats to objects left unattended. Estimates of the likelihood of theft and the cost of losing the objects help determine the amount of resources to be expended on preventing theft.

Rare book museums must protect old, delicate books from humidity and sunlight, as well as theft. Complicated climate control systems must be designed into these structures. Similarly, the manufacture of complex electronic components requires control of temperature, humidity, and dust levels. Sophisticated systems make the cost of these thing-protecting structures higher than those of most people-protecting structures.

The Whitney Museum of American Art in New York City has been designed to protect the artwork it houses. Its windows are angled to avoid direct sunlight. Each floor is wider than the one below it, so the top three floors have ample gallery space. (Marcel Breuer, 1966. Courtesy Whitney Museum of American Art)

These three houses in Belgium are built in three quite different architectural styles. Which do you think is oldest? Why?

Examples of Sheltering Structures

■ Residential Structures

Residential housing is the most common type of structure in the world. Residential housing ranges in size and cost from shacks made of cardboard, sticks, and to the great stone castles of the very wealthy. There are over five billion people in the world, and most of them sleep in some form of

This stone wall is over 150 years old and still in excellent condition. White stone is an attractive and durable building material, its weight makes it expensive to transport, and it requires regular repointing (mortar repair). (Photograph by Julia Runk Jones)

structure that protects them, to a greater or lesser degree, from the weather, animal predators and pests, and human enemies.

The Foundation ■ Foundations for houses range from nothing (building on the ground), to tons of concrete poured and formed on top of bedrock. Poles, slabs, rocks, and all-weather wood systems can also be used.

Walls ■ The walls of human shelters have been constructed of every conceivable material, including bales of hay, ice, logs, and dirt. The earliest constructed residences were made from readily available materials, such as branches, mud, and stones. All of these materials were used for human shelters in prehistoric times. Today, people throughout most of the world still build their shelters with indigenous materials.

The walls are of two major types: **frame** and **bearing.**

Frame walls have a structure of pieces which supports the rest of the wall and roof. They consist of a strong frame and of materials to cover the openings in the frame. The most common material for the frame is wood due to its availability and structural characteristics. The covering materials can range from mud and leaves to sheets of metal and modern foams such as polystyrene. Complicated frame walls contain many different materials serving a variety of purposes, such as thermal or temperature insulation.

Many African houses today are made of a frame of wood sticks with earth and twigs placed onto the frame by hand. These houses usually have roofs of grass or thatch. While easy to build, such houses are easily damaged by rain and often fail to keep animals and insects out of the house. In eastern Zaire, vipers often enter local stick and mud houses through or under the walls during the rainy season. They then seek out the warmest place in

Wood frame walls can be put up quickly. This frame structure is being built in Colorado. What covering material is likely to be applied? (Photograph courtesy U.S. Forest Service)

Outputs

the structure, which is often under a sleeping child. Many children in Zaire have been bitten and some have died after rolling over onto sleeping vipers.

Most residential walls in America are constructed of wood studs. Often, insulation is placed in the cavities between the studs. Recently, some houses have been built with 2 × 6 studs to increase the amount of insulation that can fit in the walls. Super-insulated houses have been built with stud walls up to twelve inches thick.

Posts and beams are larger wood members placed farther apart than studs. Post and beam construction is the traditional wood building method in much of Europe and Japan and is gaining in popularity in the United States.

Bearing walls bear their own weight and that of the roof without a separate frame. They can be made of stone, earth, bricks, concrete blocks, logs, hay bales, and any other materials that can be stacked or formed into a wall.

Stone is a building material that is free on many residential sites. However, stones are heavy and if there are not a lot of stones available around a building site, it is not usually worth transporting them.

Many homes have been built of earth, which is also free on most sites. However, not every type of soil will build a solid wall. If the proper combinations of sand and clay are not available near a building site, and the climate is not reasonably dry, it is usually not worthwhile to build walls of earth.

Houses made of earth are common in the American southwest and throughout the Middle East, North Africa, and the dryer regions of Mexico and South America. Houses made of adobe (earth) blocks or of rammed (compressed) earth often look the same as houses made from concrete blocks

Above: Stonehenge, in England, is the earliest example of post-and-beam construction. This is a much more recent version, using wood.
Below: Notice the flat roofs and multiple layers of adobe buildings. Where is adobe used most? (Photograph by Sarbo)

Fieldstone construction and symmetrical design give this library an air of countrified formality. (Photograph by Julia Runk Jones)

because both can be covered with a stucco layer to shed moisture and improve their appearance.

Both stone and earth are used to make houses with very heavy bearing walls that can stand for hundreds of years. One major problem with these materials is that they tend to be unstable in earthquakes. It is not uncommon for ten thousand people to die in one earthquake in areas such as the Middle East, where earth and stone buildings are common. In the southwestern United States, building codes require buildings made of earth to use concrete wall caps and steel reinforcing rod to reduce the danger of collapse from earthquakes.

Bricks are often used to build bearing walls. They are easier to work with and more stable than stones. They are stronger and they last longer than uncooked earth. However, they are heavy and expensive to transport. In many areas, concrete has largely replaced bricks as a building material. It is cheaper, can be poured, and is easily reinforced. Stacks of manufactured blocks of concrete are a familiar form of construction. Like brick, concrete is heavy and expensive to transport. It is generally used within a few hundred miles of where it is produced.

Stone, bricks and concrete provide poor insulation against the outside climate. Even walls of earth are much better insulators than bricks or stone. Underground homes, which are surrounded by earth, tend to have very low heating and cooling costs.

Almost every known material that can be stacked has been used to make bearing walls for houses. Early settlers in Nebraska often spent their first winters sheltered from the icy prairie winds behind walls made of bales of hay. Houses made of stacked sod have also been used. Logs are stacked into bearing walls in the familiar American log cabin.

Thatched roofs were common in England for hundreds of years. They are expensive to install and maintain, but are much more durable and waterproof than they may seem. Most thatch is now covered with chicken wire to prevent birds and squirrels from nesting in it. (Photograph by Claire Golding)

The Roof ■ The ideal roof is light, strong, and waterproof and spans the open areas of the house easily. The first major roofing system to be developed was thatch, which used a frame of sticks to support a bed of leaves, branches, or grasses. **Thatch roofs** are common throughout the world. Thatch roofs in England became a highly developed craft. Many are hundreds of years old and rarely, if ever, leak.

The standard modern roof system for residential structures utilizes a frame of wood covered with a waterproof layer made of asphalt shingles, slate, clay tiles or some other material. Due to the need to span open spaces efficiently, roof design is comparable to bridge design and many of the same elements have been used. These include the arch, the truss, and the beam. Stone, earth, and concrete are all very heavy and are usually only used for roofs when built into an arch.

New Wall and Roof Systems ■ New materials for housing are being tested and promoted all of the time. Ferrocement and certain plastics can be used to make rounded walls and roofs and other creative shapes. To use ferrocement, a wire mesh is erected in the shape of the house walls and roof. Then a special form of cement is sprayed on the wire frame. After it dries this cement becomes the walls and roof of the house and the wire mesh becomes the metal reinforcement.

• •

The house in the middle is made with stress skin panels. The panels, which fit together to form the house, provide frame, insulation and protective covering in one lightweight unit. (Courtesy J-Deck, Inc., Columbus, Ohio)

Stress-skin panels are panels made of polystyrene or polyurethane. They are usually covered with drywall on one side and an exterior house covering like shingles or siding on the other side. The $4' \times 8'$ panels then become the bearing walls of the house with only one 2×4 stud placed every four feet for reinforcement and alignment of the panelized walls.

Openings in Residential Structures ■ All residences must have a means for people to enter the structure. Doors are the most common way to do this. It is also desirable to admit outdoor light without admitting air when the outdoor temperature is uncomfortable. Before the invention of glass, translucent rocks such as mica and marble were used to admit light.

Glass, while expensive and fragile, is used by everyone who can afford it in their residences. Modern coatings have been developed which permit glass to block much of the ultraviolet radiation (heat) entering a residence. Other coated forms of glass perform a variety of specialized functions in controlling the light and heat transferred through them.

Windows, doors, and other openings can be opened and closed to allow ventilation when appropriate. Other openings can permit available utilities such as electricity, water, and gas to enter the structure and can allow wastes such as sewage to leave it.

Large windows in this contemporary house allow an unrestricted view, passive solar heat in winter, and good ventilation in warmer weather. (Courtesy Lindal Cedar Homes)

Sixty-four stories tall, the United States Steel Corporation building is constructed of (what else?) cor-Ten steel. A hollow outer grid contains water to cool and fireproof the building. (Harrison and Abramovitz, 1970. Pittsburgh, Pennsylvania)

■ Multistory Buildings

As noted earlier, the construction of residential structures and the construction of bridges go back before recorded history. However, the history of buildings that rise higher than four or five stories is barely a hundred years old. It was not until the late nineteenth century that the factors necessary for the construction of today's skyscrapers were all in place.

Imagine that a skyscraper of twenty stories had been constructed in 1850 and that you had been assigned an office on the eighteenth floor. What kind of problems would you have using your office? First, you would have to climb up eighteen flights of stairs to reach your office because elevators had not yet been perfected. All your furniture and water would have to be carried up by hand. If you needed a bathroom, you would have to return to the ground floor, because indoor plumbing was not well developed at this time.

· ·

Now dwarfed by its neighbors, this late nine-teenth century skyscraper was made possible by the development of the steel I-beam. (Holabird and Roche, Marquette Building, 1894. Chicago, Illinois)

After accomplishing all of this, you would probably want to get some real work done. Unfortunately, you would still have to leave the building before dark, or burn some smelly fuel to see, due to the lack of electrical lighting. Since there was no phone service, you would have to pay someone to deliver even your most routine messages by hand. Finally, there was no easy way to heat such buildings in those days and you probably would have had to deal with mountains of coal or wood to burn in the winter. In fact, you might have had to carry the coal up the eighteen flights every day with you. Doesn't sound like much fun, does it?

Buildings with more than five or six stories were extremely difficult to build until the development of Bessemer steel and the steel I-beam. However, even if ideal materials had existed, skyscrapers still were not feasible until the development of a number of supporting systems. Elevators, telephones, indoor plumbing, central furnaces, and electric lighting were all necessary to make taller buildings usable. Luckily, by 1890, all of these developments were in some usable form. Multistory buildings followed almost at once.

Early Steel-Frame Buildings ■ Dense urban areas with expensive property values are the logical places to build multistory buildings and downtown Chicago in the late nineteenth century was such an area. In addition, a major fire in 1871 had destroyed the center of downtown Chicago so there was a need for new buildings. Many were built with the new steel-frame construction system instead of the more familiar masonry construction.

The early six- to ten-story steel buildings resembled the massive masonry buildings that designers were familiar with. However, it was not long before the heights of the steel buildings were increasing, with more and more space devoted to windows. These developments eventually led to buildings of great height sometimes entirely covered with glass, such as we often see today.

Basic Structure ■ Modern skyscrapers are basically constructed of various combinations of steel, concrete, and glass. The steel is used to make the basic structural frame, which will support the entire weight of the structure and its wind loads. This frame includes the posts, beams, and floor support systems.

Concrete is used in the foundation, for the floors, and as the barrier protecting the buildings central utility core. The glass is used in large quantities in the exterior skin of the buildings. Often the glass is tinted to reduce the effect of direct sunlight on the interior spaces. Buildings with entire skins of glass were extremely popular in recent decades and they can be found in any major city.

Shafts are a necessary part of skyscrapers because they are needed to carry people and utilities between different floors. The elevator shafts, staircases, and central utility cores must be carefully designed to reduce the risk of fire and to maintain the structural strength of the building. The utility cores carry water, sewage, electricity, heating ducts, etc. In very large buildings, entire floors are devoted to providing technical services such as air condition equipment and emergency water tanks to fight fires.

A panorama of modern skyscrapers. Can you find the nineteenth century multistory building in this photograph?

Design of Skyscrapers ■ As with any construction, economic factors are the key to whether a tall building will be constructed. Given enough free land, many low buildings always provide cheaper floor space than one skyscraper. However, where land is very expensive, the tall building can provide additional floor space at a cost lower than the purchase of additional land.

. . . .

Not all multistory buildings are skyscrapers, but many of the same considerations apply. (The L&N Service Center Corporate Headquarters, Dallas, Texas)

The stability and strength of the foundation system is a key concern in the construction of any massive and heavy structure. The plastic, uniform clay soils of Chicago require different foundation structures than the rocky, uneven subsoil under New York's Manhattan Island.

The early builders of steel-frame structures in Chicago were well aware of the danger of fire due to the great Chicago fire of 1871. They considered this factor carefully in their designs. The greatest number of regulations concerning high-rise construction today relate to fire dangers. A familiar example is that any doors connecting a floor area with a shaft that joins floors must be kept closed and must close automatically when released.

Unfortunately, steel beams will melt (become plastic) if enough heat is applied. This is why the structural steel members in a skyscraper are always covered. These coverings include plaster, tiles, vermiculite, reinforced concrete and sheet metal.

The pressure of wind on a forty-story building can cause it to sway and vibrate if it is not rigid enough. In such a building, there are about ten pounds of structural steel per square foot of floor space that serves to support all of the weight of the building and its occupants. There are another ten pounds of steel per square foot of floor space that serves only to resist wind loads on the building. As a building becomes taller than forty stories, there must be even more steel per square foot for the wind loads even though the amount required to support the weight of the building remains the same.

The Sears Tower in Chicago and the World Trade Center in New York are the tallest buildings in the world. They face enormous wind loads. Both of these structures were designed to be like reinforced tubes. Each one has a steel frame around the outside, which is linked to a central steel tower by each of its many rigid steel reinforced concrete floors.

Outputs

Building Considerations ■ The steel frame can support the entire skyscraper so it is important to build the steel frame as soon as the foundation is completed. Steel beams are lifted onto the structure by cranes erected next to the building site. Workers must be skilled and fearless to walk across beams high in the air, while wrestling other beams into position and fastening them securely.

After the initial frame is completed, derricks are erected on its peak to lift all of the other building materials up to where they are needed. Workers are lifted onto the buildings by temporary elevators constructed on the outside of the steel frame. Typically, the precast concrete floor sections are added to each level of the frame followed by the ducts and wires for utilities. Then the windows, interior finish and exterior finish are completed. Construction crews of each specialty move up the structure from floor to floor performing the same tasks over and over.

■ Other Building Types

Residential structures are the most common structures on earth and skyscrapers are among the most noticed. However, there are many other types of sheltering structures. Examples include commercial buildings, stadiums, stores, farm buildings, theatres, factories and power plants.

Above: **A tower-mounted gantry crane can lift up to one million pounds of steel beams.**
Below: **The main window (called a "curtain wall") of Houston's Wortham Theater is eighty feet high. What special construction challenges might this structure pose? (Morris Architects, Houston)**

The Shakers developed round barns to store hay and grain and stable livestock. (Photograph by Claire Golding)

This geodesic dome, designed by R. Buckminster Fuller, was built from the top down, on top of a giant air bag. (Union Car Dome, Wood River, Illinois. Courtesy of George Barford)

Farm Buildings ■ Farm outbuildings are utilized worldwide to house livestock, preserve crops, and store farm tools and equipment. Traditionally, barns in the United States were made with post-and-beam wood framing and covered with boards. Many of these old barns are beautiful. Now that post-and-beam construction has become popular for houses, some of the older barns have even been recycled as houses.

Farmers in the United States today use **pole structures** for many of their outbuildings. A pole building is supported by poles set in the ground. The poles serve as a foundation and as the frame which supports the walls and roof of the structure. Pole construction is also widely used for homes built on steep slopes.

Public Buildings ■ Among the earliest public structures were the Greek **ampitheatres,** used to present plays. These were outdoor arenas consisting of rows of benches carved into a curved hill. A stage would be constructed at the base of the hill in such a way that the sounds made on stage would be projected out towards the audience. Ampitheatres are still common throughout the world.

Arenas and theatres in Europe were constructed of masonry and wooden beams until the development of iron and steel building components and reasonably priced mass-produced glass. Iron and steel permitted the construction of stronger and taller buildings, while the availability of glass allowed the buildings to be well lit inside until nightfall.

Steel framing revolutionized the construction of public buildings because it permitted far larger indoor open spaces than previous methods. This revolution did not occur overnight as it took designers and engineers time and experience to develop methods of using steel and glass effectively.

Further developments in the use of reinforced concrete and improvements in steel frames lead to a wave of large sports arenas being constructed in the United States with concrete seating areas and pillars that served to support heavy steel roof frames overhead. While the view from some seats was blocked by pillars, these arenas provided far more people access to indoor events than any previous structures.

New arenas and pavilions continue to be constructed, using a great variety of innovative designs. Geodesic domes, fabric structures, and covered stadiums are all relatively recent innovations that have not yet been fully developed.

Military Buildings and Fortifications ■ Military buildings have a long history. Groups of people have been fighting at least as long as they have been building. Once people began to build fortified structures, they soon realized that it was necessary to be able to live for some time inside the fortifications. Otherwise, attackers would just wait until the defenders had to leave the fort for food or water. The concept of the walled city was well developed in ancient times. The walled city of Troy was so well fortified that the Greek invaders had to use the trickery of the Trojan Horse to enter it.

In medieval Europe, most major towns were circled with high stone walls. Rulers and lords built themselves massive stone castles. It was found that early stone castles could be entered by undermining a corner of the wall and collapsing it. This development lead to the use of moats and to design changes in the castles themselves. Developments in society and in military techniques lead to constant changes in the design of military structures.

Early forts in the United States were usually made of wood and surrounded with cleared areas. Guns were used to shoot attackers before they could get close enough to the forts to set them on fire. Later, American forts designed for use in the nineteenth century were made of stone and concrete and were more heavily fortified to resist explosive shells.

The modern equivalent of forts are the command centers buried deep into mountainsides. These heavily fortified compounds are designed to protect the military and political leaders who will command our response to any nuclear attack. The compounds are covered with thick concrete barriers and entire mountainsides to protect the people inside from everything but a direct hit with a nuclear weapon.

Light Steel-Frame Buildings ■ Commercial buildings and factory buildings are often constructed with concrete floors, metal siding, steel-frame roofs, and either concrete block or light steel-frame walls. Such structures are easily and quickly assembled from standard manufactured components. The simplicity and ease of construction is very reassuring to businesspeople who have their money tied up with no payoff until after the building is completed. These buildings also require little maintenance.

Housing complexes such as hotels and condominium developments utilize a great deal of steel framing. Sometimes, the actual room units are manufactured in a factory and then lifted into place on the steel-framed structure by cranes. This is a form of modular construction.

This jet airplane factory is housed in a building made of light steel frame. What are some of the disadvantages of such a building? Consider extremes of temperature, acoustics, or natural hazards such as earthquakes and tornadoes.

SUMMARY

Sheltering structures protect people, animals and things from potentially harmful aspects of the exterior environment. Sheltering structures also permit the creation of controlled interior environments. Their design and cost depends on the threats expected and the degree of protection required.

Residential housing is the most common type of structure in the world. Residential housing ranges in size and cost from shacks made of sticks and cardboard to the mammoth castles of the rich and famous. All residential structures have a foundation, a wall and roof system (or systems), and openings designed to permit the controlled entry and exit of people, air, light, and, often, utilities such as electricity and water.

The history of high-rise buildings is barely a hundred years old. Inventions such as elevators, telephones, indoor plumbing, central furnaces, and electric lighting were all necessary to make taller buildings usable.

Commercial and factory buildings are often constructed with concrete floors, metal siding, steel framed roofs, and either concrete block or light steel framed walls. Such structures are easily and quickly assembled from standard manufactured components.

Study Questions

1. Would sheltering structures for people be easier and cheaper to construct if we lived in a climate with a permanent temperature between 60° and 80°F? Why?

2. Discuss the basic functions a shelter for a family would need in your area. Discuss what additional functions most shelters have.

3. Why are more and more residential structures and components of structures are being manufactured in factories instead of being constructed on-site.

4. Look around the building you are in now. What holds up its roof and floors? How about your house? Pick specific buildings and discuss how they are supported.

5. What problems had to be solved before multi-story buildings became usable?

Suggested Activities

1. Pick a sheltering structure and analyze what dangers it protects occupants from and in what ways it provides a controlled interior environment.

2. Design a structure to shelter a collection of ten antique cars. Before designing, first investigate what dangers the cars should be protected from.

3. List several different types of sheltering structures in your community and describe their functions. If you live in or near a city, name the tallest building. Find out who designed it and how it was built.

4. Design a skyscraper that rests on the ocean floor. What special problems will you have to consider in such a structure?

Glossary

Ampitheatre   An outdoor arena consisting of rows of benches carved into a curved hill initially developed by the Greeks to present plays.

Building walls   Walls that carry their own weight and that of the roof without a separate frame.

Crawl space   The space between the bottom of the house and the soil inside a perimeter wall.

Frame walls   Walls which are composed of an integrated structure of bearing pieces such as 2 by 4 studs and posts and beams.

Pole building   A structure which is supported by poles which are set in the ground. The poles serve as a foundation and as the frame.

Rammed earth   A method of building which involves compressing sand and clay inside forms to make bearing walls.

Stress-skin panels   Prefabricated building components which consist of a sandwich with polystyrene or polyurethane in the middle and such materials as drywall, plywood siding, or chipboard on the exterior.

Thatch roofs   Roofs composed of a bed of leaves, branches, or grasses, which rest on a frame of sticks.

Chapter 10

Non-Sheltering Structures

Chapter Concepts

- Supporting structures hold things up.

- Supporting structures are largely compression structures, although tensioned components are widely used for reinforcement or support.

- Examples of supporting structures include roads, platforms, towers and foundations.

- Containing structures are used to hold in or contain something.

- Dams are constructed structures used to contain water supplies.

- The four main types of dam designs are earth-fill and rock-fill, gravity, buttress, and arch.

- Directing structures are stationary structures, designed to provide pathways used to guide movements in transportation systems.

- Directing structures are constructed to guide vehicles, people, and materials.

- Examples of directing structures include railroad tracks, pipelines and tunnels.

- Transporting structures are designed to move freight or passengers from one place to another.

- Ships and mobile homes are examples of transporting structures.

Key Terms

Arch bridge	Gravity dam
Arch dam	Guy wires
Beam bridge	Lift bridge
Buttress	Movable bridge
Buttress dam	Perimeter wall
Cable-stayed bridge	Pioneer roads
Crown	Rip rap
Culvert	Slab
Drainage blanket	Suspension bridge
Eminent domain	Truss bridge

Railway bridge over the Firth of Forth. This cantilevered bridge is a mile long and 30 stories high.

Electricity is transported from the source to the user over a network of towers. The truss elements seen in the tower are common in support structures. (Photo by Stan Komacek)

lthough sheltering structures are the most important and certainly the most familiar type of structure, there are four other categories as well, based on their use:

- **Supporting structures,** such as building foundations and electricity transmission towers, hold up or support other structures or objects

- **Containing structures,** such as dams, silos, and tanks, hold in or contain substances, usually in liquid or granular form.

- **Directing structures,** such as pipelines and tunnels, provide pathways that are used to direct the transportation of passengers and freight.

- **Transporting structures,** such as ships and rockets, are structures that move for the purpose of transporting freight and passengers.

. . . .

Supporting Structures

Supporting structures are designed and constructed to hold things up. Often, the supporting structure is a substructure that supports a structure with a different purpose. The foundation of a house is a supporting substructure that supports a sheltering structure. Similarly, the footings of a concrete dam are a supporting substructure that supports a containing structure.

Other supporting structures can support equipment, people, and animals. An offshore oil rig is supported by a steel tower. Wooden fire observation towers are primarily designed to support the forest rangers who watch for fires. Roads support the weight of cars, trucks and their occupants.

There are three main types of supporting structures based on their location: underground, aboveground, and underwater. Foundations are usually constructed underground. Towers are aboveground. Footings for bridges are constructed underwater, or even under the ground that is under the water. Each environment imposes different stresses on the supporting structures.

A supporting structure rests on something and it holds something up. The three most important parts of a supporting structure are the **base,** the **compression area,** and the **top surface,** which provides the direct interface with the object being supported.

. . . .

■ Elements of Supporting Structures

The form of supporting structures is determined by their functions. Since the function of providing solid support is very old, a number of shapes have been developed to meet this function. In fact, many of the structures discussed in the chapter on basic structural elements are supporting structures or substructures. These include the post and beam, the arch, and the tower.

The triangle is another important element of supporting structures. The braces in a post-and-beam house form triangles that keep the structure from collapsing sideways. The light steel beam is designed to contain as many triangles as possible. If you carefully observe a steel tower, you will not be able to count the number of triangles it contains.

The traditional American roof is supported by rafters tied together at their base by collar ties. These also form triangles. The many types of trusses used for support in construction are all based on variations of the triangle.

Beautiful triangle braces add both decoration and strength to this post-and-beam structure.

■ Designing Supporting Structures

The design of supporting structures depends largely on what loads they are supposed to support. **Live loads** move around and thus require more support than **dead loads,** which rest permanently in one place. A person is an example of a live load, while furnaces, walls, and floor tiles are examples of dead loads.

Another important consideration in the design of supporting structures is the total weight of the load to be supported. Because supporting structures often support heavy loads, they are usually constructed of materials with a compressive strength.

In theory, a steel beam on end can resist most compression loads. In practice, however, the steel beam would tip over, because almost every supporting structure is also subject to horizontal loads caused by such factors as wind, water current, and soil movement.

Supporting structures must resist both kinds of loads. It is for this reason that many supporting structures also contain materials with tensile strength. The simplest example of this are the **guy wires** used to keep tall narrow radio towers from tipping over. It is the tensile strength of these steel wires that ultimately keeps those towers up. The wires are tightest on the upwind side and loosest on the downwind side.

The conditions under which the supporting structure must function are another key consideration in the design process. Aboveground towers are subjected to slow deterioration from the effects of precipitation. They are also subject to shifting horizontal loads from the force of the wind. Below-ground supporting structures must resist movements of the earth and potential deterioration from contact with water in the soil. Underwater supporting structures must resist damage from constant contact with water and the creatures that live in water. In addition, they must resist the powerful loads imposed by currents.

■ Examples of Supporting Structures

Typical examples of the supporting structures include house foundations, roads, and bridges.

The House Foundation ■ There are many different types of house foundations. The particular type used depends on local soil conditions, available materials, and customs. Some of the most common are the **full basement,** the **perimeter wall,** the **slab,** and **posts.**

A **full basement** provides extra space below ground level, but is quite expensive. The problem with a full basement is that water often penetrates this space and lowers its usefulness. The key issue in building a full basement is the handling of drainage. If a full basement is not designed with proper drainage, it is almost impossible to keep water out of it.

A **perimeter wall** is built on a footing. it serves to raise the building off the ground level. The space between the ground level and the bottom of the first floor of the house is called the **crawl space.** Perimeter walls cost less than full basements, but they do not provide any usable space.

Form work is necessary before slab foundations can be poured. (Courtesy of Gary Bolyard)

Outputs

Builders must be very careful to construct the perimeter wall so that the crawl space remains dry. Another common problem is that animals, particularly snakes, love the cool, dark crawl spaces to live in. The repair of the insulation or plumbing under the house can be unpleasant, difficult and dirty.

A **slab** is a flat foundation of concrete which rests directly on the soil. Although slabs have footings which extend downward around their perimeters, the whole slab rests directly on the soil and provides a large bearing area. For this reason, slabs are widely used in soft soils with low bearing capacity.

Slabs provide no basement or crawl space, which complicates the placement of heating ducts and other utilities. They also can crack over time, permitting the entry of moisture into living areas of the house.

Posts of wood or concrete provide the least expensive foundation system for a permanent house. They can be used in uneven and marshy terrain and in places where people wish to disrupt the site as little as possible. Post foundations are enclosed to create a crawl space, with the potential for pest and moisture problems. In addition, they should not be used in very soft soils because they have a relatively small bearing area.

Economically, post foundations are competitive with the other major house foundation types. However, they are usually found in the United States only in owner-built houses and certain expensive beach and dune houses. One reason for this may be that people are not accustomed to post foundations and therefore do not desire them.

◼ Roads

Roads support the weight of vehicles and allow them to travel over many different kinds of terrain. Roads vary from dirt paths passable only in the summer to modern multi-lane superhighways that cost millions of dollars per mile.

Designing and Constructing an Asphalt Road ◼ To build a major road where there is only wild country requires many steps. First, the route of the road must be surveyed carefully. Road planners attempt to minimize the cost of construction and the cost of land acquisition. They try to plan the most efficient straight road with the least number and steepness of grades (slopes).

The design and construction of roads is an extremely expensive and complicated undertaking. Economic and political factors often play a large role in determining which roads will be built. To complete a road, land must often be taken by the state from landowners who do not wish to sell. This is called **eminent domain,** the power of the state to seize private land for public use, with the amount of payment to the owner determined by the state. There have been many legal battles over the right of eminent domain.

In addition to economic, political, and legal issues, road planners try to minimize the environmental damage caused by the construction and use

Most early roads were made by just levelling the ground. In impassable areas, such as this California desert, plank roads had to be built. (Courtesy of Fort Archives, Henry Ford Museum, Dearborn, Michigan)

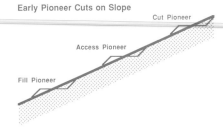

Early Pioneer Cuts on Slope

Cut Pioneer

Access Pioneer

Fill Pioneer

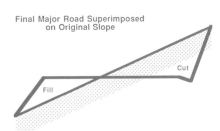

Final Major Road Superimposed
on Original Slope

Cut

Fill

A cross-section of an asphalt road. The road is layered to create a smooth, level driving surface.

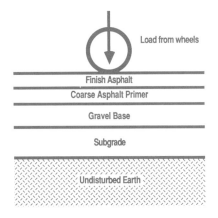

Load from wheels

Finish Asphalt

Coarse Asphalt Primer

Gravel Base

Subgrade

Undisturbed Earth

of the road. This is not easy because the construction and use of roads alters the land surface and destroys vegetation and animal habitats. The use of roads pours pollutants from vehicle exhaust into the air, endangers animals who wish to cross the road, and often kills nearby vegetation through the application of herbicides and winter road salt.

Once the road has been planned, the first step is usually the construction of **pioneer roads.** Along these access roads machinery is brought in to clear the land in the path of the permanent road. Then excavation can begin. Tons of earth are moved to prepare a flat, relatively straight subgrade on which the final road surface will rest. Often, earth is cut from slopes and then used as fill in order to convert the slopes into level roadbeds. The fill areas usually must be compacted to resist settling and erosion that could undermine the road surface. Careful planning is critical to ensure maximum efficiency while moving earth. If rock outcroppings must be moved it is often necessary to blast them loose by drilling holes and inserting sticks of dynamite.

Culverts, or large pipes, may be installed to divert water away from the road, generally to permit streams and rain drainage routes to cross under the new road.

A subgrade is not finished until all rocks larger than 3 inches have been removed from it. In rocky soil this can require a number of passes with a grader. After a flat surface has been prepared, the ditches and edges must be clearly defined.

Finally, the road surface is added to the subgrade layer by layer. First, a layer of gravel is placed on the finished subgrade. The gravel must be laid to a certain depth, watered, and compacted repeatedly until it forms a uniform and solid layer.

At this point, it is important to carefully monitor the height of the road particularly on curves where roads must be sloped to the inside of the curve to help counteract the momentum of turning vehicles. Roads are also designed to have a **crown** in the center. This slight elevation makes rain water flow off the road.

Water in subgrades is the main cause of roads heaving up in the winter. It can also cause erosion of the edges of the subgrade and the later collapse of the edges of the road. For these reasons, a primer coat of coarse asphalt is applied to the road surface to waterproof it before the final smooth asphalt layer is applied.

For smaller roads, the final asphalt coat is mixed on the road itself. A row of **aggregate** made of materials such as sand, gravel, and crushed stone is placed along the road. A crew mixes asphalt from a dumptruck with the aggregate to make the final road surface. A grader levels the mix and a roller is used to compact it.

For interstate highways and more heavily travelled roads, a portable plant hot mixes the asphalt for the road surface while a paving machine lays it down. On many roads a sealing and wearing coat is added to the top of the road to protect the structural part of the road from damage caused by wear and water.

A continuous truss bridge, Nijmegen, Holland. The brick piers support the bridge at regular intervals. (Courtesy of George Barford)

Bridges

A bridge is a structure which spans and provides passage over a river, valley, road, or other obstacle. Some bridges are designed to support only people. Others can support cars or trains. In fact, some bridges carry canals over roads and allow us to drive our cars under boats!

The first bridge was almost certainly a tree laid across a stream: an example of a **beam bridge.** This provided a means of crossing the stream without getting wet. It probably did not take long before people discovered that several trees joined together made it much easier to cross the stream safely.

Truss Bridges ■ As loads crossing the bridge became heavier, a single beam was not strong enough to support the loads. The next development was probably the **truss bridge.** A simple truss bridge consists of a long unsupported truss serving as a bridge. Simple truss bridges have been around a long time and can span surprising distances. A simple truss bridge built in 1544 was still in use in the mid-twentieth century in Bremgarten, Switzerland.

A continuous truss bridge is a series of trusses resting on piers with the individual trusses securely attached to each other so that they form a single structural unit. A continuous truss bridge can be of almost indefinite length as long as there are piers at regular spacings.

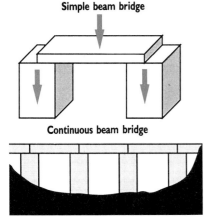

Simple beam bridge

Continuous beam bridge

• •

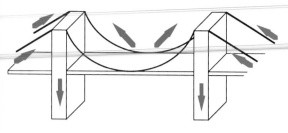

(Above:) Diagram of a suspension bridge. (Below:) Another view of a suspension bridge showing how the weight of the bridge is supported directly by the piers.

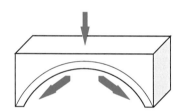

Suspension Bridges ■

Asia is blessed with a multitude of plants that produce strong vines. It was probably in Asia that the first person thought of suspending twisted vines across a ravine and constructing a simple footbridge by adding woven sticks and leaves. Such **suspension bridges** are still common in Nepal and other mountainous areas of Asia. Modern suspension bridges span the greatest distances of any bridges in the world, the longest being the Humber Suspension Bridge in Hull, Britain, which is 4,626 feet long.

A spectacular bridge design uses cables hung from piers to suspend long spans. These bridges with **cable-stayed spans** have basically replaced new suspension bridges for spans up to 1,500 feet because the cables used do not have to be anchored on land. All of the weight load of the bridge is supported directly by the piers themselves.

Arch Bridges ■

Arch bridges have been built throughout history and are still common today. Sometimes the arch is under the bridge platform and sometimes over it. The arches can be made of stone, steel or concrete. Most normal sized arch bridges constructed today are made of steel-reinforced concrete. In fact, most of the road bridges in America are made this way.

(Above:) Diagram of an arch bridge showing distribution of the load. (Below:) View showing the footing of an arch bridge.

The Rialto Bridge, Venice, Italy, was built in 1591. Arch bridges are one of the oldest forms of bridges. (Photo by George Barford)

This photograph shows two types of movable bridges: bascule bridge on left and swing bridge on right.

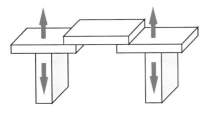

(Above:) Cantilevered bridges are balanced on each of the piers. The weakest point is the small suspended segment between the cantilevers. *(Below:)* Diagram of the cantilevered bridge at Firth of Forth, shown on page 342.

Cantilevered Bridges ■ Cantilevered bridges are balanced on piers. The heaviest construction is nearest to each of the piers to support the parts at the greatest distance. A cantilevered bridge must be built very carefully from both sides of the pier at the same time to maintain the balance of the two sides.

Movable Bridges ■ An entire technology has grown up around the construction and use of movable bridges. Many bridges over water are required to move so that tall ships can pass. This can be accomplished in several ways. The most common method of moving a bridge is to raise one end, which swings on a pivot and is counterbalanced by a weight. These are called bascule bridges. Bascule bridges are usually constructed with the deck in the raised position so as not to block the waterway.

Vertical lift bridges are designed so that the entire bridge deck is raised vertically from both ends at once. This requires construction of a tower at each end of the bridge and powerful motors. The towers are constructed first and then the deck is put in place. The deck is often assembled as a single unit on barges and then lifted into place.

A third method, less common now, is to have the deck of the bridge swing out of the way on a pivot located on a pier in the middle of the span. Swing bridges are an example of a cantilever since each end of the bridge is supported by the opposing weight on the other side of the pivot.

■ Bridge Materials

Until the eighteenth century, bridges were made of naturally occurring materials such as wood, vines, and stones. Two materials, steel and concrete, have had a major impact on bridge-making since that time. By far the most important has been steel (and iron).

The Golden Gate Bridge is greatly admired for its beauty. Few people think about all the many problems that had to be solved in its design and construction. The bridge survived the earthquake of 1989 with no apparent damage. (Courtesy of George Barford)

The first all-steel bridge was built in Glasgow, Missouri over the Missouri River in 1879 with five steel truss sections of 315 feet each. In barely fifty years, iron and steel eliminated the use of wood as a structural material in all but the smallest bridges. Similarly, steel cables opened up a new era of suspension bridge building leading to the massive spans of the George Washington and Golden Gate Bridges in the 1930s. The steel cables of the George Washington Bridge are 36 inches in diameter and contain over 26,000 parallel wires each.

Since 1960, many bridges have been built from matched precast concrete box segments. These segments allow off-site indoor casting and the use of cheaper construction methods. In fact, precast concrete segment bridge designs have won many contracts over steel bridge designs because they are usually cheaper and just as strong for spans up to 300 feet. Box segments have also permitted less intrusive and destructive construction techniques.

Reinforced concrete is a strong, formable, and relatively inexpensive material for building bridges. It is the most common type of bridge material used today on American roads. However, reinforced concrete suffers from one major weakness. The steel reinforcement is destroyed over time when road salt is used to de-ice winter roads. The salt dissolves in water, which penetrates the concrete exterior of the bridge. Many methods are being tried to make reinforced concrete bridges more resistant to the decay caused by salty water runoff.

In fact, some engineers in West Virginia are attempting to test new low-use road bridges made of wood. The expected 50–100 year lifespan of a wooden bridge exceeds what we are now getting from reinforced concrete exposed to winter salt. The idea of using wood, the oldest bridge building material, for new road bridges is considered an original, even radical, idea.

Although wood is one of the oldest bridge materials, this modern wood bridge in West Virginia is considered unusual and a little radical.

The cantilevered segment of the Linn Cove Viaduct appears suspended in mid-air. The next pier will be lowered segment by segment from the existing sections. (Courtesy of Figg & Muller Engineers, Inc.)

The Linn Cove Viaduct

The Blue Ridge Parkway is a scenic road that traverses Virginia and North Carolina through the Appalachian Mountains. It permits thousands of visitors to enjoy the spectacular beauty of this part of the Eastern United States. The problem with new roads through areas of great natural beauty is that often the road itself destroys much of the scenery around it by killing vegetation and rearranging the terrain.

As the planning for the Blue Ridge Parkway arrived at the beautiful and rugged Grandfather Mountain, the owner of the land to be traversed and the National Park Service both insisted that the road and its construction not deface any of the terrain except that directly under the road.

These conditions meant that the extensive excavation and clearing required for any road on the surface of the mountain was impossible. The only possible solution was to elevate the road and make it one long bridge.

Bridge building over land usually requires an access road on the ground large enough to carry the components of the bridge and the necessary construction equipment. Under the environmental restrictions at Linn Cove, such an approach was impossible.

The solution was to build the bridge of precast concrete segments and to add each segment from a crane resting on the already completed road segments. This permitted the new bridge itself to serve as the platform from which it was built. In this

way, construction equipment and materials were not transported over access roads cut out of the protected mountain terrain.

The Linn Cove Viaduct has won awards for its design and innovative construction methods. This extended bridge proves that it is possible to build a road through a scenic area that permits visitors to view the scenery without destroying that scenery in the construction process. It is unfortunate that building a bridge in this way is far more expensive than ordinary road construction and that so many highways have destroyed the integrity of much of our open terrain.

(Adapted from pgs 105-106 of Barcow and Kruckemeyer *Bridge Design: Aesthetics and Developing Techniques*).

Industrial minerals are often stored in containment silos. (Courtesy of Amoco Corp.)

Containing Structures

Containing structures are used to hold in or contain liquids, granular materials, and other substances. Examples of containing structures include dams, water tanks, silos, swimming pools, and nuclear-containment buildings. The form of each of these structures is designed to match the function of containing. The construction site, materials used, money spent, and building technology used is determined based on the intended use of containing.

■ Dams

Nuclear containment silo at the Oconee Nuclear Power Plant. (Courtesy of the U.S. Department of Energy)

Dams are perhaps the most interesting containing structures. Dams are barriers constructed across waterways to contain or control water. People build dams to meet their needs for public and industrial water uses, crop irrigation, electric power generation, flood control.

As society expands, so does the need for a constant, dependable supply of water. On average, each American uses approximately 135 gallons of water per day. This figure includes home, business, and industrial water use. Many industrial processes consume tremendous amounts of water. For example, processing one ton of steel requires over 65,000 gallons of water.

Dams are usually categorized by the type of materials used or by the design of the structure. The primary materials used to construct dams include earth, rock and concrete. Other materials used include metals, woods and plastics. The material used must be impervious to water. That is, it must contain water without leaking.

Dams must also be heavy and strong to resist the extreme pressures created by the huge reservoir of water. At the base of Hoover Dam, for example,

The Hoover Dam is a typical arch dam. The arch shape was chosen because of the narrow space to be spanned combined with the enormous weight of water to be held.

Before the dam is built, trial borings must be made with great care to determine the nature of the materials beneath the ground. (Courtesy Pegasus Gold Corp.)

the water exerts a pressure of 45,000 pounds per square foot. That pressure is approximately equal to the weight of a tractor trailer truck being concentrated on each one square foot of the dam surface.

The four main designs are concrete gravity dams, concrete arch dams, concrete buttress dams, and earth and rock-fill dams. The design used depends on the topographical, geological, and hydrological features of the dam construction site. When engineers chose a design, they must consider topographical features of the area, such as mountains, rolling hills, and plains. Geological features underlying the surface materials are also considered. Trial borings or drillings are made deep into the earth to determine the strength, elasticity, permeability, and ground stresses that may be present. Finally, the hydrological features, or characteristics of the ground water, are examined.

These construction site features are studied as part of a **feasibility study** that always accompanies a dam building project. In addition to examining topographical, geological, and hydrological features, a feasibility study also answers questions about the economic costs associated with building a dam, the positive and negative impacts the dam may have on the local society and environment, and the resources that will be needed to complete the project.

An important aspect of a feasibility study is the building of models of the construction site and dam. Engineers use these models to verify their calculations for forces and loads on the dam, stresses in the ground strata, reservoir water pressures on the dam, and the influence of ice build-up, silt, wind and waves, gravity, temperature extremes and earthquakes. Feasibility studies can take years to complete.

Certain generalizations can be made about which dams are best suited for certain situations. For narrow valleys with hard rock foundations and solid rock sides, the concrete arch and concrete gravity dam are best. In wide valleys with deep top soil material, and an abundance of suitable earth and rock, the earth and rock dams are best.

In the United States, over 80 percent of all large dams are made from earth and rock. In Switzerland, on the other hand, over 90 percent of all large dams are made from concrete. This is because of the typography and geology of the locations of rivers and streams. Switzerland's rivers are located in steep, mountainous regions with hard rock valleys. Most of the rivers in the United States are located in rolling hills or plains.

Grand Coulee Dam, a gravity dam, is the largest concrete structure in the world. Gravity dams must resist the force of the water by their weight alone.

Gravity Dams ■ Gravity dams are solid mass structures that resist the force of the reservoir water by their weight alone. The effect of gravity on the materials in the dam must be strong enough to withstand the force of the water. To meet this function, gravity dams are usually made from concrete, which is much heavier than earth materials on a volumetric basis.

Grand Coulee Dam in Washington state is an example of a gravity dam. This is the largest concrete structure in the world, standing over 550 feet high with a crest length of 4000 feet. Over 10.5 million cubic yards of concrete were used to build the Grand Coulee Dam.

In cross-sectional views, gravity dams are shaped like a right triangle. Typical proportions for gravity dams finds the base of the dam equal to three-fourths the total height.

Gravity dams are usually built from concrete blocks cast one on top of the other. During the casting process, overheating must be controlled. When concrete hardens, heat is generated by a chemical reaction between the cement and water. This heat can cause expansion of the concrete during hardening. When the expanded concrete cools, it shrinks. This can cause cracks and voids in the dam that could lead to leakage.

To limit this generation of heat, the dam is built in small blocks approximately seven feet high by fifty feet long and fifty feet wide. These small blocks limit the volume of concrete and the amount of heat generated during curing. Workers allow the blocks to cure and cool completely before adding another layer, which can take three to five days. Building dams with this construction technique reduces the likelihood of cracks, voids, and gaps in and between the concrete blocks. Voids still develop, however, and these

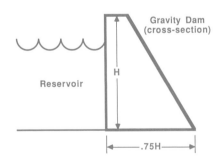

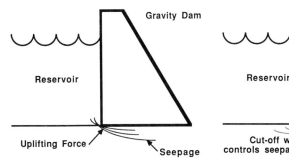

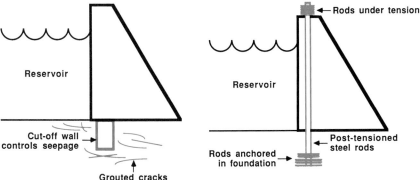

are filled with grout material forced into the voids under pressure. Rubber or metal seals are also used to plug gaps.

Problems with Gravity Dams ■ Gravity dams are subject to a number of potential hazards, including sliding off their foundation, water seepage, and overturning. Gravity dams contain the reservoir water only by their sheer weight. For this reason, these structures are usually over-designed to withstand flood waters beyond the most dramatic conditions.

Water seepage under the dam and through the foundation material must also be prevented. The obvious problem is leakage of the reservoir water directly through the dam itself. This type of seepage is difficult to control once seepage begins. A second problem from seepage under the dam is the possibility that the dam might overturn. If water builds up under a gravity dam a tremendous uplifting force is created because of the pressure of the water in the reservoir.

To prevent seepage, the foundation of a gravity dam usually includes a **cut-off** wall near the upstream face. Cut-off walls are usually made from concrete or another impervious material that limits the flow of seepage water. On solid rock foundations, a concrete cut-off wall is all that is needed. For more permeable foundations where water could seep through gaps in the rock strata, grout is usually forced into the strata to create a watertight foundation.

A relatively recent innovation used to prevent overturning are post-tensioned rods. During construction, long steel rods are built into the dam. These rods are secured into the foundation material near the face of the dam and run the entire height of the dam. When the dam is completed, the rods are put under tension and secured to the top of the dam. Post-tensioned rods help the dam resist uplifting forces from seepage water.

Buttress Dams ■ A **buttress dam** is actually a modified gravity dam. It contains reservoir water not just be weight alone as in a gravity dam, but also because of its shape. In cross-section, a buttress dam looks similar to a gravity dam except that the upstream face has a slight angle of between 25 to 45 degrees. Because of this angled face the water pressure in the reservoir helps hold the dam on its foundation. In addition, a buttress dam has equally spaced triangular buttresses on the downstream face that support

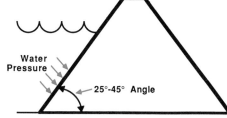

the main barrier of the dam. These are similar in principle to the buttresses used to support the walls of medieval cathedrals.

A buttress dam can be built using 40 percent to 80 percent of the total material weight used in a gravity dam, thus reducing the total cost of building the dam. Buttress dams are best suited for low, wide river valleys with solid rock foundations.

Buttress dams are subject to the same problems and hazards as gravity dams and similar construction techniques are employed.

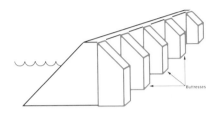

Dam buttresses serve the same function as cathedral buttresses.

Arch dam.

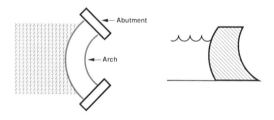

(Below:) Workers building up a layer of an arch dam by spraying wet concrete onto a wall of reinforcing wire. The characteristic arch shape is clearly seen in this picture. (Courtesy of American Public Works Assoc.)

Arch Dams ■ The **arch dam** uses the power of the arch to resist force. Unlike most arches used in construction, the arch in dams is placed horizontally rather than vertically.

Arch dams are best suited for narrow V-shaped or U-shaped river valleys. A concrete arch is constructed between two abutments which are anchored in solid rock valley walls. The arch curves upstream, and when the reservoir is full, the force exerted by the water is transmitted through the arch to the abutments. Arch dams provide a spectacular illustration of the strength of the arch shape.

Arch dams actually have a double curvature. From the plan view (top view) the arch design is obvious. In cross-section, the dam also arches to form a belly or dome shape. Such dams use the arch as the main structural element to contain reservoir water, but they also resist weight by gravity (weight of dam) and by the angle on the back of the arch, which is similar to a buttress dam.

One of the best known arch dams in the United States is Hoover Dam in Arizona.

Earth-Fill and Rock-Fill Dams ■ The cross-sectional shape of **earth-fill** and **rock-fill** dams is similar to an equilateral triangle. Typically, the upstream and downstream faces are angled at 18 degrees. Compared with concrete dams, earth-fill and rock-fill dams are relatively inexpensive to build. They are usually built where there is an abundance of suitable earth and rock materials. The materials are, therefore, readily available, inexpensive, and can easily be moved and compressed using heavy construction equipment. Earth and rock dams can also be built on a weaker foundation that concrete dams because of the lighter material used.

Earth-fill dams are built in sections. The finer earth material is placed near the center of the dam. It is then layered with gradually coarser materials, with the most coarse on the outside. Each layer of material is compressed with heavy equipment. When built on a permeable foundation earth-fill dams must have a watertight underground cut-off wall. Steel plates and concrete can be used, but clay is usually cheaper, more readily available, and easier to work.

Oroville Dam in northern California is a typical earth-fill dam. Over 770 feet high, Oroville dam contains more than 80 million cubic yards of earth and rock. The reservoir supplies the San Joaquin Valley in southern California with water for public use and farm irrigation.

Disasters Involving Dams

Dams can be very helpful by meeting needs for drinking water, irrigation, recreating, and flood control. However, throughout the history of construction, there have been many disasters involving dams that have failed.

Many of the original disasters occurred because of trial-and-error construction techniques. People were building structures that had never been built before and many errors were made in design and construction. In recent times, dam failures are a rare occurrence usually caused by unexpected events, such as extreme floods, earthquakes, or other natural disasters. Two such

failures are the Johnstown Flood and the Vaiont Dam Disaster.

The Johnstown Flood

The South Fork Dam on the Little Conemaugh River was an earth and rock-fill dam upstream from Johnstown, Pennsylvania. In 1889, the 75-foot-high dam was completely overtopped by a severe flood. The dam failed, sending a wave of water and mud through Johnstown, killing over 2280 people.

The Vaiont Dam Disaster

The Vaiont Dam, in Italy, was a concrete arch dam 858 feet high. In 1963, a mountain landslide of

over 314 million cubic yards of earth and rock completely filled the reservoir directly above the dam. A huge wave of water between 200 and 300 feet high flowed over the arch dam and destroyed the village of Longarone, killing over 2000 people. The dam, however, was damaged only slightly, thus proving the strength of arch dams. Unfortunately, since the reservoir filled with mud, the dam was left completely useless.

The Oroville Dam in Northern California. Behind this earth-fill dam is a vast reservoir irrigating a large part of our nation's crops.

Problems with Earth-Fill and Rock-Fill Dams ■ Earth-fill materials have a very limited resistance to the flow of water. Usually, there will always be some seepage through an earth-fill dam. Water in the structure creates an unstable region in the downstream face that could cause the dam to fail completely. One way to control this unstable region is to drain away the water that seeps into the dam. A **drainage blanket** can be built into the base of the dam on the foundation.

A second potential problem is seepage slides on the upstream face of the dam. During dry seasons or when water is needed in large quantities for irrigation or public needs, the water level is drawn down substantially. During these low-water periods, the seepage on the upstream face could slide off the dam into the reservoir.

During high water conditions, the weight of the water in the reservoir restrains and holds this seepage in place. However, when the water in the reservoir is drawn down quickly, the upstream face retains the seepage water and could turn into a mud slide. The dam face and a good portion of the dam could slide into the reservoir causing total failure and collapse of the dam.

To prevent this problem, rip-rap or solid slabs are placed on the upstream face of the dam. **Rip-rap** is composed of large, loose rocks. These rocks improve the drainage of water from the face and reduce the likelihood of mud slides and failure.

Solid slabs of concrete or stone can also be added to the upstream face. These slabs can prevent large amounts of seepage in the first place.

A third potential problem is seepage under the dam through a permeable foundation. As with other dams, water can seep through cracks in the rock strata under the foundation. Solutions employed are similar to those used in other dams, including grouting the cracks, incorporating an impermeable cut-off, or the use of a drainage blanket.

Rip-rap is used to control seepage and mud slides.

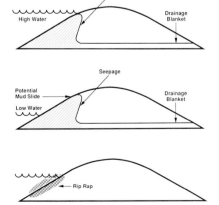

Directing structures, such as this large intake pipe, are generally expensive to build. Once in place, however, they transport materials at very little cost.

Directing Structures

Directing structures are stationary structures designed to provide pathways to guide the movements of vehicles, people, and materials. Examples of directing structures include pipelines, canals, tunnels, cattle chutes, and railroad tracks. Even the barriers used to keep people moving in lines at amusement parks may be considered directing structures.

Directing structures do not move, but they guide and enclose people and objects that are moving. Essentially, they provide guideways for transportation.

Since directing structures are always in place ready for use, they often can carry large quantities of materials. For example, an oil pipeline can carry as much oil in a day as hundreds of loaded trucks. However, the pipeline covers a fixed route. All of the oil must travel between the same two points. Trucks offer more flexibility of destination, but they also cost more per barrel of oil transported.

Directing substructures are often part of larger structures of other types. For example, almost every bridge has guardrails. The guardrails serve to direct the people and vehicles on the bridge so that they do not fall off. The guardrails are a directing substructure on a supporting structure.

■ Examples of Directing Structures

The two most common types of directing structures are pipelines and the steel rails, or tracks, that guide trains by forming the **railroad** on which the trains travel. (The railroad **beds** under the tracks are a supporting structure.) Other directing structures include tunnels, monorails, aquaducts, and canals.

Railroad Tracks ■ The rails of railroads cover the American continent and form a vital part of our overall transportation system. By forming a straight, level, and smooth guideway for trains, the rails of a railroad allow large quantities of freight to travel with a very small amount of **friction.** This means that material can be transported using only a small amount of energy.

In 1802 an Englishman named Richard Trevithick patented the idea of rails over which locomotives could run. George Stephenson, also of England, developed the first commercially feasible locomotive. His *Rocket* won a prize in 1829 for pulling three times its own weight at a speed of nearly thirty

The two most common types of directing structures. *(Above:)* Rail tracks were first laid in the U.S. to transport coal. This unit train carrier coal from the mine to the generating plant. *(Below:)* Pipelines are laid both above and below ground. (Courtesy of Chevron Corp.)

New rail systems, such as this overhead rail car, are being looked at closely by modern city planners.

miles an hour. Similar directing structures soon gained favor as a means of removing coal from underground mines. Such rail lines were quite short.

The earliest American locomotives were bought in England. In fact, by 1829, the Delaware and Hudson canal company was actually importing British locomotives to operate on its track in Honesdale, Pennsylvania.

The Americans soon came to build their own locomotives and changed the designs to better suit American conditions. Massive technical problems faced the early railroad builders as they traversed the mountains and valleys of the Alleghenies and crossed countless rivers. Railroads need to be very close to flat and straight, and the early builders had to use great skill and ingenuity to lay continuous and stable railroad tracks without the powered tools that we rely on today.

Railroad tracks must be level and stable. This track is being laid on a carefully graded bed.

Railroads are constructed using many of the same techniques as roads. A solid and level base must be constructed under every section of railroad tracks. Heavy rocks are used and the land around the track bed is carefully graded to insure that water runoff does not flow over, or undermine, the tracks. Railroad tracks must have only moderate slopes and moderate turns. Thus, planning a rail route requires extremely careful planning and access to a wide choice of land particularly when travelling over uneven countryside.

One disadvantage of railroads is that the products and freight delivered can only be delivered where there is track. Some companies now carry truck trailers across the country on railroads and then unload them to be pulled over the road to their final destinations. This can lower costs.

While trucks have taken business from railroads over the last fifty years, the railroads (and barges) are still the cheapest means of transporting large quantities of materials between any two distant points, as long as those points fall along the directing tracks.

· ·

An artist's depiction of Roman aquaducts showing the enormous scale of this ancient project. Notice the area at right where a repair to the aquaduct reveals the 3 levels of "pipes" carrying the water. (Courtesy Deutsches Museum, Munchen, Germany)

The building of the Alyeska, or Trans-Alaska, pipeline.

Pipelines ■ Pipelines have been used since ancient times. The Romans built wooden pipelines to carry water; the Chinese carried natural gas in bamboo pipes. The modern pipeline industry started with the discovery of oil in Western Pennsylvania in 1865. Welded wrought-iron pipe was used to carry crude oil to a railroad terminal. It was only 2 inches in diameter, but it required an armed guard to protect it from sabotage by the workers it replaced.

Today, pipelines are used in almost every town in the United States to carry water to homes and businesses and to remove sewage. Many towns also use pipeline systems to distribute natural gas. Much larger pipeline systems carry crude oil and natural gas across the United States and Canada.

The Trans-Alaska pipeline runs from the major oil fields of the North Slope of Alaska to the port of Valdez where the oil is loaded onto tankers. Other major pipelines carry natural gas from Texas and the southwest to the midwest and northeastern United States.

The pipeline acts a means of both transportation and storage for the company that owns the oil. The pipeline company does not usually own the oil it transports, but instead operates as a **carrier** much like a railroad or truck company.

The amount of oil a pipeline can carry is largely a function of its size. A pipeline 6 inches in diameter can carry an average of 8,000 barrels of crude oil a day, while a 12-inch pipe averages 50,000 barrels a day. Because pipelines move only their products and not accompanying vehicles, they provide one of the most energy efficient means of transporting.

The average flow of petroleum in a modern oil pipeline is only three to five miles per hour. More pumps could be installed on pipelines to increase the speed of the oil, but it would not be economical. Having the oil in the pipeline does not cost the company any extra; they just cannot sell or use it right away.

Ft. McHenry Tunnel, Baltimore, MD. Although tunnels are directing structures, they bear many of the characteristics of supporting structures, since they must bear the weight of their roofs and whatever is above them.

One major disadvantage of both pipelines and railroads is that they are so inflexible. Once they are built, at great expense, they cannot be moved or readjusted. Another drawback of pipelines is that only materials that are liquids or gases can be easily transported by pipeline. However, even coal can be crushed and mixed with water to form a slurry that can be transported by pipeline.

Like roads, proposed pipelines often face legal battles over the right to the land along the planned route. When rail rates rose after deregulation of the railroad industry, people in the coal industry in Pennsylvania and West Virginia proposed building a coal slurry pipeline to the port of Norfolk, Virginia. One reason the project was never built was because the railroad companies refused to grant the pipeline right of way over or under any of their property.

Tunnels ■ Tunnels are underground passageways permitting the movement of people, cars, trains, even water or sewage. A tunnel is primarily a directing structure but it must also support the weight of its roof and the dirt or water above it.

In 687 B.C. the Greeks built a tunnel to carry water through a ridge. The tunnel was over half a mile long and used pipes in its floor to carry the water. Similar tunnels were built in Persia (modern-day Iran and Iraq). The first of the large modern tunnels that we are familiar with were constructed for railways. These started to appear in England soon after the development of the early parallel rails and locomotives.

Tunnels for roads came later. After all, a road, unlike a railroad, could always be routed around or over an obstacle. A third major use of tunnels in the modern era is the same as that of the Greeks—to transport water to a city. In 1867, Chicago drove a tunnel lined with bricks over two miles out into Lake Michigan to ensure a supply of clean water for the city.

Many cities use tunnels for their sewage. The famous sewers of Paris are a tunnel system running under the whole city. Sometimes, it is hard to define the difference between a large sewage pipeline and a small tunnel. Both are enclosed directing structures with many of the same characteristics.

Canals ■ Canals are humanmade waterways usually used to transport freight across inland areas. Canals were constructed in great number in the

A lock on an inland canal. Notice the drop in water level below the lock.

A cruise ship passes through a lock on the Panama Canal. One of the world's greatest construction feats, the 44-mile canal cuts across the continents of North and South America. Ships sailing from New York to San Francisco save over 7,800 miles by using the canal.

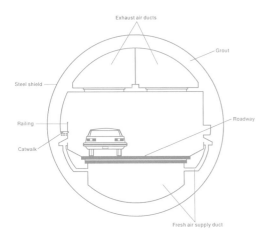

Tunnels cut through rock frequently require no lining. Underwater tunnels can be ventilated by shafts leading to the surface or by exhaust or booster fans at the ends.

United States in the middle of the 19th century. After the railway came to dominate freight transport, canals were not built any more. Many older canals have fallen into disrepair and disuse. There are now hiking trails along many of the old towpaths.

It was far easier to construct a mile of railway track than to dig a mile of canal. Railways can also climb modest slopes. Any time a canal climbs, the boats must pass through locks to raise or lower their height. Locks are expensive to construct, maintain, and use. However, locks are still used today to transport coal on some rivers and in important canals such as the Panama Canal.

■ The Design of Directing Structures

Directing structures are used to help transport people, vehicles, or things. The major design issue with directing structures is how much they will assist in the transportation and control of the people or objects being transported. This potential benefit must be weighed against the cost.

Directing structures usually cost more to construct than to operate. It is therefore critical that they be constructed between two points that will experience relatively heavy traffic longterm. Pipelines from major oil fields to refineries located near major markets are a relatively safe bet, and are often constructed because refined oil goes to many small markets (such as gas stations), it usually goes by truck, which is more flexible.

There are a number of design challenges when planning tunnels. One is how to keep a tunnel from collapsing. Another is how to guarantee sufficient clean air underground for people to breathe. Both of these problems are even more serious during the construction of the tunnel before permanent braces and fan systems are in place.

Once a tunnel for transportation is completed, the danger of collapse is small. Permanent tunnels are heavily reinforced and are surrounded with heavy casings to support the loads upon them. However, the air quality must be watched every day. Tunnels used by cars complicate the fresh air problem because cars emit carbon monoxide and other toxins. The levels of these pollutants in tunnels are always higher than they are aboveground. This only presents a danger to the people who work underground in the tunnels every day.

The cost of constructing railroads has risen so much that new rail lines are rarely built any more in the United States. In fact, every year more railroad tracks are abandoned than are constructed. The cost of land, labor, and insurance have all multiplied during a period when trucks have cut deeply into the overall business of railroads. If the government subsidized laying railroad track as much as it subsidizes road construction, the balance of new construction between rails and roads might be more equal.

The 100-Year-Old Dream

Humans have long dreamed of connecting England to mainland Europe by means of a tunnel under the English Channel. Napoleon was the first to try, but the British quashed the project. A second attempt fizzled in 1973.

In 1988, Great Britain and France agreed on a third attempt at the 100-year-old dream. With strong financing and the latest in technology, it looks as though this tunnel will become a reality. Due to be completed in 1993, with a final cost that could reach $7.5 billion, the tunnel will be the largest European civil engineering project in the twentieth century.

Plans call for three tubes: two 24-foot-diameter railway tunnels; and between them, a 15-foot-diameter service tunnel. Drive-on drive-off railway cars will zip through the tubes at speeds up to 99 mph. Trains will run in a continuous loop. A railway link to Paris would make it possible to travel by train between London and Paris in 3¾ hours, about half the current time it takes by rail and ferry. Time needed to cross the Channel by way of the tunnel will be 30 minutes.

The three tunnels will be bored through chalk marl, the lowest layer of chalk under the Channel. It is a sedimentary rock considered to be an almost perfect tunneling material. It is so soft that it will require no blasting, yet it is so stable and impervious to water that a totally unsupported 1880's excavation remains dry

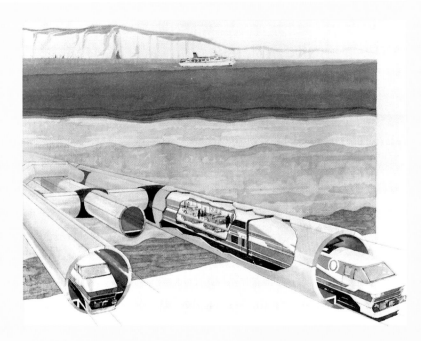

An artist's depiction of the English Channel Tunnel. Two main railway tunnels will be linked by a smaller service tunnel.

and intact. On the French side, the chalk becomes fissured chalk, shale, and clay, calling for somewhat different tunnel boring techniques, but this is not expected to present any significant problem.

Rings of precast concrete segments and cast iron will form the tunnel liner. There will be an average of 40 meters (131 ft) of cover over the tunnels, with most of the tunnel excavated 100 meters (328 ft) below sea level.

Eleven massive TBMs (Tunnel Boring Machines) will excavate the three tunnels at a rate of 1/2 mile per month. There are a number of reasons why eleven machines will be used instead of just one. The service and railway tunnels have different diameters. Tunnels under land need thicker liners than the bores under the water. And the French and British have elected to use different kinds of linings. Above all, speed is a key consideration, with con-

tract over-runs costing investors millions in interest alone.

Laser probes will keep the tunnels on line and level. These probes can be used in conjunction with microprocessors that determine a TBM's course and compare it to its planned course.

The importance of keeping the tunneling machines on line is paramount to the success of this project. If a tunneler veers a few millimeters off course and continues on that route, the machine could miss the machine that is coming to meet it from the opposite side of the Channel. Also, each tunnel must be in perfect alignment with the other two tubes so as to not distort the interconnecting passages.

A Titan IV rocket on the launch pad. Smaller vehicles, such as automobiles, are manufactured. Larger vehicles, such as this rocket, are built using construction techniques.

While financial issues are critical in the design of directing structures, there are also major environmental and technical issues. The design of the Trans-Alaska pipeline had to allow for protecting the tundra, protecting the caribou migration routes, and crossing two major mountain ranges. These types of challenges were met with unique technical solutions.

. . . .

Transporting Structures

Transporting structures are designed and constructed for the purposes of moving freight and passengers. Examples of transporting structures include large ships and airplanes, mobile homes, rockets, and submarines.

Some people say transporting structures are not constructed at all, but rather manufactured. This is because construction is often defined as the technology in which structures are built and used on a site. With this definition, all constructed structures must remain stationary. However, ships, mobile homes, and submarines are obviously large structures produced using many construction techniques, tools, and materials. In these terms, transporting structures are very similar to other structures. The distinguishing feature is their ability to move under their own power or when pulled by a vehicle.

■ Ships: The Largest Transporting Structures

Large ships are used to carry passengers and dry or liquid freight. Ships are like self-contained, floating cities. A ship must provide all the comforts of home for the crew, including sleeping quarters, food preparation and eating facilities, recreational equipment, electricity, clean water, and waste disposal. In addition, the ship must float and safely transport its freight or passengers.

The largest ships afloat today are the supertankers used to carry petroleum across the oceans. A supertanker is nothing more than a number of enormous tanks contained within the hull of a ship. The tanks are loaded and unloaded through nozzles using pumps. Because of the tremendous size of these ships, loading can take from 24 to 36 hours, even with the strongest pumps available.

Supertankers are approximately 1500 feet long, 200 feet wide, and can carry 500,000 tons of oil while traveling at 15 knots (approximately 17 miles per hour). If a supertanker could be stood on end, it would be taller than most of the skyscrapers in the world.

. . . .

Supertankers are the largest transporting structures. Stood on end, a supertanker would be higher than the highest skyscraper.

■ Naval Architecture: Designing Ships

The design and construction processes used in shipbuilding are very similar to those used for other types of structures. The first step is to design the structure.

Naval architecture, the technology of designing ships, is governed by rules and criteria established by national and international organizations called classification societies. These rules are similar to building codes established for homes, skyscrapers, and other stationary structures. Lloyds Register of Shipping in England is one of the oldest and most prestigious classification societies. In the United States, the American Bureau of Shipping established the standards for ship design and construction.

Classification society rules make the job of designing a ship easier for the architect. Ship classifications are based on payload capacity, overall ship size, and travel speed. Ship classification determines the taxes and fees paid by the ship owner. During the design process, the ship owner specifies the desired classification and the naval architect works within the society guidelines for that class.

. . . .

Wooden Shipbuilding Processes

When ships were made from wood the construction techniques were very similar to building a house. A keel (the bottom most part of a ship) was fabricated from wooden timbers on building ways. Building ways are rails on the ground angling into the water used for launching the ship. A timber frame was erected up from the keel to create a backbone (keel) and rib (frame) arrangement. Wooden cross pieces were laid between frame members for strength. Next, wood planking was attached to the outside of the skeleton

. . . .

Building a wooden ship. The timber skeleton clearly shows the keel and frame. When the skeleton is completed, it will be covered with wooden planking. (Courtesy of U.S. Navy)

Steel ships today are built by welding together large prefabricated sections. Welded steel is lighter, stronger and more watertight than riveted steel. (Courtesy Pascoula Construction)

to create the hull. When the hull was complete, the ship was slid down the building ways into the water. Once in the water, it was outfitted with the mast, rudder, sails, rigging, and sailor accommodations.

. . . .

Steel Shipbuilding Processes

Today, steel has replaced wood as the main structural materials used in building large ships. The first steel ships were fastened together with rivets and used the same processes used for wooden ships. All the components were brought to the building ways where one piece was added at a time starting at the keel and building upward.

Since 1930, welding has replaced riveting as the main fastening technique. With welding, large sections of the ship are prefabricated in buildings, then brought to the building ways and welded together to form the complete ship. This improves the speed and efficiency of constructing a ship.

Welding has other advantages, too. A welded ship is lighter since no overlapping is required for seams and the rivets themselves are eliminated. The ship is more watertight, because the pieces of metal are fused into one continuous piece rather than overlapped, so there are no gaps through which water might pass. Welding also gives the ship a smoother outside hull surface, which results in less resistance as the ship moves through the water. All of these advantages reduce the cost of building and operating a large ship.

All large ships are constructed using flat plate steel as a shell structure, rather than the wooden frame or riveted frame structure. Huge sheets of steel are lifted and moved in the shipyard by magnetic pickups on overhead

. . . .

Supertankers are constructed from large steel sheets which are welded together. (Courtesy of Amoco)

Workers installing the prop into a large ship. (Courtesy of Ameron Corp.)

cranes. The sheets must be cut to accurate specifications, since they are butted together and welded. This cutting is done using burning torches, a process that is often automated in larger shipyards. Once the steel sheets are cut to size, they are bent or rolled to form the curves on the outside of the hull. Powerful hydraulic presses are used with special forms for bending and rolling.

A ship is built in sections, called modules. The modules are prefabricated in large sheds. The formed steel plates are welded together to create a sub-assembly of the shell of the hull. Smaller sub-assemblies are joined to form the larger modules. Several different groups of workers prefabricate all the modules required to construct a ship.

As much outfitting as possible is included in the construction of the modules. The propulsion systems, including the engines and props, are installed. Pipes are installed within the floor and walls of the modules for plumbing, electrical, and communication systems. Bulkheads, doors, and compartments are also installed at this time. When the outfitting is completed, the individual modules, which can weigh several hundred tons, are moved by crane to the building ways where they are welded together to form the ship. Once the shell of the hull is complete, the ship is launched and the remainder of the outfitting is finished.

Constructing a ship in this manner requires very precise work. Because of this, many of the cutting, forming, and welding operations are controlled by computers to insure accurate alignment of structural members, floors, and utilities.

• •

The Impact of Large Ships

There is a distinct economic advantage for the marine shipping company that builds and operates large ships. One ship carrying 300,000 tons of freight can operate at approximately the same cost as a smaller ship carrying 150,000 tons. Labor, insurance, and fuel costs are about the same for each of these ships. Since the larger ship can operate for about the same costs as a smaller ship and carry twice the freight, profits are dramatically increased.

However, large ships also have many disadvantages. One is the great depth of water necessary to float these ships. Some huge supertankers require ports with water depths of 100 feet. Most ports are not that deep. Offshore, floating ports have been developed for these supertankers. Ships attach to the floating port, then pump their petroleum through pipes to land.

Another problem is maneuverability and safety. Supertankers require several miles to stop and are difficult to navigate through narrow passages. The grounding of a loaded supertanker can result in oil spills with dramatic impacts on the environment, as evidenced by the Valdez incident in 1989. Millions of gallons of petroleum were spilled when the ship ran aground near Alaska. Such oil spills can cause irreparable damage to water, land, and plant and animal life.

Supertankers are difficult to maneuver. This problem has resulted in an increasing number of accidents and oil spills. One of the worst involved the Exxon Valdez. In 1989, the supertanker ran aground in Prince William Sound, spilling 11 million gallons of oil. A diagram shows the damage to the ship that resulted in the spill.

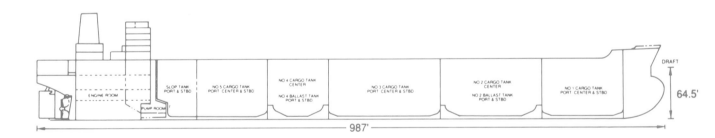

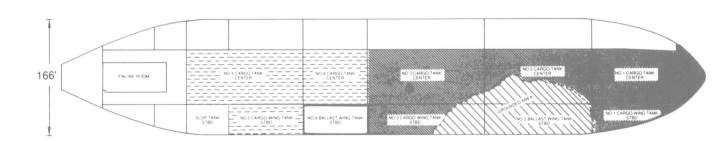

Is an escalator a directing or transporting structure? It serves both functions at once.

Multi-Function Structures

The category in which a structure is placed identifies the *principal* function of the structure and helps explain why it is constructed the way it is. However, most structures serve more than one purpose.

The typical wood-frame house is a good example of this. Obviously, the main function of this structure is sheltering. It protects people and their possessions from potentially harmful elements in the natural environment, such as heat, cold, wind, rain, snow and predators. But the structure we call a house has components that serve the functions of other categories as well. Pipelines are directing structures; walls are supporting; heat and cool air are contained by the house.

Realizing the many functions a structure serves is the first step to understanding why certain materials were used, or why the structure was erected in a particular location, or why the structural elements are arranged as they are.

From now on, when you study a structure, try to analyze its form in terms of the ways the structure is functional for people.

SUMMARY

Supporting structures hold things up. They are largely compression structures, although tensioned components are used for reinforcement or support. There are three main types of supporting structures based on their location: underground, aboveground, and underwater. The specific form a supporting structure takes depends on the loads it supports, the surface it rests on, and the materials available locally to do the job. Examples of supporting structures include house foundations, roads and bridges.

Dams are the most spectacular examples of constructed structures used for **containing.** The two main materials used to construct dams are earth or rock and concrete. Common dam designs include the earth-fill and rock-fill, concrete gravity dam, concrete buttress dam, and the concrete arch dam. The earth-fill and rock-fill dams are more commonly found in the United States. When designing a dam for a particular situation, engineers must consider a variety of factors, including the topological, geological, and hydrological features of the land. The most common problems associated with dams relate to water seepage through and under the dam. A variety of construction techniques are employed to counteract these problems.

Directing structures are stationary structures that guide the movements of vehicles, people, and materials. Essentially, they provide pathways for transportation.

Examples of directing structures include pipelines, tunnels, chutes, and railroad tracks.

Transporting structures are designed and constructed for the purposes of moving passengers and freight. The distinguishing feature of a transporting structure is the ability to move by itself or when pulled by a vehicle. Large ships and airplanes, mobile homes, rockets, and submarines are all examples of transporting structures.

. . . .

Study Questions

1. Discuss the advantages and disadvantages of dirt roads, paved roads, and superhighways as structures for supporting moving vehicles.

2. Why are steel, wood, and masonry the major materials used in supporting structures. Give examples of local supporting structures that use each of these materials. Discuss the advantages and disadvantages of each.

3. Are there any good potential routes for a directing structure such as a pipeline or railroad around your area. Remember, you need a lot of steady traffic to justify construction costs.

4. Do you think the government should subsidize railroad track construction and maintenance as it does with roads?

. . . .

Suggested Activities

1. Make a photo essay of the steps used to construct a transporting structure, such as a ship or mobile home. Contact a shipbuilding or mobile home building company and ask them for slides or photos that describe the construction processes employed.

2. Design and construct a system to transport water 5 feet over the floor with a 6-inch vertical obstacle in the center of the route.

3. Call the city and local utilities to discover what types of pipeline systems underly your town. Look at the maps of the systems, if possible.

4. Observe railroad tracks and their bed carefully and try to discover what the function of the different parts is. Later, look in the library and see if you can discover anything else about the function of the parts.

5. What are the major types of dams?

6. What are the topographical, geological, and hydrological features of your local region. Which type of dam would you construct, considering these features?

7. What are several examples of transporting structures? What feature of these structures distinguishes them from other structures described in this chapter?

8. Would you say that ships and mobile homes are manufactured or constructed? Why?

9. Try and list structures made by humans which are not discussed in this book (like treehouses). Where and why are they constructed? Which of the 5 functional categories do you think they fit into?

Glossary

Arch bridge   A bridge supported by a structural arch, usually made of wood, steel, or reinforced concrete.

Arch dam   A dam designed to use the strength of a horizontal arch to resist the force of the trapped water.

Bascule bridge   A moving bridge designed on a pivot with a counterweight so that one end of the bridge raises.

Beam bridge   A bridge supported by a single straight rigid member, such as a steel or wooden beam.

Buttress   A support that rests against the outside of masonry structures at regular intervals to help them resist buckling forces.

Cable-stayed bridge   A bridge supported by piers and cables hung from the piers to suspend long spans.

Cantilevered bridge   A bridge supported by piers designed in such a way that the loads are balanced on the piers.

Crown   The slight elevation in the center of a road that makes water flow off the road and prevents vehicles from hydroplaning.

Culvert   A pipe used to divert water away from a road or other structure.

Eminent domain   The legal process by which the government can obtain land from people who do not wish to sell in order to complete projects for the public good, such as roads and schools.

Guy wires   Wires attached to the ground which are under tension and are used to keep tall narrow radio towers from collapsing.

Lift bridge   A moving bridge designed so that the entire bridge deck can raise vertically from both ends at once.

Movable bridge   A bridge over water, designed to move so that tall ships can pass on the waterway.

Perimeter wall   A foundation system consisting of a masonry wall several feet high around the exterior of the structure.

Pioneer roads   The first paths cut through an undeveloped area, which permit machinery used for clearing the land to enter.

Slab   A foundation system that consists of a flat layer of concrete resting directly on the soil.

Suspension bridge   A bridge which is supported by ropes or cables attached to anchors in the ground at each end of the bridge.

Truss bridge   A bridge which is supported by several beams which are reinforced with diagonal cross-bracing.

ACTIVITY 21

Supporting Structures Design Brief

Reference

Chapter 10: Non-Sheltering Structures

Design Brief

Support structures are designed and constructed to "hold things up." Piers under a bridge are examples of supporting structures which support the weight of the bridge itself and the traffic that uses the bridge.

PROBLEM

Your company has decided to compete for a construction contract to build a bridge over a river. You, and the members of your company, must design a bridge which will be the most efficient supporting structure among your competitors in order for you to gain the contract.

BACKGROUND

1. Your company includes the members of your work group selected by the instructor.

2. The competitors are other work groups in your class.

3. Bridges must meet the PARAMETERS identified below.

Parameters

1. The following design specifications will be identified by the instructor:

	MINIMUM	MAXIMUM
BRIDGE SPAN:	8″	18″
OUTSIDE BRIDGE WIDTH:	2½″	5″

2. Types, sizes and quantities of the following design materials will be identified by the instructor:

STRUCTURAL MATERIALS:	1/8″ × 1/8″ Balsa Wood
FASTENERS:	White glue or hot glue (Your teacher will specify the amount of glue.)

	3. Bridge should support the maximum possible static load on its roadway or deck.
	4. A full-sized design sketch of your bridge must show the top and side views.
Research & Development	1. Consider the various bridge designs which are available in your community.
	2. Go to the library and research various bridge designs.
	3. Brainstorm with the members of your company on possible designs.
	4. Construct and test mock-up and prototype bridges before building your final bridge.
	5. Chose your company's best design and create full-sized sketches on graph paper.
	6. Construct your bridge for official testing.
Evaluation	1. Bridges will be weighed.
	2. The roadway will be used to hold a testing device. A gauge will be used to insure that bridge roadways meet the MINIMUM specifications.
	3. Bridges will then be tested with a static load on the roadway until failure occurs.
	4. Efficiency ratings will be computed using the following formula:

$$\text{EFFICIENCY RATING} = \frac{\text{WEIGHT CAUSING FAILURE}}{\text{WEIGHT OF BRIDGE}}$$

5. The best bridges, and their creators, will be identified in each of the following competitive categories:

    a. Most efficient (official testing)
    b. Most weight held (official testing)
    c. Most unique design (student voting)
    d. Best Aesthetic appeal (student voting)
    e. Highest quality bridge sketches (teacher evaluation)

6. Company with the most efficient bridge will receive the contract. (Special award to be determined by the instructor.)

ACTIVITY 22

Be A Structure

Reference Chapter 9: Sheltering Structures
Chapter 4: Structural Elements

Introduction In order to better understand how a building works, try being me! The drawing shows some possible ways to demonstrate this. (Source: Illustrations from Architecture and Children: Learning by Design by A. Taylor, G. Vlastos, and N. Harden.)

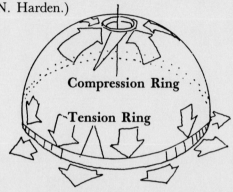

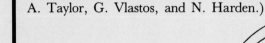

Post and Beam—To determine the strength of the beam, load books on three different types of "beams" with hands touching with hands interlocking with hands and arms interlocking. Which one works best? Why?

Dome—One student holds basketball and five others hold onto basketball and spread feet apart to each touch the others feet to form a dome.

Note: Students shoes touch as shown and this connection allows feet to remain steady.

Compression and Tension—Six students join arms in a circle, intertwining their arms with feet together. All lean back as shown in sketch.

Tension Ring—Students form circle and face the same way. Each student places elbows on their own waist and hands on waist of student in front. At the same time all sit on the lap of the person behind them. Sit as long as you can.

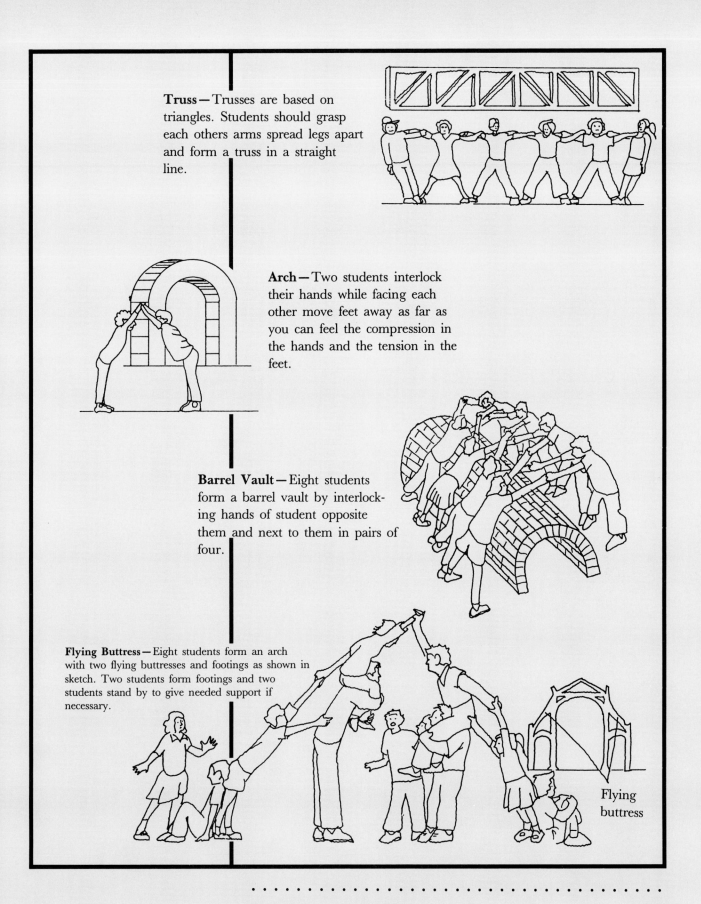

Truss—Trusses are based on triangles. Students should grasp each others arms spread legs apart and form a truss in a straight line.

Arch—Two students interlock their hands while facing each other move feet away as far as you can feel the compression in the hands and the tension in the feet.

Barrel Vault—Eight students form a barrel vault by interlocking hands of student opposite them and next to them in pairs of four.

Flying Buttress—Eight students form an arch with two flying buttresses and footings as shown in sketch. Two students form footings and two students stand by to give needed support if necessary.

Flying buttress

Part IV

Feedback

Chapter 11

Implications of Construction Systems

Chapter Concepts

■ The long-term nature of construction systems makes it essential that we understand the social, technical and environmental implications associated with the systems.

■ Historical and cultural implications allow us to maintain a cultural identity with generations that have come long before our own.

■ Social implications relate to the psychological health of the social institutions of family, community, religion, state, recreation and education, as well as the self-actualizing needs of the individual.

■ Economic and political factors are important elements related to the social implications of construction systems.

■ Access to technical means is an important part of solving some of the social problems such as our homeless citizens.

■ New ethics related to craft should be promoted in the construction infrastructure.

■ The quality of life is directly related to creative and meaningful work with the hands and mind. Mental, physical and emotional health is part of the self-actualizing equation.

■ All construction systems damage the natural environment.

■ Basic human needs such as water, food and energy are affected by construction systems.

Key Terms

aquifer	pollution
erosion	retrofit
hard energy	siltation
hierarchy of needs	sink hole
neighborhood feeling	soft energy
net energy gain	super insulation

Do you think the builders of China's Great Wall realized that it would still be an important, functioning structure over 2000 years later? (Courtesy Gerald F. Brommer)

. . . .

Long-Term Implications

The implications of construction systems are far reaching because of the long-term nature of the systems. In many cases the systems of construction will outlast all of the other technical systems. In communications we experience a day-by-day obsolescence of various communications technical systems. In manufacturing, most products deteriorate rapidly. A radio, for example, may last only 10 years before it is junked or reprocessed. In transportation, most airplanes that were built 50 years ago are grounded.

In construction, however, we have great artifacts and a living history of our past. For example, the Anasazi cliff dwellings and villages have lasted over 800 years. Some Egyptian pyramids are over 5,000 years old. Let's recall, for contrast, that the industrial revolution of the United States is only about 100 years old.

More important than the long-term nature of the physical structures of construction systems are the long-lasting social implications, technical implications and environmental implications resulting from them. Many of these patterns were rooted millennia ago.

Social Implications

In the middle ages, safety meant not only a roof over your head, but also a wall around your house. How have conditions changed since then? (Pen and ink illustrations from *German Castle* by Paul Taylor.)

The social implications of construction systems are not only tied to meeting the physical needs of contemporary social institutions (i.e. family, community, state, religion, trade, recreation, and education), but also are related to the psychological needs of people.

■ Hierarchy of Needs

Human needs and desires fall into a **"hierarchy of needs,"** according to psychologist Abraham Maslow. The lowest level deals with the basic human needs of food, water, safety and shelter. These basic human needs must be met first before higher needs can be fulfilled. If people are scared, hungry, and cold, it is difficult for them to reach their full potential. Construction systems, such as the sheltering systems (i.e. houses, apartment buildings, etc.) provide the primary safety and sheltering needs.

Around The World with History and Construction

Learning from the implications of past construction systems is important if we are to improve the future. By observing the historical social, technical and environmental implications of long-term construction systems, we can better understand the effects construction can have. Long-lasting construction systems have occurred throughout history and in all parts of world. The following examples of structures from Japan, Peru, and the United States highlight the long-term nature of construction systems.

Japan

Many recent Japanese buildings have been influenced by the work of craftspersons over 1000 years ago. These structures have carried the social and environmental patterns alongside the technical patterns. Why have the technical patterns of Japanese buildings (i.e., the skeleton structure, modular building components, open plan, sliding walls and simple beauty) lasted for over 1000 years?

Would a Japanese builder in the 8th century have guessed that the social, technical and environmental patterns of their construction would have lasted to the year 2000 and beyond?

The design of this sixteenth century Japanese castle combines Chinese and Japanese materials with medieval European fortification techniques. How does this building differ from military structures you are familiar with? (Courtesy Japan National Tourist Organization)

Peru

The Inca tribe of the Maras in Peru constructed a wonderfully sculptured theater that remains well preserved. This theater not only is aesthetically beautiful but also tells modern historians that the Incas were highly developed in their arts. This theater outlasted the Inca culture.

The theater is quite monumental even by modern standards. It could seat 60,000 people, having twelve terraces 6 feet high and 23 feet wide. Corresponding to orchestra style arrangement, the platforms range in diameter from 80 to 134 feet. Spring water was transported to the theater from a nearby mountain through stone-carved water pipes. Located 12,000 feet above sea level between Cuzco and Machu Picchu, there is no counterpart to this theater in the world.

United States

A modern-day example of long-term implications is the Hoover Dam in Colorado. Built from 1931–1936 the dam required 5,250 workers and about $165 million. The dam resembles a concave plug wedged into Black Canyon. The Hoover dam is the world's largest arch-gravity dam.

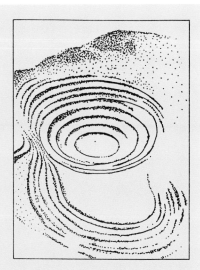

This Incan theatre is monumental in size. Compare this to today's large stadiums.

It was built for three main reasons: flood control, irrigation, and electricity. The dam produces six billion kilowatt-hours of electricity a year. Many cities throughout Utah, Arizona, Nevada and California are served by it.

However, the long term nature of the Hoover dam, does not rival the ancient theatres of the Incas. Civil engineers believe the dam will only last between three hundred and four hundred years.

Whether it is Japan's timeless structures, the theaters of the Incas or recent historical undertakings such as the Hoover dam, all construction systems have long-term social, technical and environmental implications. Because of the long-range implications associated with construction systems, future structures should be designed with full understanding of their lasting impacts.

Attractive areas near where people work or study create a sense of community, while providing space for performance, informal gatherings, displays and public ceremonies. (Photograph by Wyatt Wade)

The second level of needs addresses the psychological need for the "feeling of belonging." Construction systems on a neighborhood scale often help unite people. These may take the form of a church, a baseball park, a diner, or even a well designed street.

We all have a need for environments that provide a secure social atmosphere. As children, most of us built forts or tree houses in an attempt to create the **neighborhood feeling** among our friends.

In Maslow's hierarchy, self-actualization is the highest level. This is the need for meaningful and creative work.

Henry David Thoreau, a nineteenth-century American philosopher, believed that people should take an active role in designing and building the structures they use. Participating in the design and construction process helps a person in the self-actualizing process. In his famous book *Walden*, Thoreau wrote:

"There is some of the same fitness in a man's [human's] building his [or her] own house that there is in a bird's building his [or her] own nest."

The hierarchy of needs may also apply to a society as well. Structures are necessary to allow the social institutions an opportunity to operate in a safe and comfortable manner (fulfill basic needs of the institutions). There is a special feeling that neighborhoods should also be part of a larger whole, such as counties, states or even nations. And finally, meaningful work and purpose is required for communities to reach their full potential or become involved in the community actualizing process.

A recurring social pattern is that it is healthy for individuals and communities to participate in the construction process of the structures they will eventually use. The process of participating not only helps an individual or community to address the basic human needs of safety and shelter and the need for belonging, but may also help in the self and community actualization process.

■ Economic Implications

Virtually every economic function requires an infrastructure in the form of construction systems. The institution of trade dominates the construction infrastructure. Railroads, bridges, office buildings, factories and interstate roads do not directly serve the needs of family, community, religion, recreation, or education. These systems support the economic or trade base of a society.

The economic base generated by creating new construction systems creates new opportunities for economic growth. It might seem that this growth can

Artist Charles Sheeler portrayed the structures of trade in many of his paintings. What types of constructed elements can you find in this picture) (*City Interior*, 1936. Oil on fiber board, 27 × 22-1/8″. Courtesy Worcester Art Museum)

Skyscrapers are an attempt by architects to stretch the physical limitations of construction. As available land becomes scarce, the air above small sites becomes prime development space. (Courtesy Sears, Roebuck and Co., Chicago)

go on forever, but this is an illusion. There is no such thing as unlimited growth, not even for the economy.

Economics is actually the study of the allocation and distribution of scarce resources. There are physical limits to the earth's resources, which means that unlimited growth is actually unobtainable. If there were no physical limits on the earth's resources, then everyone would be able to live in a mansion of 20,000 square feet. As it happens, most people in the United States live in structures around 1,100 square feet. And as resources (such as land availability) become increasingly scarce, the size of the average home in the United States will continue to decline.

In addition, there are physical limitations to the earth itself. As world population increases, land for construction systems will become increasingly scarce. The Chicago School of architects thought they had the answer when they started building skyscrapers in Chicago. Now most industrialized cities of the world are lined with skyscrapers because the land has become scarce. As land becomes scarce, it also becomes expensive. Expense and scarcity are, therefore, directly related. Try buying an acre of land in New York City or Los Angeles!

The natural environment also places economic restrictions on construction systems. Pollution of the environment is as much an economic issue as it is an environmental issue. Acid rain, for example, is destroying many acres of timber used in construction in New York's Adirondack Mountains and also in Canada. As acid rain increases, scarcity of timber also increases, driving up the price of wood-based construction materials.

• •

Political Friendship and Construction

Political friendship between countries often manifests itself through a constructed project. Perhaps the most well known of these is the Statue of Liberty. Built in 1875–1886, it was a gift from France to the United States. France had long admired the freedom offered in the United States and wanted to gain international attention by recognizing the democratic system. Although this was a peacetime endeavor, it was nevertheless a powerful political statement.

The statue was made by a French sculptor named Auguste Bartholdi. After the unveiling ceremony was over, President Grover Cleveland told Bartholdi, "you are the greatest man in America today."

Ironically the statue also had political overtones of a different nature. A ship in New York's Harbor was rented by the Women Suffrage Association and during the ceremony a loud-speaker blared, "If the Statue of Liberty came to life, she would not be allowed to vote in the United States or France!" It took 34 year (1920) before the Nineteenth Amendment was ratified allowing women their voting rights.

Spacecraft such as the space shuttle require costly and complex construction systems. (Courtesy **NASA**)

■ Political Implications

Large structures intended to make political statements also have long-range implications. On October 4, 1957, the U.S.S.R. launched Sputnik, the first artificial satellite to circle the earth. The United States felt pressured to launch its own space program. President Kennedy, early in the 1960's, announced that the United States would be on the moon before the end of the decade and, in 1969, this goal was realized. The entire space program was launched by a perceived political pressure to be number one in the world. This project required huge investments in construction systems.

Military construction systems tend to initiate long-term or far-reaching political responses, based upon a real or perceived threat from these constructions. In other words, whenever "they" build something, "we" build something, and vice versa.

. . . .

Technical Implications

Participation in the technical processes associated with construction requires the knowledge of tools, materials and technical processes (i.e. technical means). This knowledge is critical, because when people understand the technical means associated with construction then they can make better decisions about the structures that will support their society. These decisions impact future generations because of the long-term nature of construction systems.

. . . .

Feedback

■ Meaningful Technical Work

Meaningful and creative work is important for a healthy society. The construction field offers many diverse jobs that allow people to utilize tools, materials and processes in a creative manner. And when the people who build the structures are the same one ones who will use them, then it is not only the skilled hands and mind that benefit, the spirit of the society itself also benefits.

■ Technical Quality

When a construction team produces a high quality structure, there is a special feeling of accomplishment. High technical quality of a construction system is a result of a work force that holds quality as a premium.

In some cases, economic criteria outweigh the technical criteria of quality and the result is a poorly built structure. "Haste makes waste," is a familiar axiom and a very accurate one in the construction industry. If concrete is "watered down" to speed up the pouring process, the result is a weakened structure. If a cheaper material is used instead of the appropriate one, the result will be a product of low technical quality. To produce high-quality technical results, a high-quality technical work ethic must be promoted. This creates a system of construction that will last for generations.

Below left:) **The construction of oil pipelines requires top-quality welding to insure against leaks. (Courtesy Alyeska Corporation)**

(Below right:) **The same technical processes essential to the construction of the nineteenth century building on the right have been used in the twentieth century building on the left. (Photograph by Rhonda Fournier)**

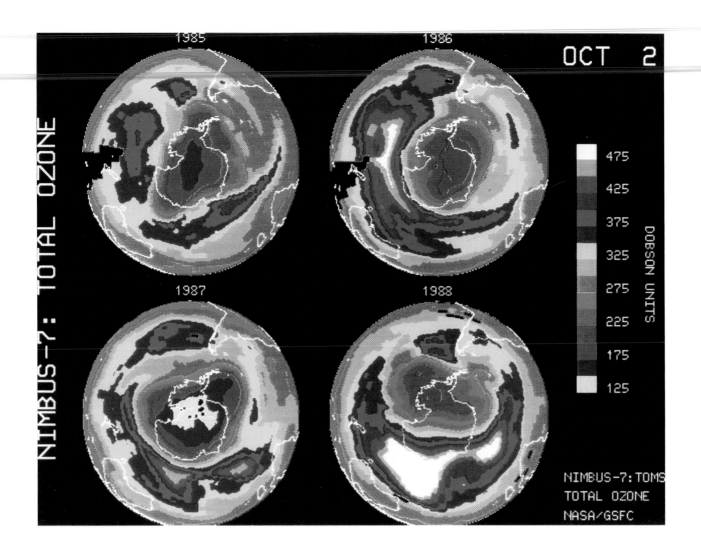

Satellite photographs from four consecutive years show the amount of ozone levels measured in Dobson units. 1985 and 1987 show far lower levels than 1986 and 1988. Concern about the destruction of the ozone layer has caused debate over the use of some construction materials, such as styrofoam. (Courtesy NASA)

Environmental Implications

All structures have a direct and significant impact on local, regional and global environments. Everything in the natural and human-made environment is interconnected through a complex web of relationships. Some of these relationships, such as the causes of the depletion of the ozone layer, are so complex that they are still not fully understood. Other relationships are so simple and direct that they are obvious to even the untrained eye.

This section discusses only a small portion of the total environmental effects of construction systems. In particular, we will explore how construction systems affect our water supply, our food supply, our demands for energy, and the relationship between construction systems and environmental contaminates (pollution).

■ Water

Every structure built on land causes flooding, water shortages and erosion.

To understand this statement you must first understand the water cycle. Water enters the atmosphere through evaporation from bodies of water and transpiration (the loss of water vapor through the leaves of plants). Water vapor collects in the upper atmosphere until conditions are right for precipitation (rain, snow etc.). As the rain falls some of the water evaporates, remaining in the atmosphere. The rest of the water falls to the ground. Once on the ground, several things can happen to the water:

- It can be consumed by plants and be eventually transpired again.

- It can soak into the ground, either remaining in the area in which it fell or moving varying amounts of distances as ground water, eventually resurfacing at a spring.

- It can remain on the surface and eventually evaporate again.

- It can run off into a network of streams and rivers.

In most natural settings all four of these options will occur. Now imagine a structure, say a house, in a rainstorm. Assuming the house is in good repair, no water enters the house. It flows off the roof down the spout. What happens to this water? Most houses do not have plants growing on their roofs, so no water is consumed by plants. The house is covering ground, so no water can soak into the ground it covers. Almost all houses have some sort of drainage system, so very little water remains on the surface to evaporate. Of the options listed above, the only one remaining is for the water to run off.

Below left:) **When more rain falls then can be readily absorbed by the ground, water remains on the surface, eventually running off into low areas. (Courtesy Johnstown, Pennsylvania Historical Society)**

(Below right:) **The 1977 flood in Johnstown, Pennsylvania caused extensive damage to houses and businesses. But structures themselves contribute to flooding, by covering open ground. How might construction systems be modified to: a) resist the effects of floods or b) reduce the amount of water than runs off a structure? (Courtesy Johnstown Historical Society)**

Is this so bad? The answer is yes and no. Yes, runoff is good; it is a vital part of the natural environment and is necessary for the formation of many rivers and streams. The answer is also no. A lot of runoff coming at the same time is a flood. Flooding kills more people every year than lightning, tornadoes or hurricanes. It also costs billions of dollars in lost and damaged homes and businesses.

Notice that streams and rivers after heavy rains are often a deep brown color. This color is caused by small particles of soil suspended in the water. The darker the water the more erosion is taking place.

Erosion is usually caused by water washing over unprotected soil. Construction sites are especially vulnerable to erosion. Most construction projects begin by removing the vegetation from the project site. This vegetation provided both a cover and an anchor for the soil. With the vegetation removed, the finer particles of soils are washed away with the first significant rain. Additional rainfall washes away more and more soil until eventually, if left untreated, the once fertile soil is washed down to bare rock. If you look at a stream bed flowing near a construction site, you may see a heavy layer of fine soil or silt covering the bottom and sides of the stream bed.

Erosion does not stop once the construction is finished. A completed structure still causes erosion. A building causes increased runoff and decreases the amount of plants and soil that can soak up the water. Water drainage from the area then receives more runoff during rainfalls. Since there is less water retained in the ground, these drainage areas receive less water during periods of no precipitation.

In effect, the streams in a very developed area are converted into storm sewers, flooding when it rains and dry when it doesn't. This flood-drought pattern is very hard on the stream banks and beds. In undeveloped areas, streams tend to remain somewhat even, with a steady flow of groundwater during dry periods and only moderately high water during rains. This allows plants and other vegetation to grow around the stream protecting its banks from erosion.

If erosion is only dirt being swept away, then why is it a problem? There is plenty of dirt and there is plenty of water to wash it away. Right?

Wrong. Some organizations that study trends and problems of the nation and the world say that erosion is one of the greatest environmental problems facing this country and the world.

Erosion is costing us money every day. Not only does it undermine homes and other valuable real estate, and cause sedimentation or damage to waterways, it is possible that food production, both in the United States and worldwide may seriously decrease because of it. The first soil to be washed away are the smaller lighter particles. These are the ones containing most of the nutrients. Farms having even small amounts of erosion need costly fertilizers to replace the nutrients that are washed away. This cost is passed on to the consumer in the supermarket. Soil is not easy to replace. Topsoil forms naturally, but only very slowly. It can take hundreds of years to form one inch of topsoil.

Topsoil that is washed into streams and rivers often settles out of the water when the water stops moving. This sediment often carries pesticides,

Exposed ground without vegetation is especially vulnerable to erosion. (Photograph by Gene Alexander, Soil Conservation Service)

Feedback

Damming a Dream

President Shehu Shagari of Nigeria had a dream—a dream of a great dam spanning the Sokoto and Rima rivers. This dam would provide the regional farmers with two certain harvests instead of one uncertain harvest per year.

The plan was simple: build a dam large enough to contain the flood waters that come every year with the rainy season. The vast lake created by this dam would allow a steady, reliable source of water for agriculture. But before this dream was complete, it would become a nightmare, complete with riots and deaths.

The area surrounding the dam site is sub-Saharan savanah, meaning it is very hot, dry, flat grasslands. It is relatively well populated, primarily by poor farm families that live in mud (adobe) homes.

The dam was designed and constructed by the Italian firm Impresit, the construction division of Fiat. The original estimate of the project was 110 million naira (about $150 million). The final price tag for construction alone soared to a whopping 400 million naira (about $550 million).

The project encountered great social as well as financial problems. The biggest opponents to the project were the same inhabitants that this project was designed to help: the local farmers. They had been farming the same area, in the same way, for generations. Although their life was not easy (rains could be light, crops could fail), it was none-the-less the life they were used to.

The residents that lived downstream of the dam, the ones that were supposed to receive the most benefit from the project, were also very upset. Their plots of land were taken by the government and leveled for the irrigation system. Smaller plots were reallocated to them, again unsuitable to the form of agriculture they had been using all of their lives.

To protect the dam, the displaced inhabitants staged a revolt. Large groups established roadblocks, bringing construction to a stand still. It was not until the government sent in large police forces that the road blocks were broken and the work resumed. The cost of this action was an official death toll of nineteen and compensation to the construction company of 23 million niara (approximately $31 million) for their lost time.

The total profit from this project is hard to determine as of yet. More time is needed in hopes that the locals will adopt the farming techniques that might maximize the productivity of this region. The total cost of this project is somewhat easier to estimate:

- $550 million dollars in outright payments to the construction company (average cost of $20,000 per irrigated hectare)

- Nineteen lives
- Thousands of people forceably removed from their homes

- Millions of dollars for police and bureaucrats.

The total cost of the project will also include supporting bureaucrats and maintenance and repair to the dam system. This dam, like all others, eventually will fill with the silt, requiring very costly dredging or the abandonment of the entire project.

It is also important to note that the total agricultural productivity of the region may eventually decrease as a result of the dam. The yearly flooding is not only a source of water, it is a valuable source of nutrients that are carried by the flood waters and deposited on the farmlands as the water recedes. With this new dam in place, the cycle of yearly flooding is disrupted for all of the farmers that live below the dam past the area of the irrigation system.

President Shagaris' dream did not happen the way he had planned it. Can blame be placed on any factor or group? Certainly some people would try to blame the local farmers, but the real blame lies with the design and implementation of such a large project without incorporating the people most affected by the project into the planning stage. The design of any construction system must work *with* people and the environment to be effective.

Average Annual Cropland Erosion

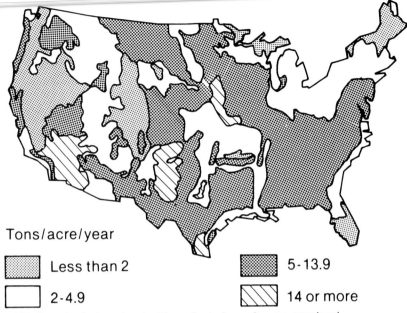

Tons/acre/year

☐ (dotted) Less than 2 ☐ (dark) 5-13.9

☐ 2-4.9 ☐ (diagonal) 14 or more

1982 data. Includes sheet, rill, and wind erosion on cropland.

phosphates and other chemical pollutants. Sedimentation also makes it difficult for fish and other aquatic life to breathe, often destroying commercial and recreational fishing areas.

This **sedimentation,** or **siltation,** is a particular problem where dams and reservoirs have been constructed. We are already finding dams that were designed and built to last for a hundred years being rendered useless because the lakes formed by these dams have filled completely with sediment after only a few decades.

The same pattern of flood/drought that helps cause erosion also contributes to some areas losing their water supply. Just as streams dry up in developed areas, so do the underground lakes and rivers **(aquifers).** As aquifer levels drop, people and communities must drill deeper and deeper to obtain water. Aquifers drop so low in some areas that it becomes too expensive or impossible to drill any farther. This situation is accelerated by the construction of new homes and businesses. Not only do they use more and more water, they also intensify the flood/drought pattern.

Other serious problems can arise from the lowering of aquifers. In coastal areas, salt water from the ocean will sometimes intrude into the water supply as the level of fresh water in the aquifers drops. Salt water is almost useless for homes, businesses and agriculture.

The underground water supply of some regions actually helps support the weight of the ground. As this water is used up, the ground loses its support, causing **sink holes** or land subsidence. The ground drops to fill in the areas once filled with water. This may be a very slow decline, causing cracking and breaking of buildings, foundations, and water, gas and sewage lines. Sometime it happens suddenly. Subsidence can cause huge

U.S. Water Use (1985)

Based on consumption of 1400 gallons per person per day

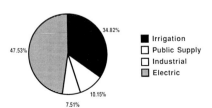

34.82%

47.53%

10.15%

7.51%

■ Irrigation
☐ Public Supply
☐ Industrial
☒ Electric

Dams, although built as flood control structures, can cause devastating floods themselves if their walls are damaged or weakened by earthquakes, or faulty construction. (Courtesy Sacramento Metropolitan Water District)

Can you think of any drawbacks related to preserving farmland? If the majority of agricultural land were developed, what economic impact would we feel?

craters more than 100 meters (327 feet) across to open overnight and swallow entire buildings.

Although all structures disrupt the water cycle, some have an overall positive impact. Dams, in particular, are often built as flood control structures. By catching huge amounts of water during heavy rains, dams can prevent flooding downstream. This water is either slowly released as the flooding stops or held in lakes to provide recreation areas for boating and fishing. Other dams are built with several objectives in mind. One dam can control flooding as well as providing water for recreation, agriculture, domestic use and/or hydropower.

■ Construction Systems and the Food Supply

As national and global populations increase, both the number of constructed structures and the amount of food that is produced must increase as well. Unfortunately, construction systems and food production often compete for limited resources. This competition creates problems, particularly for those involved in agricultural production.

There are three notable dilemmas facing food production in the U.S. today:

■ The erosion of top soil and nutrients, as discussed above.

■ The dropping of the water levels in some of the nation's aquifers.

■ The loss of valuable agricultural land to development.

Farming and Aquifers ■ Much of the agriculture of the midwestern states is based on intensive uses of this ground water. Unfortunately, this water is being used much faster than it is being replenished. If this trend continues, much of the farming in this region will either have to be eliminated or supported by new, expensive irrigation techniques.

Development of Farmland ■ When most people think of building a house, they have visions of a home with a nice, flat, green lawn. They think of being close to good roads and they think of a mild climate with plenty of water and sunlight. Unfortunately, this description of a dream house matches a description of a dream farm. Land that is good for homes is also usually just as good for farming.

An estimated 1,000,000 hectares (3,900 square miles) of land undergo development in the U.S. every year. The United States has over three and a half million square miles of territory. Simple mathematics indicate that the U.S. could continue to expand at this rate for hundreds of years without running out of space.

· ·

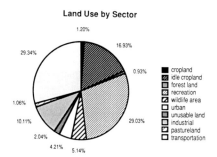

Land Use by Sector

1.20%
16.93%
29.34%
0.93%
29.03%
1.06%
10.11%
2.04%
4.21%
5.14%

■ cropland
▨ idle cropland
▥ forest land
▨ recreation
▨ wildlife area
□ urban
▤ unusable land
□ industrial
▨ pastureland
□ transportation

Unfortunately, it is not so simple. To estimate the potential land area that could be used for construction development, considerable amounts must be subtracted from the total land size. Subtract land that is already developed (cities, homes sites, business areas and roadways), land that can not easily be developed (tundra, lakes, marshes, deserts and mountains) and land that cannot be developed (historic areas, national parks, forests and game reserves). The total remaining amount of land usable for either agriculture or construction is actually relatively small.

Urban sprawl is the term given to the increasing size of urban and suburban areas. Many factors cause urban sprawl. People who work in urban areas often view the suburbs as an escape from the crowding, crime, high expense and other undesirable elements of city living. As more and more people migrate outwards, the suburbs increase in population and begin to develop the same undesirable urban characteristics people are trying to avoid. As one area becomes crowded, the development moves down the road a little bit farther.

When people are deciding on a new house site, an important consideration is the daily commute to work. For most people, the question is not one of distance, but rather of time. A person living in the city might take 45 minutes to travel 10 miles across town. Someone else, living further out but near a major highway, might take 30 minutes to travel 20 miles. Most people would prefer the longer, quicker drive. Problems arise when more and more people opt for that drive. As the number of commuters increase, so does the traffic and the time it takes to cover those miles. As the traffic

As population and traffic in an area increase, new roads must be built and existing ones widened. (Courtesy John Deere and Co., Moline, IL)

Feedback

The coal that fuels this coal-burning power plant is becoming more and more expensive to mine. What source of power might take its place? (Courtesy New England Power Co.)

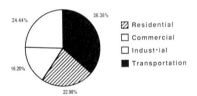

U.S. Energy Use By Sector

36.38%
24.44%
16.20%
22.98%

☑ Residential
☐ Commercial
☐ Industrial
■ Transportation

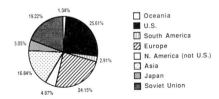

World Energy Use (1985)

1.34%
19.22%
25.61%
5.05%
2.91%
16.84%
4.87%   24.15%

☐ Oceania
■ U.S.
▦ South America
☑ Europe
☐ N. America (not U.S.)
▨ Asia
▨ Japan
■ Soviet Union

increases, so does the demand for new or improved highways. With new highways come new commuters, which need new highways, that bring new commuters, and the cycle continues.

Most U.S. cities were originally sited near major agricultural areas, because in the early years of this nation's development, agriculture was the basis of trade and commerce. Today as these cities sprawl outward, it is these nearby farmlands that are paved over.

The overall effect of highway development, urban sprawl and new communities is a steady loss of prime farmland. In this country, as in so many others, the economy depends on a strong agricultural base. The potential long-term effects of this loss of valuable land is uncertain, but the possibilities are not pleasant.

■ Construction and Energy

Energy has many uses, among them:

- To transport people and goods

- To produce fertilizer

- To power agricultural machinery

- To pump and purify water

- To provide heating and cooling

- To produce and manufacture consumer goods

- For lighting and appliances

- For communication devices

If a switch was thrown today that cut off all sources of produced energy, what would the world be like tomorrow? The first thing you might think of is the lack of electricity in your daily life. No more electric lights, heating, radios or television. But it would go far, far beyond that. Energy is used for everything we consume or buy.

All sources of energy may be categorized as being either "hard" or "soft." **Hard energy** sources use non-renewable resources, fuels that exist only in limited supplies, and once used cannot be replaced. Petroleum, coal, natural gas and uranium (for nuclear power) are hard energy sources. **Soft energy** sources can used over and over again. Solar, wind and water power are examples of soft energy.

All technologically advanced countries must have a cheap and reliable source of energy. But cheap and reliable sources are becoming more and more difficult to find. This is particularly a problem in the United States,

Public distrust of nuclear power has increased dramatically since the 1979 accident at Three Mile Island in Pennsylvania and the 1986 Chernobyl (Soviet Union) disaster. Here a technician measures the Chernobyl plant's outdoor radiation level. (Courtesy Sovfoto)

Why do you think so little research and development funding has been directed toward soft energy sources, such as this Hawaii wind farm? (Courtesy EDCH and Hawaii Electric)

which uses over a quarter of all the energy produced in the world, although it has only 5–6 percent of the world's population.

Sources of hard energy are becoming increasingly unreliable. The United States reserves of petroleum and natural gas are not large enough to maintain energy consumption for much longer. Imported oil is subject to many uncontrollable factors, particularly in the politically turbulent Middle East. Domestic coal reserves are becoming increasingly expensive to mine and the quality of the coal is decreasing. Nuclear power is suffering greatly from staggering cost overruns and, in the wake of the 1986 accident in Chernobyl, USSR, it also faces hostile public and political pressure.

Unfortunately, the outlook for soft energy sources is not much brighter. Lacking the huge funding for research and development that has been invested in hard energy sources, soft energy systems are still not well developed or cost efficient. Hydropower (produced from dams) is one notable exception. Although providing only about 3 percent of the total energy used in this nation, it is nonetheless an important contribution to our country's energy independence.

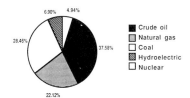

World Energy Production (1985)

■ Crude oil
▦ Natural gas
☐ Coal
▨ Hydroelectric
☐ Nuclear

4.94%
6.90%
28.46%
37.58%
22.12%

Energy-Efficient Buildings ■ Conserving energy should be important to everyone. Conserving energy saves money, decreases the nation's dependence on foreign imports, reduces pollution, delays the time until we must implement new, more expensive energy sources and promotes a stronger national economy.

One way to conserve energy is to design and construct buildings that are energy efficient. The most energy efficient buildings are not primarily in the United States. For example, Swedish homes are, on the average, twice as well insulated as homes in northern Minnesota (with a similar climate). Swedish homes can stay warmer throughout the winter and still be cheaper to heat than their American counterparts.

There are two ways of increasing residential energy efficiency:

■ The first is to **retrofit** (add on to, improve or modify) existing homes.

■ The second is to use energy-efficient designs in new structures.

Solar panels are one way to retrofit an existing house and significantly increase its energy efficiency.

Solar Air System

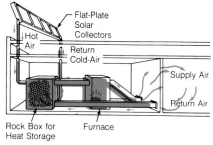

Flat-Plate Solar Collectors
Hot Air
Return Cold-Air
Supply Air
Return Air
Rock Box for Heat Storage
Furnace

Solar Liquid System

Furnace will run only when solar-heated water is not hot enough to provide heat.

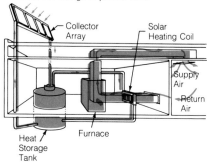

Collector Array
Solar Heating Coil
Supply Air
Return Air
Heat Storage Tank
Furnace

Home Energy Consumption in British Thermal Units (1985)

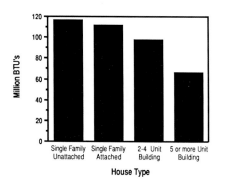

A well designed retrofit project can make life more comfortable for people living or working in a building. In addition, it can pay for itself in as little as four years. After those four years the retrofit is not only paid for, but starts to save money for as long as the building is used. Retrofits can be as simple as adding storm windows or insulation. Retrofits can also be more elaborate, such as adding on a sunroom or a new layer of siding. *Adding storm windows may not seem significant, but it has been estimated that if the U.S. could eliminate energy loss through windows, the energy saved would be about the same as the usable energy in all the oil that flows through the Alaska oil pipeline!*

The real need for energy efficient design is in new structures. We already have the technology to make new buildings that use between one-tenth to one-third the energy of existing structures. The key to these new structures is in **"super insulation,"** greatly increasing the amount of insulation and adding an airtight seal or "vapor barrier" around a building. Some of these buildings are so airtight that they need mechanical ventilation to provide fresh air.

Super-insulated building are so energy efficient that even body heat and the heat generated by appliances provide significant heat. Additional heat is produced by heat pumps, stoves, conventional furnaces and/or solar energy. During the summer months these buildings keep out the heat of the day. During the night, they cool themselves by circulating fresh, cool air. This provides the occupants with a very comfortable, yet inexpensive shelter.

The amount and kind of energy used *after* construction depends on the design, use and location of the structure itself. For example single-family dwellings require much more energy than do townhouses or apartments. During construction of single-family homes, more energy must be spent providing extra road surface, utilities (water, sewer, and electric lines) and landscaping than is required for each family in a multiple-family structure.

After completion, single-family homes continue to require more energy. A single-family home has all four sides and the roof exposed to the heat and cold. This means more energy is required to maintain a comfortable environment inside. Sprawling tracts of single-family homes make public transportation much less cost-efficient simply because customers are widely spread. Energy costs associated with other forms of transportation are also greater. School buses, trash services and other public services must travel farther between each home. Simply going to the store is a longer trip in areas that are dominated by single-family housing.

Although the construction and maintenance of any structure requires energy, some structures have a **net energy gain.** This means that in the long run these structures save more energy than they consume. A bridge on a busy highway that shortens the distance drivers must travel, a subway system that reduces the number of commuters traveling by automobile, and a canal that reduces shipping distances are all excellent examples of structures with a net energy gain.

■ Contaminates

No discussion of the environmental effects of construction systems could be complete without including a section on **pollution.** Pollution is one of those words that everyone knows but few can define.

Although no definition of pollution is entirely correct, perhaps the best definition is

Contamination of the air, water or soil with undesirable amounts of material or heat.

Note that this definition does not distinguish between natural and man-made substances or between living and non-living contaminates. It also does not specify the source of the contamination.

Construction systems generate pollution during the manufacture of materials, the construction process, and the use of the completed structure. Even the structure itself becomes a form of pollution after it is no longer in use.

Practically every object or material produced causes some form of negative environmental impact. Sometimes these impacts are relatively harmless. Other times they are so serious that regulations must be enacted to prevent great damage to the environment and/or to people.

There are few easy answers to environmental problems caused by the production of building materials. A good example of this problem is styrofoam, or structured plastic panels. The production and use of styrofoam creates some serious problems. Manufacturing styrofoam can create chloroflourocarbons (CFCs), which are a major culprit in the breakdown of the ozone layer. During its use, styrofoam continues to emit a low but steady stream of CFCs. Finally, styrofoam does not break down; it lasts

• •

Home Sickness Is More Than Missing Mom's Cooking

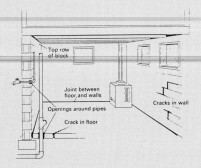

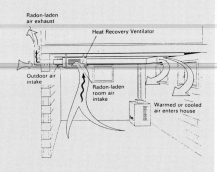

The air is thick with all sorts of toxic chemicals. Every breath takes in a host of chemicals that include formaldehyde, carbon monoxide, radon, volatile organic compounds, phenols, ozone, sulfur dioxide and countless other harmful agents. What is this place? A chemical factory? A toxic waste dump? It may be that this place is a home, a school or a local office building.

They are called sick buildings, and they are being found everywhere. Even a Washington D.C. office of the Environmental Protection Agency has been found to be "sick". It is not the buildings themselves that are sick; the people who live or work in them are getting ill. Due to poor design or attempts to reduce heating and cooling costs some building are improperly sealed. Ventilation is reduced, and there is not enough fresh air circulating inside. Various chemicals emitted into the air inside these buildings accumulate to sometimes dangerous levels.

These chemicals come from a variety of sources. Radon has received much attention in the past few years. Radon is a odorless, colorless, radioactive gas produced by the radioactive decay of naturally occurring radium in the soil. It can enter a building through the basement and be held in the stagnant air inside the home. Enough exposure to radon can cause cancer.

The materials used to build and furnish buildings can also cause serious indoor pollution problems. Formaldehyde is emitted in low levels by such things as plywood, particle board, foam insulation, carpets and fabrics. If formaldehyde levels are allowed to build up inside a building, they can cause irritation of the eyes, nose, throat and lungs. More serious effects include loss of sleep, headaches, depression and dizziness.

When students in an Oakland, California, high school began complaining of constant headaches, sore throats and tiredness, parents dismissed it as "back-to-school blues," especially when the headaches would disappear over the weekend. When almost half of the students in the school showed the same symptoms, they were taken more seriously. An investigation revealed that the school had 145 times the acceptable level of formaldehyde in its air. the source was found to be new particleboard shelves in the school library.

Cancer is not the only problem. Volatile organic compounds can cause kidney or liver damage. These compounds are released into indoor atmospheres by paints, cleaning solvents, plastics and waxes. The effects of secon-

dary smoke from cigarettes are magnified by poor indoor circulation as are the effects of the other pollutants mentioned above.

The solution to this problem is to minimize materials that emit harmful chemicals to provide proper ventilation and to periodically monitor buildings for high concentrations of pollutants.

Does this mean that buildings must sacrifice heating and cooling effectiveness for clean indoor environments? Not necessarily. This soft of accumulation of pollutants occurs only in buildings that are very "tight," buildings that allow almost no air to slip in through cracks in the wall or around windows.

Installing air-to-air heat transfer systems are an ideal, and usually inexpensive, means of allowing plenty of ventilation without excessive loss of heating or cooling. These systems can be as simple as inserting one aluminum pipe inside a larger pipe. One brings in fresh air the other is used for exhaust. As the air travels through these pipes the heated air gives off energy that warms the cold air. The end result is fresh air that is heated or cooled by the air that is being exhausted from the building.

Asbestos was widely used in transporting structures such as this steam locomotive. Workers were exposed to large amounts of asbestos during such operations. (Courtesy Arthur D. Little)

almost forever and releases dioxins and other harmful fumes when incinerated, making it extremely difficult to dispose of.

But styrofoam is an important building material. It provides great insulation and can be bought in easily installed sheets or even in large blocks that become the actual walls of a building. Is it better to use styrofoam insulation, saving energy but creating toxic waste, or is it better not to use it and consume more energy, creating other environmental problems, such as acid rain, smog, and depletion of resources?

It is sometimes difficult to identify what is and what is not a pollutant. Asbestos was used widely for decades before it was identified as being a carcinogen (a cancer-causing material). Even after it was identified as such, it was still argued that its benefits (such as fire protection) outweighed its risks (cancer). Even today, years after it has been recognized not only as a cause of cancer, but also of emphysema and other lung diseases, asbestos is still in the process of being removed from schools and other public buildings.

The debate over the use of materials such as styrofoam and asbestos are excellent examples of the concept of **trade offs.** There may be good reasons to not use a particular product or device, but there are often equally good reasons to use the same product. It is hoped that the positive aspects of a technology outweigh the negative aspects, but no matter how many positive aspects there are, there are always at least some negative aspects.

The process of examining new materials for their potential negative side effects is very time consuming and expensive. New materials are constantly being developed. The government agencies responsible for the testing and evaluation of these materials simply cannot keep up.

• •

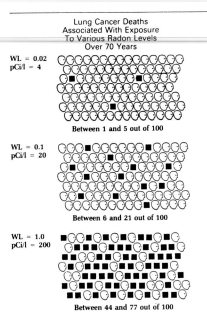

Lung Cancer Deaths
Associated With Exposure
To Various Radon Levels
Over 70 Years

WL = 0.02
pCi/l = 4

Between 1 and 5 out of 100

WL = 0.1
pCi/l = 20

Between 6 and 21 out of 100

WL = 1.0
pCi/l = 200

Between 44 and 77 out of 100

If these same 100 individuals had lived only 10 years (instead of 70) in houses with radon levels of about 1.0 WL, the number of lung cancer deaths expected would be:

WL = 1.0
pCi/l = 200

Between 14 and 42 out of 100

a material used does present a potential health problem, it is often very hard to prove that it is actually harmful. This is especially true with cancer-causing agents. Cancers sometimes take years to develop, so if exposure to a material does cause a cancer to form, it is often not noticeable for a long time. When a person dies years after exposure, it is extremely difficult to point a finger at a particular cancer-causing material.

A poorly designed building can also create interior pollution. If a building is designed or used without adequate ventilation, the air inside can become quite polluted. The materials used in the construction of the building, the furniture, even the people using the building can all emit small amounts of pollution. If these pollutants are not ventilated, they can build up to harmful levels.

After a building has served its purpose and is no longer needed or wanted, it becomes a large accumulation of trash. Some of the materials in an old structure (such as brick) can be salvaged, but most of the structure is not recyclable. Concrete generally is not reused at all. Most of the wood from old buildings is no longer usable for new structures and usually is burned or buried. The common method of destroying old buildings is to first remove what is reusable or saleable, then simply bulldoze, knock down or blow down the remaining structure. The huge pile of scrap left is then loaded into trucks and hauled to a land fill. The majority of the material will sit, mostly unchanged, for centuries. The portion that does break down may reenter the atmosphere as pollutants either in the air or in the water supply.

The debris of construction can also be considered archaeological treasure. This excavation shows the ruins of the oldest city on earth: Jericho, in Israel. The circular tower (bottom left) is part of the city wall, built about 9000 years ago!

SUMMARY

There are important social, technical and environmental implications related to construction systems. In many cases these implications are very serious because of the long-term nature of construction systems. What people design and build today will very likely outlast the people responsible for their construction. Comprehension of the social, technical and environmental implications is important because many construction systems will continue to affect us for a long time.

All construction systems product some negative environmental impacts. Some of these impacts present a serious danger to the health and safety of the people building these structures, the people using these structures, and sometimes for the public at large. These impacts can also present a threat to the economic well being of individuals, businesses and nations.

Construction systems disrupt the natural water cycle by increasing the amount of land surface covered by buildings and pavement, the demand for water, the amount of contaminates found in the water and the rate and extent of the erosion of topsoil. Food production is jeopardized by the disruption of the water cycle, and the development of agricultural lands.

The energy used and the pollution produced by a structure depends on the location, type and design of the structure, the quality of construction, the materials used, and how the structure is used.

. . . .

Study Questions

1. Describe a structure you know that creates a "neighborhood feeling."

2. The long-term nature of construction systems is important for historical and cultural reasons. Why?

3. How is technical quality related to meaningful work?

4. What responsibility does a contractor or builder have in regards to maintaining a healthy environment?

5. How does a new highway create more traffic?

6. How do construction systems help and hurt your local environment?

7. How does the quality of the environment affect your life?

. . . .

Suggested Activities

1. List the ways that energy is used in your own home or school. What can be done to reduce the amount on energy used in each of the ways listed?

2. Find out where and how the energy used in your area is produced.

3. Design and construct a cardboard model of a house that would have as little impact as possible on the land, water, air and use as little energy as possible.

Glossary

Aquifer   An underground water-bearing layer of rock, sand or gravel.

Erosion   Stripping away of soil or rock due to the abrasive action of water or wind.

Hard energy   Energy produced from non-renewable sources such as oil, coal or uranium.

Hierarchy of needs   Levels of human needs from the most basic physical needs such as food and water to more complex needs such as secure social and professional environments.

Neighborhood feeling   Secure social atmosphere found in interactive communities.

Net energy gain   A positive energy balance found in structures that save more energy than they use.

Pollution   Contamination of air, water or soil with undesirable amounts of material or heat.

Retrofit   To add on to, improve or modify an existing structure.

Siltatation   The process whereby bodies of water such as reservoirs become choked with fine-grained sediments eroded from the land.

Sink hole Depression in the land caused by subsidence of the water table.

Soft energy Energy produced from renewable resources such as the wind, sun and water.

Super insulation A technique using vapor barriers and other materials to make buildings very energy efficient.

Chapter 12

The Future of Construction Systems

Chapter Objectives

■ New office systems affect the design and construction of office buildings.

■ New developments in HVAC systems have helped control rising energy costs.

■ Describe some of the problems associated with the building and use of large buildings.

■ Computers have affected the design and daily operations of buildings.

■ Manufactured housing will continue to grow in the construction industry.

■ New materials and products entering the construction industry will change the way buildings are constructed and used.

Key Terms

CADD	Modular houses
Cogeneration	Panelized houses
Economizer cooling	Precut houses
HVAC	Smart buildings

Architects and engineers are aiming higher and higher in their quest for the tallest building. The proposed *500-story building* would stand 6,864 ft., well over a mile high! What are the advantages and disadvantages of such structures? (Designed by Robert Sobel, courtesy of Emory Roth & Sons, P.C.)

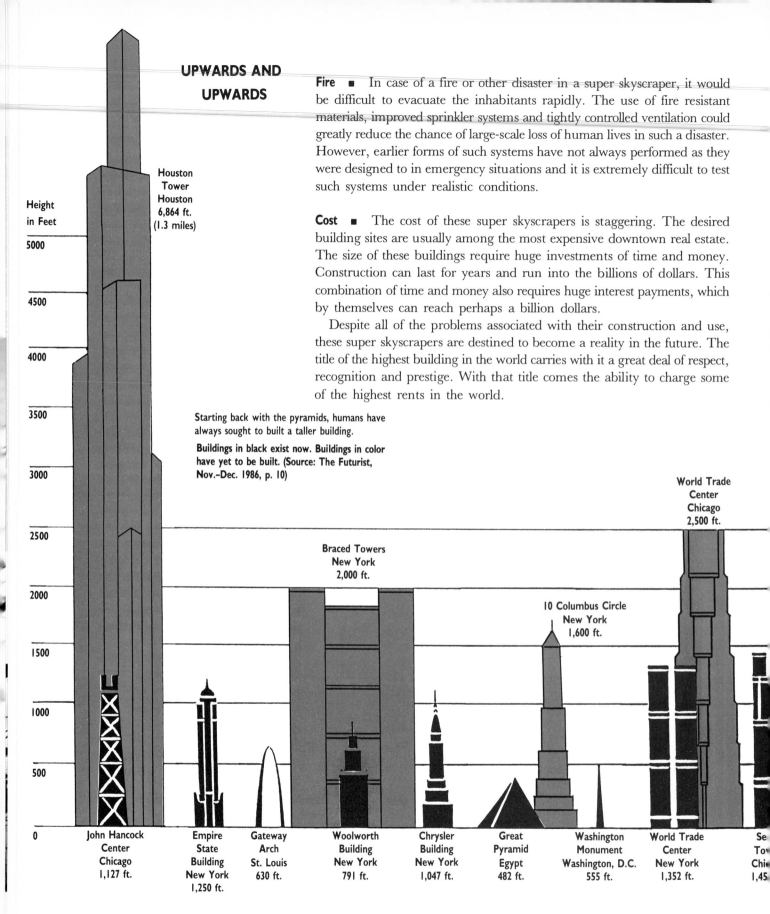

UPWARDS AND UPWARDS

Fire ■ In case of a fire or other disaster in a super skyscraper, it would be difficult to evacuate the inhabitants rapidly. The use of fire resistant materials, improved sprinkler systems and tightly controlled ventilation could greatly reduce the chance of large-scale loss of human lives in such a disaster. However, earlier forms of such systems have not always performed as they were designed to in emergency situations and it is extremely difficult to test such systems under realistic conditions.

Cost ■ The cost of these super skyscrapers is staggering. The desired building sites are usually among the most expensive downtown real estate. The size of these buildings require huge investments of time and money. Construction can last for years and run into the billions of dollars. This combination of time and money also requires huge interest payments, which by themselves can reach perhaps a billion dollars.

Despite all of the problems associated with their construction and use, these super skyscrapers are destined to become a reality in the future. The title of the highest building in the world carries with it a great deal of respect, recognition and prestige. With that title comes the ability to charge some of the highest rents in the world.

Starting back with the pyramids, humans have always sought to built a taller building.

Buildings in black exist now. Buildings in color have yet to be built. (Source: The Futurist, Nov.–Dec. 1986, p. 10)

Height in Feet

Houston Tower Houston 6,864 ft. (1.3 miles)

World Trade Center Chicago 2,500 ft.

Braced Towers New York 2,000 ft.

10 Columbus Circle New York 1,600 ft.

John Hancock Center Chicago 1,127 ft.

Empire State Building New York 1,250 ft.

Gateway Arch St. Louis 630 ft.

Woolworth Building New York 791 ft.

Chrysler Building New York 1,047 ft.

Great Pyramid Egypt 482 ft.

Washington Monument Washington, D.C. 555 ft.

World Trade Center New York 1,352 ft.

Se Tov Chic 1,45

Smart Building Systems

There is increasing interest in computerized buildings, known as "smart" or "intelligent" homes and offices. A **smart building** has an elaborate electronic system integrated by one or several small computers.

The use of the term "smart" is misleading. A computer or computerized system cannot be "smart" any more than a car or any other machine can be. Yet, the full use of these systems could give the occupants the feeling that the building does, indeed, have a mind of its own. Certainly the development of these systems will have a significant impact on the use of completed structures and will mandate a completely new form of wiring and appliances for buildings in the not too distant future.

In its simplest form a smart building can use existing wiring techniques to control appliances, heating, air conditioning, security and lighting through a central control panel. This is by no means new. What is emerging as a new building technology is the increased use of microcomputers to supplement the human control of these systems.

The new generation of smart homes replaces the web of electrical, telephone and cable television wires with a single, continuous cable. The current passing through this cable differs from traditional wiring in two ways: The destination and amount of the current is completely controlled by a central command unit, and this current is direct current (DC) rather than standard alternating current (AC). The standard two-prong wall socket would be replaced by a multi pronged module.

These changes makes a number of improvements possible:

■ Any appliance or electronic device could be plugged into any wall socket. The central command unit would "recognize" the appliance and transmit the correct signal to it. For example, a television would receive cable hook up in any room of the house merely by plugging it in; stereo speakers plugged into any wall socket would receive signals from a separate tuner plugged into another wall unit.

■ Appliances would receive only the amount of electrical power they needed at any given moment.

■ "Unauthorized appliances", such as a baby's fingers, would not be recognized by the command unit and would receive no current, thus eliminating the dangers of electrical shock.

■ Light bulbs could be set to emit only as much light as desired for a particular situation.

Smart houses are controlled by a network of computerized systems. These systems are programmed from a console such as the one shown at the right. (Courtesy of GE Plastics)

"Sorry, unless you can convince me you are a vacuum you won't get any juice from me"

Smart building systems can control electrical current to outlets. This safeguards infants against electrical shock.

Made To Order

The solution to his problems at work came to him in his sleep. He awoke with a feeling of insight. Sitting up in bed, John, his voice still hoarse from sleep, said "June, what time is it?" June's soft voice almost immediately replied "It is 3:17 in the morning". Desite the hour John knew that he should run down to the office and enter his new brainstorm onto the office computer.

Still feeling groggy, John commanded June to make him coffee and asked about the weather. Within seconds, June had started the coffee brewing and had given John the current weather forecast.

"June, I need a hot shower, about 103 degrees, and make some toast. It's a little cold in here. Warm it up about 5 degrees, turn on the lights in the bathroom and while I shower read me the latest headlines."

Almost before John had finished talking, the bathroom lights flickered on. By the time he had reached the bathroom door, warm air was flowing from the heating vents. As he showered, June read him the lead stories from a newspaper published only minutes before in a town hundreds of miles away. After his shower, John wolfed down his toast and coffee and headed out the door. He paused to say "I am going to the office now; forward any of my calls there. Start up my car for me, turn the heat back down, turn off all the lights, lock all the windows and doors as soon as I am gone and do not let any one in until I return. Oh, and transfer $200 from savings to checking and pay the phone bill. Check all of the newspapers and magazines. If there is any news on the Wochick Enterprise merger, have a printout when I get home." June repeats all of John's instructions and wishes him a good day. As John closes the door behind him, he hears the engine of his car jump to life and the bolt on the door slide shut.

Walking into his office building, John presents his identification card to Jim at the security station. The elevator car is waiting with open doors in the lobby. Jim has already informed the elevator what floor to take. Jim has also turned on the lights inside John's office, activated his computer and brought the room temperature up to the level that John prefers.

John walks straight to his office. If he was to take too long or try to enter an office that was not his, Jim would immediately inform security. While in his office, everything that John does is faithfully recorded by Jim. If John's boss should ask, Jim can give a complete recounting of John's every move: when he arrived, what files he examined, what programs he utilized, what he entered on the computer, to whom he talked on the phone, even how much time he spent in the bathroom.

John does not get angry at Jim for snooping any more than he is grateful for the help June provides around the house. John could not carry on a real conversation with either Jim or June. In fact, he has never seen either one of them. Jim and June are both computer systems. The house he lives in and the building he works in are called "smart" buildings.

June, as a computer, is not terribly sophisticated, having computing power, speed and memory not much above that of the average personal computer. What is remarkable is the extent to which the system can control the house and its contents. Commanded either by voice or keyboard, the June system can control the operation of every electrical, water or gas appliance in the house. Sensors and small robots provide both simple housekeeping duties and security. By using the telephone lines, June can interface with various database systems to obtain a wide variety of news and information from around the globe.

Jim, although larger and with more sensors and operations, is still less sophisticated than the computers currently being used by most companies. Jim functions much the same way as June. One important distinction between the two is that while the home unit is a convenience item, and represents a significant cost to its owner, the office building computer unit was bought to save money for its owners. An office system such as the one described can substantially reduce utility bills to the point of paying for itself in a few years, as well as providing increased security, comfort and fire protection for its inhabitants.

This might sound like a forecast of what houses might be like in the future, but in fact, houses and offices like those described exist today. The number of such systems is very small due to high cost and lack of demand, but as these systems evolve and become less expensive their numbers will almost surely increase.

- Loud appliances, such as vacuum cleaners could be automatically shut off and the volume of television or stereo sets reduced when the phone rings are made or visitors arrive.

- Adding voice recognition and voice synthesizers would permit the systems to hear commands from specified people and to respond to these commands with a voice style selected by the owner.

- Such systems hooked up to telephone lines would enable owners to send instructions to the house by phone. For example an owner could call home and tell the computer to turn up the heat, turn on certain lights and start the oven.

- Doors and windows could be locked simultaneously. If an intruder was present, the house could be programmed to notify the police, emit an alarm, and alert the occupants. These systems would be able to distinguish between a true intruder and a pet or family member walking around the house late at night.

- The heating, ventilation and air conditioning cost of a home could be drastically reduced by using outside air for heating or cooling when sensors deem appropriate. Additional savings would be achieved by heating and cooling only those rooms in use and by setting temperature limits for each room individually.

. . . .

Computer-Aided Design and Drafting

This designer is creating a new window design using computerized equipment. (Courtesy of Andersen Corp.)

Computers are changing the way structures are designed. With the advent of computer-aided design and drafting **(CADD),** the days of an architect laboring over a drawing board are rapidly fading. Most architects and architectural firms today have installed CADD systems. Since the cost of computing power is decreasing and the abilities of CADD systems are increasing rapidly, this trend is expected to continue. In the future it will probably be rare to find a professional architect who does not use a CADD system.

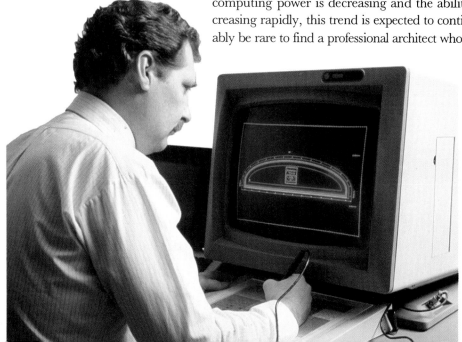

What Is a CADD System?

The first CADD systems were little more than high-tech drawing boards allowing the architect to make lines and figures faster and to rearrange these lines in a variety of ways. (Imagine a cross between a computer and an Etch-a-sketch.) CADD systems also allow an architect to store and retrieve plans and portions of plans to be used on other projects. CADD systems of the 1980's are in some ways similar to word processing systems. Instead of communicating with words, CADD systems communicate with drawings.

A higher order of CADD systems, integrated into the entire construction process, is beginning to emerge. From the architect's initial drawings the computer will be able to produce specifications, construction documents, estimates and construction schedules. Some factories that produce buildings and building components are already using CADD systems to produce drawings and transfer this information directly to the robots that perform the assembly line production. Future CADD systems using holography will most likely make solid models of a structure obsolete. By merely pressing a few buttons, the computer could produce a three-dimensional image of the structure.

Some **CADD** systems allow the creation of highly three-dimensional, color drawings. (Courtesy of AT&T)

A CADD system is similar to a word processor. Just as a word processor manipulates words and sentences, a CADD system manipulates drawings and figures. Below is a partial list of some tasks a word processor can accomplish and similar tasks that a CADD system can perform.

Word Processor	*CADD System*
Move a word.	Move a stairway.
Change the margins of the paper.	Change the size of the building.
Copy a paragraph from another document and insert it on to the paper that is being written.	Copy a kitchen layout from a house that designed last year and insert it into a new house.
Produce dozens of form letters, each identical except for the name of the person that it is addressed to.	Design a hotel with dozens of identical rooms.
Move sentences around a page.	Move rooms around a building.

Advantages of CADD

- Eliminates much of the repetitive work in design and drafting.
- Decreases the time involved to take an idea to finished blueprint.
- Decreases the cost of the design and drafting stage of construction.
- Decreases the amount of risk, in terms of time and effort, on the part of the architect, to experiment with a new concept or design.
- Allows for increased standardization of design.
- Allows architects freedom from long hours at a drafting table.
- Allows for more comprehensive planning of the construction process.
- Advanced CADD systems allow for greater safety from human error by evaluating design.

Disadvantages of CADD

- Increased time needed to learn complex computer systems.
- Architect becomes more of a computer operator than a skilled artist.
- Decreases the number of architects needed for any given job, thereby decreasing the creative input of different individuals.
- Allows for increased standardization of design.
- Requires architects to spend long hours in front of a computer screen.

◼ CADD Pro and Con

The CADD system offers great new possibilities, but, like any new technology, it also creates new problems. Before any discussion of the pros and cons of CADD systems, it is important to recognize that CADD systems are being adopted. Professionals in the field believe that the benefits outweigh the disadvantages. CADD systems are currently being used by more than 90 percent of the architectural firms in the United States.

With or without CADD, the job of an architect is not an easy one. Even after years of schooling and a long apprenticeship, most architects are still learning. The great architects generally produce their greatest designs only after decades of work. Most people, particularly younger ones working in a design office, are involved in producing detailed construction drawings and documents, not, as many think, in the creation of ideas that transfer to drawings. It is important to remember this when discussing CADD systems. CADD requires months of specialized training and perhaps years of use to become truly proficient. During this time architects are learning to be computer operators, not architects.

Apprentice staff take the ideas generated by the more experienced architects or designers and produce detailed drawings and documents. These younger "detailers" represent about 80 percent of the work force in a design team. Higher order CADD systems can eliminate the vast majority of these positions. For the individual company this can represent a great savings on their payroll and this cost can be passed onto the buyer or builder. The

This **CADD** system highlights each story of windows in a different color. (GEOCAD® perspective drawing courtesy of Rudolph Horowitz and Associates, Architects. GEOCAD is a registered trademark of Rudolph Horowitz and Associates, Architects.)

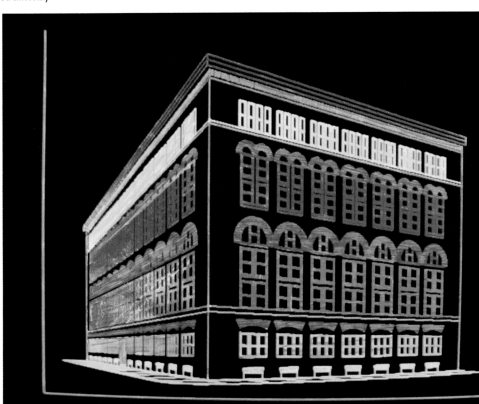

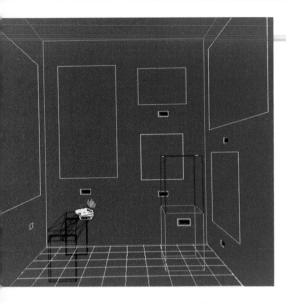

CADD programs allow for a linear, "see-through," depiction of constructed interiors. (Courtesy of AT&T)

long-term implications of this action for the entire profession may not be as desirable. If you remove the learning jobs for less experienced architects, where will the older, more experienced architects of the future come from?

As CADD systems become more common there may be an accompanying change in the style of buildings. CADD systems make it very easy for an architect to copy a building or portion of a building. This encourages the production of "cloned" buildings, each being the exact twin of others. However, it also gives the designer the opportunity to try different combinations of existing plans, which could create a greater diversity of structures than we enjoy now.

The decreased time and effort required to produce drawings also can have a positive or negative effect. On one hand, if experimentation requires less risk, then there would be more incentive to try new ideas or designs. However, decreased time may also mean less money would be budgeted for design. This would put greater pressure on the architects to produce quickly and may remove the freedom to experiment with new designs.

■ CADD Systems in the Future

The number of firms using CADD systems is likely to increase until it becomes almost universally accepted. CADD systems will have greater abilities to integrate with other computers to perform a large variety of functions, both in the construction process and in the use of the buildings.

However, it is likely that there will be an overall decrease in the total number of jobs available in the design field. The new positions created by CADD will be highly specialized.

Although CADD systems allow greater freedom for the architect to experiment with new and innovative design, the extent to which this ability is utilized will depend on economics and management. The total percentage of the construction budget spent on architecture and design probably will decrease.

With the ability of advanced computer systems to check designs for adherence to codes and regulations and to perform complex calculations, the buildings produced by CADD systems are more likely to be designed safer and of higher quality than those designed with more basic systems or without computer assistance. There is great potential for improved design of basic services such as heating, air conditioning and lighting, making the completed structure more versatile, comfortable and energy efficient.

This computer graphic shows the structure of a multiple radial tent structure. (Courtesy of Geiger Berger Associates, P.C.)

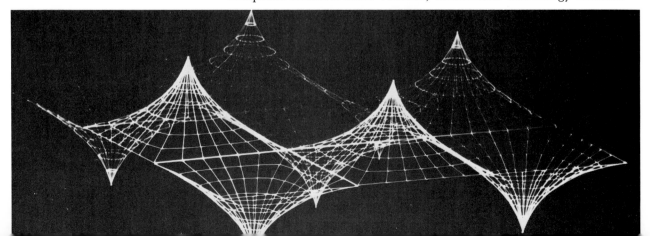

Manufactured houses are more efficient and therefore cheaper to produce. Notice the different stages of construction including framing and sheetrocking. (Courtesy of Coachmen Industries)

Manufactured Housing

As large numbers of servicemen returned from World War II eager to start a family, there was an unprecedented demand for new housing. One method used to meet this demand was manufactured housing. In simplest terms, manufactured housing means that all or part of the house is produced in a factory instead of on the house site. This experiment of the 1940's was not long lasting and was relatively unsuccessful.

Today there is a demand in the housing market for homes affordable by the average citizen. Again, the industry is looking into manufactured housing. This time it appears that the experiment is no longer an experiment, but the wave of the future in home construction.

Manufactured houses come in three basic forms:

Modular houses are built almost entirely in the factory. When these homes leave the factory they often have electrical, plumbing and heating systems installed. Some manufacturers even include finish work such as wallpaper, paint, wood trim and major appliances in their models. Shipped by truck, these modules are connected together on the house site, often in only one day, to form full-sized homes. The only work needed at the home site is the placement of the foundation and hook up of the utilities. The traditional mobile home is one type of modular home. Today, and in the future, modular homes can far surpass the "metal boxes" that characterize the mobile home. Once finished it is often difficult to distinguish a modern modular home from one built on site. The quality of construction can be, and often is, superior to that of on-site built homes. The manufacturing process presents fewer "surprises" to the workers than an on-site built home. These surprises (sometimes remedied by the judicious use of a large hammer) often decrease the quality and soundness of a structure.

Panelized houses arrive at the job site in wall, floor and ceiling units. Workers assemble and connect these units on site to form the completed structure. These units may arrive with electrical, plumbing and heating components enclosed in the units, referred to as "closed" units. "Open" units require the wiring, plumbing and duct work to be done on the job site.

Precut houses, or house kits, arrive at the job site much like a very large model plane kit, complete with instructions. The materials are cut or formed so that they can be assembled with minimal time and effort. Some of the smaller components, such as stairs and windows, are preassembled at the factory. These precut units may contain only the parts necessary to form the outer shell and basic wall units, or may be very complete, including such things as paint, wallpaper and fixtures. These units are especially appealing to people who wish to build their own homes without excessive expense or knowledge of construction techniques.

■ Advantages of Manufactured Houses

The primary advantage of manufactured houses is cost. Some manufacturers are able to build, deliver and finish a home for less than half the cost of a comparable traditionally built home. In addition, the time spent in the construction process is greatly reduced, therefore the interest on building loans is reduced.

Habitat '67 in Montreal is composed of mass-produced, pre-cast concrete units. Each unit is a complete apartment. Individual families can order different sizes and different interior arrangements. Each floor has a play area for children. This structrure resembles the early pueblos of the Southwestern United States. (Courtesy of Moshe Safdie & Associates)

I'll Take a Hamburger, French Fries and a Two Bedroom Rambler

After years of saving, John and Jane Moore have finally saved enough money to buy their first home. The day has finally come when they can actually look for their dream home. Years ago, their parents would have spent weeks talking to realtors, looking through the real estate section of the local newspaper and countless hours driving around the area looking at homes. Such antiquated practices are out of the question for John and Jane. They, like all of their friends, avoid realtors and newspapers by going to the house store.

Once in the store the smiling salesperson shows them aerial photographs and detailed drawings of new housing areas that are being developed. After selecting their site from these photos and drawings, the Moores start on the house itself. The salesperson shows the Moores a thick catalog of homes already built by that company. Selecting just those parts of the homes that appeal to them, and adding quite a few ideas of their own, the Moores finally decide on a floor plan they consider just right for them.

The salesperson works patiently with the Moores through a long list of options. These options include such things as amounts of insulation, paint and wallpaper colors, window size and placement, siding material, trim work, heating and air conditioning units and

(Courtesy of Coachmen Industries)

carpeting. These lists completed, the Moores can "see" their home, presented in 3D, on the computer screen.

The computer then totals the cost of the lot and home, with the selected options and compares this figure to the credit rating of the Moores. If the final price and design is acceptable to the Moores, and the computer decides that it is within their credit limits, the deal is completed.

The salesman pushes a button or the computer keyboard that sends the completed details of the house and its location to the computers in the factory. Machinery and workers are dispatched to the house site to excavate and pour the foundation. At the factory, the master computer receives the Moores order and immediately issues orders to dozens of smaller computer systems. Some of these computers locate, organize and transport the thousands of parts and materials needed for the house while other computers handle the actual assembly of the house. From the time the first two pieces were put together the Moores' house does not stop traveling at a

steady rate of fourteen feet per minute until it emerges at the end of the assembly line. Even before the form work of the foundation is finished, the house arrives at the site on four tractor trailers. Once the foundation is finished, a crane is brought in to unload the house. A crane operator and a crew of five workers assemble the four sections of the house in less than six hours. A different, smaller crew complete the finish work and hook up all the utilities in less than two work weeks.

Only weeks after they placed their order the Moores have their dream home completed and ready to inhabit. Far from being a cheap, rickety shelter, this home is not only tightly sealed and insulated, it is able to withstand earthquakes and hurricane-force winds. The house, designed, built and finished to their exact specifications, is everything that the Moores hoped it would be.

This may seem like a science fiction, but it is in fact, almost exactly the way some new homes are being produced today in Japan. As a manager of one of these house factories put it: "We are building houses the way we build cars".

The quality of construction of a manufactured home can be far superior to that of an on-site built home, but this is entirely dependent on the quality of the work done by individual manufacturers and builders. The quality of work is often difficult for the average home buyer to determine. Most buyers therefore rely upon reputation, word of mouth, uninformed impressions or blind faith in determining the quality of construction.

Strictly as a business, the benefits of manufactured versus on-site built homes are overwhelmingly in favor of factory-built homes. There is much less waste, in terms of materials and lost time in a manufacturing operation. In a factory there are no lost days due to weather conditions and there are fewer management problems, such as plumbers waiting for electricians or long waits for vital parts. Materials are bought in large quantities, often made or cut to order and the majority of the labor force is non-union, semi-skilled, permanent workers. All these factors plus the added financial saving of assembly line production, create a product that is vastly less expensive than traditionally built structures.

Disadvantages of Manufactured Houses

Japan and European countries successfully use modular construction techniques to assemble large homes and even mansions. In the United States, however, most modular homes are relatively small "double-wide" structures. Because they are transported on the highways, road conditions limit the maximum width of modular units to 12 or 14 feet. A double-wide home is two of these structures assembled together. Zoning restrictions in many urban and suburban areas require a house size much larger than this. Therefore, most modular homes are built in areas that have lax or non-existent zoning regulations.

The public often identifies modular homes with mobile homes, thus creating the impression of small, poorly constructed boxes. This perception is no longer valid, yet it presents a major public relations obstacle to the manufactured housing industry.

As the percentage of manufactured housing units increases, there will be a direct decrease in the demand for skilled labor and craftspeople. In an assembly plant, there are no true carpenters, cabinet makers or plasterers; there are only assembly line workers who handle wood or plaster.

The movement towards manufactured housing has been strongly protested by some traditional builders. Small scale contractors and home builders can see themselves being edged out of the market by manufactured housing companies. The housing industry has the potential to develop into a system very similar to the automobile industry, with smaller operations being eliminated by larger and larger corporations until only a handful of companies produce the majority of the new homes.

Exposure tests try to determine how various materials withstand weathering. (Courtesy of Andersen Corp.)

This insulating glass has a nearly invisible metallic coating that keeps the heat out in summer and the heat in during the winter. (Courtesy of Andersen Corp.)

Materials

The construction industry is perhaps the slowest industry to adopt new materials. Structures are built with the longest life expectancy of any major technological good produced. This, and the high cost of any full-scale construction project, makes the economical and practical risks of using a new material very high. With so much at stake, there is little incentive to use a material that has only been tested in a laboratory and only for a limited amount of time.

Laboratory testing techniques can subject a material to a wide variety of conditions that can simulate years of normal use in a relatively short period of time. These testing techniques are by no means perfect; they can only hope to approximate real use conditions. The reliability of these tests also depends on the life expectancy of the product being tested. It is much easier to simulate real conditions for a product intended to last only a few years, such as a small appliance. It is more difficult to simulate real world conditions for goods intended to last for longer periods and it is virtually impossible to accurately simulate these conditions for products intended to last for decades, such as most structures.

The industry as a whole is more likely to adopt materials that are easier to replace, present less of a risk and represent a smaller capital investment. Windows, interior and exterior trim and finish materials are the most prevalent of these.

■ Windows

The traditional single glass pane window is extremely inefficient at blocking the flow of heat into, or out of, a structure. Double pane windows are more than twice as efficient as single pane, but are still much less efficient than the rest of the average wall. Just as clear glass is very good at allowing sunlight to enter a structure, thereby warming it, it is also almost as good at allowing heat to flow back out, particularly at night.

New windows that attempt to control the passage of heat and light are either coming onto the market now, or are being developed.

Electrochromic Windows ■ Electrochromic windows can change from completely clear to completely dark with the flip of a switch. These windows have microscopically thin layers of indium tin oxide, magnesium fluoride and amorphous tungsten trioxide sandwiched between glass panes. When low voltage current is applied to these materials the flow of electrons causes the tungsten to absorb light, particularly the red wavelengths. As the level of this absorption increases, the glass becomes visibly darker. The glass remains dark even after the current is stopped. When the polarity of the current is reversed, the window loses its light-absorbing capabilities.

Another variation of electrochromic windows is the use of electrically-sensitive thermoplastic windows. A switch changes these windows from clear to translucent. (Courtesy of GE Plastics)

Plastic is a primary material of this 3,000 square foot experimental house. It is being used as a laboratory to explore the feasibility of wide-spread use of polymers (plastic) in construction. (Courtesy of GE Plastics)

Although still only in the research and development stage, electrochromic windows have the potential to greatly reduce energy demands and increase comfort of buildings, in the not-to-distant future. The installation and proper use of these windows could conceivably reduce the heating and cooling costs of a building by as much as 25 percent and lighting costs by as much as 50 percent.

Vacuum Windows ■ The "dead air" space between double or triple pane glass is a good insulator. A vacuum space (having no air at all) between the panes would be even better. Developing such a vacuum space has two major technical complications. Sealing the seams of these panes in a vacuum would be difficult and if such windows were built, they would have a tendency to implode (explode inward) due to the atmospheric pressure pressing against the outside of the glass.

Both of these problems have been solved, at least in laboratory conditions. Lasers have been used to form leak-proof seals around the glass. This technique needs to be refined to make it economically feasible. Implosion problems can be eliminated by using extremely small (one half of a millimeter) glass beads as spacers between the panes. These beads would provide enough support to keep the panes from collapsing inward and are small enough to be nearly invisible.

■ Plastic

The term "plastic" has long been associated with cheap, poor quality materials. This is becoming a misconception as plastics technology rapidly improves. Plastic components are already being substituted for wood and steel in products ranging from automobiles to home appliances. In the future, the amount of plastic based products found in the construction field is expected to dramatically increase.

Although some plastics, and particularly fiberglass reinforced plastics, are already stronger, pound for pound, than most woods, metals and concretes, it is not expected that they will replace these materials in structural components in the foreseeable future. The use of plastics in non-structural applications, however, is already increasing.

Some applications for plastic products in construction systems include:

■ Below grade concrete form walls that would be left in place to provide waterproofing. These form walls may also be produced with insulation, providing the concrete form, insulation and waterproofing all in one operation.

■ Foam-insulated plastic siding that provides a finished exterior surface, weatherproofing, insulation and vapor barrier in one component.

■ Foam-insulated plastic roofing panels and skylights.

- Interior wall boards with built-in air channels to circulate hot or cold air, as a supplement to, or in place of, forced air heating and cooling.

- More thermally efficient and versatile foam insulations.

- Stronger, more impact- and shatter-resistant alternatives to glass.

It should also be noted that one of the more promising products of the emerging plastics recycling industry is a mixture of various plastics formed into dimension "lumber". These products have one inherent advantage and disadvantage: they last practically forever. These materials can be cut, nailed and formed in much the same way as many woods. They are immune to warping, cracking and are highly water resistant. Although the technology is still new and primarily in the experiment and testing phase, the use of this plastic lumber is likely to become more and more commonplace. This trend will be accelerated by the decreasing amounts of available quality lumber and the increased need to find alternatives to placing plastics in land fills. It is entirely probable that the person entering the construction industry today will see the wooden 2 × 4 completely replaced by recycled plastic, at least for interior framing.

Recycled plastic can be used to make shingles as well as other elements such as dimension lumber. (Courtesy of GE Plastics)

▪ Recycled and Waste Materials

Besides the use of recycled plastics to form dimension lumber, there is an increasing interest in using other materials previously considered waste as a source of building materials. These materials are not only residential waste, such as plastics, but includes industrial and construction waste as well. Coal-fired electrical power plants produce huge amounts of fly ash, a fine powdered coal ash. Research is being conducted to find new and innovative means of using this material for such applications as an aggregate for concrete and bedding for foundations and roadways. With increased efforts for cleaner emissions from these plants, the amount of sulfur recovered will constitute millions of tons. This sulfur also has great potential as an aggregate and for roadways.

Wood scrap and unfavored tree species were considered waste products and were either left to rot or burned until recently. With the advent and increased use of high strength adhesives these waste products are turned into chip board, particle board and strand board. These products not only create new applications, and allow new construction methods, they also reduce the economic and environmental expense of harvesting new trees.

Solar energy will play an increasingly important role in residential and commercial buildings. (Courtesy of Meridian)

Future Trends

There is no shortage of predictions for the future. Just about everyone involved in any profession seems to have their own version of what the future will bring. These predictions range from the thoroughly ridiculous to the thoroughly plausible. Besides those already discussed in this chapter, there are several trends and events that fall within the plausible category.

- Despite short-term fluctuations, real estate prices will continue to increase. This is a direct result of increasing populations and increased wealth of these populations.

- Energy prices will significantly increase, at least for the next few decades. This trend will increase the interest in more energy efficient buildings and components.

- If energy prices rise as expected, there will be large demands for home remodelers and renovators specializing in energy efficiency and intensive energy auditing.

- These increased real estate and energy prices coupled with the increase in the number of senior citizens, will create larger demands for smaller, more energy efficient, easier-to-maintain dwellings.

- Mass transit systems will see a revitalization due to increased commuting time and cost, deteriorating air quality and urban congestion.

- Solar energy, particularly passive solar space heating, will become more commonplace in both homes and larger buildings.

- Increases in computer and communication technologies will help contribute to the significant rise in the number of people working at home. These "telecommuters" will increase the demand for homes with office space attached or included in the home design. There is also expected to be an accompanying rise in the demand for home renovation companies specializing in home office design.

- There will be a general decrease in the demand for traditional construction trade workers. There will be an partially offsetting increase in the demand for specialized construction trade workers, particularly in the fields of electronics and heating, ventilation and air conditioning (HVAC).

- Computers will have an increasing role in virtually every phase of the construction process. This will create a greater demand for computer professionals that specialize in the construction field.

Sometimes, It Is Better To Put All Your Eggs In One Basket

A relatively new and emerging trend in residential area development is called **clustered communities.** Clustered communities are an alternative to traditional large tracts of detached single-family home suburban development.

When developers buy a tract of land, they will usually divide the entire plot in small, individual lots. On each of these lots an individual home is placed, each with its own lawn and driveway.

Rather than building individual homes on quarter or half-acre lots, clustered communities have all the homes built in adjoining groups or townhomes. By doing this, a developer can still site as many homes on a given parcel of land but in much smaller area. The rest of the land can be used for parks, recreation and public areas.

Social Advantages of Clustered Communities

- Reduced cost of care and maintenance of yards and homes.
- Greater social interaction with neighbors.
- Greater diversity of recreational facilities (tennis courts, golf courses, horseback riding, nature trails, bike paths, basketball courts etc.).
- Better quality of recreation areas (playgrounds instead of backyard swing sets).
- Greater access to green areas.
- Requires greater community cooperation for management of community areas.

Technical Advantages of Clustered Communities

- Lower cost, per unit, of homes.
- More efficient installation and maintenance of water, gas, sewage and electric utilities.
- More efficient public transportation.
- Greater efficiency of trash collection and other services.

Environmental Advantages of Clustered Communities

- Reduced energy consumption for heating and cooling individual homes.
- Reduced consumption of petroleum resources for transportation.
- Less land space devoted to roads and driveways.
- Decreased surface runoff of water.
- Decreased soil erosion.
- Reduced destruction of animal and plant life.
- Reduced destruction of waterways.
- More advanced community sewage treatment.

Disadvantages of Clustered Communities

- Loss of large yard space, which is considered a source of social status by some individuals.
- On-going maintenance cost of community areas.
- Requires greater community cooperation for management of community areas.
- Loss of some degree of privacy due to closer proximity of neighbors.

Three views of a typical New England village: undeveloped, conventionally developed, cluster-zoned. (From *Design Manual,* Center for Rural Massachusetts, by Harry Dodson. Drawings by Kevin Wilson)

There are no certainties in regards to the future. Any, or even all, of the trends discussed could be drastically changed by unforeseen events.

If these trends do continue as predicted, then it seems clear that the role of computers in the construction field will greatly increase. Like any tool, the computers can only produce what the human controlling it wants. Individuals considering entering construction, or any technological field, should acquire a basic understanding of these machines. This understanding does not need to be extensive, only enough to remove unresonable fears and assure a basic familiarity with their use and applications.

The construction industry tends to lag far behind other technological fields in terms of adopting new processes and materials. Nevertheless, the number of new products and processes available will continue to grow. Some of these will hold great potential; others will not.

Individuals entering the field of construction today will have a much greater opportunity to pick and choose from new innovations than ever before possible.

Study Questions

1. Does the trend towards the use of computer aided design (CADD) have a positive or negative impact on the construction industry as a whole? On society and the individual consumer?

2. Should the federal government offer tax breaks, funding or other financial incentives to companies that conduct research into more energy efficient windows and/or building components?

3. Does the trend towards manufactured structures have a positive or negative impact on the construction industry as a whole? On society and the individual consumer?

4. Should the federal government offer tax breaks or other financial incentives to companies that utilize recycled products in the construction of buildings or structures?

5. Would you, as an individual:
   (A) Purchase a manufactured home your own residence?
   (B) Live or work in a super skyscraper?
   (C) Work in a building manufacturing plant?
   (D) Use new, untested building materials in a house?
   (E) Live in a clustered community?

Suggested Activities

1. As a class pick or create a design for a small house or structure. One half of the class will construct individual scale models of the structure while the other half manufactures the models using assembly line techniques. Each team should produce one model for each member. When the models are completed, discuss the following questions related to process of assembling these models.
   (a) Which group produced the models fastest?
   (b) Which group's models are of better quality construction?
   (c) If these models were full sized, and the class members were paid workers, which group would produce the structure with the least expense?
   (d) Which process was the most enjoyable?
   (e) Which group learned the most from this activity?

2. Using a specified amount of cardboard, tape and "popsicle" sticks each member should attempt to construct a structure as tall as possible. When completed these structures should be tested by:
   (a) Turning on a box fan located four feet away from the top of the structure.
   (b) Gently shaking the base of the structure.
   (c) Adding small weights to the top floor of the structure.
   (d) Determining the capacity (volume) of the building.

3. Individually design a layout for a community of the future, include roadways, pathways and mass transit, industrial areas, office areas, residential areas, recreation areas, commercial areas and civic areas.

4. Pick a time in the future, anywhere from 5 to 25 years from now. Write a list of the changes you expect to see in communities and construction systems by this time. Be prepared to defend your predictions to the rest of the class.

Glossary

Economizer cooling   The pumping of outside air directly into a buildings ventilation system during times of cool temperatures.

HVAC   Heating, ventilation and air conditioning.

Cogeneration   The use of waste heat produced by electrical generation to warm a structure.

Smart buildings   Structures utilizing computers to control the HVAC and electronic operations occurring within.

CADD   Computer aided design and drafting.

Modular houses   Homes that have entire rooms or sections manufactured in a factory and joined together at the job site.

Precut houses   Houses that arrive at the job site with all materials pre-cut or formed for quick assembly.

Panelized houses   Arrive at the job site with wall, floor and roof units prefabricated.

ACTIVITY 23

Building Modern Structures

Reference

Chapter 12: The Future of Construction Systems
Chapter 4: Structural Elements

Concept

Space Frames
Many modern structures use principles of construction referred to as space frames.

Related Concepts
Hyperbolic parabaloid, space frame, folded plate, parabolic, hyperbolic.

Objective

On completion of this activity the class will have constructed models of several space frames and be able to (1) describe the importance of the structural members reinforcing each other, (2) describe what contributes to the strength of lightness of the structure and (3) describe some of the advantages and disadvantages of the different space frames.

Considerations

1. The ice cream cone was the first edible structure. Is the ice cream cone despite its age, a modern structure?

2. Many modern structures are based on mathematical forms. Can you think of any mathematical shapes that you have seen used in buildings?

3. Modern structures use the least amount of material possible while achieving the greatest strength possible. What does this statement mean?

Materials and Supplies

Group A
activity box
manila file folders
glue
small weights

Group B
round tooth picks or cotton swab sticks
1 piece of ¼" plywood, 4" × 4" for test pad
small weights

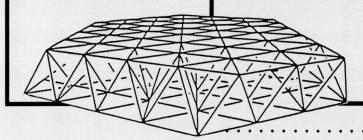

Group C
long thin balloons
sheet of rubber or plastic (24″ × 30″ minimum)
tacks
tape
nails
string
glue
tire pump

All Groups
Structure Capability Test Form
drawing materials

1. Break the class down into three work groups. Each group will complete a part of the planned activity. Groups A, B and C.

Group A

1. Cut a 4″ × 11″ piece from the manila file folder. Hold the piece as shown in figure 2 to see if it will hold its own weight.

2. Fold the piece of cardboard lengthwise and repeat the test. Can the cardboard support its own weight? Can it support the weight of an object such as a pen or a small bolt? This simple exercise shows the major principle of the folded plate.

3. Lay a manila folder on top of an activity box as shown in figure 3. Place some light weights on the folder and observe what happens.

4. Make a pattern on the file folder with parallel lines placed 2″ apart. Fold the cardboard to make an accordian shape. (See figure 4) Use a second manila folder to cover the box. Do not glue the folders together because that would give additional strength. Now place weights on the roof and observe what takes place. Would the roof be stronger if the folds had been made with 1″ segments?

5. Cut out a saw tooth support for the roof and set it on top of the wall of the activity box. Once again test the roof with the 2″ segments (and the 1″ segments if you did that part of the activity).

6. Construct the circular folded plate roof shown in figure 5 and test its strength in comparison to the conical roof of the same size made of the same materials. (In this case you will have to glue pieces of cardboard together because of the size and the shape of the roofs.)

Procedure

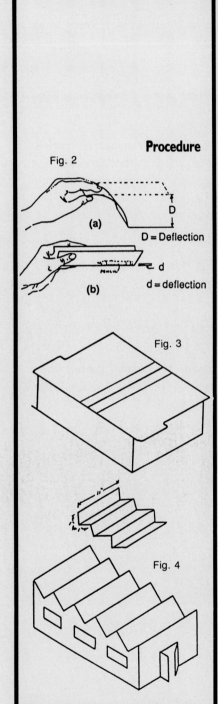

Fig. 2

(a)

D = Deflection

(b)

d = deflection

Fig. 3

Fig. 4

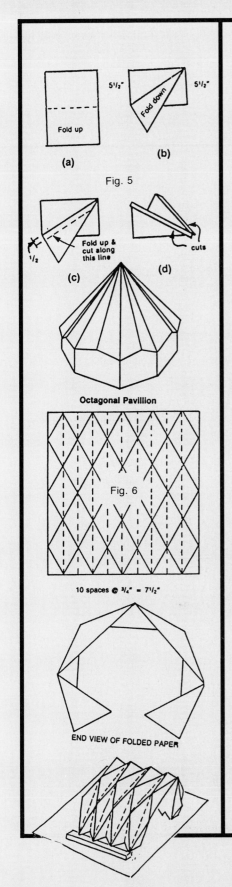

Fig. 5

Octagonal Pavillion

Fig. 6

10 spaces @ 3/4" = 7 1/2"

END VIEW OF FOLDED PAPER

7. Mark out the pattern shown in figure 6 and fold the paper into the intricate folded plate structure shown.

Group B

1. Using round toothpicks, cotton swab sticks or the materials your teacher provides glue together a square pattern 18″ × 18″ as shown in figure 7. (You will need to cut the toothpicks down to 2″ long.)

2. Build a pyramid as shown in figure 8 over each square in the pattern.

3. Continue the process until each square in the base has a pyramid built over it.

4. Connect the tops of the pyramids to form another square grid at the top. (See figure 9) You have just built a space frame called a Takenaka truss.

5. Repeat the process described above but this time make the base out of 2″ triangles. (See figure 10) Build a triangular pyramid (this is actually called a tetrahedron) over each of the triangles in the base.

6. Connect all the points of the tetrahedrons to form a new triangular pattern for the top.

7. Support each of the trusses by placing a block at the four corners. Place 4″ × 4″ × 1/4″ plywood in the center of the structure to serve as a pad for the test weights. Add weights to each of the structures to see which is the strongest. Which one held the most weight? Why do you think that one was stronger?

Group C

1. Attach a sheet of hardboard or plywood to the bottom of an activity box and tape the edges to ensure an airtight fit.

2. Drill a hole in one of the ends to fit the hose from a bicycle pump.

3. Tack and tape a sheet of heavy plastic to the sides of the box then tape the edges of the plastic to ensure an airtight fit. (Be sure to leave some play in the plastic so that it can blow up like a balloon.)

4. Divide the long length of the box into three sections and drive two nails into each side and one nail in the middle at each end. Leave each nail head sticking out about 1/4″. Tie a string loosely between each of the pairs of nails and inflate the structure as shown in figure 11.

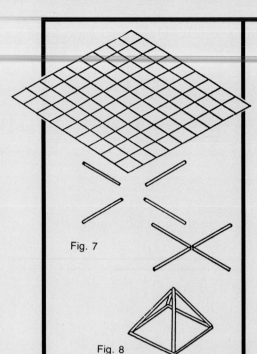

Fig. 7

Fig. 8

Assessment Activities

Student Analysis

Suggested Indepth Study

5. Blow up enough long thin balloons to cover the top of an activity box. Tie each end of the balloons to the walls of the box to form a curved balloon arch. (See figure 12)

6. Continue this process until the entire box is covered with a balloon arch roof.

7. Tape or tie the balloons together as shown in figure 13. You are ready to begin the testing of the two air structures for their strength and stability. Which of these structures is able to hold the most weight? What advantages does each have over the other?

8. Organize your findings on the structures you built and tested. Be sure to identify some of the advantages and disadvantages that each structure has.

All Groups

Meet again as a large group. Make your individual and small team presentations. make sure that you get copies of your classmates reports and drawings.

Complete the Structure Capability Test Form.

1. Determine what weight each structure can support and what weight causes collapse.

2. Determine which space frame could be made most energy efficient.

3. Determine which of the structures appears to be the strongest with the least materials (as determined by weight).

1. Photograph buildings in your community that use one of the space frames.

2. Design a large enclosed recreationasl area using a space frame.

3. Build a display model of one of the space frames.

4. How are architects currently using the space frame in buildings?

TAKENAKA TRUSS

COMPRESSED BARS

Fig. 9   SUPPORTED BOUNDARY

HORIZONTAL LOWER
DIAGONALS TIEING   INCLINED DIAGONALS
LOWER VERTICES

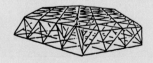

Fig. 10

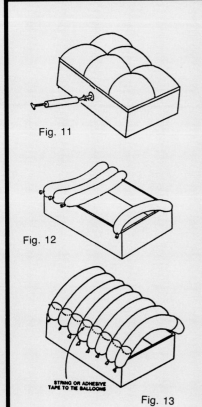

Fig. 11

Fig. 12

STRING OR ADHESIVE
TAPE TO TIE BALLOONS

Fig. 13

STRUCTURE CAPABILITY TEST FORM

Structure	Weight Supported	Weight Causing Failure	Least Surface Area for Volume	Most Volume for Materials (by weight)	Least Fabrication Required		Least Materials Required	Most Easily Transported
Flat Folded Roof								
Octagonal Pavillion								
Folded Plate								
Takenaka Truss								
Tetrahedron Truss								
Air Support								
Other								
Other								

ACTIVITY 24

Future Structures Design Brief

Reference

Chapter 12: The Future of Construction Systems

Design Brief

Several nations have plans to construct space stations that will shelter workers and house space industries. As these space stations become a reality, many changes will be made in proposed structural designs to accomodate people and make them feel "at home."

Problem

You are the member of a design team working for W.O.S.C. (Worldwide Organization for Space Construction). Your team has been given the responsibility of designing a mock-up (model) space station for the first colonization of space in quadrant EMOH-1, targeted for the year 2030.

Parameters

1. The model should be tabletop sized and can be suspended or mounted in any manner.

2. You must give a presentation of your design to the WOSC that will address the following factors:
   a. Space Station Materials:

      - space or Earth-made
      - loads & forces

   b. Environmental Considerations:

      - gravitational needs
      - oxygen generation

   c. Social Institutions:

      - family sheltering
      - government/laws
      - trade/economics
      - education
      - religion
      - recreation

   d. Technological Systems

      - Production (food, goods, etc.)
      - Communication
      - Transportation

Research & Development

1. Go to the library and research current proposed space station designs.

2. Write to NASA about their plans for space stations.

3. Research the problems associated with living for extended periods of time in a space station (oxygen, food, water, shelter, recreation, family, etc.)

4. Brainstorm with the members of your design team on possible designs.

5. Sketch various designs and consider the feasibility of modeling the space station.

6. Gather various materials that may be useful in constructing a model space station.

7. Chose your team's best design and create full-sized sketches on graph paper.

Evaluation

1. The members of the class will role play as members of the WOSC and evaluate space station designs during the in-class presentations.

2. The WOSC will vote for the best of the following:

    a. Space Station Design (ideas)
    b. Space Station Design (modeling)
    c. Presentation

3. In order to be considered for selection as the "best", design teams must address all of the factors listed under PARAMETERS above.

Index

· ·